The Realistic Spirit

Wittgenstein, Philosophy, and the Mind

D1548221

Representation and Mind
Hilary Putnam and Ned Block, editors

The Realistic Spirit

Wittgenstein, Philosophy, and the Mind

Cora Diamond

A Bradford Book
The MIT Press
Cambridge, Massachusetts
London, England

First MIT Press paperback edition, 1995
© 1991 Massachusetts Institute of Technology

This book was set in Palatino by Compset, Inc. and was printed and bound in the United States of America.

Library of Congress Cataloging-in-Publication Data

Diamond, Cora.
    The realistic spirit : Wittgenstein, philosophy, and the mind /
Cora Diamond.
        p. cm.—(Representation and mind)
    Includes bibliographical references and index.
    ISBN 0-262-04121-9 (HB), 0-262-54074-6 (PB)
    1. Wittgenstein, Ludwig, 1889–1951. 2. Realism. 3. Philosophy of
mind. I. Title. II. Series.
    B3376.W564D52   1991
    192—dc20   91-7117
                                                                          CIP

To A.D.W.

Contents

Preface

I have been reading Wittgenstein since 1965, and the papers published in this collection have come out of that reading. There is an obvious way to divide them: seven are explicitly about Wittgenstein, and three about the philosopher who most strongly influenced him; the other five, in which Wittgenstein is hardly mentioned, are about ethics and are done in a way which reflects what I have learned from him. But in fact the papers are connected more closely than that suggests. I found, in trying to make clear their relations to each other, that I was trying to show how the unity of Wittgenstein's thought had been refracted through my own discussions now of this, now of that. So the difficulties of trying to write an introductory essay were in part those of understanding the development of Wittgenstein's thought and of presenting it so that what was central could be seen as such. The result has been two introductory essays. Both essays take the change of perspective between Wittgenstein's early and his later work as pivotal; both connect that change with what I call "the realistic spirit" (and thus treat "Realism and the Realistic Spirit" as the central paper of the collection); both are critical of the attempt to understand that change through the contrast between philosophical realism and anti-realism. The first essay treats the change in perspective as a change in the philosophical treatment of the mind and thus gives a reading of the collection as a whole as in philosophy of mind, though perhaps in a queer sense. The second contrasts the realistic spirit with metaphysics and connects the papers of the collection to the character of philosophy and the significance in it of the laying down of philosophical or metaphysical requirements. The two essays are poor bastards this way: they are not self-contained essays on the development of Wittgenstein's thought; nor are they neat, brief explanations of how fifteen essays of mine make sense together.

Of the fifteen papers, three have not previously been published. For the most part, I have made only minor stylistic changes in the papers that have already appeared; "Wright's Wittgenstein" has been shortened. I have added a postscript to "Throwing Away the Ladder" commenting on a startling remark of Gilbert Harman's. I have also added something to "Riddles and Anselm's Riddle." Of the papers collected here, that is the one that now seems to me most in need of reworking. Every year for more than a dozen years I have taught an undergraduate class in philosophy of religion and have discussed Anselm's *Proslogion*. What changes most from year to year in that class is what I find I can say about Anselm and "that than which no greater can be conceived." One thing in the paper's discussion of Anselm, though, that still seems to me right is the connection between riddles and Anselm's understanding of what it is to speak about God. He makes the connection himself in the *Monologion*; and the fact that he does so might have found its way into my paper, had it not been written while I was in Shetland, dependent on a few books which I had with me and the generous help of the library in Lerwick. I have now added a short paragraph about the *Monologion*.

For several reasons I have not included in this volume some recent papers of mine on ethics, nor two essays on Wittgenstein, essays which go on in different ways from where the papers in this volume leave off. "Rules: Looking in the Right Place" gives a reading of Wittgenstein's remarks on rules and connects that reading with Rush Rhees's discussions of Wittgenstein; "Ethics, Imagination and the Method of Wittgenstein's *Tractatus*" considers the implications of treating seriously Wittgenstein's claim in the *Tractatus* that besides ordinary senseful propositions there is only plain nonsense.[1]

The papers reprinted here are not in chronological order; the order corresponds roughly to the organization of the first introductory essay. But I should point out that two of the papers—"Secondary Sense" and "The Face of Necessity"—are very much earlier than the rest and draw on a more limited reading of Wittgenstein's work. "Frege Against Fuzz" is later than "Frege and Nonsense" and "What Nonsense Might Be"; its arguments imply that some of the points in the two earlier papers need to be revised or hedged about with qualifications.

Several of the papers are critical responses to things I had read; two were invited commentaries: "Missing the Adventure" is a reply to Martha Nussbaum's "'Finely Aware and Richly Responsible': Moral Attention and the Moral Task of Literature"[2] and "Having a Rough Story about What Moral Philosophy Is" was written as a discussion of several other papers in an issue of *New Literary History* on Literature and/as Moral Philosophy.[3] "Experimenting on Animals" was originally written for a symposium at a meeting in 1977 of the British

Psychological Association and was rewritten for a collection addressed to a general audience.

For their comments and suggestions, I am very grateful to Martha Nussbaum, Richard Rorty, James Conant, and Anthony Woozley. I am indebted also to Judy Mitchell for preparing the bibliography and to Anthony Woozley for helping with computers, printers, and programs.

Notes

1. "Rules: Looking in the Right Place" is in D. Z. Phillips and P. Winch, eds., *Wittgenstein: Attention to Particulars* (Basingstoke, Hampshire, 1989), pp. 12–34; "Ethics, Imagination and the Method of Wittgenstein's *Tractatus*" is forthcoming in *Wiener Reihe* **5** (1991).
2. *Journal of Philosophy* **82** (1985) pp. 516–29, reprinted with revisions as " 'Finely Aware and Richly Responsible': Literature and the Moral Imagination" in Martha Nussbaum, *Love's Knowledge: Essays on Philosophy and Literature* (Oxford, 1990) pp. 148–167.
3. Vol. **15** no. 1 (Autumn 1983).

Acknowledgments

The author and publisher wish to thank the editors, journals, and publishers who gave permission to reprint eleven of these essays: to Harvester Press for "Frege and Nonsense," from C. Diamond and J. Teichman, eds., *Intention and Intentionality: Essays in Honour of G. E. M. Anscombe* (Brighton: Harvester, 1979); to Cambridge University Press for "What Nonsense Might Be," from *Philosophy* **56** (1981), for "Throwing Away the Ladder," from *Philosophy* **63** (1988) and for "Eating Meat and Eating People," from *Philosophy* **53** (1978); to J. E. R. Squires and Basil Blackwell Ltd. for "What Does a Concept-Script Do?" from *The Philosophical Quarterly* **34** (1984) and for "Wright's Wittgenstein," from *The Philosophical Quarterly* **31** (1981); to The Aristotelian Society, which holds the copyright to "Secondary Sense," originally published in *Proceedings of the Aristotelian Society* **67** (1966–67) and to "Riddles and Anselm's Riddle," originally published in *Proceedings of the Aristotelian Society* supp. vol. **51** (1977); to Basil Blackwell Ltd. for "Anything but Argument?" from *Philosophical Investigations* **5** (1982); to John Wiley & Sons Ltd. for "Experimenting on Animals: a Problem in Ethics," from D. Sperlinger, ed., *Animals in Research: New Perspectives in Animal Experimentation* (Chichester: John Wiley, 1981); to *New Literary History* for "Having a Rough Story about What Moral Philosophy Is," from *New Literary History* **15** (1983–84). "Realism and the Realistic Spirit" (to which I retained copyright) appeared in S. Shanker, ed., *Ludwig Wittgenstein: Critical Assessments,* vol. **4,** 1986.

Abbreviations

Full details of work referred to in this collection will be found in the general bibliography at the end. Abbreviated titles used only in a single essay are explained in the notes to the essay.

Works by Wittgenstein

BB   *The Blue and Brown Books* (Oxford, 1964).

PI   *Philosophical Investigations* (Oxford, 1958).

RFM   *Remarks on the Foundations of Mathematics* (References
                in the various essays make clear which edition is
                meant.)

Tractatus   *Tractatus Logico-Philosophicus*, trans. D. Pears and
                B. McGuinness (London 1961).

Notebooks   *Notebooks, 1914–1916* (Oxford, 1961).

Works by Frege

Grundgesetze *Basic Laws of Arithmetic* (Berkeley and Los Angeles,
                1967).
                References to *Grundgesetze* in "Frege Against Fuzz"
                are to selections from *Grundgesetze der Arithmetik* in
                P. T. Geach and Max Black, eds., *Translations from the
                Philosophical Writings of Gottlob Frege* (Oxford, 1966).

Grundlagen   *Foundations of Arithmetic* (Oxford, 1974).

Introduction I

Philosophy and the Mind

There is a sense in which the entirety of this book lies within philosophy of mind. Frege once said of logic and mathematics that neither of them investigates the minds, the contents of consciousness of individual men. "Their task," he went on, "could perhaps be represented rather as the investigation of *the* mind; of *the* mind, not of minds."[1] Thus his own argument that what can be true or false—thoughts—must be independent of individual men, that thoughts are not ideas, which like pains or sensations belong to us as individuals—that argument helps bring out what belongs and what does not to investigation of *the* mind.

The theme of this book, viewed as a book within the philosophy of mind, is that we misunderstand our relation to that fundamental idea, that distinction, of Frege's. We may think that the only choices we have are to take it seriously or to debunk it, to reject it for a thoroughly empirical view of thought and the logical relations between thoughts. To understand the distinction, the first thing that is necessary is clarity about what it was for Frege. Such clarity requires that we see what he believed would be accomplished by a language specially suitable for the clear expression of thoughts. In doing so, we come up against the problem that the logical distinctions built into the language cannot themselves be the objects of thoughts. This means that there are features of thought which cannot be put into true or false sentences. It seems, then, that philosophy, as it deals with *the* mind, is in a peculiar way stymied: its subject matter has essential features that escape it. Or consider the difference between what makes sense and what does not. It is tempting to see this as a distinction which is like that between truth and falsity in one respect, namely, that it applies, or some version of it does, both to sentences and to what sentences express. Treating in that way the distinction between sense and nonsense, we may think that nonsensical sentences are expressions of thoughts which are logically faulty, and that a philosophical account of *the* mind will therefore distinguish between nonsensical thoughts and those which make sense. It is part of the philosophical view of *the* mind, in Frege and in the *Tractatus*, that there is no nonsensical thought expressed by a nonsensical sentence. Similarly for vagueness (at least on Frege's view; Wittgenstein's would require a different characterization): there are vague sentences, and there are individual people who think, as it were, in fuzzes, who fail to entertain any definite thought. But *the* mind has no fuzzes and no logically confused thoughts; there are, on this view, no translations, strictly speaking, of fuzzy or logically confused mental contents; and so far as philosophy deals with *the* mind, it will not have, internal to its subject matter, any distinction between the fuzzy and the sharply defined, or between the nonsensical and what makes sense. Such remarks as it contains about vagueness or nonsense can belong only to the setting out of what it is *not* concerned with.[2]

Wittgenstein, in the *Tractatus*, entirely shared Frege's view that logic and mathematics have nothing to do with the contents of consciousness of individual people. But on the matter of whether they are investigations of *the* mind, the issue how he resembles and how he differs from Frege is complex. On the one hand, logic and mathematics cannot be described as investigations of *the* mind because they are in a sense not (as they were for Frege) investigations of anything. The propositions of logic, the equations of mathematics, lack content, deal with nothing, express no thoughts. On the other hand, the *Tractatus* does not break the connection in Frege between *the* mind and logic-and-mathematics. The connection emerges this way: the propositions of logic and the equations of mathematics show what Wittgenstein calls "the logic of the world," and that *is* for them to show the possibilities that belong to the mind or the self considered in a non-psychological way. The relation between Wittgenstein's views and Frege's can be seen if we go back to our starting point: Frege's idea of the significance of conceptual notation. It is one of the glories of his notation that the way logic and mathematics penetrate *all* thought is shown in the notation: in the notation itself, you can see what it means to say that the task of logic and mathematics is the investigation of *the* mind. What is fundamental in the notation is the construing of concepts and relations as functions, and the concomitant analysis of indicative sentences into expressions for functions and for their arguments. The analysis into function and argument is applicable to *all* thought and leads directly to an understanding of logical terms: through the use of quantifiers, e.g., we represent whether the value of a function is the true for any argument, or for all arguments, or for exactly so-and-so many arguments. You can see directly in the symbolism the relation between the function-argument character of thought and the possibility of logical inference. The nature of *the* mind is thus put before us in logic and mathematics. The connection between logical inference and the function-argument character of thought is formulated differently by Wittgenstein in the *Tractatus* (at 5.47), but it is equally central to what it means for logic and mathematics to treat the mind or self non-psychologically.

I have been taking a view opposed to that of Bernard Williams, who suggests that when Wittgenstein said that there is a sense in which philosophy can talk about the self in a non-psychological way, he meant that it could speak of the self as it speaks of anything, i.e., without sense.[3] But no. Wittgenstein's remark about how philosophy can talk about the self is a consequence of "the world is my world" and "logic fills the world." Because logic 'fills' *the* world and because the possibilities of *the* world are the possibilities for thought, for the self considered non-psychologically, philosophical talk will be 'about the self' in its analysis of ordinary propositions about any and every ordinary subject matter. Since ordinary propositions are expressions of thought, an analysis of "The pot is on the stove" would be a contribution towards making clear the limits of thought 'from the inside': by making clear a particular thought it goes some way, however little, towards making clear what can be thought. In doing so, it shows (in a non-psychological way) something about the self or the mind. Russell's Theory of Descriptions is, in the sense intended by *Tractatus* 5.641, philosophy talking about the self in a non-psychological way; so is the presenting of any expression by a propositional variable (which makes clear the propositions in which the expression can appear); so is the presenting of the general form of proposition, or the presenting of the general form through which propositions can be generated from other propositions.[4] *What* is thus 'spoken about' is not made clear by words like "the mind," "the self," "the I," "the subject"; to take logic in the way Wittgenstein has in mind will, though, be to give up certain uses of those words. Wittgenstein's remark about philosophy's being able to talk about the self in a non-psychological way is one of the remarks that has to be *überwindet*: we must win out over it, throw away the ladder of which it is a rung (*Tractatus* 6.54). The same would apply to the account I gave of why we can take the analysis of ordinary propositions as philosophy's talking about the self. The final step in the philosophical journey that takes us to the seeing of philosophical analysis as philosophy's non-philosophical presentation of the self leaves us without that description or any supposedly unspeakable understanding corresponding to it. The question of the relation between logic and the mind or the self takes us to the question how the *Tractatus* is to be read, to questions about its final characterization of itself as nonsense. (The question how the *Tractatus* is to be read is the main topic of "Throwing Away the Ladder" in this volume; in "Ethics, Imagination and the Method of Wittgenstein's *Tractatus*,"[5] I discuss some implications of my answer to that question.)

In being concerned with the significance of logic for Frege and for Wittgenstein's early writings, five papers in this collection[6] are about what it is for there to be a non-psychological approach to the mind. (I am not suggesting that the *Tractatus* is a philosophical account of *the* mind via some ineffable metaphysics; I criticize the idea of it as metaphysical in Introduction II.)

Wittgenstein's perspective changed radically around 1930. I have in mind the change he describes in *Philosophical Remarks* this way:

> Here we come to the apparently trivial question of what Logic is to count as a word, whether the ink-mark, the sound, whether it's necessary that someone connects or has connected a sense with it, etc., etc.—And obviously the crudest conception must be the only correct one here.
>
> So I will speak once more of 'books'; we have words here; should some squiggle ever occur I'd say: that's not a word, it only looks like one, obviously it wasn't intended. One can treat this only from the position of a sane human understanding. (It's remarkable that precisely in this there lies a change of perspective.)[7]

What then is the result of this change of perspective on philosophy as it treats of the mind? The older approach—Frege's and that of the *Tractatus*—can now be seen to have two elements: (1) the distinction between an empirical or psychological approach to the mind and one that is not psychological, and (2) a mythology of that distinction. What is essential in the change of perspective is that the distinction is kept but the mythology is recognized for what it is.

Mythology: I mean, for example, Frege's mythology of thoughts, eternal, unchangeable, uncreated by us; Wittgenstein's mythology of logic as a realm in which the nature of the naturally necessary signs speaks for itself. These conceptions belong to a mythological treatment of the distinction between a psychological and a non-psychological approach to the mind.

Just as Wittgenstein's understanding of logic, in its relation to the limits of language, is central in his earlier philosophical, non-psychological treatment of mind, so his understanding of grammar, and of what a philosophical investigation is, is central to the later philosophical, non-psychological treatment of mind. The change of perspective involves a change of method: attending to what we do, attending (that is) to what we may think *cannot* be relevant to a non-psychological treatment of the mind, attending to what we think must mean that we should be giving up Frege's distinction. We can see the significance of Wittgenstein's later discussions of what it is to follow a rule as part of the working out of a non-psychological treatment of the mind from this changed perspective, in which the timelessness of what belongs to a rule (the timelessness that characterizes logic) is brought into connection with the look of human life containing rules. It would be misleading to say that rules are what constitute *the* mind, but something akin to that is true. The capacities picked out by "*the* mind" are those for coherence and commitment in thought and language[8]; they are capacities characteristically exercised in going on intelligently and intelligibly, in giving and following rules, inventing kinds of rules, applying rules in matter-of-course ways and in penetrating, imaginative, and unexpected ones, and in play with rules, as for example in crossword puzzle clues that play with what *definition* is.

"Realism and the Realistic Spirit" is the central paper in this collection as a whole, in that it shows how Wittgenstein's attention to what we do is compatible with respect for Frege's distinction between what empirical psychology might show us of people's minds and what belongs to *the* mind, and in fact enables us to look in a realistic spirit at thought, at the coherence, the commitments, and connections that belong to it as thought. The paper is concerned with the question what it is that stops us looking at those details to which Wittgenstein would have us turn our attention. The answer I give is in terms of a notion of philosophical fantasy (what I am here calling mythology), explained in part by reference to Berkeley's diagnosis of the confusions of scientific realism. I make use, that is, of a partial analogy between Berkeley and Wittgenstein. Each criticizes and gives diagnoses of philosophical views often thought of as 'realist'; the criticisms in each case may appear to involve a denial of some reality important in our thought, a denial of some distinction the recognition of which belongs to the logical character of our judgments, their inferential relations to other judgments. It may seem that, if Berkeley draws our attention to the observations which we do in fact go by, which we treat as relevant or decisive, in establishing the truth of our judgments about real cows or horses, he is looking away from that independent reality with which such judgments are concerned, looking away from what gives those judgments their logical characteristics. Logic cannot be *there*, in what we do. Well, the argument of "Realism and the Realistic Spirit" is that it *can* be, and that it is something like fantasy that stops us looking there. That is, the paper attempts to show how the arguments of philosophical realism transform distinctions that, as I might now put it, belong to *the* mind into philosophical fantasy, a transformation that begins with the kinds of question we ask, the conception we form of what knowing about our concepts would be like.[9] The aim of the paper is then to show how what belongs to *the* mind may be seen without fantasy.

I want now to bring out how "Realism and the Realistic Spirit" is connected with "The Face of Necessity" and "Wright's Wittgenstein." Both those papers criticize the idea, originally Michael Dummett's, of a clash between realism and anti-realism, and the ascription of an extreme form of anti-realism to Wittgenstein. The idea that there is such a clash, and that Wittgenstein was on one side in the *Tractatus* and on the other in his later writings, involves failure to understand his change of perspective and failure to grasp the significance of his use of the notion of grammar. Wittgenstein's criticism of what I have called mythology or fantasy—in particular, his criticism of the mythology attached to logical necessity—is read as if it were rejection of the mythology as a *false* notion of how things are. That reading of Wittgenstein is tied to insistence on the question *when* it is fixed that such-and-such is logically necessary, or that such-and-such is in accord with a definition we have given or a rule we have formulated. The question appears to give us no choice but to say either (a) that necessity (or what follows from a definition or is in accord with a rule that we have formulated) is independent of and prior to our recognitions and our habits of inference, or (b) that necessity comes into existence when we explicitly accept the sentence at the end of a proof or when we decide to accept an application of a rule or definition as 'what we meant', and that *until* the acceptance or the decision we were, as far as logic is concerned, quite free. But treating *"When was it fixed?"* as the subject of philosophical dispute is not seeing it as a grammatical issue. Whether the question *"When* does it become true (or necessary) that p?" makes sense is a grammatical question about p. Wittgenstein wanted us to see that the grammar of atemporality has application in a life which *looks* like *this and this and this;* that is, he shows us life with definitions that fix meaning, life with formulations of rules that do (in an unmysterious sense) contain all their applications. If we do not see him as drawing attention to the face of necessity, the face of life with logic (logic that penetrates all thought just as much as ever it did in the *Tractatus*), we shall see him instead as repudiating the hardness of the logical 'must' and giving up Frege's distinction between logic and psychology. We shall miss altogether the kind of philosophical criticism in which he was engaged.

The way we look at things changes. It is possible to consider such changes empirically and psychologically: these novels make people think about the world or life differently; these proofs make people give up their attempts to trisect angles with rulers and compasses. But what works on people is one thing, and what is a good proof is something else again. We can judge that the proof is sound or that it is confused or fallacious independently of our knowledge of the conditions in which people exposed to it retain and those in which they change their old attitudes toward trisecting angles. It was once argued to me that I should not criticize Peter Singer's arguments about vegetarianism because they work—"He's bringing in the converts." That point depends on the distinction between what persuades people to change and what is genuinely or properly convincing. Several of the papers in this collection are concerned with that distinction, as applied not just to proofs, but, more generally, to the things we say or do in leading people to look at things differently, the things we ourselves think in coming to see them differently. Our commitments to rationality, to thinking well, have a variety of forms, but one bad effect of mythological versions of the distinction between logic and psychology is that our myths, at the same time as they appear to explain the applicability of the distinction to some types of case, appear to rule out its applicability to other sorts of case—I mean particularly to cases of creativity and imagination in thought. That effect of the mythology can be seen plainly in Frege's idea that what thoughts there are there are timelessly (Frege, the creator of new kinds of thought) and that all languages have the logical capacity to express all thoughts; it can be seen in the *Tractatus*, in the idea of logical space, of the structure of logical relations between propositions, the structure that must be in place for the sense of any proposition to be determinate, for it even to be determinate what combination of signs it is. In the *Tractatus*, that myth of what it is for sense to be determinate is, at the same time a myth of essential changelessness. There is no possibility of genuinely new thoughts or sorts of thought. (If there were, the sense of no proposition would be determinate, since new thoughts would be inseparable from the old propositions standing in new logical relations, i.e., *not* having determinate sense.) Alternatively, the mythology may lead to the idea that rationality may be found when we operate *inside* a system of thought but can have no application to a movement to a new system; in such cases, the mythology allows there only to be persuasion or conversion, but not genuine exercise of thought or reason. Myths attaching to rationality make it seem inconceivable, in the case of the *Tractatus*, that our ways of thinking or understanding can change; in the alternative sort of case, that if they can change, the distinction, essential to logic, between how people may be inclined to go and how, thinking *well*, they ought to go, can apply. The two papers most directly concerned with these issues are "Riddles and Anselm's Riddle" and "Anything but Argument?" but "Secondary Sense," "The Face of Necessity," and "Missing the Adventure" are relevant too.

We live with many kinds of criticism of the ways people set out proofs and arguments. Such-and-such setting out of some proof suppresses an important premise; such-and-such version of some argument needs to be reformulated to be convincing; such-and-such version of a proof (on an examination, by a student) is a mere sketch, and it has not been made clear how the proof might be more fully set out. The variety of kinds of criticism belongs to the life of logic; and Wittgenstein, in his later writings, was concerned to combat the idea of *the* full, *the* adequate setting out of argument or proof, an idea inseparable from the myths attached to the idea of what follows from what. His criticism of such ideas focused on the form they took in Frege's and Russell's work on the foundations of mathematics. One characteristic element in the criticism is his insistence that our ordinary calculations are not given any underpinning by being tied to logical proofs; if, in carrying out a calculation in Russell's system, we actually got a result different from that which we get in ordinary arithmetic, the result would have no tendency whatever to show that ordinary arithmetic was questionable.

We find in ethics a fascination, comparable to Frege's and Russell's, with an ideal, an ideal of ethical rationality thought of as underlying ethical arguments whenever they are more than appeals to prejudice or parochial sentiment, whenever they are not mere attempts to shift our views but respect our capacities as thinking beings. It is indeed part of the life of ethical thought that some considerations are treated as irrelevant, that charges of bias may be made, evaluated, replied to. But there is then a philosophical idea of something underlying ethical argument as such, an ideal of unbiasedness. The construction of arguments under the influence of this ideal is like the construction of Russellian versions of ordinary calculations: if there is disagreement between the Russellian calculation and the ordinary one, or if there is disagreement between moral arguments constructed under the influence of a supposed ideal and arguments we might in ordinary moral thought regard as good or penetrating or reasonable, there is no basis for thinking that we *ought* to choose the supposed ideal and that going with the ordinary calculation or argument is giving up on logic and going over to intellectual arm-twisting or seduction. The commitments we incur in thinking cannot be worked out from myths of *the* mind.

An argument close to the one I have just given is in "Eating Meat and Eating People"; the point underlies my discussion in "Experimenting on Animals." "Anything but Argument?" is addressed to a related question. The distinction between what merely effects conversions and what comes up to appropriate standards may be taken to imply that such standards can be applied only to arguments and proofs. Just as mathematics can be done by proof but also (as Wittgenstein mentions) by drawing something and saying, "Look at this," so ethical thought goes on in argument and also *not* in argument but (e.g.) in stories and images. The idea that we have not got *Thought* unless we can rewrite the insight as argument in some approved form is a result of a mythology of what is accomplished by argument.

I have connected several of the papers on ethics with Wittgenstein's change in perspective on the contrast between logical and psychological treatments of thought, as I understand it. I have not said anything about "Having a Rough Story about What Moral Philosophy Is," nor have I tried to connect my papers on ethics with Wittgenstein's remarks on ethics in the *Tractatus* and elsewhere. There are connections, but I can give only a brief indication of how they go. A starting point is the remark in the *Tractatus* "There is only *logical* necessity" (6.37, 6.375). That remark is essential in ruling out any treatment like Kant's of *the* mind, in which there are necessities internal to thought other than those reflected in logical propositions and mathematical equations (conceived as in the *Tractatus*). It is not only that logic and mathematics show us the space thought has (and in doing so show us *the* mind), but there is *no other* treatment of *the* mind. The remark that there is only *logical* necessity is central not only in the *Tractatus* as concerned with *the* mind; it is also central in the *Tractatus* as ethics. One way of explaining how that remark belongs in ethics is to refer to G. K. Chesterton's *Orthodoxy*. Writing some years before the *Tractatus*, and lacking any but a psychologistic notion of logic, Chesterton nevertheless brought out the relation between an ethical conception of the world as marvel, of life as adventure, and there being only logical necessity. In order to understand "There is only logical necessity" as at the same time ethics and philosophy concerned with *the* mind, it is important to see the contrast between two ideas of ethics: ethics as a subject of discourse and ethics as not having some particular subject matter. An ethical spirit, an attitude to the world and life, can penetrate any sort of talk or thought. Chesterton, like Wittgen-

stein, contrasts two types of attitude to the world. For him they may
be characterized as the spirit of attachment or loyalty and that of dis-
loyalty. Wittgenstein speaks of the happy and the unhappy: the
world of the happy is a different one from that of the unhappy;
Wordsworth speaks of those who live in a world of life and of others
in a universe of death. We are used to ethics as subject of discourse;
that conception of what ethics is is built into our idea of philosophy
itself as something with branches, including ethics; it is thus built into
our idea of ourselves as philosophers discussing ethics. But a rejection of such a view of ethics is inseparable from the *Tractatus* as concerned with *the* mind. That logical analysis presents the possibilities
in *the* world, which is *my* world, that the world and life are one,
should be taken as expressing the understanding of life which belongs to ethics, not as subject of discourse but rather as primarily tied
to the sense of life. We may be inclined to think of it almost as a joke
or a kind of philosophical eccentricity that Wittgenstein said that the
Tractatus (a work plainly, as we think, in philosophy of logic or philosophy of language) was a work in ethics; and we may see as bearing
on ethics some remarks in the book, some lines of argument; but if
we see it so, that is because we start from an idea of ethics utterly
opposed to the spirit of the book (and from a conception, different
from Wittgenstein's, of the relation between philosophy and its
branches). This may all seem mystifying in its apparent lack of connection with what we take to be central in ethics: what we *do*. The
connection may be seen in the work of many writers. Chesterton is
one, but it also comes out particularly clearly in Hawthorne's "The
Birthmark," which is ethics of the sort I am discussing. The central
character of that story is shown as, in Wittgenstein's sense, unhappy.
The world does not meet conditions he lays down. That ethical spirit
is shown in the story in relation to the doing of evil. The story is a
kind of ethics by geometrical construction: extend the line (of this
character) far enough and it destroys life, goodness, beauty. My object in going over Wittgenstein's ethics in the *Tractatus* is in part to
show the difficulties there are in thinking about how the change in
perspective in his philosophy works itself out in his later thought.
Many philosophical treatments of ethics, which seek to apply the
philosophical methods of *On Certainty, Philosophical Investigations,* or
Remarks on the Foundations of Mathematics, take for granted the idea of
ethics which the *Tractatus* rejects: ethics as branch of thought, ethics
as kind of discourse, ethics as about right or wrong things to do and
what things are good, and what it means to speak about such matters. Five papers in this collection touch on these issues.[10] "Throwing
Away the Ladder" gives the understanding of the *Tractatus* underly-

ing what I have just said; "Secondary Sense" is about Wittgenstein's Ethics Lecture (in which his view of ethics was close to that in the *Tractatus*). "Having a Rough Story about What Moral Philosophy Is" discusses the defining of ethics in such a way as to exclude vision of life, and it connects that exclusion with questions about how literature may bear on ethics; "Riddles and Anselm's Riddle" is about not just mathematics and ordinary riddles but also what Wittgenstein called *the riddle* (*Tractatus*, 6.5), "the riddle '*par excellence*'"; and "Anything but Argument?" comes round, at the very end, to the connection between wonder and ethics, as expressed in, e.g., Wordsworth's "We live by admiration and by love." The last sentences in "Realism and the Realistic Spirit" express a hope that it is possible to do more.

Notes

1. Gottlob Frege, *Collected Papers on Mathematics, Logic, and Philosophy*, ed. Brian McGuinness (Oxford, 1984), pp. 368–69.
2. See Joan Weiner, "On Concepts, Hints and Horses," *History of Philosophy Quarterly* **6** (1989), pp. 115–30.
3. Bernard Williams, "Wittgenstein and Idealism," in *Understanding Wittgenstein*, Royal Institute of Philosophy Lectures **7**, ed. Godfrey Vesey (London, 1974), pp. 76–95.
4. See also Peter Winch, "Language, Thought and World in Wittgenstein's *Tractatus*," in *Trying to Make Sense* (Oxford, 1987), pp. 3–17, at p. 16.
5. Forthcoming in *Wiener Reihe* **5**, 1991.
6. "What Does a Concept-Script Do?" "Frege and Nonsense," "What Nonsense Might Be," "Frege Against Fuzz," and "Throwing Away the Ladder."
7. §18; the translation is Michael Feldman's. See also *Philosophical Investigations* I, §108.
8. For this point as it appears in Frege's thought, see Thomas Ricketts, "Objectivity and Objecthood: Frege's Metaphysics of Judgment," in *Frege Synthesized*, ed. L. Haaparanta and J. Hintikka (Dordrecht, 1986), pp. 65–95 and Ricketts, "Generality, Meaning and Sense in Frege," in *Pacific Philosophical Quarterly* **67** (1986), pp. 172–95.
9. See Warren Goldfarb, "I Want You to Bring Me a Slab: Remarks on the Opening Sections of *Philosophical Investigations*," *Synthese* **56** (1983), pp. 265–82. In Introduction II, I consider the kind of understanding we seek in philosophy.
10. I have also discussed them in "Ethics, Imagination and the Method of Wittgenstein's *Tractatus*"; see note 5.

Introduction II

Wittgenstein and Metaphysics

This introduction connects "Realism and the Realistic Spirit" with our desire for philosophical explanations. We may want an explanatory account of the relation between thinking and the standards proper to it. So we may look for metaphysical truths to which our thinking ought properly to correspond; or we may argue that there are standards for thinking which are not set by anything external to it but by its own intrinsic nature. If, in philosophy, we seek to understand such things as how our thoughts can be true or false at all, what makes their logical character possible, what makes it possible for there to be adherence to a definition, we may take the details of what we say, what we do, to be irrelevant to the understanding we seek. What I call the realistic spirit aims not to provide that sort of understanding but to change our idea that *it* is what we seek.

The relation and the difference between the two introductions comes out this way. We may make meaning, thought, inference, proof into mysterious achievements that indeed call for philosophical explanation. Seeing them as they are in our life and giving up the desire for such explanations go together. In this introduction I emphasize Wittgenstein's view of philosophy, his criticism of philosophical theories and explanations; in Introduction I, I argue that giving up what I there called mythology is not giving up what it was a mythology *of*. The link, and the difference, between the introductions may be seen in the use in them of an image of Wittgenstein's, that of a 'physiognomy'. It comes from *Philosophical Investigations* I, §235, where Wittgenstein says of his remarks that they serve to show you what belongs to the physiognomy of what we in everyday life call 'obeying a rule'. In Introduction I, I use the notion of necessity as having a face, of life with logic as having a complex *look* characterizable by its details, in arguing that Wittgenstein's attention to what we do, to what we accept, is not a giving up of the distinction between the logical and the merely psychological. In Introduction II, I appeal to the image in showing that, in his discussions of what we do, es-

pecially his discussions of privacy, criteria and agreement in following a rule, Wittgenstein is not giving philosophical explanations of
how our words mean anything definite, how what we say has consequences. He provides no new theories to replace the old. (A different way of seeing the relation between the two introductions would
emphasize their ties to a linkage of ideas in Frege—the linkage, which
Thomas Ricketts has brought out, between Frege's attack on psy-
chologism and the impossibility of treating ontological notions as independent of and set over against logical ones.)[1]

This introduction has five parts. In Part I, I sketch an argument
against my own reading of Wittgenstein, an argument that presents
him as an anti-realist about the existence of metaphysical facts. Part
II is about the contrast, which I here treat as central, between metaphysics and the realistic spirit. Part III explains how the papers on
ethics reflect what I take to be Wittgenstein's view of philosophy, and
Part IV is about the papers dealing explicitly with Frege and Wittgenstein on logic, language, and mathematics. Part V draws things
together.

I

> A picture is conjured up which seems to fix the sense *unambigu-
> ously*. The actual use, compared with that suggested by the pic-
> ture, seems like something muddied. Here again we get the same
> thing as in set theory: the form of expression we use seems to
> have been designed for a god, who knows what we cannot
> know; he sees the whole of each of those infinite series and he
> sees into human consciousness. For us, of course, these forms of
> expression are like pontificals which we may put on, but cannot
> do much with, since we lack the effective power that would give
> these vestments meaning and purpose.
>
> In the actual use of expressions we make detours, we go by
> sideroads. We see the straight highway before us, but of course
> we cannot use it, because it is permanently closed.[2]

> When . . . we are out of agreement with the expressions of or-
> dinary language (which are after all performing their office), we
> have got a picture in our heads which conflicts with the picture
> of our ordinary way of speaking. Whereas we are tempted to
> say that our way of speaking does not describe the facts as they
> really are. As if, for example, the proposition "he has pains"
> could be false in some other way than by that man's *not* having
> pains. As if the form of expression were saying something false

even when the proposition *faute de mieux* asserted something true.

For *this* is what disputes between Idealists, Solipsists and Realists look like. The one party attack the normal form of expression as if they were attacking a statement; the others defend it, as if they were stating facts recognized by every reasonable human being.[3]

I used both those passages in "Wright's Wittgenstein," where I argued that Crispin Wright's ascription of anti-realist views to Wittgenstein was confused. Here, as in that paper, I want to connect the passages with disputes about the past and its reality. The road that seems to be permanently closed is (in the case of the past) the road giving us access to the past event *itself*; the sideroads we are forced to use instead are memory and evidence. When we reflect on the fact that we have merely memory and evidence and not the past fact itself, it seems that we merely say things in the past tense when certain present conditions are fulfilled, but we never have, cannot have, the fact that would genuinely stand behind the saying and make what we say true. For there *are* no such past facts; the past "is not and cannot be."[4] Since what makes us count a sentence in the past tense as true is not the fact itself that could genuinely make it true, our form of expression is here deceptive, untrue to the reality we are representing in our words.

Wittgenstein's ironic presentation of that sort of dispute should (this was my argument) lead us to question Wright's picture of him as an anti-realist. But it might well be argued against me that those very passages I quoted, despite their irony, show him to be implicitly committed to a profoundly anti-realist view. The argument might go like this:

Wittgenstein describes us as "tempted to say that our way of speaking does not describe the facts as they really are." And this is not because he thinks that it *does* describe the facts as they are, but rather because he takes our mode of speaking not to describe any facts at all. More strongly: if we had a different way of speaking, we should not be getting something in reality wrong that we are now getting right, nor should we be getting something in reality right that we are now getting wrong. There are no metaphysical facts to make our way of speaking right or wrong; there is nothing *out there* to make the necessities we have built into our language correct or incorrect.

Let me illustrate that point with an example. It may be held that it is *because* the past cannot change that, having heard some noise, you cannot have all over again *the hearing of that noise,* and that therefore any rule of ours according to which "having the same noise again" counts as an impossibility is *correct*. Something like that view was taken by Ronald Butler, arguing against Wittgenstein's ideas as they had been presented by Elizabeth Anscombe.[5] Butler does what Wittgenstein in §402 of *Philosophical Investigations* describes as defending the normal form of expression, as if in doing so he "were stating facts recognized by every reasonable human being." But how exactly should we see Wittgenstein's view in relation to such a defence of our forms of expression? There may seem to be a sort of tension built into Wittgenstein's response. On the one hand, there is the ironic distance at which Wittgenstein places himself from defender and attacker of our forms of expression; on the other hand, he appears to deny something that a person like Butler clearly believes, and thus, against Butler, to be taking a specific sort of anti-realist view. That is, Butler believes that a fact about the past—that it cannot change—can make certain features of our form of expression (our counting certain things as logically necessary) correct. And Wittgenstein's distancing himself from any dispute about whether the facts about the past make our form of expression correct or incorrect seems to depend upon his taking the view that there are no facts about the past of a sort that *could* make our form of expression correct or incorrect. *There is nothing* for our forms of expression to get right or wrong. So the situation appears to be this: Wittgenstein is genuinely involved in a dispute at one level about whether there are metaphysical or philosophical facts about the past that we can get right or wrong in our forms of expression; and, given the side that he takes in *that* dispute, the anti-realist side, he can then distance himself or present his philosophical position as distant from *all* the disputants who, taking for granted that there *are* metaphysical facts, argue about the relation between our forms of thought or forms of expression and those metaphysical facts. There are any number of discussions and arguments in Wittgenstein which may seem to lead us to such a reading. In particular, he repeatedly raises questions of the form: "What would go wrong if our form of expression were different?" "What would be wrong if we recognized different logical laws?" And the answer seems to be: we should not, in such cases, be getting the essential facts about the nature of what we were speaking about wrong, we should be speaking *about something else.* Wittgenstein seems to be committed to the idea that our forms of expression are not answerable to any facts because there are none for them to be answerable to. In the case of the irrevocability of the past, what this means is that if we were to *introduce* talk of having again the very same hearing of the very same noise that we had heard earlier, or of doing something and then making it the case that it had not been done, we should be altering the grammar of our talk of events, but we should not be getting the nature of events wrong. Repeatability, or changeability, would belong to the kind of thing we were now speaking of. The unchangeable character of the past cannot *explain* why we cannot have the very same noise twice, since there is no fact of irrevocability capable of playing such an explanatory role. But the absence of certain kinds of facts itself does play an explanatory role in this account.

Such a reading of Wittgenstein may seem forced on us. But there is a main theme of his writing with which it is in conflict, the theme sounded most strongly and clearly in *Philosophical Investigations* in §§126–33.[6] As Wittgenstein understands what he is doing in philosophy, it does not lead us to philosophical discoveries, to the unearthing of something of which we might previously have been ignorant. And there being, or there not being, metaphysical facts like the irrevocability of the past would be a discovery of the sort philosophy (as he says he does it) is supposed not to provide. He says "If one tried to advance *theses* in philosophy, it would never be possible to debate them, because everyone would agree to them" (§128). The anti-realist view which is ascribed to him on the reading I have just sketched, the denial that there are metaphysical facts for our forms of expression to get right or wrong: *that* can hardly be described as something with which everyone would agree, something impossible to debate. So the reading of Wittgenstein as a profound anti-realist about what underlies our modes of thought and expression, the ascription to him of the view that there are no facts down there to do the underlying, requires one to set aside his remarks on what philosophy does; it requires one either to discard them altogether, or to treat them as applicable only to *some* things in philosophy, or to regard them as evidence of some kind of failure to think through the position he wanted to take.

The idea that Wittgenstein was an anti-realist about facts underlying the logical features of our forms of expression goes very naturally with a particular way of taking the *Tractatus*, and of seeing its relation to the later writings. We may think of Wittgenstein as having gone from taking a realist view of such metaphysical facts in his earlier writings to an anti-realist view afterwards. Here I need to explain what I mean by the ascription to him of a realist view in the *Tractatus*. Wittgenstein is read as holding in the *Tractatus* that there are certain fixed possible ways in which the objects forming the substance of the world can combine with each other. These possibilities are fixed in the nature of things, independently of language; language then mirrors these possibilities in what it makes sense to say. Thus certain metaphysical features of reality underlie the logical features of language. Wittgenstein is read as denying that we can put these metaphysical features of reality into intelligible language, but as meaning to convey that they are nevertheless there, however unsayable or unthinkable their thereness may be. That conception of what Wittgenstein held in the *Tractatus* goes then with the idea that the metaphysical fixing of possibility is dropped in his later thought. These readings of early and later work depend, both of them, on failure to take seriously what Wittgenstein says about philosophy itself. Both readings take for granted that there is a genuine philosophical question whether there are or are not metaphysical features of reality underlying structural or logical characteristics of language, and they see Wittgenstein as giving first one answer and then another. "Throwing Away the Ladder: How to Read the *Tractatus*" is an attempt to show what is involved in taking seriously what the *Tractatus* says about the remarks of which it is composed and, more generally, about philosophy and the possibility of philosophy. If we do not see how the *Tractatus* asks us to read it, we cannot understand what Wittgenstein later came to think was wrong with it. In Part II of the introduction, I shall go further into the question how we should understand Wittgenstein's remarks, in his later work, about philosophy, and in doing so I shall make clear how the papers in this volume are connected with each other.

II

I need first to ask whether there is a sense in which the *Tractatus* might be described as metaphysical, even though it is not concerned with features of reality underlying sense, with things that are the case although they cannot intelligibly be said or thought to be the case. It is metaphysical, I want to suggest, in holding that the logical relations of our thoughts to each other can be shown, completely shown, in an analysis of our propositions. It is metaphysical in holding that it is possible for propositions to be rewritten in such a way that these logical relations are all clearly visible, and that, by rewriting them in that way, *what* propositions our propositions are, what combinations of signs, would also be clear, as would be what all propositions have in common. This is not a view about what there is, external to language or thought, but about what they essentially are (despite appearances), and about what we can do, what it must be possible to do. The belief that there must be a certain kind of logical order in our language (the belief reflected in our seeing that order as already *there*, given the understanding we have of the signs we use (*PI*, I, §§101–

2)): this is a belief also in what we must be able to do, given that we understand sentences and use them, where using them is saying things in determinate logical relations to each other; and these relations are what (totally laid out) shows us *what* sentences we use, as Russell's analysis of sentences containing definite descriptions showed us in part.

What is metaphysical there is not the content of some belief but *the laying down of a requirement*, the requirement of logical analysis. We do make sense, our propositions do stand in logical relations to each other. And such-and-such *is required* for that to be so. The metaphysics there is not in something other than language and requiring that it be like this or like that; *that* sort of metaphysics the *Tractatus* uses only ironically: it uses apparently metaphysical sentences, but in a way which is disposed of by the sentences which frame the book, in the Preface and the final remarks. The metaphysics of the *Tractatus*— metaphysics not ironical and not cancelled—is in the requirements which are internal to the character of language as language, in their being a general form of sentence, in all sentences having this form. The metaphysics of the *Tractatus* is a kind of metaphysics that does not involve what is unsayably the case outside language, except so far as sentences which, as one might say, 'appear to be about such things' help us understand the requirements which are internal to a sentence's having a use, i.e., being some entirely determinate combination of signs. The attempt to take the *Tractatus* as metaphysical in a straightforward sense (as in Norman Malcolm's recent *Nothing is Hidden*)[7] yields plain nonsense or plain self-contradictions, like "There is a fixed form of the world, but it is not a *fact* that there is a fixed form of the world."[8] That is a sentence of the form "There is a buggle-wuggle, but it is not a fact that there is a buggle-wuggle." Whatever we choose to mean by "buggle-wuggle," the sentence remains a plain self-contradiction; replace "buggle-wuggle" by "fixed form of the world" and you have not expressed something deeper, not come any closer to gesturing at something ineffably so. Wittgenstein does not ask that his propositions be understood, but that *he* be; the reading of the *Tractatus* as giving us 'assumptions' or 'conceptions' which cannot be put into what officially count as propositions, but which can nevertheless be conveyed to us or grasped by us, reflects a resolute insistence on understanding the propositions and not the author, and on not taking seriously that what cannot be thought cannot be thought.[9] I have gone over this here because I need to make a contrast between the metaphysical spirit and what, in "Realism and the Realistic Spirit," I call the realistic spirit; the contrast depends upon a prior understanding of the contrast between metaphysics of the sort the *Tractatus* does not contain, although it works by using sentences that look like that sort of metaphysics, and the metaphysical 'must' that it does contain: the 'must' of logical analysis, of total determinacy of sense. In Part IV of this introduction, I shall discuss an objection to my reading of the *Tractatus*, namely, that its arguments require that we understand the propositions composing those arguments and that those propositions cannot therefore really be nonsensical.

The contrast which runs through this collection of papers lies between the realistic spirit and metaphysics, where I understand by metaphysics the laying down of metaphysical requirements, whether in the form of views about what there is (as in Peirce's claim, discussed in "Realism and the Realistic Spirit," that there are real generals in nature, and that there must be if there is a genuine distinction between causal and accidental regularities) or in the rather different form exhibited by the *Tractatus* and also (as I believe) in Frege's work, as for example in his views about determinacy of concepts and the possibility of logic (on which see "Frege against Fuzz").

"Realism and the Realistic Spirit" may be treated as central in this collection in that it lays out the relation between the metaphysical demand and Wittgenstein's kind of response, which is that of the realistic spirit. The criticism of the metaphysical demand by Wittgenstein is never that what is demanded *is not there*, that there are no facts of the kind which is necessary if the demand is to be met. Our needs *are* met, but how they are met we can see only by what Wittgenstein calls the "rotation of the axis of reference of our examination about the fixed point of our real need" (*PI*, I, §108). We shall not understand Wittgenstein's critical response to metaphysical demands if we do not see the kind of criticism he makes of the *Tractatus*. If we read the *Tractatus* as containing metaphysical claims about reality, if we take the metaphysics that we think we find in it to be joined with the idea that metaphysical claims cannot be put into genuine propositions, we shall miss entirely the character of Wittgenstein's later philosophy. We shall see it as rejecting a metaphysical account of reality, the rejection being dictated by a shift from one set of philosophical requirements on language to another. Whereas what I am suggesting is that the criticism of the *Tractatus* may be viewed as a criticism of the *laying down of philosophical requirements*. That is, a radical understanding of the *Tractatus* itself, as metaphysical only in an extremely exiguous sense (it lays down philosophical requirements on language and does not look at the phenomena of language), is necessary if the radical character of Wittgenstein's criticism of it is to be understood.[10]

Here I need to turn to an objection, namely, that Wittgenstein himself, in his later work, lays down this requirement or that: for something to be language, publicity of some sort is required; or for such-and-such else, agreement in judgment is required, or whatever it may be. Where, however, Wittgenstein speaks of what is or is not *possible*, what he says has a quite different significance. The point is illustrated by his remarks about grief and hope: when he says that only those who have mastered the use of a language can hope (*PI*, II, §i), he does not mean that hoping is a logical achievement of some sort, dependent upon mastery of language, but rather that, as he puts it, "the phenomena of hope are modes of this complicated form of life" (that is, of life with language). In the discussion of private language, Wittgenstein's aim is to let us recognize calling into question whether a definition has been followed, and establishing whether or not it has, as phenomena of the life in which we apply words together, as parts of that life. What we call applying a definition has *this* or *this* or *that* position in our lives, has *these* connections. (Compare *Zettel*, §533.) Call any phenomena you like "following a private definition," take seriously the invitation to do so, and you will find that there is nothing you want to call that. The laying down of philosophical requirements, the characteristic activity of the metaphysical spirit, may be contrasted with looking at the use, looking at what we do. Thus, for example, there is on the one hand what we might lay down, in some philosophical theory, as essential to rule-following, to something's being in accordance with a rule; in contrast there is description of the face, the physiognomy, of what we call "obeying a rule" in everyday life, of all that belongs to that face.[11] The philosophical theory lays down, without looking, what must be present in following a rule, while Wittgenstein's talk of what is possible is entirely different. Imagine such-and-such a change, he will say; and with the face of the activity thus altered, do you still want to call this following a rule? The important thing then is not what answer you give, but your willingness to look, i.e., your not laying down general philosophical conditions.

Only if we understand Wittgenstein's aim in relation to metaphysical requirements will we see the point of his urging us to look at what we do. We shall get a wrong idea of the sense in which philosophy "leaves everything as it is" if we ignore that aim. Thus, for example, it is sometimes argued, against Wittgenstein, that, after all, philosophical discussion constitutes a language-game or group of language-games. So, it is asked, why does he not leave such games alone? Why are *they* subject to criticism, if 'what we do' is supposed to be all right? What a misunderstanding that is! The sense in which philosophy leaves everything as it is is this: philosophy does not put us in a position to justify or to criticize what we do by showing that it meets or fails to meet requirements we lay down in our philosophizing. If there are language-games we engage in because we think that playing them, or playing them in such-and-such ways, will enable some philosophical requirement to be met, we shall indeed no longer want to play such games, or to play them in those ways—the interest of doing so will be gone—if we understand what Wittgenstein was trying to make clear. And we may indeed also no longer go in for the game of discussing whether and how philosophical requirements can be met. Nothing in Wittgenstein's writing or practice suggests that his work would not *in such ways* lead to changes in language-games. The idea that there is some inconsistency in Wittgenstein's saying that philosophy "leaves everything as it is" and his criticizing philosophy itself (which is part of 'everything') is a result of removing remarks like the one about leaving everything as it is from their context: the discussion of philosophy's interest in 'foundations'. Here it is useful to turn to Wittgenstein's treatment of the philosophy of mathematics, which is important in his work for a number of reasons. One of them is that it is possible to see there the relation between the kinds of criticism he thinks can be made of a practice that we go in for (like developing set theory) and 'leaving everything as it is'. Leaving everything as it is is consistent with showing that the interest of a game rests on mythology or fantasy or a failure of understanding of what it is for our own real needs to be met.

III

The papers in this book are connected with the attempt in our reflections on logic and ethics to lay down philosophical requirements. Kant's influence is evident in the requirements in both cases, although that influence has come down to us in ethics in one way and in logic in quite another. There is indeed a sense in which Kant provides this collection of essays with its unity, but I cannot here try to show how the realistic spirit is related to Kant's conception of philosophy.

In the papers on ethics, I am concerned with our philosophical ideas about what the role of universality and universal principles must be in moral thought and discussion; also, with a view (which we may take to be essential in moral thought) of the self, of what we as moral agents must be taken to share; and also with what concepts can be morally relevant. The papers are, then, all attempts to think about ethics in a realistic spirit, i.e., not in the thrall of metaphysical requirements. They make two sorts of claims about the effects of such thralldom. The requirements which we lay down stop us seeing what moral thought is like; further, they lead us to construct stupid or insensitive or crazy moral arguments, arguments which are capable of hiding our own genuine ethical insights from ourselves and of giving others good grounds for identifying philosophical argument in ethics with sophistry. What I mean by "stupid or insensitive or crazy" may be brought out by a single word, the word "even" in this quotation:

> We have seen that the experimenter reveals a bias in favor of his own species whenever he carries out an experiment on a non-human for a purpose that he would not think justified him in using a human being, even a retarded human being.[12]

There is a philosophical requirement on what constitutes ethical rationality underlying the structure of that argument and the idea that experimenting on retarded people is relatively easier to justify than experimenting on normal people. The idea is that, if the scientist can justify experimenting on animals in preference to experimenting on people, it must be by appeal to something which we have and they lack, or to something which we have more of than they. Any such justification will thus proceed in terms of intellectual capacities (since there is nothing else which can plausibly be made out to be morally relevant and which we have and they lack or which we have more of than they). But since retarded people lack those capacities, or have them to a lesser degree than normal people, the justification for experimenting on animals in preference to people is a justification for experimenting on retarded people in preference to normal people. Not to accept the latter is to reveal as a fraud the supposed justification for experimenting on animals; one reveals a bias in favor of one's own species. In "Eating Meat and Eating People" and in "Experimenting on Animals" I criticize the mode of thought to which such arguments belong, but in fact all the papers on ethics are concerned with the conception of ethical rationality reflected in the remark about experimentation.

Putting these points another way: in *The Brothers Karamazov*, the evil heart of a central character is revealed by what he does to the village idiot, a girl cared for by others in the village, who lacks even the capacity any normal animal has to look after itself; "everyone in the village was willing to look after her as being an idiot, and so specially dear to God." Any competent reader of Dostoyevsky must draw on an understanding of Karamazov's act as specially vile in its abuse of the specially vulnerable girl; but that understanding is not something a competent reader of moral philosophy is expected to be able to draw on. It is thus possible for moral philosophy to contain arguments like the one I have sketched, remarks like the one I have quoted, which will seem (to those drawing on the capacity for moral thought and understanding expected by Dostoyevsky) to evince utter blindness to what common humanity recognizes. One reason, then, why a theme of the papers on ethics is the relation between moral philosophy and literature is that literature shows us forms of thinking about life and what is good and bad in it, forms of thinking which philosophical requirements on the character of thought, mind, and world may lead us to ignore.

Wittgenstein believed that Russell's and Frege's work on the foundations of mathematics, and the work of mathematicians in set theory, depended on illusions about the significance of those intellectual developments. The aim of the papers on ethics in this volume has analogies to Wittgenstein's aims in relation to both set theory and Frege's and Russell's work on foundations. That is, although I want to argue that we are blind to what moral thought and discussion are like, what *we* are like in our engaging in them, I do not simply want to say "look at the use." Looking at the use may help us see that ethics is not what we think it must be. But ideas about what it must be have shaped what it is, shaped what we do; and looking at the use is not, on its own, enough. In "Realism and the Realistic Spirit," I try to show how the laying down of metaphysical requirements is connected with our thinking that what we want lies somewhere, while it in fact lies somewhere else, that it is dependent on something which it is not dependent on. Thus, e.g., Hylas, in Berkeley's *Three Dialogues,* wants there to be a distinction between real things and chimeras; Peirce wants there to be a distinction between causal and accidental generalities; a moral philosopher may want there to be a distinction between reasonable moral discussion and effective propaganda or between biased and unbiased thought. The aim of the realistic spirit is that of Philonous in relation to Hylas: to show him that what he wants is not where he thinks it can only be, nor dependent on what he thinks it must depend on.

So far as our ideas about what ethics must be like have shaped what we actually do, the realistic spirit, if it frees us from such ideas, will change what we want to do in ethics. Of our own accord we may leave off some kinds of ethical thinking, the attraction of which was inseparable from illusions about ethical rationality. (Compare *Wittgenstein's Lectures on the Foundations of Mathematics,* p. 103.)

Two of the papers on ethics, "Missing the Adventure" and "Anything but Argument?", are directly concerned with philosophically induced blindness. The first takes as an example William Frankena's philosophical blindness to the character of Socrates's moral thought. (The passage I look at comes from a particularly important kind of context, the beginning of an elementary textbook; my argument in the paper bears, therefore, not just on blindness but on blindness as something which we teach.) I want here to make a connection between that paper and another one in this volume, "Riddles and Anselm's Riddle." The discussion of riddles is about how what is in one sense plainly before us may be hidden from us, and about how words can both hide and reveal. In the *Crito*, Socrates's redescription of what he is doing makes it into something in his life and in that of his friends and his sons, something which Crito had not seen it was possible for it to be. The redescription is itself 'set' to Crito as a sort of riddle: "If we go away from here without persuading the city to let us go, do we treat some badly, and those at that whom least of all we should treat badly—or not? Do we stand by our agreements (if they are right) or not?"[13] Crito does not understand and cannot answer, just as he might be unable to answer the riddle. "Do you or do you not have that which, if we catch it, we do not keep, and which, if we do not catch it, we do keep?" Revealing the character of what we might do, as Socrates reveals the character of what he will do, is in some ways like finding or giving the solution to a riddle; riddle-thinking, as one might call it, like the creative and penetrating use of proverbs, stories, jokes, and so on, goes to shape what moral life is like (is part of the face of moral thought), especially in cultures in which such modes of thought are not looked down on in comparison with the use of explicitly formulated principles and arguments.

By turning briefly to Kant, I can show more clearly the connection between the sort of blindness within moral philosophy that is a topic of these papers and riddle-thinking (and the like). In a passage in the *Logic*, Kant makes a contrast between active reasoning and the lazy imitativeness of the use of proverbs, which he associates with the ill-educated. This lazy imitation of the thought of others, this passivity, supports prejudices; and, even if the prejudices turn out (as they sometimes may) to be true, it involves an improper use of our faculties.[14] The insightful and creative application of proverbs is a form of thinking that cannot be fitted into the types, allowed for by Kant, of reasoning about moral things. At the beginning of *Proverbs*, the capacity to understand proverbs is linked with the capacity to understand figures or parables, the sayings of the wise and their riddles.[15]

These capacities, which are prized in some cultures, to turn words, to penetrate them, and thus to bring illumination to something, or (as it may be) to conceal it, cannot be thought of (from a Kantian point of view) simply as belonging to rational capacity as such; they are distributed in an obviously contingent way. Part, though, of Kant's conception of what it is for reason to be actively employed in moral thinking is the requirement that the capacity for such active employment be present in everyone, considered simply as moral agent. Any contingently distributed capacity must be irrelevant to moral rationality. Given this requirement, it is not surprising that proverb-thought is regarded by Kant as passive and imitative. He does not look at moral life and find that people who use proverbs are always mere passive repeaters of the sayings of others; rather, his philosophy allows no place for an active moral self to come to a deeper, or even just a different, understanding by the insightful turning of words. His philosophy can, of course, treat such activities of the mind as a kind of wit; my point is not that Kant cannot see that such verbal play goes on, but that philosophical requirements blind him to its non-decorative place in moral life. An image, a riddle, a proverb, *cannot* be what really brings moral understanding; it can only be inessential trim.

The paper "Anything but Argument?" was also meant as a discussion of philosophical blindness to modes of moral thought, blindness produced by philosophical requirements about what such thought must be like. It is about Onora O'Neill's review of Stephen Clark's *The Moral Status of Animals,* and was misread by Professor O'Neill, who ascribes to 'Wittgensteinians' a view about what makes moral reasoning possible.[16] I do not know how what she says applies to some of the philosophers whom she describes as Wittgensteinians. What concerns me is that it seems to reflect an idea of what philosophy is, an idea which leaves no room for what I have called the realistic spirit, which is what I contrast with the laying down of requirements. In any case, she sees Wittgensteinians as laying down certain characteristic kinds of requirement for moral discourse. Neither in the paper of mine which Professor O'Neill treats as an example of a Wittgensteinian approach to ethics nor in any other do I say or imply that moral discourse about examples can take place only within a context of shared moral traditions and practices within which genuine moral disagreement is merely preliminary and dispellable, that if it persists we have non-communication, or that the only permanent possibilities are moral agreement and lack of moral communication. It is not just that I have never said such a thing and am naturally somewhat aggrieved at its being ascribed to me. I had attempted to describe certain features of what moral life *is* like, without saying anything at all about what it must be like. But blindness to what philosophy itself may be like resulted in that paper's being read as yet another imposition of some set of requirements, namely, 'Wittgensteinian' ones.

I wrote in that paper about ways in which we go on, in ethics, beyond just saying what we think is so; against Professor O'Neill, I claimed that there are *various* ways of going on beyond mere saying, and that, besides argument (which is one such way) there were such things as the telling of stories. The paper sets various non-argumentative ways of talking *alongside* argument; it does not treat them as a recourse when argument—or any other sort of communication—has broken down. Professor O'Neill, however, conceiving 'Wittgensteinians' to have certain views, takes me to hold that, when we are confronted by cases of incommensurable practices, confronted (that is) with the breakdown of moral communication, we can seek to enlarge or reshape the moral structure or outlook of the other person by such things as telling stories, and in that way we may hope to move to a situation in which moral communication becomes possible, i.e., a situation in which agreement can be reached. It is extremely difficult to respond to that with anything short of an oath, but let me simply say that telling stories, or writing novels, is not what people do because communication (moral or other) has broken down. Talk about moral things may include the telling of stories; as much as anything is, the telling of stories is communication or what we hope will be communication. (Communication about moral things, like that about many other things, includes exploration of what will enable the participants to reach each other: that is not 'given' by the existence of a 'practice'. Our practices are exploratory, and it is indeed only through such exploration that we come to see fully what it was that we ourselves thought or wanted to say.) I did speak of stories as capable of changing the ways we look at things, but telling a story in the hope of altering someone's way of looking at things is hardly what we do when we regard someone as "beyond the pale of moral communication"[17]; changing someone's way of looking at things is one perfectly ordinary aim of much communication. That is not just what I take to be the true view; it is also clearly Wittgenstein's. Unfamiliarity with his discussions of mathematics might contribute to someone's missing his view. In those discussions he says that giving someone a proof changes his way of looking at things; and giving someone a proof is hardly what we do because mathematical communication has broken down and we are trying to bring someone outside of our mathematical practice into it. What could be more a part of our mathematical practice than offering mathematical proof?

(Another kind of example is provided by John Wisdom's memorable case of the woman who says to a friend trying on a hat and studying her reflection in a mirror, "My dear, it's the Taj Mahal."[18] This is plainly not a case in which communication has broken down, but the way the woman sees the hat may be radically changed. The remark itself is an exercise of imagination of a sort not entirely different from those I was considering.)

Professor O'Neill thinks that, for 'Wittgensteinians', all justification is relative to locally accepted practice. Story-telling and so on must then (if spoken about by a 'Wittgensteinian') be taken to be among the ways we get people into the locally accepted practice, after which we and they can reason together and reach agreement. Again, it is hard to respond without impatience. Justification, in ethics as anywhere else, goes on within lives we share with others, but what we make count in that life is not laid down in advance. The force of what we are able to say depends on its relation to the life of the words we use, the place of those words in our lives; and we may make the words tell by argument, by image, by poetry, by Socratic redescription, by aphorism, by Humean irony, by proverbs, by all sorts of old and new things. And the judgment whether we produce illumination or obfuscation by doing so, the judgment whether there is truth in our words or self-deception, is not in general something on which there will be agreement. Ethics *is not* like mathematics; the role of agreement, the kind of agreement that there is in ethical thought, is not to be laid down in advance on some general Wittgensteinian principles. We need to see—in ethics as in mathematics—what agreement *belongs to* the intelligibility of the language we use. (Compare the use of *gehören zu* in *PI*, §242.)

I have written with some feeling about all this, although in "Anything but Argument?" I argued that my arguments were in a sense useless, and that, if someone lays down requirements from which it follows that there can be no room for any cases except of some limited kind, one cannot hope to make clear, by a description of cases, what else may be included in our moral lives. But what has made me respond with such strong feeling is the interpretation of that piece as itself simply an imposition of a different, 'Wittgensteinian', set of requirements. The aim of philosophy, as I see it, being in a kind of liberation from laying down this or that requirement, no reading could have seemed more deadly. That reading is based, indeed, on what Stanley Cavell once spoke of as a 'Manichean' conception of a contrast between what supposedly lies 'inside' and what lies 'outside' social practices[19]; and part of the frustration I felt on reading Professor O'Neill was no doubt due to the sense that Cavell had, more than twenty years ago, said all that needed to be said about such ideas. My reason for going into this matter in the introduction is that Professory O'Neill's response to "Anything but Argument?" demonstrates the imposition on philosophical writing of a requirement: that it impose philosophical requirements—the requirement that it say "Regardless of what things look like, if we are to have or do such-and-such, there must be so-and-so."

IV

I turn now to the papers on logic, language and mathematics, i.e., to those explicitly about Wittgenstein and Frege, and to the notion of 'use' in those papers. Earlier I said that Kant's influence was evident in the metaphysical requirements I discuss in the papers here, both those on ethics and those on logic. The Kantian influence I have specially in mind in philosophy of logic is that of Kant's attack on psychology in logic. In this section, I take up the theme of the first introduction, the importance of separating psychology and logic, and show how it bears on Wittgenstein's philosophical aims.

Joan Weiner, in her recently published study of Frege, points out that Frege virtually paraphrases Kant's remarks about the absurdity of messing up logic with questions of how we *do* think.[20] One remark of Kant's which she quotes is particularly striking and important:

> In logic we do not want to know how the understanding is and thinks and how it hitherto has proceeded in thinking, but how it ought to proceed in thinking. Logic must teach us the correct use of the understanding, i.e., that in which it is in agreement with itself.[21]

That idea of the understanding as, in its correct use, in agreement not with some external thing but with itself, is central in my reading of Frege and Wittgenstein. But I should not say "that idea," as if it were a *single* idea, which they all shared. What I want to suggest is rather that there are, in Kant's thought, in Frege's writings, and in the *Tractatus*, different workings out of what it is for the understanding to be 'in agreement with itself' and for logic to teach us what that is. These different workings out are themselves tied to the shifts from Kant to Frege to Wittgenstein in how logic itself is conceived, in what it is for logic to be necessary for all thinking, and in what it is for logic to be non-arbitrary and totally distinct from empirical psychology. (See, on this, Joan Weiner's discussion of Frege's reconstrual, in the light of his own new treatment of logic, of the distinction between analytic and synthetic judgments.)[22] While these ideas about logic are important for both my introductory essays, in this one I am concerned with their relevance to what can be accomplished by philosophy, how its task may be conceived.

A principle for reading Frege and the *Tractatus* can be put this way: look at what particular shape is being given to the notion of the understanding as, in its correct use, in agreement not with some external thing but with itself. The starting point is (as in Introduction I) what Frege thought he had accomplished with his concept-script. I argue in "What Does a Concept-Script Do?" that, on Frege's view of logical categories, they are not fundamental properties of the things we think about, such that we might in our thought get them right or wrong. The idea of logical categories as giving a genuine classification of our objects of thought treats the grasp of categories as if, in it, the understanding were in relation to something external to itself. We can fail to be clear about these categories, a failure which may be reflected in or dependent on a language which does not show them systematically, as Frege's concept-script does; but adequacy and inadequacy of language are a matter of language's revealing what is internal to it *as* language, what belongs to it as capable of expressing thoughts, what belongs to thought as thought. That paper on Frege takes for granted a particular distinction: between logical categories, which show themselves in a good logical notation but cannot properly be put into words (for reasons which I go into in the paper),[23] and the laws of logic, which Frege thinks can be expressed in language in propositions which are significant and true. My reading of the *Tractatus* (in "Throwing Away the Ladder") presents it as an attempt to take further the notion of the internality of logic to the understanding. In Wittgenstein's working out of that notion, it is incompatible with the Fregean conception of the laws of logic as themselves genuinely significant propositions.[24] Just as Frege thought that logical categories are not *classifications of things,* Wittgenstein, taking further the same sorts of consideration, thought that logical laws are not *statements of anything that is so.* The confusions that both Frege and Wittgenstein take themselves to be fighting arise from attempts to represent what is internal to the understanding as if understanding were in agreement with something else.

The notion of logic as giving what it is for the understanding to be in agreement with itself is connected with a way of thinking about the significance of *use.* You cannot see what logical kind of thing I am thinking about except by grasping the role it has in my thoughts. You cannot, as it were, first mentally grab hold of the thing I mean, and then find out if in my thoughts I manage to get its logical characteristics straight. For logical categorization to be internal to thought is for there to be no such thing as *genuinely thinking something* about a thing, and getting its logical character wrong: you may come up with nonsense, but in coming out with nonsense, or saying it to yourself, you are not *thinking* something which disagrees with how things logically are. When you utter nonsense, your words fail to mean anything, but not because they mean something that cannot make sense[25]; the idea of nonsense as a getting wrong of the logical characteristics of things is the idea of logic as a matter of the understanding's being in relation to something external to itself. There is a fundamental connection between Kant's attack on letting psychology into logic and the idea in Frege and Wittgenstein that there is no getting hold of what you are talking about and *then* making propositions about it. What we are talking about by a word is given only via the use of the word in propositions, i.e., in making sense, expressing thoughts.

At the end of "What Does a Concept-Script Do?" I connected the idea of use as showing what we are talking about with the idea of philosophy as freeing us from the "bewitchment of our intelligence by means of language," that is, with the idea of philosophy that we see in Wittgenstein's later work.[26] Frege gave expression, in the Preface of his *Begriffsschrift*, to a hope that the concept-script described in his book would be *liberating*, that it would aid the philosopher in one of his tasks, which is "to break the domination of the word over the human spirit by laying bare misconceptions almost unavoidably arising through ordinary language and by freeing thought from that with which the means of expression of ordinary language saddle it."[27] The Fregean conception of philosophy as liberating is related to that in the *Tractatus*. For both Frege and Wittgenstein (in the *Tractatus*), a conceptual notation is liberating in that it will not be possible in it to put together combinations of signs which, because of the misleading analogies they have to other signs, leave us either unable to recognize what we mean (as when we think we are thinking about a concept but are thinking about something else, and as when we think we have spoken twice of the same thing but have spoken of two different things) or unable to recognize that we are thinking nothing at all. A concept-script in which we can express every thought and in which there is no putting together of signs in ways which leave us unable to recognize ambiguity or nonsense (ambiguity and nonsense of the sort made possible by ordinary language) will thus help break what Frege spoke of as the domination of the word.

My reason for summarizing that view of philosophy as liberating is its close connection with the main theme of this book as a whole. What I need now to do is to explain the contrast between two conceptions of philosophy as liberating: the one I have just sketched and that in Wittgenstein's later philosophy. The way philosophy liberates is—in the *Tractatus and* in Wittgenstein's later philosophy—connected with the significance of 'use' and of willingness or unwillingness to look to the use for what it enables us to see. In the *Tractatus* the notion of use ("logico-syntactical use") is tied to that of an adequate conceptual notation and that of complete logical analysis. In Part I of this introduction, I said that confusion was created by thinking of the shift from the *Tractatus* as any kind of shift from realism to anti-realism. I need now to return to that point. The thoughts expressed in the *Tractatus* are not thoughts expressed by its propositions. The metaphysical-sounding propositions of the book should be seen as they would by someone who has had the thoughts expressed in it, i.e., who will not treat those propositions as expressing any thoughts at all, neither thoughts in a supposed technical *Tractatus* sense nor non-thoughts in that sense but nevertheless indications of something that is unsayably so. "What cannot be said" is not something that is unsayably so. The *Tractatus*, that is, is not an attack on metaphysics as merely unsayable. What cannot be thought cannot be thought, and not cheating on that means not treating "cannot be thought" as meaning *unsayably so*. My point now is that we can see in the *Tractatus* a working out of the Kantian idea that logic is a matter of the understanding being in agreement with itself, a working out which undercuts any idea of *metaphysical being the case*, being sayably or unsayably so, just as we can see an earlier working out of the Kantian idea in Frege's view of logical categories and the significance of a concept-script, a working out which leaves Frege with insoluble difficulties about the logical laws themselves.[28] The Kantian demand that logic be absolutely distinguishable from what empirical psychology can tell us of the natural laws of human thinking is important for both Frege and Wittgenstein—important for the ways in which they show that philosophical confusion can arise from treating the non-arbitrariness of logic as if it were a matter of agreement with something external to the understanding. My argument now is that central to Wittgenstein's later work is the dramatic shift in the idea of what it is for our real needs to be met: what it is for logic to be rigorous, for mathematics to be mathematics, for there to be a difference between following a rule correctly and thinking that one is doing so, for the understanding to be in agreement with itself, a dramatic shift that went with a profound criticism of the *Tractatus*, not a rejection of its 'realist' metaphysics, or of its 'ontology' of this or that, but of a Kantian element of a different sort, a Kantian spirit which lays down, not some ontological conditions for making sense, but internal conditions of language's being language, of thought's being thought. The notion in the later philosophy of philosophy as liberating is thus tied to an ability to look at the use without imposing on it what one thinks must already be there in it. The notion of use itself and what is meant by giving or presenting it thus also changes: an expression is not presented timelessly—its use is not given—by the general form of the propositions it characterizes; use can be seen only as belonging to the spatial, temporal phenomenon of language.[29]

I need to touch briefly on one main feature of many of the papers in this volume, a feature considered also in Introduction I. What is characteristic of language, of using words, is that we do new things. I gave a very simple example in "Riddles and Anselm's Riddle": a baby, having learned to do things in response to "Kiss your hand," "Kiss Mommy's nose," and so on, may be told "Kiss your ear"; an example Wittgenstein uses is the question, set to someone who knows how to say what color things are, "What color is the looking glass?" Many of the papers in this volume are about new things in language, of various sorts, new things which may be trivial or not so. It would be a confusion (analogous to some of the confusion I discuss in Introduction I) to think that when we do something new, this is to leap out of some practice into a non-practice, or out of shared life-with-language, or something of the kind. *Look.* Take riddles, for example; take the riddle in Act IV, Scene ii of *Measure for Measure.*

> Every true man's apparel fits your thief: if it be too little for your thief, your true man thinks it big enough; if it be too big for your thief, your thief thinks it little enough: so every true man's apparel fits your thief.

"Apparel" is here given a new use: this apparel is not cut with shears, not sewn or woven or knitted. My edition of the play says in a footnote to the description of this apparel, which is not explicitly presented as a riddle, "Interpretation uncertain,"[30] but it is 'uncertain' only because the editor has not revived in himself the familiarity he once had (if he was a child like the rest of us) with the language-game of riddling, i.e., of making and playing with new uses in certain ways. The language-game we learned with "apparel" does not contain a rule that a coffin counts as apparel; and, if one wants to say that the 'rules of riddling' allow it to count as apparel, that is a way of obscuring from oneself how very different are what one is calling "rules" in the two cases. Speaking of any coffin, however large or small, as neither too large nor too small for the thief, and thus as fitting him, is a new use of "fit," and so is speaking of a proposition as fitting a fact. We might put alongside *that* use of "fit," the use of "agree" in "Logic must teach us the correct use of the understanding, that in which it agrees with itself." A reflexive use of "agree," like Kant's, moves on from, and takes for granted familiarity with, what itself was once a new sort of move, namely, using "fit" or "agree" for thought in relation to what it is about. What I earlier called workings out of the idea of logic as showing us that use of the understanding in which it is in agreement with itself could just as well have been described as solutions to the riddle: "When does the understanding agree with itself?"

Moves in new directions from what we have done with words are themselves a motley. There is nothing in Wittgenstein's writings, in particular nothing in the kinds of criticism he brings to our philosophizing, which implies that moving with words beyond what we have done with those words in the language-games in which we learned to use them has anything the matter with it, or is not something we can judge as appropriate or inappropriate, worth the doing or not. The idea of Wittgenstein's philosophy as inherently *conservative* is nutty. At the heart of his discussion of that most profoundly rule-governed of all our intellectual activities, mathematics, is his account of interesting mathematical questions and the mathematical developments that are initiated by them as involving kinds of new move that can illuminatingly be compared with riddles. The interpretation of his philosophy as conservative results in part from lack of attention to what he says about mathematics; but it is supported also by what I earlier described as the imposition on philosophy itself of the philosophical requirement that it lay down requirements. And that is the refusal of the kind of liberation that he hoped philosophy might bring.

I can now turn back to a difficulty, alluded to in Part II, for my reading of Wittgenstein. (A corresponding difficulty can be raised about my reading of Frege.) I have often heard it argued, as if it were some kind of absolutely knock-down claim, that it is ridiculous to take seriously the idea that the propositions of the *Tractatus* are nonsensical. The claim is that, if they were nonsensical, they could not form part of an argument (as they do) and could be replaced by any other nonsensical propositions, for nonsensical propositions clearly cannot differ in sense. "Riddles and Anselm's Riddle" contains not so much a reply as an indication of what sort of reply is possible. In that paper I discuss riddle-reasoning: the derivation of conditions that the solution to a riddle must meet, a kind of derivation that can be given even if we have no idea what the riddle-phrase means. Applied to mathematics there is a corresponding but stronger point: the derivation of conditions from what may be treated as analogous to a riddle-phrase (e.g., "the rational number p/q which squared gives 2") does not depend upon the riddle-phrase's being anything but a linguistic construction. Movement from phrase to phrase goes on the basis of linguistic analogies; the use of the riddle-phrase in the development of these analogies is all there is, at that stage, to its meaning. That account is developed in the paper on riddles; my point now is that an account of the role of nonsensical propositions in the argument of the *Tractatus* can be given in terms of a kind of riddling, a play with sentences of a certain construction, the result of which is the rejection of such sentences as meaningless. The reasonableness of that ultimate rejection of the sentences does not require that the sentences themselves are anything more than constructions resembling other, senseful, propositions of the language. Overconfidence in the power of the argument that the *Tractatus* propositions must make sense (because they form an argument that we understand) has various sources. One may be found in what it shares with the idea of the editor of *Measure for Measure* that the interpretation of the executioner's words in Act IV, Scene ii is uncertain, and with Kant's idea that the use of proverbs is merely imitative. We have forgotten how far riddles go or have chosen to turn our backs on our knowledge.[31]

The *Tractatus* and the *Investigations* have this in common: they do not invite us to give up the making of philosophical propositions *because* such propositions are nonsensical (because they are a priori, or departures from some language-game, or in whatever other way fail to meet some supposed requirement). They both treat philosophical propositions as constructions we make on the basis of linguistic analogies, patterns, or images in our language. We may come to see that we do not want to go on doing anything with these linguistic constructions; the satisfaction of our needs does not lie that way. We abandon them; we leave them unused; we say "These we *do not* want." To call them nonsensical is to exclude them in that way from the commerce of our lives.

V

I want to draw together three themes of this introduction by juxtaposing four quotations. The themes are Wittgenstein's later view of philosophy as laying down no philosophical or metaphysical requirements; Kant and a Kantian spirit in ethics and logic; and riddles and riddle-thinking. The first of the four quotations is Kant's, already given, on logic as showing us the correct use of the understanding, in which it is in agreement with itself. The second is a fragment of the quotation, at the beginning of Part I, from *Philosophical Investiga-*

tions §402: "When . . . we are out of agreement with the expressions of ordinary language. . . ." The third is from Frege; I use it in "Frege against Fuzz": "Just as it would be impossible for geometry to set up precise laws if it tried to recognize threads as lines and knots in threads as points, so logic must demand sharp limits of what it will recognize as a concept unless it wants to renounce all precision and certainty."[32] And so too for Kant in ethics: there are limits to what ethics will recognize as moral rationality unless it wants to renounce the necessity that belongs to the moral law. No threads or knots in logic or ethics! "Back to the rough ground!" is Wittgenstein's reply; and that is my fourth quotation.[33] "Back to the rough ground": that is, we have a false idea of how our thready, knotty lives can stand in relation to the rigor of logic, the bindingness of ethics, the necessity of mathematics. We are dazzled, Wittgenstein says, by ideals, and fail to understand their role in our language.[34] When we are thus dazzled, we are "out of agreement" with ourselves, our language, our lives of threads and knots. I have suggested that we treat the quotation from Kant as a riddle, that we see Kant, Frege, and the *Tractatus* as giving us solutions to "What is it for the understanding to be in agreement with itself?" Wittgenstein's later philosophy does not turn away from that riddle; it turns it round: asking it as we had been, we were "out of agreement" with ourselves. Philosophy can return us to "agreement with ourselves" where we least thought to find it. The solution to the riddle was right there in the knots and threads.

Notes

1. Thomas Ricketts, "Objectivity and Objecthood: Frege's Metaphysics of Judgment," in *Frege Synthesized*, ed. L. Haaparanta and J. Hintikka (Dordrecht, 1986).
2. *Philosophical Investigations*, I, §426.
3. *Philosophical Investigations*, I, §402.
4. See G.E.M. Anscombe, "The Reality of the Past," in her *Metaphysics and the Philosophy of Mind* (Minnesota, 1981), pp. 103–19, especially p. 103.
5. Ronald J. Butler, "A Wittgensteinian on 'The Reality of the Past'," *Philosophical Quarterly* 6 (1956), pp. 304–14, at p. 307, discussing G.E.M. Anscombe, op. cit., especially pp. 113–116.
6. The claim that he thinks that there are no facts to which our forms of expression are answerable is also in conflict with his discussion of the answerability of forms of expression to reality in *Wittgenstein's Lectures on the Foundations of Mathematics: Cambridge 1939*, ed. Cora Diamond (Ithaca, 1976; reprinted Chicago, 1989), Lectures XXV–XXVI.
7. *Nothing is Hidden* (Oxford, 1986), chapter 2.
8. Compare Malcolm, p. 24.
9. About such an interpretation, Thomas Ricketts says that what the *Tractatus* calls 'showing' "is thus made over into a special sort of saying"; he gives a detailed argument against such a reading of the *Tractatus* (in "Facts, Logic, and the Crit-

icism of Metaphysics in the *Tractatus*," unpublished). For related arguments against such readings of the *Tractatus*, see Warren Goldfarb, "Objects, Names, and Realism in the *Tractatus*" (unpublished); Peter Winch, "Language, Thought and World in Wittgenstein's *Tractatus*," in his *Trying to Make Sense* (Oxford, 1987), pp. 3–17; Brian McGuinness, "The So-Called Realism of the *Tractatus*," in *Perspectives on the Philosophy of Wittgenstein*, ed. Irving Block (Oxford, 1981), pp. 60–73; Hidé Ishiguro, "Use and Reference of Names," in *Studies in the Philosophy of Wittgenstein*, ed. Peter Winch (London, 1969), pp. 20–50; Rush Rhees, " 'The Philosophy of Wittgenstein'," in his *Discussions of Wittgenstein* (London, 1970), pp. 37–54.

10. My account of the critical bearing of Wittgenstein's later thought on the *Tractatus* is related to Warren Goldfarb's reading of §§1–20 of *Philosophical Investigations* in "I Want You to Bring Me a Slab: Remarks on the Opening Sections of *Philosophical Investigations*," *Synthese* **56** (1983), pp. 265–82. The exiguousness of what I call metaphysical in the *Tractatus* can be connected with the primitiveness of the steps in our philosophizing which are, on Goldfarb's view, the objects of Wittgenstein's criticism in those sections of the *Investigations*. What I call the realistic spirit in philosophy thus involves the sort of critical attention, described by Goldfarb, to the misconceptions that accompany the beginnings of our philosophizing.

11. See *Philosophical Investigations*, I, §235.

12. Peter Singer, *Animal Liberation* (New York, 1975), p. 82.

13. *Crito* 49e–50a; trans. A.D. Woozley, in his *Law and Obedience* (London, 1979).

14. Immanuel Kant, *Logic*, trans. Robert S. Hartman and Wolfgang Schwarz (Indianapolis and New York, 1974), pp. 83–86.

15. *Proverbs* 1.6.

16. Onora O'Neill, "The Power of Example," *Philosophy* **61** (1986), pp. 5–29, at pp. 13–15.

17. op. cit., p. 14.

18. John Wisdom, "The Modes of Thought and the Logic of God," in *The Existence of God*, ed. John Hick (New York, 1964), pp. 275–298, at p. 277.

19. Stanley Cavell, "The Availability of Wittgenstein's Later Philosophy," in his *Must We Mean What We Say?* (New York, 1969), pp. 44–72, at p. 47.

20. Joan Weiner, *Frege in Perspective* (Ithaca, 1990), chapter 2.

21. Kant, op. cit., p. 16. I have altered the translation. Kant speaks of the *mit sich selbst übereinstimmenden Gebrauch des Verstandes*.

22. Joan Weiner, chapter 2.

23. See also P.T. Geach, "Saying and Showing in Frege and Wittgenstein," *Essays on Wittgenstein in Honour of G.H. von Wright*, ed. Jaakko Hintikka, *Acta Philosophica Fennica* **28** (Amsterdam, 1976), pp. 54–70.

24. See on this matter also Thomas G. Ricketts, "Frege, The *Tractatus*, and the Logocentric Predicament," *Noûs* **15** (1985), pp. 3–15. In two other papers, Ricketts shows how Frege's anti-psychologism shapes his notions of objectivity and of the significance of logic so that there can be no question of a gap between language or thought and reality: "Objectivity and Objecthood: Frege's Metaphysics of Judgment," *Frege Synthesized*, ed. L. Haaparanta and J. Hintikka (Dordrecht 1986), pp. 65–95; "Generality, Meaning, and Sense in Frege," *Pacific Philosophical Quarterly* **67** (1986), pp. 172–95.

25. See *Philosophical Investigations*, I, §500, discussed in "What Nonsense Might Be" in this volume.

26. See *Philosophical Investigations*, I, §109.

27. Gottlob Frege, *Begriffsschrift*, trans. Stefan Bauer-Mengelberg, in *From Frege to Gödel*, ed. Jean van Heijenoort (Cambridge, Massachusetts, 1967), pp. 1–82, at p. 7.
28. See Ricketts, "Frege, The *Tractatus*, and the Logocentric Predicament."
29. *Philosophical Investigations*, I, §108.
30. S. Nagarajan, ed., in *The Complete Signet Classic Shakespeare* (New York, 1972), p. 1163.
31. A further account of the philosophical method of the *Tractatus* and its use of nonsensical propositions is in my "Ethics, Imagination and the Method of Wittgenstein's *Tractatus*," forthcoming in *Wiener Reihe* **5**, 1991.
32. Gottlob Frege, letter to Peano, 29.9.1896, *Philosophical and Mathematical Correspondence*, ed. Gottfried Gabriel et al., trans. Hans Kaal (Oxford, 1980), pp. 114–15.
33. *Philosophical Investigations*, I, §107.
34. *Philosophical Investigations*, I, §100.

Chapter 1
Realism and the Realistic Spirit

Not empiricism and yet realism in philosophy, that is the hardest thing.[1]

Wittgenstein directed that remark against F.P. Ramsey, but he was at the same time making a general point about philosophy. That general point is what I shall discuss. My account may also be read as a reply— of sorts—to Saul Kripke.[2] In recently published works Kripke has expounded a reading of Wittgenstein as formulating sceptical solutions, in the manner of Hume, to sceptical problems.[3] In particular he takes Wittgenstein, in his discussion of rules, to be setting forth a sceptical paradox, "the fundamental problem of *Philosophical Investigations*." But sceptical problems *and* their solutions (sceptical solutions or those of philosophical realism) are, for Wittgenstein, signs that we have misconstrued our own needs in philosophy. How do we come to do that? That *is* one of the fundamental problems of Wittgenstein's philosophy. A discussion of the remark about realism, with which I have begun, can cast some light on it.

"Not empiricism and *yet* realism": this may seem puzzling. For whatever exactly we mean by realism in philosophy, we should usually have in mind a view which in some way or other emphasized the significance of what is independent of *our* thought and experience; and whatever exactly we mean by empiricism, empiricism would seem to deny the significance of what is independent of our experience, if indeed it even admits that it is intelligible to speak of such an independent reality at all. So what can be meant by "not empiricism and *yet* realism"? The suggestion appears to be that empiricism is something we get into in philosophy by trying to be realists but going about it in the wrong way, or not hard enough. But what sort of attempt at realism can empiricism be thought to be?

We can try to answer the question by looking at some of the non-philosophical uses of the term "realism." We may tell someone to "be realistic," when he is maintaining something in the teeth of the facts, or refusing even to look at them. Or again if he knows what the facts *ought* to be, either from a theory or wishful thinking, and will not take the world to be something capable of shaking his belief. We also speak of realism in connection with novels and stories; and here again we often have in mind certain kinds of attention to reality: to detail and particularity. We are not, that is, handed too many characters who are simply given by their labels: a Manchester factory owner of the 1840s, let us say, where the details of the behavior are merely illustrations of the way a person of that type would be expected to behave. We are not given lots of sentences like "Like all Russian officials, he had a weakness for cards."[4] The weakness for cards of a character in a realistic novel may be shown us, but it will be shown as it is in him, and will not simply be a *deduction*. We expect in a realistic novel something you might call a phenomenalism of character: it is built up out of observed detail, and in a sense there is nothing to it over and above what we are shown. That is evidently an oversimplification. To make it less of one, I should have to say something about how what is said about a character, when it goes beyond what we have been shown, may be tied to what is actually there in the story. I should have to develop the parallel between going on beyond what we see of a character and going on beyond—in the way the phenomenalist thinks we can—what we perceive, in our talk of chairs in an unoccupied room. But that is not my present concern; I want to indicate only that once we look outside philosophy, the idea of connections between what is *there* called 'realism' and what we associate with empiricism becomes less puzzling.

A further characteristic of realistic fiction, which is relevant in the same sort of way, is that certain things do not happen in it. People do not go backwards in time, pots do not talk, elves do not do chores while shoemakers sleep, and holy men do not walk unaided over the surface of lakes or oceans. We all know that if God sells wine in an English village, we do not call the story realistic; and if the devil turns up in a realistic novel, it is within what we can take to be some extraordinary experience of one of the characters, say in a dream or in delirium. Magic, myth, fantasy, superstition: in different ways are terms used in making contrasts with realism. And again with this non-philosophical use of "realism" there is a connection with empiricism, with its characteristic attempts to banish from philosophy (or from our thought more generally) myth, magic, superstition of various sorts, or what it sees as that.

There is a third characteristic of realism outside philosophy, related to both of the others, and this is the significance of consequences, of causation. A man wanting to bring about some social reform will be said to be unrealistic if he does not attend to how politics *works*; he might be said to be realistic if he gives not just moral arguments but statistics showing that the injustice he is protesting against actually does not pay. Similarly in a novel; it is unrealistic if the plot proceeds by a series of improbable events, incredible coincidences, and the like; rather, in a realistic story, events develop out of each other, characters respond to circumstances and so on: there is operative a conception of how things work in our lives, what leads to what, what sorts of things do in actual fact determine how events proceed. It is connected with this that a novel in which vice is defeated and virtue flourishes in the end is often felt as unrealistic: that is not how things are determined. The duke does not reveal himself, and the king's messenger does not come riding up. I shall show later why this aspect of realism, its insistence on consequences, on realistic coherence, has close connections with empiricism.

We may ask whether it is likely—or even possible—that Wittgenstein had in mind anything like the things I have been talking about when he suggested that empiricism could be taken as an attempt at realism. Here are two pieces of evidence, supporting a claim that it is at least possible.

(1) Although he normally uses "realism" and related terms in the ordinary philosophical way, he did also use "realistic" in the non-philosophical sense. He wrote, in an earlier section of *Remarks on the Foundations of Mathematics:*

> The conception of calculation as an experiment tends to strike us as the only *realistic* one.
> Everything else, we think, is moonshine. In an experiment we have something tangible.[5]

Later in that passage, he uses "obscurantism" to make the contrast with realism. Denying that a calculation is an experiment (or that mathematics is about signs, or that pain is a form of behavior) seems like obscurantism "because people believe that one is asserting the existence of an intangible, i.e. a shadowy, object side by side with what we all can grasp."[6]

(2) Wittgenstein's remark, I mentioned, was directed against Ramsey—who took a view of logic which Wittgenstein rejected, as giving a wrong place to the empirical. Ramsey held that whenever we make an inference (of any sort) we do so according to some rule or habit. These processes by which we form opinions may be criticized: our mental habits are to be judged "by whether they work, i.e. whether the opinions they lead to are for the most part true, or more often true than those which alternative habits would lead to."[7] What Ram-

sey calls the general conception of logic is of a science telling men how they should think; i.e., it is engaged in just such criticism of habits of thought, and thus even the principles we use in mathematical calculation and in formal logic can be criticized: do they *work*? If other ways of calculating or other rules of inference turned out to be more reliable, we should have reason to change. For Wittgenstein this was the *wrong* way to show the bearing of empirical data on logic. But, still, granting (as I think is clear in the context) that it is *that* view of Ramsey's that Wittgenstein is criticizing, why should his empiricism be thought of as a kind of realism or an attempt at realism?

It is Ramsey himself who provides an answer. In one of his last papers, Ramsey defended an empiricist view of causality, a view closely related to Hume's.[8] Part of it is an account of such propositions as "All men are mortal," which he refers to as variable hypotheticals. Ramsey was concerned to deny the intelligibility of two alternative philosophical views about such propositions: one view takes them to express real connections between universals, and the other takes them to express infinite conjunctions (even though if we think of them as conjunctions they would go beyond anything we could express *as such*). What drives people to such views, Ramsey says, is certain misleading analogies, and the emotional satisfaction which they give to certain kinds of mind. He adds, "Both these forms of 'realism' must be rejected by the realistic spirit."[9] Rejected by the realistic spirit, that is, *for* an empiricist account. We have a picture here of the philosophical 'realist' as someone misled by phantoms, by what appears to make sense but is really nonsense, by what could make no difference to us in any case. Earlier in the paper Ramsey had made the same sort of point in contrasting "All men are mortal" with "The Duke of Wellington is mortal."[10] The latter, which expresses what Ramsey calls a "belief of the primary sort" is

> a map of neighboring space by which we steer. It remains such a map however much we complicate it or fill in details. But if we professedly extend it to infinity, it is no longer a map; we cannot take it in or steer by it. Our journey is over before we need its remoter parts.

Considered as a proposition, what it would be saying (if we can make sense of that idea at all) would be something useless to us; and Ramsey then argues for an account of these variable hypotheticals as not strictly speaking propositions at all.

Ramsey's contrast between the philosophical 'realist' and the realistic spirit, the former taken in by illusions which the latter can see to be illusions, irrelevant to any distinction which we might have the least use for—this contrast may make us think of Berkeley. For Berkeley is concerned to show us that *matter* in the philosophical sense will be seen by the realistic spirit to be nothing but a philosophical fantasy. In the *Three Dialogues*, Hylas is portrayed exactly as someone who has to be brought back to the modes of thinking of the realistic spirit, has to be helped to remove the false glasses that have been so painfully obstructing his vision of reality.[11] That image, of glasses which we do not see that we can remove, is in Wittgenstein too,[12] used by him in somewhat different ways, but there are important similarities. Hylas has taken himself all along to be like someone wearing distorting spectacles: he has (or so he has thought) only the dimmest grasp of things as they really are, independent of perception, because he knows them only indirectly, through perception. The removal of the glasses is the recognition, through philosophical discussion, that his perceptions never were something between him and the real: he has all along (unbeknownst to his bemused self) been perceiving what *is* real. With the 'removal' of the glasses, he is able to take a totally different view of the reality of what he perceives; he no longer peers vainly for something beyond it.

In Wittgenstein's use of the image, the philosopher who takes himself to be wearing irremovable glasses does not take these to be *distorting* his view. The 'glasses' here are the underlying logical order of all thought, the philosopher the author of the *Tractatus*. Because he is convinced that all thought *must* have this order, he is convinced that he is able to see it in the reality of our actual thought and talk, even though the ways we think and speak do not (to what he takes to be a superficial view) appear to exhibit such an order. (Imagine, for example, a philosopher visiting France, where they draw a line through the name of a town on a sign one can see as one leaves. He thinks "The line is a sort of negation sign, but since one cannot negate a name, what is really negated by

> [Mont~~éli~~mar]

is not the name but the sentence 'You are now in Montélimar'." Where in actual use there is a name, he sees there to be *really* a use of an abbreviated sentence.)

What is common to both uses of the image of the glasses is that the philosopher who takes himself to be in them misrepresents to himself the significance of what is before his eyes, and takes himself to be concerned rather with the *real* nature of something, where that real nature is not open to view. The *removal* of the glasses is his being able to see properly what always was before him; what stood in the way of his removing them was a confused understanding of language. In what sense that understanding of language is 'unrealistic' is a point I shall return to. I shall first continue with the characterization of the realistic spirit, as we may see it embodied by Berkeley in Philonous.

A very striking passage in the second *Dialogue* begins

> Look! are not the fields covered with a delightful vendure? Is there not something in the woods and groves, in the rivers and clear springs, that soothes, that delights, that transports the soul?[13]

And so it continues. One may say that Philonous, in this and other passages, is *celebrating* the reality of the world of the senses; and this is portrayed as a response from which poor Hylas is quite alienated. Taken in by philosophical principles that "lead us to think all the visible beauty of the creation a false imaginary glare," he is convinced that there is nothing whose real nature we can know.[14] For him the things we actually experience have at best a merely secondary and derivative sort of reality, where the real reality is something which causes our sensations and whose character—? Well, can we know it? Perhaps we can arrive at it through science, perhaps not at all—who knows? This is the 'being in pain' about the unknown natures and absolute existence of things which Hylas ascribes to himself and which cuts him off from the kind of response we see in Philonous. (For an earlier version, in Berkeley, of the contrast between the attitude of the 'realistic spirit' to the world and that of the philosophers, we may look at the *Philosophical Commentaries* [517a]: "N.B. I am more for reality than any other Philosophers, they make a thousand doubts and know not certainly but we may be deceiv'd. I assert the direct Contrary.")

Philonous's attitude to the world of the senses could be put by paraphrasing a remark of Wittgenstein's. In reply to the suggestion that one might be said to *believe* of another person that he is not an automaton, Wittgenstein says, "My attitude towards him is an attitude towards a soul (*eine Einstellung zur Seele*). I am not of the *opinion* that he has a soul."[15] The attitude of Philonous, of the realistic spirit, to the world as he knows it in sense perception is an attitude to the real: to the real real enough that there is no question of something missing from it, no question of something else beyond it in virtue of which it is perception of the real. This *Einstellung zur Wirklichkeit* is inseparable, that is, from the idea that whatever more you might think you wanted would not make any real difference at all. "Whatever more": and it is indeed left vague. Hylas's claim is that *matter* is the needed 'more', but how exactly that is to be understood is not something on which he is willing to be pinned down. But whether or no there is such a thing as this 'matter' that he thinks is essential to the reality of what is perceived, *it would make no difference*—or so Philonous believes. Matter, then, has exactly the character of an 'idle wheel', to use Wittgenstein's expression: part of his criticism of the idea that we must keep hold of a mental sample of pain to fix what we mean by the word "pain." But someone who could not keep hold of such a thing might be none the worse for it, might use the word as we all do; and the mental sample, the supposedly crucial thing, has in fact no work to do.

We have there, in Berkeley and in Wittgenstein, a sort of philosophical criticism of a concept, quite different from the criticism based on ontological parsimony which one finds in Russell, for example. The difference hinges on the distinction between *mistake* and *fantasy*. In what I have just called Russell's ontological parsimony, a refusal to accept the existence of entities which one *can* do without is justified on the ground that it is safer; you are diminishing the risk of error.[16] But 'matter' in Berkeley, the 'private object' in Wittgenstein, are not hypotheses which are unsafe and, because also unnecessary, better dropped. Rather, if you think that some significant distinction rests on whether there is or is not something *x*, and you are shown that the presence or absence of *x* *could* make no difference of the sort you wanted it to make, this is puzzling in a way an unnecessarily risky hypothesis would not be; it shows that you were in some unclarity about the distinction that you were trying to explain to yourself,[17] and that you had in a sense substituted a fantasy for the real difference. You *knew* what ought to be, what *had* to be, the basis of the distinction, and so you did not look to see how the distinction actually is made, what that is like.

So much, one might say, for generalities, for the merely suggestive: what does this sort of criticism actually *come to*? I shall try to answer, but before the generalities are over, here is another—about how the terms of criticism I have been talking about differ from Russell's. The idea of the idle wheel is of something trundled onto the stage and said to be what is doing the work, but in fact that is just a label stuck on it; if we were to look behind we should see that the thing had no connections with the mechanism at all. But these terms of criticism, that we have here a fantasy of how things work, not (as in the Russellian criticism) an overelaborate conception of them, belong with ideas outside philosophy of what it is to think or write realistically. In particular, the idea of the idle wheel as a tool of criticism belongs with the third strand in realism that I mentioned earlier: attention to the way things actually do work. It is not unlike, for example, the idea of the fairy godmother, as used by George Orwell in criticizing some of Dickens's novels.[18] He speaks of the role in these novels of the character of the good rich man as that of a fairy godmother, scattering guineas instead of waving a wand to solve problems; and Orwell's point is that in these novels there is a *fantasy* of what it is to act in such a way as to change a situation or resolve a problem: this in works invoking standards which make such fantasy inappropriate. There is a loss of a sense of the real, of which the writer is not aware. It is important that this is not a criticism of the writer's idea of how things happen, that he is *mistaken* about it, but rather that he has lost hold of the idea that he has to show things being made to happen and not just say that they have been made to. That is, the 'fairy godmother' criticism, like that of the 'idle wheel', depends on the distinction between mistake and fantasy.

To return to the case of matter and the attack on it by Philonous, the realistic spirit. The claim that the absence (or presence) of matter would make no difference at all goes with an attempt to enable us to see how we actually make the distinctions which we called in matter to explain. Take for instance the distinction between what there really is and what is merely chimerical, a product of imagination or whatever. We are in a muddle about this distinction, we misrepresent it to ourselves; and one characteristic feature of the muddle is our belief that the distinction *must* depend on something beyond what we perceive. Berkeley's attempt to deal with the confusion has two parts: description and diagnosis, as it were. The description is meant to show us that exactly where we thought the distinction *could not* be made, it *can* be, and indeed is; and the diagnosis aims to explain how the confusion arises from a fantasy of the way language itself works. (The diagnosis is explicit only in the *Principles of Human Knowledge*, but can be seen to apply to much that is put into Hylas's mouth in the *Three Dialogues*.) There is a similar two-part procedure—of description of the sort of details which we are inclined a priori to think *cannot* be what is involved, and diagnosis of why we are inclined that way—in Wittgenstein, when he discusses the problem of the relation between a word and what it stands for. He says that "in order to see more clearly, here as in countless similar cases, we must focus on the details of what goes on; must *look at them from close to*" (§51). He goes on

> If I am inclined to suppose that a mouse has come into being by spontaneous generation out of grey rags and dust, I shall do well to examine those rags very closely to see how a mouse may have hidden in them, how it may have got there and so on. But if I am

convinced that a mouse cannot come into being from these things, then this investigation will perhaps be superfluous.

But first we must learn to understand what it is that opposes such an examination of details in philosophy (§52).

The realistic spirit does not then know so well that you cannot get a mouse from rags that it will not *look at* the rags. What I am suggesting is that Berkeley's aim is like Wittgenstein's: to show that philosophers miss the details, the rags, that a philosophical mouse comes out of, because something has led them to think that no mouse *can* come out of *that*. Berkeley's mouse—the one we are concerned with—is the distinction between real things and chimeras. For Hylas, real existence is existence distinct from and without any relation to being perceived; and so if the horse we see (in contrast to the one we merely imagine) *is* real, it is because its sensible appearance to us is caused by qualities inhering in a material body, which has an absolute existence independent of our own. The judgment that the horse is real and not imaginary, not a hallucination, is thus a hypothesis going beyond anything we might be aware of by our senses, though indeed it is clear on Hylas's view that we must use the evidence of our senses in trying to *tell* what is real. Still, it is not what we actually see or hear or touch that we are ultimately concerned with in such judgments; and this because *however* things appear to us, it is quite another matter how they *are*. Philonous, in reply to Hylas's question what difference there can be, on his views, between real things and chimeras, describes how we do tell the difference. The important thing is the general point: "In short," Philonous says to Hylas,

> by whatever method you distinguish *things* from *chimeras* on your own scheme, the same, it is evident, will hold also upon mine. For it must be, I presume, by some perceived difference, and I am not for depriving you of any one thing that you perceive.[19]

Our actual ways of handling different sorts of perceived differences (e.g., coherence with "the preceding and subsequent transactions of our lives" and lack of such coherence): these are the rags we will not look at, so convinced are we that no mouse can come into being from them.

In other words, Philonous takes Hylas to have a picture in his mind of what is involved in telling honest things from chimeras (a picture which leads Hylas to think that Philonous is in no position to tell the difference), and contrasts it with the methods, whatever they may be, which Hylas actually uses. Describe any procedure that you actually use—and of course Philonous can use it too. And what then is it that he was supposedly *unable* to do, not picturing the difference as Hylas did?—The philosophical technique is one of great power, which surprisingly is often missed. That is, a philosopher will make a claim open to the kind of attack Philonous makes, without seeing the necessity to protect himself on that side at all. C.S. Peirce, for example, argues that unless we suppose active general principles in nature, we have no way to distinguish a mere coincidence from a uniformity on which we can rely, on which we can base a prediction. The reply of the realistic spirit is that an active general principle is so much gas unless you say how you tell that you have got one; and if you give any method, it will be a method which anyone can use to distinguish laws from accidental uniformities without having to decorate the method with the phrase "active general principle." Peirce of course knows that there are such methods, but assumes that his mouse—properly *causal* regularity—cannot conceivably come into being from the rags: patterns of observed regularities.[20]

At this point someone might wish to raise an objection. I have called attention to Berkeley's technique, exemplified in the reply to Hylas about how things may be distinguished from chimeras, and have described it as powerful. *But*—this is the objection—what is this technique but the familiar verificationist technique of challenging anyone who comes up with some distinction between A's and B's to say how it is established that something is an A and not a B? What in our experience—the verificationist asks—counts as establishing such a claim? For if the question cannot be answered, then—the suggestion is—the claim lacks cognitive content; and whatever cognitive content it has is to be seen in the ways its truth or falsity can be settled.

And—the objection now continues—if there is a resemblance between things in Wittgenstein and this element in Berkeley, is that not simply a reflection of the fact that there is a verificationist streak in much of Wittgenstein's post-*Tractatus* writings? Does this not explain the resemblance without there being any need to appeal to a notion of realism which has to be explained by reference to literary and other non-philosophical talk of realism? And, finally, is it not extremely misleading, to say the least, to take this element of verificationism in Wittgenstein and the empiricists and start calling it—of all things— realism? Given, that is, the established philosophical uses of that term, which have in common (if anything) a spirit opposed to just exactly what you have been calling the realistic spirit and what would better be called the reductivist spirit?

To which my reply is: Wait a minute.—That objection came as an interruption. I had been in the middle of Berkeley's discussion of the distinction between real things and chimeras. He describes roughly how we do distinguish them; and it was my account of that that led to the objection just now. But he is also concerned with *what* stops us looking. And what I want to do is leave the objection temporarily and turn to what I have called his diagnosis.

Berkeley conceives our state of mind here as more or less like this. What we are *doing* is not attending to our actual ways of telling what is real—which do not involve an *idea* of being real. We look *past* the variety of different ways of handling experiential data, because we take ourselves to be on to something beyond it, beyond anything as muddy and untidy as that.[21] We think that our practice—whatever it is—is just a way of getting at something we have an idea of: what really *is*, what really is out there and independently real; and it is that notion of reality that we call in matter to explain. That is, the not looking at the details of our methods of judging what is real goes with the idea of something that we are really after, whatever the details may be of how we try to get *it*. The details appear irrelevant, because we think we can make out something *else*, which, if we did not have it or at least believe that we did, would make pointless our actual practices of using evidence as we do in judging what is real. To think, though, that we are on to something else here, that we have an idea of what it is to be real which is what guides us in our practice—this is to think that the term "real" means something besides what we should see if we looked at how we tell real things. To conceive the matter in this way reflects, Berkeley thinks, a fundamental confusion about language, about what it is for a term to be kept to a fixed meaning, for there to be anything guiding us, constraining us, in our actual use.

A diagnosis of the same kind could be given of the passage I quoted in Peirce. Peirce thinks that we must suppose there to be "active general principles" in nature if we are to distinguish causal from accidental regularities. The practices of distinguishing as we do, of making predictions in the case of some regularities and not in others, must reflect a conception of something over and above the regularities. We have to believe in something *real* to which the formula we use in making a prediction *corresponds* (it is Peirce who uses italics on these words); else we should have to regard *all* observed regularities as equally due to chance. Any observed regularity might be mere accident, a weird coincidence not to be betted upon to happen again; to take it to be *not* that, as we do in predicting, is to believe in something *else,* the connection underlying the observed regularity. The "real generals" (or "active general principles in nature") to which our formulations of natural law correspond play the role for Peirce that matter does for Hylas; because he is so convinced that we need them in order to distinguish as we do, he is convinced that he is aware of them, and that no one who was not could reasonably believe that the next stone he dropped would fall. Without matter, we should have—it seems—to take all appearances as equally *mere* appearances, without "real generals," all regularities as equally mere chance. In all this, Peirce shows himself—from the point of view of a Berkeley—a sufferer from the disease Belief in Abstract General Ideas. Its most characteristic symptom is his way of conceiving the connections between events. The only reason there can be for accepting a prediction is belief in a connection supposed to be *real,* in the sense of independent of our thought,[22] and for which the observed regularity is evidence. But "real connection," as thus conceived, is as much an abstract idea (in Berkeley's sense) as "absolute existence" is in Hylas.

Berkeley, I said, thinks that the source of the disease is a wrong idea of what it is for a term to be kept to a fixed meaning. That wrong idea leads us to think that we need something that we do not need: matter or whatever it may be; it also leads us to think that we have *got* what we need, in order to be making sense, when we do not. We use a word as if it had a meaning, whereas in fact we have not specified any. Our view of what meaning is stops us from noticing that the word is actually floating free: we have only the surface of sense. We so far impose upon ourselves, Berkeley tells us, as to imagine that we *believe* all sorts of things about matter, when we are merely repeating sentences empty of meaning.[23] That we can be taken in in such a way by misunderstandings about language, can *imagine* ourselves to believe something—this in Berkeley should be compared to Wittgenstein, to his reply "You do indeed *believe* that you believe it!" to the man who takes himself to have had again Something, of which he has given himself a private definition.[24]

I want to say more about this last point, to show its connection with realism—realism, that is, in the sense in which I have been using that term. I want to take the conception of language which Berkeley says is to blame for our philosophical difficulties, and to suggest that his criticism of that conception of language comes to saying that it is a *fantasy* of how words work. In short: a fantasy of what it is for a term to mean something is what leads us to philosophical fantasy about what we are getting at when we distinguish the real from the chimerical, or the causal from the coincidental, or about what length or motion or color is, and so on. So we have a structure here: of unrealism in discussing some philosophical question having its source in unrealism about language or meaning. Can such a relation be made out? And what exactly has it to do with what we call unrealistic outside philosophy?

Take, to start with, an example of a mode of description of the world—medieval hagiography—which does not attempt to be realistic. Its not being realistic is partly a matter of the kind of events described; but I want to look at something else, the style of description common to ordinary and extraordinary events in such narratives, taking *The Little Flowers of St. Francis* as an example.

First, an extraordinary event. We are told that in an ecstasy Brother Pacificus saw the soul of his brother ascend direct to heaven at the moment it left his body.[25] We are told that that is what he saw, but we are not told at all what it was like to see such a thing. In fact we do not have any idea what he saw and how he knew it was his brother's soul. But in the context of the narrative, that is not something that is felt as an omission. I do not mean that there is nothing that we could imagine here if we were asked to fill in the story, but simply that what we have is a narrative style, a texture of story, in which such gaps are not felt as gaps. (Cf. also the story of the miraculous transportation of St. Clare from her cell to church and back to her bed.[26] What is it *like* to be miraculously transported?)

There is something similar in the narration of perfectly ordinary events. We are told of St. Francis that he "did his utmost" to conceal the miraculous wound in his side, and are told of the ways in which some of the friars nevertheless got to see or find out about the wound.[27] The methods of discovery were not very ingenious, and anyone who was so easily found out as St. Francis appears to have been cannot very well be described as having tried his utmost to conceal his wound. Now although it would seem that the words "St. Francis tried his utmost" would have to be withdrawn or modified, in the light of what follows in the narrative, unless some explanation were given how someone trying his utmost could so easily have been found out, the difficulty is simply not noticed by the writer. But his not doing so is no slip; it is rather a characteristic of the texture of the stories that realistic coherence is not demanded, and its absence is not felt as a fault.

That kind of unrealism in description is in some ways like the case I mentioned at the beginning: "Like all Russian officials, he had a weakness for cards." St. Francis's attempt to conceal the stigmata is a matter of a characteristic which *saints have*: they conceal the signs of divine favor. The phrase, as used of St. Francis, was never arrived at by people noticing something odd in his behavior, guessing that he was trying to conceal something, and then somehow finding out what it was, and so on. The description has been as it were set free from the kinds of constraints which ordinarily operate, and in virtue of which terms like "trying one's utmost" mean what they do. In this case, the freeing of the term from constraints—from ties to evidence, from the need to consider what counts against its application—means that the apparently contradictory evidence is not felt as something that calls into question the description of St. Francis or as something that requires explanation or even comment.—Indeed the very next paragraph contains another apparent contradiction which also causes no discomfort: St. Francis would grant Brother Ruffino anything he desired, Brother Ruffino wanted to find out about the stigmata, and it appears that that is not something Saint Francis would grant him. This case is like the other two from *The Little Flowers*: it is not a sloppiness in the writer but a style in which our words are in some ways set free from ordinary constraints. Here descriptions of St. Francis's particular activities do not bear on the applicability to him of the general characterization: he would grant Ruffino anything he desired. But we know what it means to say that St. Francis would grant Ruffino anything he desired only if we take it to be called into question by the mention of something which Ruffino wanted and St. Francis seemingly would not give him. *That* has been taken away from us, but how then is the characterization of St. Francis to be understood? What is going on here?

The writing of saints' lives, it has often been said, aims not so much at history as at edification.[28] I have been suggesting that that is reflected in a characteristic use of language, distinct from that of ordinary historiography, or indeed of ordinary descriptions of things around us. The *language* of description is used, but without some of its normal ties: to consequences on the one hand, to evidence on the other. Hippolyte Delehaye compares hagiographers to poets, and more interestingly to painters. He asks us to think of

> an old edition of the *Aeneid*; in accordance with the custom of his time the printer has prefaced it with an engraving representing Virgil. You do not hesitate for a moment, do you, to say that it is not a portrait? And nobody will take you to task for so lightly deciding a question of likeness, which calls for a comparison between the original and the representation. You for your part will not say that the man who wrote Virgil's name under a fanciful picture is a swindler. The artist was following the fashion of his time, which allowed conventional portraits.[29]

In the writing of saints' lives we have just such portraits, constructions of objects for contemplation; and if we think of words and phrases detached from their normal ties to evidence and consequences as linguistic 'surfaces', we may say that these writings are constructions from such surfaces: words without the body of their connections to the world.

Delehaye's remarks suggest a further point. Someone may have a picture of the Baptism of Jesus which shows, besides one man pouring water on the head of another, a dove above their heads, and above that the head of an old man; perhaps there are some people with wings on the sides. For the man who has the picture, it is 'how he pictures the Baptism of Jesus'; but he may never have asked, it has never been a question for him, *how* such a picture would be compared with what it represents. Just as a certain engraving may be for me my picture of Virgil, without my thinking of it as a good or bad *likeness*, the picture of the Baptism may represent the scene for someone who does not consider in what way he takes it to be *like* what he would have seen. Saints' lives, like tales of heroes, may be read or repeated in a similar spirit. And when someone says that such a story is *true*, this sometimes means only that that is his picture of the saint's life. According to the widow Keelan, in Tara, in 1893

> St. Columcille never had a father. The way it was was this: St. Bridget was walkin' wid St. Paathrick an' a ball fell from heavin', an' it was that swate she et it all up, an' it made her prignant with Columcille, an' that's what a praste towld me, an' it's thrue.[30]

But it is *not* true—and even if it were part of the conventional representation of Columcille that he was so conceived, or of Irish saints in general that they were, that would not make it true.—Let me look further at this matter of conventionality and truth. Delehaye points out (using the comparison to the engraving of Virgil) that the saint's life is not a realistic portrait, and that we can recognize that it is not without actually having to compare it with the facts. It is rather a conventional portrait, where this means (among other things) that such sentences as "St. N hid signs of divine favor" may be put into N's *vita* simply because that is how one describes saints. Perhaps the guides for writing saints' lives (it is thought that there were such things)[31] specified such matters in detail. But now we should note two things.

(1) To say that such a sentence as "St. N hid signs of divine favor" is a *conventional* element in the description of N, that the

rules for writing the *vita* of a saint allow it to be put in without worrying about the facts, is not to say that it reflects a necessary truth about saints, or what was taken to be one, any more than it is a necessary truth, or was thought to be one, that the Virgin Mary wore a blue mantle. It is perhaps worth pointing out that *these* 'conventions of description' are not conventions of the sort Wittgenstein occasionally speaks of in connection with necessity. The rule that you can describe a saint as having or doing such-and-such, that you can just put that into his *vita*, is not like a rule "If someone does *not* hide signs of divine favor, he can be no saint"—which might be used in handling the data, in judging whether someone really *is* a saint. The conventions I am concerned with in hagiography have nothing to do with how we make judgements on the basis of our investigations of the facts. There has been a certain amount of confusion of these very different sorts of convention in some philosophical writings influenced by Wittgenstein.

(2) Someone nowadays who wants to write an accurate biography of a medieval saint may be concerned to sort out what is true in the older *vitae* from what is not. On the one hand, some of what is said may be supported by good contemporary documents; on the other, a *vita* may clearly have been stuffed by its author with (let us say) ready-made descriptions of fantastic tortures undergone by the saint, or with bits and pieces taken from other *vitae*, from folktales or Biblical narratives.[32] The point is obvious: what is conventionally put into a saint's *vita* may by no means be true, and we recognize this when we make use, in judging the truth of what is said, of our techniques for weighing and sifting evidence. The fact that these techniques would not have been of interest to the author of the *vita*, who was not attempting to produce an accurate life, nor to his audience, does not mean that our judgments about what is said in the *vita* are in any way out of order or conceptually confused. In dealing with the material in the *vita*, we may perfectly properly adopt a sort of realism: the existence of rules or conventions concerning what may appropriately be *said* and indeed *thought* about a certain matter, here saints' lives, leaves open the question what is *true* about those matters. The practices—here, of embroidering saints' lives in such-and-such ways, of describing them as having certain features, whatever the documents may say, or in the absence of any evidence, or the presence of contrary evidence, of ignoring questions of coherence—are one thing, whether what is said in adhering to these practices was actually true is another. (And

indeed in some cases it may not even be clear what it would be for it to be true.) Our elementary realism (as we may call it) has at its heart that contrast between what is said, adhering to the practices, the conventions, governing the writing of saints' lives, and what the facts were.

Let me indicate briefly why there is nothing confused about the contrast. In connection with *The Little Flowers* I said that we might regard saints' lives as constructions out of what I there called 'linguistic surfaces', sentences used independently of the ties to evidence and consequences which characterize the ordinary application of the expressions which they contain. But if the hagiographer uses sentences with such ties cut, they can nevertheless be used so that the ties are intact, and (in the case of many of them) they can thus be compared with reality; we can use the available evidence to determine whether things were as represented. If it were not for the fact that the hagiographer's sentence about St. Francis (for example), that he "tried his utmost" to hide signs of divine favor, made use of expressions ordinarily tied to evidence and consequences as our English expression is, we could not translate the Italian as we do, we could not take the hagiographer to mean what we should. But it is just such ties then which make it possible for the critical historian, painting a portrait answerable to the facts, intelligibly to ask of things said in an older *vita* whether there is good evidence for them. That last claim would need some qualification and some filling in of details, but I shall instead take up here again the comparison to painting. St. Mark (to use another example of Delehaye's) might be represented in a painting as dipping his pen into an inkwell held by a kneeling disciple as he takes down a sermon of St. Peter's in shorthand.[33] The representation was not meant to be taken as an accurate portrayal of how things were—but because what it shows is indeed St. Mark dipping a pen into an inkwell, we *can* ask, irrespective of any conventions for representing St. Mark, whether he did actually use such things. Conventions of representation of the sort we have been concerned with, in painting or in writing, do not settle truth; and elementary realism simply expresses that point.

I have dwelt on this at some length because of what I want to show about *philosophical* realism, in contrast with elementary realism. I want to suggest that the philosophical realist attempts to take up a position analogous to that of elementary realism—but confusedly. The philosophical realist's conception of *room for* a position analogous to that of elementary realism: *that* is fantasy. And empiricism, often enough, is an attempt to show that it is. We can then see empiricism as Ramsey does; as putting scare quotes on the "realism" of "philosophical realism," and as *itself* the expression of a *properly* realistic spirit. That is, it is empiricism (seen as he does) which takes up a critical position *genuinely* analogous to that of elementary realism.

But here I am ahead of the story. What I needed the discussion of elementary realism for was my account of Berkeley. Berkeley, I said, thought that the philosophical belief in matter, as well as other philosophical confusions, depended on misunderstandings about language. I can now try to explain that.

The fundamental point in elementary realism, applied to hagiography, was: whatever may be the practices and conventions of description used in writing saints' lives, the *truth* about their lives is another matter. However the medieval writer may have been instructed to write up lives in the *Guide for Hagiographers* (if there were such a thing), the *true* description is the one that fits the facts, not the one produced in following the *Guide.*—Philosophical realism about the external world tells us that whatever our actual practices may be—our saying that there are *real things* with such-and-such characteristics, when *appearances* to us have certain features—the truth about real things is another matter, and depends on what is the case independent of the appearances to us. Whatever guidance we may be offered in the *Sense-Data Users' Guide,* whatever it may tell us that we should say given such-and-such appearances, the true description is what fits the facts, not the one produced in following the *Guide.*

Berkeley's view is roughly this. The *Sense-Data Users' Guide* is a guide to thought about reality, more precisely to one of the two main kinds of reality. Elementary realism, e.g., about the writings of hagiographers, could, following Berkeley, be treated as a consequence of what is pointed out in several of the chapters of the *Guide.* There will be a chapter on the use of documents, giving much of the critical apparatus of the historian; there will be a section, a Guide to Handling Human Testimony, within the chapter on Human Nature, dealing with such topics as credulity, and the tendency of legends to become more marvelous as they are passed down. There will be a chapter on Logic, A Guide to Coherence; for Berkeley thinks that coherence has a central place in our ordinary ways of judging what is real. The *Sense-Data Users' Guide* thus itself shows us how we can take up a realist view of what is said in saints' lives.

With *some* of that, the philosophical realist can agree. But he attempts to turn it in a different direction. That is, he indeed insists that the *Sense-Data Users' Guide* contains in many of its chapters instructions how to correct what the evidence seems to point to: it enables us to distinguish the way things may appear to us from how they are.

There are whole chapters on perceptual illusion and distortions, and how to avoid being taken in by them. Further—and he emphasizes this—it has a chapter How to Establish a Scientific Account of Perception. Whether we depend on the Ordinary Man's version of the *Guide*, or more advanced versions, our application of the *Guide* will lead us to accept that how things appear to us as observers depends on what impinges on our bodies, and how our bodies work.—Having emphasized these points, the philosophical realist will now go on to claim that the *Guide* leads us into incoherence. For it allows us to describe things—like stones—as actually themselves having the qualities, like color, that we are aware of in our experience; it allows us to describe ourselves as aware, in our perceptual experience, of real things themselves. But the chapters showing us how to correct perceptual errors, and the chapters on how to give scientific accounts of perception, make clear that we do not observe stones themselves, but only their effects upon us,[34] and that most of the qualities we ascribe to objects they do not themselves really have. We ordinarily ignore the incoherence that following the *Guide* leads us into; we may be just as happy, believing that we actually observe real things *and* that how things appear to us is entirely determined by what impinges on our bodies and how they work, as hagiographers and their audiences were with the incoherences which the *Hagiographers' Guide* led them to tolerate unconcernedly. But tolerated incoherence is incoherence still; our ordinary practice is no way to the truth.

How does that philosophical view rest, according to Berkeley, on misunderstandings about language? We—philosophers—tend to think that when language is not being used to communicate information about particular matters in the world as we know it in experience, it is used to communicate information about something else: that is one misunderstanding. Further, when we can follow a bit of language, we take it that we must have in our minds an *idea* of *what* it is the words we understand stand for. The two tendencies can be illustrated by an example of Berkeley's: the notion *force*. The word "force" occurs in propositions and theorems of very extensive *use*. The doctrine of composition and resolution of forces (e.g.) enables us to arrive at numerous rules directing men how to act, and explaining a great variety of phenomena. By the doctrine of force we arrive at many inventions, and frame engines, by which we accomplish what we otherwise could not; and we can also explain celestial motion. But instead of recognizing propositions about force as guides to action and speculation, we construe them as giving information about facts of a sort not accessible to our senses. Since we understand and use these propositions, we take it that we must have an *idea* of what it is "force" stands for. Since it does not stand for any idea of a perceptible thing, we ascribe to ourselves an idea of something in reality, distinct from what is perceived. Taking the sentence as conveying information, we generate a realm it reports on; taking words like "force," "mass," and so on to stand for ideas, we take ourselves to have ideas of the items to be found in this realm.[35]

When the philosophical realist imagines that there is a basic incoherence in the *Sense-Data Users' Guide*, he is subject to the same kind of illusion. There was a section in it: How Things Look Is Not Always The Best Guide to How They Really Are, which Berkeley reads as containing rules guiding us in our expectations. When it tells us that an oar in water may appear bent while really being straight, he reads it as advising us: Don't expect to see a bent oar when you pull it out of the water; don't expect it to *feel* crooked.[36] The philosophical realist, though, takes the chapter as conveying information which helps us map the realm of Things As They Really Are, Distinct From Our Perception; he takes himself to have an *idea* of what it is to be Absolutely Real, an idea of Existence independent of being perceived. In a similar way, he misconstrues the chapter on how perception depends on our bodies and their environment, taking it to imply that we do not perceive material objects but only their effects. The objects themselves have not got the qualities that we are aware of, but only the capacity to produce such awareness in us. Here the philosophical realist is engaging in the purest fantasy. He *thinks* he thinks of objects with non-sensible properties and unknown natures, he *thinks* he thinks of matter, a substratum of the objects of sense, but all he has is a construction of *words*, linguistic surfaces, as far removed from any practice of comparison with the world as is the story of Saint Columcille's conception. He has, by mistaking the force of words "framed by the vulgar for conveniency and despatch in the common action of life, without any regard to speculation,"[37] ensnared himself in a net. Embarrassed by difficulties of his own construction, he cannot see what is before his eyes.

If my concern in this paper were to expound Berkeley's views, I should need to look in much greater detail at his criticism of philosophical thought. My aim, however, has been to explain how empiricism might be taken as an attempt at realism, treating Berkeley as an example, and looking briefly at the account he gives of specific philosophical errors and their source in confusion about language. "Fantasy" is not a term of criticism Berkeley uses, but I have suggested that the misconstruing of language which he thinks underlies philosophical difficulties could be described as a fantasy of how language works. The philosopher who takes himself to believe in a material substratum of objects of sense is not so much like someone who has a linguistic construction, with the words in it cut free from the ordinary constraints, for amusement or edification, but rather like someone who puts together such a construction while deluded about what it is he is doing. He takes himself to be offering a realist's criticism of the irresponsible ways of talking and thinking of the vulgar, but he leaves for empiricism—or so the empiricist may see it—the task of genuinely realistic criticism.

In the course of this exposition, I have mentioned an objection, that what I have called realism is really just what we already know as verificationism; and I have postponed replying to it. The objection can be answered in a few sentences, but there is one matter which must be cleared up first. Wittgeinstein's remark was "Not empiricism and yet realism in philosophy, that is the hardest thing." The question is: What is wrong with empiricism as an attempt at realism?

One thing wrong with it is that the *Sense-Data Users' Guide*—or, rather, what I have used it to represent—is itself a fantasy. I have used it to stand for a variety of empiricist views, including Berkeley's, which have in common that what is *given*, the basis of our knowledge of the world, is sensible appearances. In Berkeley's case the *Sense-Data Users' Guide* represents what he would himself have thought of as a directory for understanding God's language. The *signs* of that language are such things as the look of the tree from here, the taste of the cherry. To someone who has learned to understand and use these signs, the tree-look suggests "distances, figures, situations, dimensions and various qualities of tangible objects," just as, to someone who has learned to read, the printed characters in a book, which in strictness of language are all that is seen, "suggest words, notions and things." In strictness, I see only the tree-look; if I say that I see a tree ninety feet high, I speak as if I *saw* what is merely suggested to me by the tree-look.[38] It would be possible to consider what is wrong with such a view, taken as an attempt at realism, but I shall go another way.

Wittgenstein's remark was, as I mentioned, directed against Ramsey, and I want to indicate what is wrong with empiricism as an attempt at realism by turning back to Ramsey and asking: What is the matter with *his* empiricism as an attempt at realism?

Ramsey thought of philosophy as directed at the clarification of our thought, the clarification of what we mean by the terms and sentences we use. A clarification of what we mean can sometimes proceed by unselfconscious attention to the objects that we are talking about, as for example if we were to ask whether we mean the same or different things by "horse" and "pig." On the other hand, there are terms and sentences the clarification of which cannot proceed in that way. In order to explain what we mean by a variable hypothetical like "All men are mortal," we must look at the way such expressions are used, where this means looking at our own *mental states*.[39] Ramsey means that in such cases we have to look at the relation between things in our experience and the making of such statements, and at the relation between making such statements and our habits of making judgments about further items in our experience.

His investigation of the meaning of variable hypotheticals is at the same time an investigation of what we mean by "P is a law of nature," and of what we mean when we speak of an unknown causal law, or of one described but not stated. He reaches this view of what it is for there to be an *unknown* causal law: it is the existence of certain singular facts which would lead us by a psychological law to accept a causal generalization. The generalization must be one which when made would not be misleading: i.e., it must hold within the scope of our possible experience (and that would have to be spelled out, though Ramsey does not go into this, in terms of such things as there not being singular facts which would lead us, through certain psychological laws, to withdraw the generalization). Accepting the generalization is a matter of asserting it and of forming a habit of making certain judgments about particulars. There is a psychological law in virtue of which those judgments would be made: the connection between asserting the generalization and the habit of forming beliefs about particulars depends upon the psychological law which makes the meaning of the word "all."[40]

So there we have an empiricist account of causation (or, rather, a central part of such an account), tied closely to an empiricist view of what philosophical clarification of meaning consists in. (Since for Ramsey explication of meaning is essentially causal, the account of causation itself is not a mere example of philosophical analysis). Why might Ramsey's account be thought not to be genuinely realistic, or not realistic enough? We can answer that by considering an objection that Ramsey himself comes near discussing, and to which he has at least indicated a reply.

Here is the objection. To say that there is an unknown causal law governing the occurrence of such-and-such (connecting people's chromosomes and their characteristics, to use one of Ramsey's examples) cannot be to say that there are singular facts which would lead us in virtue of psychological laws to a generalization, because we need to exclude things like our becoming *unhinged* by our knowledge of the singular facts and in that way reaching some mad generalization. The existence of facts that would lead us in virtue of *some* psychological law to a mad generalization, one which no singular facts within the scope of our possible experience would (given our psychology) lead us to give up, is quite clearly not what we mean by there being an unknown causal law.

Ramsey's reply would be that the psychological laws meant are "the known laws expressing our methods of inductive reasoning"[41]: the existence of an unknown causal law is the existence of singular facts which by the known psychological laws of our inductive reasoning would lead us to a generalization that we should stick to in the light of whatever other singular facts there may be that we might actually turn up. But the distinction Ramsey needs to make cannot be made by contrasting the psychological laws, known or unknown, of our inductive reasoning and possible unknown psychological laws of mad generalizing.

It may be puzzling that he should say that the psychological laws in virtue of which go from singular facts to causal generalizations are *known*. But it should be less puzzling if we note that he does not mean laws belonging to theoretical psychology, which have, he thinks, no place in philosophical analysis. (And in any case the theoretical psychology of inductive inference could not enable us to explain what we mean by the existence of an unknown causal law.) The laws he means he thinks we know, in that we know how we infer and can turn our attention to our own mental states and processes. Indeed, if we can describe some case—some set of possible observations—and say "I should conclude so-and-so," we are relying at least implicitly (he thinks) on a causal generalization about our own inductive reasoning. Ramsey's notion of "known psychological laws," was reflected in something I mentioned earlier, that it is a psychological law which makes the meaning of "all." This, too, is not a law, known or unknown, of theoretical psychology, but one which we know in that we know how we infer from statements using "all" to singular statements.

Wittgenstein's criticisms of Ramsey are directed against such views of his as those we have just seen: Ramsey treats logic as if it were a matter for a kind of empirical knowledge. We know empirically what our habits of thought are, and can then investigate empirically whether these habits are useful or perhaps improvable. But let us leave aside general criticisms of such empiricism and continue. It is plain that Ramsey's account will not do. Even if there are singular facts that might, looked at in *some* way, lead someone, with great insight, to a causal generalization, there need be no reason whatever to think that I or others, given knowledge merely of those facts, would in virtue of the psychological laws (known to us, as he would

have it) of our methods of inductive reasoning, be led to assert anything whatever. When we say that there is an unknown causal law of
some sort, we do not mean that we should be able to come to it by
knowledge of singular facts and by whatever ways we now know
ourselves to be able to move from singular facts to causal generalizations, by—that is—whatever we now take to be our inferential
'habits'. But if we need not be able to find in ourselves knowledge of
habits of inference which would take us to *any* as yet unknown causal
law, the difference between going to a new causal law by some as it
were helped insight from another person and going to a mad generalization through becoming unhinged by knowledge of new singular
facts cannot be explained in Ramsey's style: in terms of what we
know of our own mental life, in terms of what we are able to observe
of regularities in it when we turn our consciousness towards our
mental states and processes.

The reference to known psychological laws cannot do what it was
brought in to do. It cannot underpin a general account of what we
mean by causal terms; it is as much an idle wheel as matter, or the
active general principles in nature of Peirce's discussion of causal regularities. Ramsey's account is intentionally realistic in *his* sense, in its
rejection of anything like Peirce's 'realism':

> The world, or rather that part of it with which we are acquainted,
> exhibits as we must agree a good deal of regularity of succession.
> I contend that over and above that it exhibits no features called
> causal necessity, but that we make sentences called causal laws
> from which (i.e. having made which) we proceed to actions and
> propositions connected with them in a certain way, and say that
> a fact asserted in a proposition which is an instance of causal law
> is a case of causal necessity. This is a regular feature of our con-
> duct, a part of the general regularity of things . . .[42]

We make sentences called causal laws—when we have learned to reason inductively. To have learned to do so is indeed to have learned
to behave in a certain way, and causal generalizations are what we
come up with when we behave that way. But what counts as behav-
ing *that way* is not specifiable in terms of any psychological laws, unless they are specified—totally unhelpfully—as those proceeding
according to which is reasoning inductively.

Consider what has led us here. Ramsey has, in what he takes to be
a realistic spirit, rejected the idea that what we call causal laws express real connections of universals: that idea depends on misleading
formal analogies between the sentences expressing such laws and
propositions properly so called.[43] The misleading appearance can be

seen to be merely *that*, if we attend, not introspectively to what we take ourselves to mean, but to the *use* of causal terms. But, as we have seen, by attending to the use Ramsey means attending to the causal relations between our experience of the world and our making of general statements, and between our making of general statements and our going on afterwards to form beliefs about other particular items in our experience. This, for him, is what counts as being realistic in our philosophy: clarifying what we mean by the terms that give rise to philosophical problems by showing the causal connections between the utterance of sentences containing those terms and what else goes on in our mental life; sense experience, decisions, habits of expectation and of utterance, and the like. What underlies this conception of philosophical method is the idea that the terms that give rise to problems, like other terms, are used in a *regular* way, and that these regularities in our use are knowable like any others; they are there to be known.

But we cannot, in general, make clear to ourselves what we do in following a rule if we try to do it in terms of a causal generalization which we ourselves are specially placed to know. For, if a rule tells us to do so-and-so in such-and-such circumstances, we shall take ourselves to be following it when we take the circumstances to be such-and-such, and ourselves to be doing so-and-so. And so we can tell ourselves that there is a generalization that we know to fit our behavior: we do so-and-so whenever such-and-such. But *whatever* we do in following that rule, we shall take that generalization to apply. Our 'knowledge' is merely a misleading way of putting the fact that in what we do, we are taking ourselves to be following a rule. The point applies to our knowledge of the psychological laws that—supposedly—make the meaning of our words. Any application of a term that seems appropriate to us will also seem to belong to the regularity that our use of the term exhibits to us, or appears to, when we take ourselves to be attending to our own use as Ramsey does. He thinks he knows such laws because what he takes to be realism requires that there be such laws: causal regularities that the fixity of meaning of our terms consists in; and since "in philosophy we analyze *our* thoughts,"[44] these regularities are ones open to *our* view of ourselves and not for theoretical psychology to discover.

Ramsey's conception of philosophical method depends on an idea of the *given* that he shares with Berkeley, who said that we cannot be wrong in what we take to be regularities within our own thought. To grasp the similarities and differences of whatever passes within our minds, nothing more is needed, according to Berkeley, than an attentive perception directed towards our own mental life.[45]

Let me make clear what I am suggesting by turning briefly to a different case. Before Hylas was confronted with Philonous, he explained to himself the distinction between real things and chimeras by the mythology of 'matter', but what is he supposed to do afterwards? He is supposed to turn his attention to what is open to his own view, and what he cannot be mistaken about: the patterns within his mental life, and the ways in which his expectations of further patterns are shaped by what he experiences. *There* he will be able to see what is involved in the distinction between real things and chimeras.

Ramsey's account of philosophical method is not Berkeley's; he does not recommend that we try to consider the items of our mental life "bare and naked," keeping out of our thoughts the words united with them by constant use. But his picture of what is directly available to us in our philosophical thought is close to Berkeley's. Like Berkeley, he rejects a conception of what it is for the meaning of a term to be fixed, a conception that leads to philosophical 'realism', but what is there left then for a genuinely realistic account of meaning to look to? Ramsey takes it that we can explain how we use the terms and sentences of our language by considering what is given in mental life, the graspable characteristics and relations of the items in it; and so, in our example, the distinction between the rules we follow in causal reasoning and our suddenly starting to generalize in a totally unhinged way must lie in psychological laws we know to cover our behavior. These are explanations we can only administer to ourselves, and Ramsey comes closest to Berkeley when he makes clear that if we are thinking of other people's minds we have not got *facts* as we do when we consider our own, but only *theories*.[46] That means that our philosophical explanations of the terms we use, got by attention to our own use, can be of interest to others only so far as they, making use of their theories, are given hints towards what they can establish through attention to their own thought.

I tried to show earlier that Ramsey's claim that we have knowledge of the psychological laws of our methods of inductive reasoning was empty, and I want now to connect that with the remark that Wittgenstein put immediately after the remark, against Ramsey, about it being not empiricism but nevertheless realism that was the hardest thing.

> You do not yourself understand any more of the rule than you can explain.[47]

"Explain" there means explain to someone else, in the ordinary course of things, as when you tell him what you are doing, e.g., in developing a series, or when you explain how you are using a word. Ramsey thinks that in such cases, our minds work essentially according to what he calls "general rules or habits,"[48] if we are not proceeding in some merely random way, there is a causal regularity which we ourselves must be able to grasp. I want now to suggest that we can see, in the account he gives of what we mean by an unknown causal law, the way empiricism fails to be realistic.

Ramsey takes us to understand, or to be capable of understanding, *more* than we could in the ordinary sense explain: the *un*realism lies there. He wants a realistic understanding, to be got by attention to honest facts and honest regularities, attention to something that is there for us to observe. He construes our experience using language, our experience reasoning about the world, as taking place for each of us in a realm open to our observation, containing the honest facts and regularities we need. That he thinks he knows them itself reflects his idea of what kind of understanding philosophy seeks: that is where the fantasy lies.

What I have said certainly does not *demonstrate* that Ramsey's method is not genuinely that of the realistic spirit. I shall not try to prove it, but shall instead ask: If someone were to object to empiricism, in something like the way I have done, that it does not achieve the realism it tries for, what on earth could he have in mind as realistic? What, after all, it might be asked, does Wittgenstein himself do? Does he not simply replace the empiricist's conception of the given with a different idea of the given? Does he not take as the given what goes on in a community's shared social life and customs, where their language is taken to be part of that? And if he simply substitutes what goes on in their social life—as the given—for what goes on in one's own mental life, why should *that* be taken to be more realistic?—What has come to the surface here is the problem I had been postponing, about whether there was any significant difference between what, on Wittgenstein's view (if I am correct), counts as realism and verificationism in its various forms.

Remarks like ". . . the given is—so one could say—forms of life"[49] have been taken to show that Wittgenstein's dispute with the classical empiricists and their descendants is over what we should understand to be the given, that in terms of which philosophical clarification can proceed. And Wittgenstein's actual methods have also contributed to such a view. That is to say, the attention he gives to what we actually do has been taken to mean that the facts of what we actually do have for him the role that the facts of our mental life have for Ramsey: we should be able to see by attention to such facts what we mean by the terms giving rise to philosophical difficulties.

But the unrealism to which Wittgenstein was trying to draw our attention was not that of failing to see what the given really is, or ought to be for us in our philosophical thinking. The unrealism was in the questions we were asking. We ask philosophical questions about our concepts in the grip of an unrealistic conception of what knowing about them would be. Let me take a short passage from *Remarks on the Foundation of Mathematics* as an illustration of these points.

> I can train someone in a *uniform* activity. E.g. in drawing a line like this with a pencil on paper:
>
> — • • — • • — • • — • • — • • — • • — • •
>
> Now I ask myself, what is it that I want him to do, then? The answer is: He is always to go on as I have shewn him. And what do I really mean by: he is always to go on in that way? The best answer to this that I can give myself, is an example like the one I have just given.
>
> I would use this example to shew him but also to shew myself, what I mean by uniform.
>
> We talk and act. That is already presupposed in everything that I am saying.[50]

An enormous amount of Wittgenstein's philosophy is there in that passage—if we can only see it properly. In particular, let us ask what the point is of saying that the best answer one can give onself to "What do I really mean by: he is always to go on in that way?" is an example of a perfectly ordinary sort. For there are very different answers that we might think that we want, and might think that we should be able to get. *One* sort of answer would indeed be Ramsey's, and it is a natural answer to give if we think of ourselves as empiricists rejecting philosophical 'realism'. Essential to an answer in Ramsey's style is the idea that we are in a position to explain to *ourselves* what it is that we want him to do (we know the psychological laws of our own rule-governed behavior), but can only give *him* examples which will, we hope, cause him to behave similarly. Wittgenstein, in the passage quoted, clearly means to exclude any answer like Ramsey's which implies that we know what we mean by uniformity in a way which goes beyond the explanations we can offer another.

But it might be thought that Wittgenstein himself tells us something like this. One cannot indicate to oneself what it is one means by "he is always to go on in that way" by pointing inwardly. It is *public agreement* which constitutes something as going on *that* way. If within the community in which the teaching goes on it is natural to continue in a certain way from the example I gave, and if he then does go on in the way the community accepts, his behavior has the uniformity I wanted to teach him. This understanding of Wittgenstein goes a certain distance then with Ramsey: in philosophy we analyze *our* thought. But in such an analysis we look not inwards but towards what the community does.

In reaching such a view of what Wittgenstein holds, philosophers go against the remark about the best answer I can give myself. I want to show (a) that that misreading of Wittgenstein involves *un*realism, in the sense in which I have been using that term, (b) what is meant by saying that realism is "the hardest thing" and—very briefly then— (c) why it is not akin to verificationism.

We reach such a reading of Wittgenstein in something like the following way. We say: he teaches us that someone, given just the same examples as were used in teaching, might go on in quite other ways, and yet take himself to be going on in the same way, understanding differently what those examples show. If I recognise that possibility, I cannot explain to myself what I mean by "he is to go on in that way" simply by examples which I know might be taken in a variety of ways. Suppose I draw an initial segment of the line, continue it a bit further, then again, and then again. Each continuation I have made stands in any number of describable relations to what was already drawn; there is no such thing as *the* relation which each stands in to what is already there. I cannot then explain the particular uniformity I have in mind by saying that further continuations should stand in the same relation to what goes before them as *that* relation in which the continuations I made stand to what went before them. Someone who knew only that there is *some* relation which all the continuations he had been shown stood in to what went before, and such that his continuations should stand in *that* relation to what went before *them*, would not yet know what he was to do. My own understanding of what I want him to do cannot then be represented merely by examples of the sort that might be used in teaching, if Wittgenstein is right about how examples may be taken. And it is at this point that we take Wittgenstein as providing, implicitly at any rate, an account of what constitutes going on in a particular way in terms of communal agreement. (This description is based in part on Christopher Peacocke's argument about a related but slightly different case.)[51]

When Wittgenstein says that the best answer I can give myself to "What do I really mean by: he is to go on in that way?" is an example, he does not mean that although it is the best answer I can give myself in the ordinary way, philosophy can give a better answer, a proper account of what is meant by: he is to go on in a particular way. He means that the inclination to think that there is some better answer philosophy can give is confused. It is the mouse and the rags again. The best answer we can give ourselves is—this is Wittgenstein's point—one we cannot imagine is an answer at all. What we are concerned with here is his notion of what the real difficulty is in philosophy.

To develop the comparison between *this* case and the mouse-and-rags cases I considered earlier, recall the distinction between real things and chimeras as Berkeley discusses it. Philosophers, Berkeley thinks, are unable to believe that our distinction can be understood by looking at our ways of *using* "real" in some cases of sense perception and not in others (the 'rags') because by "real" they mean (so they would say) something whose existence is wholly independent of appearances to us. They think that they mean something by *that*. In fact the basis of the discriminations we make among sensible appearances—these of real things, those not—is the needs we, active beings, have to form expectations and plans. As philosophers, though, we take those discriminations to reflect beliefs that some of the appearances are and others are not caused in certain ways by things not themselves appearing directly to us; the appearances are merely manifestations of something *else*. So we have then a link between the ignoring of the 'rags', the thinking that they are irrelevant to our *philosophical* needs—and the idea that in our thought about the real we mean something totally independent of what has actually to be watched out for in human life-with-perceptions.

To go back now to the present case: explaining what I mean by "he is always to go on in that way." I want to explain it—and I do not want, do not think I want, something that would in fact, *does* in fact, *do* to explain to someone how to go on. I know—we may imagine—that I showed someone how to continue performing some uniform activity; I gave him a few examples, he did something, and I was satisfied.—Those are the rags. If I think that no mouse—no satisfactory account, no elucidation, of what I mean by his always going on in that way—can come from them, that is because I take it that a specification of what I really mean picks it out, not as might be for another human being, but in a sense absolutely, from *the* possibilities. If I need to explain something to another person, it is true that *certain* possibilities may need to be ruled out; certain ambiguities will create problems in certain circumstances. There might at some time be a question whether someone is to continue this − • − • • in this way − • − • • − • − • • or in this − • − • • − • • − • • • − • • •. But the idea of a philosophical account of what I really mean by "he is always to go on in that way" is of an account addressed to someone on whose uptake, on whose responses, we are not at all depending.—Or again I might show you why, in some particular case, I had criticized someone for *not* continuing correctly. I might give you the examples I had given him, and then show you what he did: I can give you *that* sort of explanation. But in philosophy I want to know what really justifies any claim I might make that he went wrong. I want something different from anything I might actually give you to justify my remarks in particular circumstances. I want to know what his going wrong really consisted in. *How* was the determination of what I meant him to do such that what he then went on to do was excluded?

The questions that we ask are in fact verbal elaborations of ordinary questions, to which we reject, as inadequate, ordinary answers, in the belief that we are asking something that passes those answers by. An adequate elucidation of what I meant by "he is always to go on in that way" must pick out something in the realm of things-that-might-possibly-be-meant: not possibly-in-human-practice but in some other sense, not dependent on what goes on in our lives. The fact that someone very different from us might take the explanation by examples differently is read as an indication of what there is, absolutely speaking, in the space of things-that-I-might-possibly-mean, so that an adequate account, adequate to represent what I mean, must make plain that those possibilities are excluded. What I *do* with examples, what I *do* in explaining, may be essential in making manifest what I mean, but the explanation of what I mean cannot be given by examples, because they *cannot* adequately represent my relation to what is possible.

Realism in philosophy, the hardest thing, is open-eyedly giving up the quest for such an elucidation, the demand that a philosophical account of what I mean make clear how it is fixed, out of all the possible continuations, out of some real semantic space, *which* I mean. Open-eyedly: that is, not just stopping, but with an understanding of the quest as dependent on fantasy. The purpose of Wittgenstein's drawing attention to the use of examples is to let us see there, in that use, "explaining what I mean" *at work*, in order that we can see that in philosophy it idles, and that we can learn to recognize the characteristic forms of such philosophical 'idling'. The demands we make for philosophical explanations come, seem to come, from a position in which we are as it were looking down onto the relation between ourselves and some reality, some kind of fact or real possibility. We think that we mean something by our questions about it. Our questions are formed from notions of ordinary life, but the ways we usually ask and answer questions, our practices, our interests, the forms our reasoning and inquiries take, look from such a position to be the 'rags'. Our own linguistic constructions, cut free from the constraints of their ordinary functioning, take us in: the characteristic form of the illusion is precisely of philosophy as an area of inquiry, in the sense in which we are familiar with it.

One remaining point, about verificationism. *Given* the demand that a philosophical account of what I mean make clear how it is fixed, out of all the possible continuations, *which* I mean, it is indeed natural to read Wittgenstein as saying that communal agreement, or whatever is the natural continuation for members of the community, fixes it. Communal agreement on what counts as continuing in a particular way justifies, underlies, any claims that someone has gone wrong. This reading makes his view analogous in significant ways to verificationism: he shows us that what we mean when we indicate to someone how to go on *comes down really* to facts of some unproblematic sort. The given (on this interpretation) is patterns of communal response; in terms of these patterns of response we can explain philosophically what it is for there to be a correct continuation of some regular activity, and what justifies calling other continuations incorrect. But the hardness of realism is in not asking the questions; and then we shall not see Wittgenstein answering them either.

What about realism in moral philosophy? Might one say: "Not utilitarianism but still realism in moral philosophy, that is the hardest thing." It seems to me a question worth asking.[52]

Notes

1. Ludwig Wittgenstein, *Remarks on the Foundations of Mathematics* (ed. G.H. von Wright, R. Rhees, G.E.M. Anscombe) (Oxford, 1978), p. 325.
2. I am grateful to Hilary Putnam for pointing out that the paper could be seen as such a reply. It was not written with that intention; I became familiar with Kripke's interpretation of Wittgenstein only after work on the paper was completed. I discuss Kripke's interpretation of Wittgenstein in "Rules: Looking in the Right Place," in D.Z. Phillips and Peter Winch, eds., *Wittgenstein: Attention to Particulars* (Basingstoke, Hampshire, 1989), pp. 12–34.
3. Saul A. Kripke, *Wittgenstein on Rules and Private Language* (Oxford, 1982); Saul A. Kripke, "Wittgenstein on Rules and Private Language" in I. Block (ed.), *Perspectives on the Philosophy of Wittgenstein* (Oxford, 1981).
4. See Frank O'Connor, Foreword to Nikolai Gogol, *Dead Souls* (New York, 1961), p. ix.
5. Ludwig Wittgenstein, op. cit., pp. 201–2.
6. Ibid., p. 202.
7. F.P. Ramsey, *The Foundations of Mathematics* (ed. R.B. Braithwaite) (Totowa, N.J., 1965), pp. 197–8; cf. also pp. 191–6.
8. "General Propositions and Causality" in F.P. Ramsey, ibid., pp. 237–55.
9. Ibid., p. 252.
10. Ibid., p. 238.

11. *The Works of George Berkeley* (ed. A.A. Luce and T.E. Jessop) (Edinburgh, 1948–57), Vol. II, p. 262.
12. Ludwig Wittgenstein, *Philosophical Investigations* (Oxford, 1958), §103.
13. George Berkeley, *Works*, Vol. II, 210–11.
14. Ibid., pp. 211, 227.
15. Ludwig Wittgenstein, op. cit., p. 178.
16. Bertrand Russell, "The Philosophy of Logical Atomism," in Robert C. Marsh (ed.), *Logic and Knowledge* (London and New York, 1956), pp. 221–2.
17. Cf. Rush Rhees, "The Philosophy of Wittgenstein," in Rhees, *Discussions of Wittgenstein* (London, 1970), p. 52.
18. George Orwell, "Charles Dickens," in Orwell, *A Collection of Essays* (Garden City, N.Y., 1954), pp. 59–60.
19. George Berkeley, op. cit., p. 235.
20. *Collected Papers of Charles Sanders Peirce* (ed. Charles Hartshorne, Paul Weiss, Arthur W. Burks) (Cambridge, Mass., 1931–58), 5.93–5.101. Cf. also 6.98–6.100.
21. Cf. Ludwig Wittgenstein, *Philosophical Investigations*, §426.
22. Peirce, *Collected Papers*, 5.93–5.101. On Peirce's realism, see Susan Haack, "Pragmatism and Ontology: Peirce and James."
23. George Berkeley, *Principles of Human Knowledge*, 54, *Works*, Vol. II, p. 64.
24. Ludwig Wittgenstein, *Philosophical Investigations*, §260.
25. *The Little Flowers of St. Francis* (Baltimore, 1959), chapter 45, p. 125.
26. Ibid., chapter 34, p. 103.
27. Ibid., pp. 175–6.
28. See Brian Stock, *TLS* February 1977, p. 224; Hippolyte Delehaye, *The Legends of the Saints* (New York, 1962), chapter 1; Paul Maurice Clogan (ed.), *Medievalia et Humanistica*, New Series, Number 6, 1975, preface.
29. Hippolyte Delehaye, ibid., pp. xviii–xix.
30. The story is recounted by J.T. Fowler, in his edition of Adamnán's *Life of Columcille*, quoted in William W. Heist, "Irish Saints' Lives, Romance and Cultural History," in Paul Maurice Clogan, op. cit., p. 38.
31. William W. Heist, ibid., p. 26; cf. also Nora K. Chadwick, *The Age of the Saints in the Early Celtic Church* (London 1961), p. 156.
32. See Hippolyte Delehaye, op. cit., chapter V.
33. Ibid., p. 179.
34. Cf. Bertrand Russell, *An Enquiry into Meaning and Truth* (London, 1940), p. 15.
35. For Berkeley's general views on misunderstandings about language, see the Introduction to *The Principles of Human Knowledge*, *Works*, Vol. II, pp. 36–8, *Alciphron*, Seventh Dialogue, *Works*, Vol. III, pp. 291–3. For the discussion of force, see *Alciphron*, Seventh Dialogue, pp. 293–5.
36. George Berkeley, *Three Dialogues between Hylas and Philonous*, *Works*, Vol. II, p. 238.
37. Ibid., p. 246.
38. George Berkeley, *Alciphron*, Fourth Dialogue, *Works*, Vol. III, pp. 154–6.
39. F.P. Ramsey, *The Foundations of Mathematics*, p. 267.
40. Ibid., pp. 240–5.
41. Ibid., pp. 244–5.
42. Ibid., p. 252.
43. Ibid., pp. 252–4.
44. Ibid., p. 266.
45. George Berkeley, Introduction to *The Principles of Human Knowledge*, *Works*, Vol. II, p. 39.

46. F.P. Ramsey, op. cit., p. 266.
47. *Remarks on the Foundations of Mathematics* (Oxford, 1978), p. 325.
48. F.P. Ramsey, op. cit., p. 194; cf. also pp. 195–6.
49. Ludwig Wittgenstein, *Philosophical Investigations*, p. 226.
50. pp. 320–1. The passage precedes by a few pages the remark about realism from which I began.
51. Christopher Peacocke, "Reply [to Gordon Baker]: Rule Following: The Nature of Wittgenstein's Arguments," Steven M. Holtzman and Christopher M. Leich (eds.), in *Wittgenstein, To Follow a Rule* (London, 1981), pp. 91–2.
52. I am indebted to Hidé Ishiguro and to A.D. Woozley for comments on an earlier version of this paper.

Chapter 2

Frege and Nonsense

O dieses ist das Tier, das es nicht gibt.
(Rilke)

Frege says that it is impossible to assert of an object the sort of thing that can be asserted of a concept.[1] If, for example, we were to take a sentence asserting of a concept that there is something falling under it (say, "There is a King of England"), we may attempt to construct a corresponding sentence about an object; the result will be a sentence of sorts ("There is Queen Victoria"), but what corresponds to it will not be an illogical thought, but no thought. It will not say of the object named that it has something that as a matter of logic only concepts can have.—I shall raise some questions about Frege's view, with the aim of making clear what it involves and how it is related to the abandoning of a psychologistic account of meaning. The starting point for me was Professor Anscombe's illuminating discussion of Wittgenstein's later view of nonsense.[2] I wanted to see how far that view could be found in the *Tractatus,* and that led to the question whether its roots were not to be found in Frege.

Let us ask first whether it is possible to describe "There is Queen Victoria" as a putting of an expression for an object—a proper name—where one for a concept should go. That is, is it possible to identify an expression as a proper name when it occurs in the wrong place, or what we want to call that? Frege thinks a proper name cannot be used predicatively; our question is whether, in a place where only a term used predicatively would make sense, we can identify a proper name at all. Take "Chairman Mao is rare," an example of Michael Dummett's. Explaining Frege's views, he says that this is senseless because "rare," although it looks like an ordinary adjective expressing a first-level concept, really expresses a second-level one—and so the idea is that we get a meaningless sentence when we put a proper name where the argument term should go. But suppose it were said that we do not always get nonsense that way: "gold" Frege takes to be the proper name of an element,[3] and "Gold is rare" is not senseless.—Well, whatever its role may be elsewhere, *there* it is not a proper name but means what not everything that glitters is. Frege himself points out that the same word can be used in some contexts as a proper name, and in others as a concept word; he says this in discussing an example somewhat like the present one.[4] But now, I can certainly say "There isn't much Churchill in our present lot of politicians," and someone might equally use "Chairman Mao" to mean a certain sort of political intelligence, which might indeed be rare. So how is it possible to tell whether, in "Chairman Mao is rare," we have the proper name or a concept word? One indication Frege gives is this: if the expression in question ocurs with an indefinite article or a numeral, or in the plural without an article, it is in that context an expression for a concept.[5]

But here we can see two problems. First, the shift of a word from proper name to concept word is exemplified for Frege by the shift from "Vienna" the name of the city to "Vienna" as used in "Trieste is no Vienna." Here, Frege says, it is a concept word, like "metropolis"—but more specifically it is a word for a countable kind of thing. Shifts like that from "gold" the proper name of an element to "gold" used predicatively are not mentioned by Frege but are—it would seem—possible too. The occurrence of what is normally a proper name in a context in which an expression for a *countable* kind of thing would make sense (where this is shown by an indefinite article, the plural, or a numeral) is taken by Frege—or so it seems—as a sufficient condition for treating the term as in that context a concept word and the occurrence as a predicative one; we must ask why the occurrence of what is normally a proper name in a context where a word for a *stuff* concept would make sense is *not* taken by Frege to be a sufficient condition for regarding the term as in such contexts a concept word. However, it now seems there may be a problem whether we can describe our original case as one in which the proper name "Queen Victoria" has been put in the place where a concept word belongs. There will not be any examples of putting a proper name where a concept word belongs if the fact that a concept word belongs in a place is a sufficient condition for treating *whatever* is put there as in that context a concept word.

Let us look at Frege's own examples. He treats "There is Julius Caesar" as nonsense, but "There is only one Vienna" not as nonsense but as a shift in the use of the word "Vienna."[6] What makes this possible is not that there is an established use of "Vienna" as a concept word but that there is an established possibility *in the language* of using what are normally proper names as concept words. (If that were not so, the use of the indefinite article, the plural, or a numeral could not be taken as Frege does: for example, "As soon as a word is used with the indefinite article or in the plural without an article, it is a concept word.")[7] But now, what if we do not know what it is for something to be a Vienna? If this has not been settled, would the sentence still be describable as one in which "Vienna" has the role of a concept word? If that were Frege's view, the question would be why "There is Julius Caesar" should not be treated analogously. It seems it could be. For "There is gold" ("Courage is rare") makes sense: why should we not say that "There is Julius Caesar" ("Chairman Mao is rare") contains a concept expression whose reference has not been made clear? The first problem then with Frege's suggestions about how to tell when what is normally a proper name is being used as a concept word is that he does not treat in the same way all cases which could be regarded as involving a shift in the logical category of the term in question, and does not make clear the basis for this difference in treatment. (I do not mean that there is no basis. But I shall return to this question later.) The second problem arises immediately we take him to be allowing that "There is only one Vienna" contains a concept word whose reference may be unclear. For if all cases apparently similar were treated in the way Frege treats that sentence, there would be no such thing as putting an expression into a place where an expression of a different logical category was required. There would instead, in all cases in which it was clear what logical category was required, be expressions whose logical category was clear from the context but whose reference might or might not be fully determined, expressions which in other contexts had a different categorial role and a fully determined reference. We could not then identify "a proper name in the place where a concept word belongs" as a *proper name*; to speak of such an expression as a proper name at all would only be to refer to its role elsewhere, or to the role it was intended to serve. On this view, there would not merely be, as Frege clearly believed, no illogical thoughts (no such combinations of senses), but also no ill-formed sentences (no combinations of expressions violating categorial requirements), even in ordinary language—and this he clearly did not believe. In fact the possibility of ill-formed constructions in ordinary language is precisely one of the marks of distinction between it and Frege's symbolic language. And so it seems that if Frege takes a consistent view we have not yet found what it is.

The argument just given overlooks something. It *is* true that Frege believed that incorrectly formed names (including here sentences) were possible in ordinary language. But what is meant by 'incorrect formation' is less clear; the problem is that we may see in Frege a way of understanding 'incorrect formation' which is not there. Frege explains the correct formation of a name this way in the *Grundgesetze*, when he is stating the requirement for his symbolic language, that correctly formed names must always have a reference: "[A name is correctly formed] if it consists only of signs introduced as primitive or by definition, and if these signs are used only as what they were introduced as being: thus proper names as proper names, names of first level functions of one argument as names of functions of this kind and so on. . . ."[8] It is clear from this passage that we can use such terms as "proper name" to speak of the role an expression was introduced to serve, or to speak of its use in a particular context, the role it serves there. If the reference of a name in its intended use is fixed, but it is then used in some context in an entirely different way, it will be possible to form complex expressions containing it whose reference will not be determined, and it is this which Frege is concerned to avoid. We *can* speak of such uses of terms as 'violations of category requirements' but that expression is itself ambiguous. We may mean that an expression introduced as a term of one sort has been used with a different role, but a 'violation of category requirements' in this sense will not necessarily be nonsense: "Trieste is no Vienna" is of this sort. To respect category requirements in this sense is simply to avoid cross-category equivocation. But we may also speak of a 'violation of category requirements' without suggesting that any term has been used in some other role than that for which it was introduced. That is, we may want to say that, *given* the role of the terms in some combination, the combination is nonsense—meaning that the trouble arises precisely *because* they have those roles: it is the fact that they have the roles, say, of a proper name and a second-level predicate, that prevents their being joined together to produce anything but nonsense. Here we have implicitly a sense of "incorrect formation" different from that explained in the *Grundgesetze* passage, and a different notion of the violation of category requirements. The idea is intuitively of a 'clash' of the category of the terms combined, and it thus depends on the possibility of identifying the categorial role of a term outside the context of legitimate combination. In particular, it assumes the possibility of identifying the categorial role of terms in a context in which (putting this in Fregean language) the reference of the parts does *not* determine the reference of the whole. In contrast, the *Grundgesetze* account does not assume that it is possible to identify the categorial role of a term, to say it has a sense of such-and-such a logical sort, in an incorrectly formed expression—except in the "Trieste is no Vienna" sort of case, in which all that is necessary to assure a reference for the whole is that a reference for the parts be settled. The fact that Frege did believe that there could be ill-formed sentences in ordinary language does not then settle the question whether he thought there could in ordinary language be sentences which violated category requirements in the second sense (clashes of category as opposed to category-equivocations). The very questionable assumption on which that second sense depends was, I believe, rejected by Frege—and the rejection of it marks an important continuity in his philosophy of language, and between his and Wittgenstein's.

I shall discuss three points bearing on the question of Frege's view; two are considerations counting for and one apparently counting against what I take him to mean. First, that Frege does not think there can occur category violations in the second sense, even in ordinary language, fits well with the account he gives of the justification of a *Begriffsschrift*, of its advantages over ordinary language. In *Über die wissenschaftliche Berechtigung einer Begriffsschrift*, he puts great emphasis on the presence in ordinary language of equivocation—equivocation of a particularly dangerous sort if we are to think clearly: the use of the same word to symbolize both a concept and an object falling under it. A main advantage of a *Begriffsschrift* is the rigorous avoidance of such equivocation. There is no mention of the presence in ordinary language of category error in the second sense, nor of its absence in a *Begriffsschrift*.[9]

Second, and more important, the view I am ascribing to Frege is closely related to the *Grundlagen* point that we must ask for the meaning of a word only in the context of a sentence. The force of that principle is not clear, but it can be explained in terms of the notion of a logical part, a notion Frege contrasts with that of simplicity in *Grundgesetze* §66.

> Any symbol or word can indeed be regarded as consisting of parts; but we do not deny its simplicity unless, given the general rules of grammar, or of the symbolism, the reference of the whole would follow from the reference of the parts, and these parts occur also in other combinations and are treated as independent signs with a reference of their own. In this sense, then, we may say: the word (symbol) that is defined must be simple.[10]

If we take a logical part of an expression to be one on whose reference the reference of the whole depends, in accordance with the general rules of the symbolism, we shall be making use of the notion of reference which Frege developed only after the *Grundlagen*. The notion of a logical part can also be explained in terms of the *Grundlagen* notion of content: a logical part of a sentence would be one on whose content the content of the whole depends in accordance with the general rules of the symbolism. 'Content' does not here correspond either to 'sense' or to 'reference'. When used of a concept word, relational term, or proper name, it is close to the later notion of *reference*, but the content of a *whole* sentence, a 'judgeable content', corresponds neither to the truth-value of a sentence nor to its sense; it is much more like a Russellian proposition than is anything in Frege's later thought. Although this notion was not ultimately a useful one, it gives us as much as we need here: a reference-like notion, such that the whatever-it-is of the logical parts of a sentence determines the whatever-it-is of the whole.

Frege's original point, that we must ask for the meaning of a word only in the context of a sentence, reflects the idea that properly speaking it is only as a logical part of a sentence that the word has such-and-such a meaning; apart from such an occurrence we cannot even say that it is a concept word or a proper name. Thus take "Vienna," which we may suppose to have been introduced as the proper name of a city. When it occurs in "Trieste is no Vienna," the rules of English grammar make the content of the sentence depend on *what it is to be a Vienna*—and that is why we can say that it there appears as a concept word, and that it stands for whatever it is to be a Vienna. It may be totally undetermined what it is to be a Vienna, and in that case "Vienna" would still be a logical part (because the rules of the language make the content of the sentence depend on whatever concept it has as content)—but it would then lack content, and so would the sentence. We may contrast the occurrence of "Vienna" in "Schlick founded the Vienna Circle." Here it is not a logical part at all, and we cannot ask after *its* meaning in the strict sense.

On this view, to give the logical role of an expression in a sentence is to characterize the way general rules of the symbolism determine the content of the whole sentence: if they do it via whatever item of such-and-such a sort (concept, say, or object or relation) is the content of *any* expression of some determinate pattern in that place, then the role of the expression is to stand for that sort of item. The expression occurs, for example, as a proper name if it occurs in a place where the content of the whole sentence depends on what object the expression there stands for. It cannot thus be identified as a proper name, or be said, strictly speaking, to have such a sense, if the content of the whole sentence does not depend on what object it stands for—in other words, if it occurs anywhere but in a suitable place. Nonsense of the category-clash type would then not be a possibility, even in ordinary language.

I have taken Frege's point to be that we must not ask, for example, of "Vienna" what *its* meaning is, not taking it as a logical part of any sentence. He said that to ask for the meaning of a word in isolation led easily to a psychologistic account of meaning—and we can see one way it does so if we consider any word which can be used in more than one role; "Vienna" will do. We suppose it to occur apart from any context of which we can say something like this: the content of the whole depends on whatever such-and-such (concept, object or relation) "Vienna" has as its content. And suppose we think of its occurrence as that of *a proper name*. That it *can* occur as a proper name does not account for its being one here in isolation; for it can also occur as a concept word. If we want to say it is one rather than the other, it is almost inevitable that we turn to the realm of the psychological for some connection between *this* use of the word and the possibility it has of standing for a particular city in ordinary sentences. Perhaps it is a matter of my thinking of the city as I say the word. But it is not in virtue of any such psychological connection that the word is a proper name in an ordinary sentence—and I may think of the city Vienna all I like when I say "Trieste is no Vienna" and it will not on that account be a proper name there. We do not improve matters by saying I may describe "Vienna" as referring to the city if I think of the class of sentences in which it does so. Thinking of a use does no more than thinking of a city to justify the ascription of a reference to a term in isolation. The same kind of appeal to the realm of the psychological is necessary if we think we can identify "Vienna" as a proper name in a context of supposed 'category-clash'. *Ex hypothesi*, the content of the whole combination of words does not depend on the object "Vienna" stands for. In virtue of what then is it supposed to be a proper name there?—What I am claiming is that exactly the reasons Frege had for saying that we should not ask for the meaning of a word in isolation are reasons for thinking the very idea of a category clash is confused.

These arguments depend on the way I have explained the *Grundlagen* point, and it may be said that Frege's insight should better have been put this way: that it is because an expression *can* occur as a logical part of sentences that we can unconfusedly ask for its meaning. That would allow for the significant occurrence, for example, of proper names on their own as greetings and so on—and would also allow the possibility of clashes of category. Simple versions of such a view may involve an implicit appeal to a psychological account of meaning in the way I have just sketched. However, I shall postpone discussion of the matter and instead ask what happens to Frege's insight if we treat sentences in the way he came to do, as merely a case of complete names.

One not unnatural move to try is to replace the *Grundlagen* principle with: ask for the reference of a word only in the context of a completed function expression. Here then the logical parts of completed function expressions might have reference in the strict sense, and the categorial role of such a part would depend on the kind of rule-governed contribution made by its reference to the reference of the whole. What about completed function expressions themselves? Are there any conditions that would have to be met for us to ask for *their* reference? In fact, if we say that only logical parts of such expressions have reference, we shall already have included all complete names on their own. Any Fregean proper name, including ordinary proper names, would count as a case both of a completed function expression and of a logical part of a completed function expression: it can be regarded as a completion of an expression for the identity function by itself.[11]—The difference then between the earlier and the later views lies in part in where we can identify logical parts; they agree, though, in making the identification of the logical role of an expression depend upon the possibility of taking its occurrence as that of a logical part. And they agree in making an extremely close connection between the possibility of unconfusedly ascribing a reference to an expression and its occurrence in a context with a certain sort of logical complexity—it is the characterization of this complexity which shifts.

I can now turn back to the question I raised earlier, about whether we should take Frege's insight to be that the essential thing for a term to have reference is the *possibility* of occurrence in a sentence as a logical part. The attractiveness of reformulating it in some such way is that (a) it allows for the ascription of reference to a proper name on its own, for example in greetings (as the original version of Frege's principle does not, but the revised version I just gave does), and (b) it makes clear the special significance of occurrence in *sentences* (as the original version does, but the revised version does not). But if it is stated as simply as I have done, it loses altogether a central feature of *both* versions, that it is only to an expression occurring in a context with a certain kind of logical complexity that reference can be ascribed. The use of an ordinary proper name in greeting someone, for example, could be taken to have the requisite complexity. *Who* it is one greets does not depend on the reference of the expression used in the greeting—when someone mistakenly uses my sister's name in greeting me, it is still I that am greeted. But what we might call the correctness or incorrectness of a greeting does depend on the reference of the expression used, and substituting terms with the *same* reference in the context of greeting someone or something will keep the 'correctness-value' of that greeting constant. In part, then, because it is a function of the reference of the expression used in greeting, it can be treated for certain purposes as the 'reference' of the greeting.

It is not my purpose to develop an account of the use of proper names on their own, but simply to suggest that accounts are possible which would not at the same time allow for 'category clash'. What leaves open the possibility of 'category clash' is taking as a sufficient condition for a word to have a reference that it *can* be used in a sentence as a logical part; but there are good reasons for wanting to avoid so weak a condition independently of the question about category clash. In any case, I am arguing now not that Frege was *right* in restricting reference to the logical parts of expressions with the kind of complexity exhibited by sentences (whatever exactly that kind of complexity is) and to what itself has such complexity, but that in so restricting reference, he was himself committed to a 'no category clash' view.

I have given two considerations in favor of thinking Frege did not allow the possibility of category clashes. But there is something apparently on the opposite side to which I shall now turn. For a long time, I thought that Frege's treatment of "There is Julius Caesar" showed that he did not take the view I have been suggesting is his. For I thought the alternatives were only (a) that "There is Julius Caesar" contains what is elsewhere a proper name, used as a concept word, and hence that it is no more senseless than "Trieste is no Vienna," and (b) that it contains the proper name "Julius Caesar" where a concept word ought to go and is senseless for that reason. As Frege was clearly not taking the first alternative, he had to be read as taking the second or something like it, and hence as allowing the possibility of category-clashes. But that was wrong.

What Frege actually says about "There is Julius Caesar" is simply that it is senseless. But what kind of senselessness is it? To answer that, I must explain why Frege takes such things as the presence of the indefinite article to indicate that a word is being used as a concept word. We may note that in the *Grundgesetze*, Frege says that we may form the name of a function (including here concepts and relations) by removing from a complex proper name (including here sentences) either a proper name forming a part of it (or coinciding with it) or a function name forming a part of it—in such a way that the argument place remains recognizable as capable of being filled by a name of the same sort as the one we removed.[12] The expression for a function is not recognizable as such without its argument place—and this is true even of ordinary language. Frege's *Grundgesetze* statement implies that we have not picked out a function expression unless we have associated with it a way of recognizing completions of that function expression as such. It is in part by means of the articles, numerals, and so on of ordinary language that we do so. Thus take:

(i) Anastasia lives in Charlottesville.
(ii) Another Anastasia lives in Charlottesville.
(iii) Another the King of France lives in Charlottesville.

Here (i) may be regarded as the completion of a first-level concept expression by the proper name of the last Tsar's daughter; (ii) cannot be taken to be the completion of *that* expression by "Another Anastasia." That is, the concept expression completed by "Anastasia" in (i) can be recognized there because what precedes "lives in Charlottesville" in the sentence is a noun in the singular on its own with *no* article, numeral, etc. The point is not that we can recognize the concept expression because there is a *proper name* before it. For any singular noun placed before 'lives in Charlottesville' on its own with no article etc. has one of the syntactical markers by which we tell that a term is being used as a proper name. I am not saying "Any such noun in the argument place will be a proper name," because the argument place is not as it were a *place* at all. It is a place *for* a proper name or a bound individual variable, and if it has not got in it what has the syntactical marks of use-as-a-proper-name or use-as-a-bound-individual-variable, the 'place' simply is not there to be seen. That is, we cannot look to see what sort of expression is in the place where an expression for an argument ought to go: we can look at a combination of words to see whether it can be construed as such-and-such a concept expression *with* its argument place. If we have not got the syntactical markers of the argument place, we have not got the argument place *or* the concept expression.

On this account, (ii) cannot be taken to be the first-level concept expression "x lives in Charlottesville" completed by an argument expression, since a singular noun with "Another" does not have the syntactical marks of use as a proper name. (It is not enough to point out that it *does* have the marks of use as a concept word; as we shall see, the syntactical markers of different sorts of terms in ordinary language may not be entirely distinct.) "x lives in Charlottesville" occurs in (ii) as part of the second-level concept expression "Another ( ) lives in Charlottesville," which is completed by "Anastasia," here a first-level concept word. (To be an Anastasia might be to be one who claims to be the Tsar's daughter Anastasia.) There is simply no such thing as putting the proper name "Anastasia" which we see in (i) into the argument place of the second-level concept expression in (ii). I am not saying that any word or phrase that fills the argument place filled by "Anastasia" in (i) would be used as an expression for a concept if we put it between "Another" and "lives in Charlottesville." Frege's view is that "the King of France" could fill the argument place filled by "Anastasia" in (i), but it is not, in (iii), in the argument place of "Another (   ) lives in Charlottesville." In (iii), that is, we do not have an expression of the wrong sort in the gap filled by "Anastasia" in (ii); the gap filled by "Anastasia" in (ii) is simply not recognizable in (iii). The concept expression "Another (   ) lives in Charlottesville" has, written into it, the means of recognition of the argument place—not through what kind of thing the expression there must stand for, but, with complete generality, what sort of expression it must look like. Whatever expression is there of that pattern, the reference of the whole will depend on the first-level concept it stands for—and that is what it is for it to be a term for such an item. On this view, then, (iii) does not contain any expression *in a gap in* another: it is simply a mess.

We can now note an ambiguity in the whole of the earlier part of this paper, which could not have been made clear earlier: I have spoken often of a 'place' where a term of a certain sort 'belongs', but what it is to 'belong in a place' is two distinct things. In (iii), we can turn the whole combination into sense by putting a singular noun where "the King of France" is. In *a* sense, then, we can say that "the King of France" does not belong there, and that it is its being there that makes nonsense of the whole. But it is not the case that "the King of France" does not belong there on account of its logical category and the logical category of the rest. In (iii), what is left when "the King of France" is removed has *no* logical category: it is not a concept expression of any sort and is not "incomplete" in Frege's sense. In (ii), on the other hand, an expression for a first-level concept *belongs* in the argument place of "Another (   ) lives in Charlottesville." This is very different from saying that if such an expression is put there, the whole will make sense. If a singular noun is put there, or certain noun phrases, these expressions *will be* first-level concept expressions; that gives their use. If certain other noun phrases are put there, we shall not be able to identify the argument place and we shall not have put into a place requiring a first-level concept expression something that does not belong there. So in the sense in which we can say that a first-level concept expression belongs in a place, there is no method of identifying the place where it belongs, such that the place would *still* be identifiable if what were there could not itself be identified as a first-level concept term or appropriate variable.

In a *Begriffsschrift* there will be completely unequivocal ways of making an argument place recognizable—but not so in ordinary language. That is, although it is possible (on the view I am ascribing to Frege) to make clear how the argument place of any concept or relational expression is indicated, even in ordinary language, there is no guarantee that argument places of fundamentally different kinds will always be marked in distinct ways. Frege himself points out, for example, that the (German) singular definite article does not always indicate that the noun which follows it stands for an object, and he suggests that what the plural definite article indicates is even less capable of simple formulation in a rule.[13]

Dummett has claimed that natural language constantly violates Frege's principle that a function expression cannot occur without its argument place or places—and he takes this to be consistent with Frege's principle.[14] I have been taking an opposite view: that the principle is not compatible with the identification of a function expression in natural language except *with* its argument place or places; that whatever the general form of the syntactical indicators of its argument places may be, that general form is part of the expression for the function. Natural language is *untidy* in its argument place indicators—hence the untidiness, and indeed incompleteness, of Frege's remarks about the definite and indefinite articles, numerals and plurals. A full account of the argument place indicators of, for example, the second-level concept expression we see in "There is a book" would be quite long, and there was no reason for Frege to mention more than a few of its most conspicuous items.

How does this explain what Frege says about "There is Julius Caesar"? Let me summarize my argument: Frege mistakenly thought that the only sort of argument place ever marked by the occurrence of a noun in the singular without an article or numeral or other explicit indicator is that of a first-level concept or relational expression. The second-level concept expression we can recognize in "There is a horse" cannot therefore be recognized if we replace "a horse" by a noun with what we might call the null indicator, like "Julius Caesar." It can also be argued that we cannot take the sentence as a first-level concept expression completed by "Julius Caesar." If it cannot be described as the completion of any expression by another—as a first-level concept term with a proper name, or as a second-level concept term with a first-level one, or in any other way—it is nothing but a word-hash, in no way logically different from a mere string of randomly chosen words. No logical role can be assigned to any of its parts, which are not logically parts.

What I shall argue more fully is the claim that Frege failed to recognize that the null indicator with a singular noun *may* mark a predicative use. In German as in English, a null indicator with a singular noun does normally show that the noun *as thus used* does not form a plural; it may, though, form a plural in other uses. Take "brandy" as an example:

(i) Brandy has a higher alcoholic content than wine.
(ii) There is brandy but no soda.
(iii) That drink he finished in such a hurry was a brandy.
(iv) Cognac is a brandy and so is Armagnac.

"Brandy" as used here in (iii) and (iv) is predicative and forms a plural; as used in (i) it is (at least arguably) a proper name and does not form a plural. ("Brandies have a higher alcoholic content than wine" contains "brandy" as used in (iv), not as used in (i).) As used in (ii), "brandy" does not form a plural—and yet, I should say, it is as obviously a predicative use as "There are horses" is of "horses." Why should there appear to be any problem about this? What exactly is the connection between the capacity to form a plural and a predicative use—if, as I should say, that is at the root of Frege's blind spot about cases like (ii)? Frege does allow that not all concepts determine a principle for counting what falls under them, but when he discusses such cases he has in mind adjectives like "red" and not stuff words.[15] What he says about "red" is important: "To a concept of this kind no finite number will belong." His idea can be explained if we imagine constructing a list. If *A*, say, is some apple and is red, we may start our list with it, and if *B* is red and is not *A* (is a different apple or not an apple), we add it. (It might be the surface of *A*, or some particular patch on it.) I may go on with the list (making use each time of the criteria of identity associated with the names already on the list)— and suppose I am asked, when I have ten things on it, how many distinct things are red. I can say that *at least ten* are—but it is evident that a list so begun has no end. The significant thing for us is the contrast Frege wanted to make between on the one hand count nouns and adjectives, and on the other stuff words. I can have a horse, and *another* horse; something red (the apple), and something *else* which is red (its surface). It is just this feature which stuff words lack, on Frege's view. When I have told you that what is in *this* bottle is brandy, and what is in *that* one is brandy, I have given you the proper name of a substance, twice—*the* substance which is in both bottles. (Compare "This plant is *Cassiope hypnoides*"—the 'is' is not the copula.) There is not an 'another' in the offing (except "another bottle of brandy," but Frege would say that all that that gives us is a predicate of which the proper name "brandy" is part); we have not got *two* things both of which are brandy, as we may have two apples or two things, however miscellaneous, both of which are red.—This account rests on Frege's "Gold and gold and gold is never anything else but gold," a remark made in characterizing the use of a proper name as such.[16]

If I am correct that that was Frege's view of stuff words, what is wrong with it is that Frege has made too close a connexion between (a) the possibility of ascribing a predicate to one thing and then to *another* (where possibility means grammatical possibility, not necessarily freedom from contradiction) and (b) the possibility of forming a plural from the predicate, either directly ("apples") or, if the term is an adjective, through attachment to a plural noun. But when I say "This is brandy and so is that," there *are* two quite different things that are said to be brandy, even though there are not two brandies nor two brandy things: the three ounces of liquid in here, and the twelve ounces of liquid over there—and the "is" *is* the mere copula.[17]

The point, though, is not whether the view I have ascribed to Frege about stuff words is correct, but whether it is plausible to ascribe it to him. If it was his view, that would explain why he did not treat "There is Julius Caesar" as he treated "There is only one Vienna." If singular-noun-with-null-indicator never indicates a predicative use, "There is Julius Caesar" cannot be taken to contain the second-level concept expression we have in "There is a horse" completed by "Julius Caesar" used as a stuff word with no clear sense or reference. It would not contain the second-level concept expression *at all*—that is, the attempt to say of Julius Caesar what "There is a horse" says of a concept does not *even* succeed in putting together expressions whose senses are unsuited to each other.

There are other passages in Frege—the last but one paragraph in "On Concept and Object" is a good example—which may seem to count against the view I have ascribed to him, and which (with the "There is Julius Caesar" passage) originally led me to think he *did* allow for the possibility of clash of categories. But rather than discuss in more detail how such passages should be taken, I shall consider two views closely related to the 'no-category-clash' view.

> (i) There is *not*, in addition to the sort of nonsense we may produce by using a word or words with no determinate meaning, and the sort of nonsense we may produce by failing to adhere to the syntactical rules of ordinary language, another (and more

philosophically interesting) sort of nonsense we may produce by putting together certain combinations of words violating no syntactical rule of ordinary language and using no word without a meaning. I shall call this putative sort of nonsense "w-f," for "well-formed"—well-formed, supposedly, in ordinary language, though ill-formed in some deeper way.

(ii) It is *not* a difference between ordinary language and a *Begriffsschrift*, an adequate conceptual notation, that we cannot form in it sentences that correspond to the w-f nonsense of ordinary language.

Here (ii) is clearly a consequence of (i), and (i) is a consequence of the *Grundlagen* principle that a word has meaning only in a sentence. Thus, to take an example from a philosopher who makes use of a somewhat different system of logical categories from Frege's, there is Carnap's claim that "Caesar is a prime number" is nonsense though syntactically well formed and without any meaningless words: he gives it as an example of what I am calling w-f nonsense.[18] Carnap believes "x is a prime number" is predicable only of numbers, which is to say in part that the truth or falsity of sentences resulting from completion of that expression by a name depends on what *number* the name stands for. But—applying a version of the Frege principle—if the truth or falsity of some sentence containing a name "*a*" depends on what such-and-such "*a*" is a name of, the role of "*a*" in *that* sentence is that of the name of a such-and-such. So in Carnap's sentence, "Caesar" is the name of a number, and since it is not determined *what* number it is the name of, "Caesar is a prime number" is not w-f nonsense after all, because it contains a number word with no determinate meaning.

I want to suggest that belief in w-f nonsense shows either failure to keep in mind possibilities of cross-category equivocation or an appeal to a psychologistic account of meaning. A clear case of the latter is Carnap's discussion of Heidegger on Nothing.[19] Carnap here too wants to persuade us that we have nonsensical sentences that break no rules of ordinary syntax and contain no meaningless words, and so he must dispose of the idea that Heidegger has, in saying all those weird and wonderful things about Nothing, simply departed from the ordinary meaning of the word. Now, prior to the sentences Carnap objects to, Heidegger has a sentence in which "nothing" is used in the ordinary way. This shows, Carnap says, that in the passage as a whole, we should take the word "nothing" to have the usual meaning of a logical particle serving for the formulation of negative existential statements. So when Heidegger says that "the Nothing is prior to the Not" and what not, we are to take "Nothing" as having the same meaning it has in "There is nothing outside." But what on earth *is* it for it to have the same meaning there? There is a gross misconception here of the role that can be given to a writer's intentions in settling what he means. One can no more look to a previous sentence to determine whether "Nothing" is used as a logical particle in *this* one than one can look in one sentence to tell whether "is" is the copula in another.

That belief in w-f nonsense may reflect failure to pay adequate attention to the possibilities of cross-category equivocation is illustrated by Dummett's discussion of "Chairman Mao is rare," which he uses as an example of what I have called w-f nonsense.[20] The source of the difficulty here is not in any direct appeal to a psychologistic account of meaning. Rather, Dummett's claim is that "rare" has the sense of a second-level predicate—that is a matter of the rules of the language. What then of its role in the sentence? Dummett takes the sense of a word in a sentence to be fixed by the general rules determining the sense of the word independently of any context, except in cases of ambiguity, where the rules of the language are not themselves sufficient to determine the sense the word has in particular sentences.[21] The kind of case he has in mind is that in which we have to guess from the context what the sense of a term is; but the sort of cross-category equivocation we have been concerned with is entirely different. In a case like "Trieste is no Vienna" there is no question of *guessing* from the context or anything else what the role of "Vienna" is. Further, we can recognize such cross-category equivocation even when the term in question has not antecedently been given two senses. That is, even if "Vienna" has only been given the sense of a proper name, the last word in "Trieste is no Vienna" is not a word whose sense is that of a proper name, occurring with the wrong sort of role or in the wrong sort of place. That word, there, is a concept word, and has, on our hypothesis, no specified sense as such. It has no logical relationship to the proper name "Vienna." The rule determining the sense of the proper name, the only sense determined for the word by the rules of the language, has no bearing on the sentence.

The case of Chairman Mao's rarity is similar. The *word* "rare" has, in a sense, no sense. "Rare" the second-level concept word has a sense, "rare" the first-level concept word has several, and there is no such thing as combining the second-level concept word "rare" with a term with the sense of a proper name. For the sake of simplicity let us forget, as Dummett does, that "rare" has actually got several uses as a first-level concept word (including the "O rare Ben Jonson" use), and let us ignore the "Gold is rare" sort of case, too. Assuming, then, that "rare" has no other use in the language than that of second-level concept word, we still cannot without further ado take the sense it has as such to have any logical connection with the *word* "rare" in some sentence—and in particular we cannot assume it to have any connection with the word as it occurs in some nonsense sentence. In "Chairman Mao is rare" we can in fact recognize the second-level concept expression "Chairman Mao is ( )" completed by "rare," which is there recognizable as a first-level concept word (it occurs in the argument place of a second-level concept expression with appropriate syntactical markers) as easily as the first-level concept word "Shirley Temple" is recognizable in "I'm going to have a blow-out on a Shirley Temple."[22] We need not know what these first-level concept words mean in order to recognize them as such in these occurrences. If "Chairman Mao is rare" is to be taken as w-f nonsense, we need to think that the sense both of "rare" and of "Chairman Mao," determined by the rules of the language (taking the one as second-level concept word and the other as proper name), have *some* connection with that sentence. But the rules determining the sense of those two terms in that way cannot *both* be brought to bear on that sentence. And whether or not the word "rare" has an established use as first-level concept word, the sentence can be taken as containing the word used in that way.

What then of the idea that an important part of the point of a good symbolic notation is that it excludes the w-f nonsense of ordinary language? Many philosophers have held such a view—and it has been ascribed to both Frege and Wittgenstein. But its ascription to them is more an indication of the hold the idea is capable of exerting on our minds than of any of their actual views. To make the issue here clear, consider the 'translation' into a symbolic notation of "Trieste is no Vienna." To be able to write this in a symbolic notation, the essential thing we need to know is that "Vienna" is there a first-level concept word. The important difference between ordinary language and a *Begriffsschrift* in the treatment of "Trieste is no Vienna" comes out only when we put alongside the two versions, ordinary language and *Begriffsschrift*, of "Trieste is no Vienna" a sentence of ordinary language containing the proper name 'Vienna' used as such and a *Begriffsschrift* version of *that* sentence. "Trieste is no Vienna" in *Begriffsschrift* differs from "Trieste is no Vienna" in English in not containing anything that looks like the term that stands for the city in the other sentence. What is excluded from a *Begriffsschrift* is only misleading appearances. It is not possible to take a sentence which is syntactically all right in English and say that something corresponding to it will be excluded from a good notation.[23] Whatever it is, it will go over as easily as "Trieste is no Vienna," but its *Begriffsschrift* equivalent will lack any resemblance to the *Begriffsschrift* equivalents of those sentences of ordinary language which had only superficial resemblances to the original sentence. The opposite view is a hangover of the kind of thinking most clearly exemplified by Carnap's idea that something logical particle-ish adheres to "Nothing" in "The Nothing is prior to the Not." (Compare the idea in much *Tractatus* exegesis that something formal concept-ish adheres to "object" in "A is an object"—which is then taken to be a sentence which could not be rewritten in a good symbolic notation.)

I want now to bring out more sharply the contrast between Frege's approach and the idea that the w-f nonsense of ordinary language is excluded in a *Begriffsschrift*. The view I have ascribed to Frege implies that there are two ways in which an expression may be identified as a part of (or 'coinciding with') another:

(i) It is recognizable as in the argument place of some expression of level *n*, and is thus being used as one of level *n*-1.

(ii) It is an incomplete expression of level *n*, recognizable syntactically as completed by an expression or expressions used as expressions of level *n*-1.

(For the sake of simplicity I have omitted from both (i) and (ii) the case of unequal-levelled functions.)

The first method is the only one available for proper names: that is, there is no way of identifying the occurrence of a proper name in a sentence or in any other context except in the argument place of an incomplete expression of first level (including the identity function). This is a part of what Frege meant when he spoke of the decomposition of a sentence into a 'saturated' and an 'unsaturated' part as a logically primitive phenomenon, which must simply be accepted and cannot be reduced to anything simpler.[24] Thus, although Frege himself tells us that we can form incomplete expressions by removing one expression from another, for example a proper name from a sentence, we get an incomplete expression as a result only if what we remove was *in an argument place*. We can, for example, distinguish the kind of pattern there is in "Smith has Bright's disease," "Smith has Parkinson's disease," "Smith has Hansen's disease," from that in "Smith has Bright's hat," "Smith has Parkinson's hat," "Smith has Hansen's hat" by recognizing that only in the latter set are "Bright," "Parkinson," and "Hansen" in an argument place.

I have been arguing that it is not possible on Frege's view to identify the parts of a sentence or other complex expression independently of each other as expressions with certain logical powers. A complete knowledge of the sense or reference or both of all the expressions forming a sentence is not what enables us to recognize them in the context, since what has sense and reference is only expressions recognizable through function-argument decomposition as having a certain role in the context. But now, take the opposite view and ascribe it to Frege: we *can* identify the parts of a sentence independently of each other as expressions with certain logical powers, which may then be appropriately *or* inappropriately combined. A sentence that makes sense will result only if we combine parts whose logical powers fit each other, and any other combinations will yield nonsense. If we know the rules fixing the sense of an unambiguous term, we can recognize it in any sentence in which it occurs and grasp its contribution to it.—If we understand Frege that way, we shall find it impossible to take him literally when he says that an incomplete expression cannot occur without its argument places. This has to be interpreted to mean: *in an adequate notation,* an incomplete expression cannot occur without its argument places. Exactly the same happens with Wittgenstein. The idea that we can identify the role of an expression in a sentence via its role in the language, independently of the function-argument structure of the context in which it occurs, makes it impossible to believe he meant to be taken literally when he said that there is no need for a theory of types because "what seem to be *different kinds of things* are symbolized by different kinds of symbols which *cannot* possibly be substituted in one another's places."[25] These plain (I should have thought) words are taken to express the view that *in a correct notation,* different kinds of things are symbolized by different kinds of symbols which cannot possibly be substituted in one another's places. In the case of both Frege and Wittgenstein, statements about what is impossible in *any* language are taken to be about what is impossible in a special notation.

The discovery that, although we can put words together so that they make no sense, there is no such thing as putting together words with a certain role in the language, or with certain logical powers, so that on account of these roles or these powers, the whole is nonsense—this is surely one of the great things in Frege, and one of the most important things owed to him by Wittgenstein.[26]

Notes

1. G. Frege, "On Concept and Object," in *Translations from the Philosophical Writings of Gottlob Frege,* ed. P.T. Geach and M. Black (Basil Blackwell, Oxford, 1966), p. 50.

92   Chapter 2

2. G.E.M. Anscombe, "The Reality of the Past," in *Philosophical Analysis*, ed. Max Black (Cornell University Press, Ithaca, 1950), pp. 52–6.
3. G. Frege, *Foundations of Arithmetic*, trans. J.L. Austin (Basil Blackwell, Oxford, 1974), pp. 49–50.
4. "On Concept and Object," p. 50.
5. *Foundations of Arithmetic*, p. 64, taken with "On Concept and Object," p. 50.
6. "On Concept and Object," p. 50.
7. *Foundations of Arithmetic*, p. 64.
8. G. Frege, *Basic Laws of Arithmetic*, ed. M. Furth (California University Press, Berkeley and Los Angeles, 1967), §28, p. 83.
9. G. Frege, "On the Scientific Justification of a Concept-script," *Mind*, 73 (1964), pp. 155–60.
10. *Translations*, p. 171.
11. *Basic Laws of Arithmetic*, §26, p. 81. See also P.T. Geach, "Saying and Showing in Frege and Wittgenstein," in *Essays on Wittgenstein in Honour of G.H. von Wright*, ed. J. Hintikka (North Holland, Amsterdam, 1977), pp. 59–60.
12. G. Frege, ibid.
13. "On Concept and Object," p. 45.
14. M. Dummett, *Frege, Philosophy of Language* (Duckworth, London, 1973), pp. 50 1, 178–9). Dummett's point is not easy to make out. He maintains in both passages that ordinary language does not adhere to the restriction that an incomplete expression can occur only with its argument place or places, but he also asserts that an expression can be identified as one with a certain sort of incompleteness only *with* its argument places. But whatever it is that is incomplete (for no word or words needs completion), *that* cannot appear without its argument place in ordinary language or anywhere else, on Frege's view. Dummett treats ordinary adjectives in attributive position as cases of expressions which are incomplete in virtue of their sense occurring without their argument places—which makes it seem as if the *word* "blue" (say) has a sense of a certain sort which then requires it (and this requirement is then not adhered to in ordinary language) to come accompanied by an argument place of a certain sort. But what has such a sense cannot be identified with something that can occur without its argument place. The troubles here are those discussed by P.T. Geach in "Names and Identity," in *Mind and Language*, ed. S. Guttenplan (Clarendon Press, Oxford, 1975), pp. 147–50.
15. *Foundations of Arithmetic*, p. 66. See also P.T. Geach, *Reference and Generality* (Cornell University Press, Ithaca, 1968), pp. 38–9 and G.E.M. Anscombe and P.T. Geach, *Three Philosophers* (Basil Blackwell, Oxford, 1963), p. 86.
16. G. Frege, ibid. p. 50.
17. See P.T. Geach, *Reference and Generality*, pp. 39–40.
18. R. Carnap, "The Elimination of Metaphysics Through Logical Analysis of Language," in *Logical Positivism*, ed. A.J. Ayer (Allen & Unwin, London, 1959), pp. 67–8.
19. R. Carnap, ibid. pp. 69–71.
20. M. Dummett, *Frege, Philosophy of Language*, p. 51.
21. M. Dummett, op. cit. p. 268.
22. *The New Yorker*, 3 July 1978, p. 74. It is mostly ginger ale.
23. We should note that on Frege's view, a sentence, like "The moon is divisible by 2" fails to express a thought, not because it is illegitimately constructed but because no adequate definition has been given of "x is divisible by y." A corresponding sentence is constructible in a good notation, and if the principles of

definition are adhered to, it will express a thought. Again, we have in ordinary language, on Frege's view, sequences of grammatical sentences no one of which expresses a thought on its own. The whole sequence of such "pseudo-sentences" does express a thought, and a single sentence of a *Begriffsschrift* would correspond to it. See G. Frege, "Über die Grundlagen der Geometrie," 1906, Part II, in *On the Foundations of Geometry and Formal Theories of Arithmetic,* ed. E-H.W. Kluge (Yale University Press, New Haven, 1971), pp. 69–103.

24. G. Frege, "Über die Grundlagen der Geometrie," 1903, Part II, in Kluge, op. cit., p. 33.

25. Letter to Russell, January 1913, *Notebooks 1914–1916* (Basil Blackwell, Oxford 1961), p. 121.

26. I am indebted to Peter Geach and Glenn Kessler for helpful comments on a draft of this paper.

Chapter 3

What Nonsense Might Be

There is a natural view of nonsense, which owes what attraction it has to the apparent absence of alternatives. In Frege and Wittgenstein there is a view which goes against the natural one, and the purpose of this paper is to establish that it is a possible view of nonsense.

There are all sorts of ways of categorizing the sentences and strings of words that may be called nonsensical. Since the two views I want to contrast classify nonsense in different ways, I shall start with a categorization of nonsense which reflects the natural view. This is Annette Baier's, in the article on Nonsense in the *Encyclopedia of Philosophy*.

(1) What someone says on a particular occasion may be said to be nonsense if it is obviously false, if it flies in the face of the facts.

(2) A remark may be said to be nonsense if wildly inapposite; often with such remarks who or what is being spoken *of* is quite unclear.

(3) Sentences involving category errors will be nonsense of another sort. Mrs. Baier gives as one example here Lewis Carroll's

> He thought he saw a Garden-Door
> That opened with a key:
> He looked again, and found it was
> A Double Rule of Three.

(4) We get yet another sort of nonsense when we have strings of words which lack any clear syntactic structure, or even any oddball and unclear syntactic structure. One way you can get this sort of nonsense—usually—is by taking the first word of ten consecutive pages of a book.

(5) In the fifth category we have nonsense of the sort you can produce by taking a respectable sentence and replacing one or more words (but not too many) by nonsense words. An example G. E. Moore is said to have used is "Scott kept a runcible at Ab-

botsford."[1] The most familiar example in English of this sort of nonsense is perhaps "Jabberwocky."

(6) Finally we have gibberish: strings of nonsense words without discernible syntax.

Let us consider a sentence belonging to the third kind of nonsense, an example of Carnap's:

(C) Caesar is a prime number.

Someone might want to hold that this is not nonsense at all, or that it is nonsense only in the sense in which anything obviously false may be said to be nonsense. And this might be for either of two reasons: either because he thought merely that it was a bad example of the third category of nonsense, or more interestingly because he thought that the third category collapsed entirely into the first, the category of obvious falsehoods. Anyone who does not find the particular example a convincing one but thinks there *can* be cases of the third sort of nonsense may make up his own example. But if someone were to say that in all cases of category error so-called, the resulting sentence is false and not in any strict or interesting sense meaningless, that would be to take a view distinct both from the natural view and from the one I am concerned with in this paper. I mention it to help me locate the latter, which I shall simply call the Frege–Wittgenstein view. It has this much in common with the natural view: there are some sentences, which on the natural view belong in (3), and which on both the natural view and the Frege–Wittgenstein view are indisputably nonsense in a stronger and more interesting sense than the sentences in (1) and (2). So the Frege–Wittgenstein view and the natural view are both contrasted with the view that would reduce category errors so-called to a case of falsehood.

I shall not be further concerned with this third sort of view—one expressed by Arthur Prior and others, and sometimes called 'falsidal'.[2] I should want to claim that it and the Frege–Wittgenstein view are the only serious contenders for Most Plausible View of Nonsense and that the natural view is a poor third; but my present aim is more limited.

The difference between the natural view and the Frege–Wittgenstein view can be explained by looking at the contrast between the third kind of nonsense and the fifth kind, since that contrast is explained entirely differently on the two views. I shall stick to "Caesar is a prime number" as my example of type (3) nonsense, although it is a bad example in one respect, namely that Frege himself would have regarded it as simply false. (A corresponding example, given the categories recognized by Frege, would be "Caesar exists.") I shall so far as possible ignore the complications created by differences in the actual category distinctions recognized by different writers. I shall use Moore's sentence

(M) Scott kept a runcible at Abbotsford

as an example of type (5) nonsense. What makes it nonsense is not the meaning of the word "runcible" but its *absence* of meaning. It is clear that if we defined "runcible" in a suitable way, we could turn the sentence from nonsense to sense—if for example we defined "runcible" as a kind of cow or a kind of shop.[3]

The natural view of (C), and Carnap's view as well, is that the case is exactly the opposite. Here the nonsense is not a matter of the *absence* of meaning of some word in the sentence, but of—precisely— the meanings the words *do* have. "Caesar" is a proper name (or title) of a person, and *that* such-and-such is a prime number can be said truly or falsely only of numbers. We cannot say of a person either that he is a prime number or that he is not. The meanings of the parts of the sentence do not fit together to make sense. Putting the same point in the way Professor Baier does: such a sentence attaches to its subject term a predicate which is unsuitable.[4] Michael Dummett expresses the same point using the notion of logical valency: the idea is that there are "different categories of expression, governed by rules determining that expressions of certain categories will fit together to form a sentence, while expressions of certain other categories will not"[5]—any more than calcium and sodium will form a compound.

The natural view of nonsense thus yields a simple account of the contrast between (C) and (M). If we do not give such an account, what alternative is there?

I shall approach that question in an indirect way, starting from a famous passage in Frege's *Grundlagen der Arithmetik,* in which he listed the three fundamental principles to which he had adhered in writing that book. The first is always to separate the psychological from the logical, the subjective from the objective; the second is that the meaning of a word must be asked for in the context of a sentence and not in isolation; and the third is to keep in view the distinction between concept and object.[6] The three principles are closely linked, but this linkage is especially clear in the case of the first two: if we disobey the second principle and ask for the meaning of a word in isolation, we shall almost certainly look for an answer in the realm of the psychological—we shall explain what it is for a term to have a meaning in terms of mental images or mental acts, and that will be a violation of the first principle. Frege's idea then is that if we want to focus on the work done by the (as it were) working parts of a sentence, those in virtue of which the whole sentence means what it does, then (a) what we are looking for has to be discussed without reference to psychology, and (b) what we want is not to be seen at all if we look not at the working parts in action in the sentence but at the mere isolated word. If you look at the words alone, nothing that can pertain to them in isolation will be relevant to what the words do as working parts of a sentence. You may use the word "meaning" in any way you like, but nothing that logically can be a characteristic of a word in isolation can help to explain its meaning in the sense of "meaning" in which what a sentence says depends on the meaning of its working parts.[7] Let me illustrate this point with a pair of sentences:

> Smith has Parkinson's hat.
> Smith has Parkinson's disease.

Suppose I say both these things, and I know Parkinson well. I have when I say each of the sentences a very vivid idea of him, and if you say to me "Whom did you mean when, in saying that about Smith, you spoke the name 'Parkinson'?" I could tell you whom I had meant. The important point is that the word "Parkinson" is a working part of one sentence, the first, and is not a working part of the other. However, everything that one might want to think of as connected with the meaning of the word "Parkinson" spoken in isolation could be present in both cases: that is, all the ideas we might associate with the word, all the acts of intention we might perform when we uttered it aloud or to ourselves. None of that helps us get a grip on the work done by the word "Parkinson" in the first sentence. There it is doing the work of standing for a person in a sentence; it is not a working part at all of the second sentence, in which the two words "Parkinson's disease" together work as a logical unit.

I shall not try to defend this view; I want simply to draw something from it. A word which in many sentences does the work of standing for a person can occur in another sentence in which it does not do that work at all, although the psychological accompaniments, if any, of uttering that sentence may be no different from what they are when it stands for a person. Whether it is doing the work of standing for a person in a sentence is dependent in a way which I have not explained at all on the general rules of the language. (Actually, in getting clear about the kind of work a working part of a sentence does, we should need to keep clear the distinction between concept and object, Frege thought, and that is one reason he introduced the third principle with the other two.)

Before turning back to questions about nonsense, I need to point out one other thing. It is a characteristic of ordinary language, as opposed to artificial and specially devised notations, that the fact that a word has one sort of use is in general no impediment to giving it quite different uses. Thus for example a Shirley Temple is a kind of drink, although "Shirley Temple" started off life as the proper name of a person. This sort of thing happens all the time, and can even happen to whole sentences; e.g., there is a shop called "I was not Lord Kitchener's valet." The point can be put in a slightly different way; just as we can take a nonsense word like "runcible" and give it a definition if we choose, we can also take words which already have one sort of meaning and assign them another, as with "Shirley Temple."

I can now turn back to the distinction between the two sentences (C) and (M) and to giving an alternative account of it. Take (C) first. It contains the word "Caesar" all right. And that word is normally taken by speakers of English to be a proper name of a person or perhaps a title—a complication we may ignore.

It is perfectly true that if I say "Caesar is a prime number" my state of mind, my intentions, and so on, may be exactly the same as when I use the word "Caesar" to refer to some or other person. But suppose we follow Frege and distinguish sharply between the psychological and the logical. We can then see that from the fact that my state of mind or intentions are the same, it does not follow that the word "Caesar" as it occurs in the context "——is a prime number" has the logical role of standing for a person, the role it does have if for example I ask you when it was that Caesar crossed the Rubicon. What I am driving at is this: that if we accept Frege's principle of always separating the psychological from the logical, there must at the very least be a question for us whether "Caesar" in "Caesar is a prime number" is working as the proper name of a person; and *this* question is not to be settled by the fact that the word occurs ordinarily as the proper name of a person nor by the fact that when I say the sentence I would say if asked that I had meant "Caesar" as the name of a man. And something similar could be said of the last four words of the sentence. The speaker may well intend that those words shall mean what they do when he says of 53 that it is a prime number; but on Frege's principle, that sort of thing cannot settle whether the words do mean the same, or indeed whether they mean anything.

Having suggested that it is at any rate not obvious that the first word in "Caesar is a prime number" means what it does in "When did Caesar cross the Rubicon?" or that the last four words mean what they do when used about numbers, I shall now turn back to "Scott kept a runcible at Abbotsford." I pointed out earlier that this sentence could be cured of what ails it if an appropriate meaning were given to "runcible"; that is something which could be accepted whether one held the natural view or the Frege–Wittgenstein view. However, the natural view holds, as the Frege–Wittgenstein view does not, that it is possible to assign a meaning to "runcible" which would clash with the meaning of the rest of the sentence. Here the idea is that "Scott kept a——at Abbotsford," which is a feature of both "Scott kept a cow at Abbotsford" and "Scott kept a runcible at Abbotsford" means the same in both; and to make sense of the latter sentence what one has to do is give "runcible" a meaning which can combine to make sense with the meaning the rest of the sentence *already* has, and not one which will clash with that meaning.

On the Frege–Wittgenstein view, if a sentence makes no sense, *no* part of it can be said to mean what it does in some other sentence which does make sense—any more than a word can be said to mean something in isolation. If "Caesar is a prime number" is nonsense, then "Caesar" does not mean what it does when it is in use as a proper name, and the last four words do not mean what they do in sentences which make sense. And "Scott kept a runcible at Abbotsford" does not have in common with "Scott kept a cow at Abbotsford" what that has in common with "Scott kept a tiger at Abbotsford."

The point can be explained by considering simpler sentences in a schematic way. Suppose that the rules of the language assign some meaning to Logical Element 1 and Logical Element 2, where these are (in a sense which I have not yet explained) the sort of item out of which sentences are constructed. To fix the meaning of these Logical Elements is to fix their contribution to the sentences of which they are—in this unexplained sense—parts. Let us suppose that these meanings are such that a sentence constructed in some specifiable way out of these Elements will say of some object that it has such-and-such a property. Now *only* if a sentence is taken to say that, can we say that it *is* Logical Element 1 combined in that way with Logical Element 2. Only in that way can we identify the expressions which we see or hear in the sentence with those Logical Elements to which the rules of the language actually assign a meaning, a possibility of contributing in a fixed way to any sentence in which they occur. The expressions we see or hear can be identified with the items to which a definite meaning has been given only in a sentence which does make sense. In general, then, what the assignment of meaning to Logical Elements does is connect a sentence's being constructed out of these Elements in some definite way with its expressing some definite sense. We can then take particular perceptible sentences as logical combinations of those Elements, expressing the sense which the rules determine for the whole sentence via the meanings fixed for the Elements. If I know the rules of the language, I know what a sentence composed in such-and-such a way out of such-and-such Elements says; but I do not know (there is no such thing as knowing) that what I see or hear *is* this Element, unless the whole of which it is part has a sense to which the meaning of this Element contributes in the way determined by the rules.

I have already touched on this view in discussing the difference between "Smith has Parkinson's hat" and "Smith has Parkinson's disease." The term "proper name" can be used, as Frege for example does, as a term for one kind of Logical Element. In this sense, the proper name "Parkinson" occurs only in the first sentence. To say that is to put in other terms my earlier remark that only in that sentence of the pair does "Parkinson" do the work of standing for a person in a sentence. It can only do that in a sentence that makes sense: a proper name cannot occur where it would make no sense for it to occur, although a *word* which in some contexts can be identified (by its use there) as a proper name may occur anywhere one pleases.

We can now apply this account, first to "Scott kept a runcible at Abbotsford" and then to "Caesar is a prime number." Among the sentences in which the complex Logical Element "Scott kept a —— at Abbotsford" means what it does in "Scott kept a cow at Abbotsford" there will be some which consist simply of that Logical Element completed by a term-for-a-keepable-kind-of-thing; any such sentence will say Scott kept such a thing at Abbotsford. We can introduce a rule by which "runcible" will stand for some such thing—not the word "runcible" but the Logical Element "runcible," a term-for-a-keepable-kind-of-thing. The sentence "Scott kept a runcible at Abbotsford" will then say that Scott kept such a thing at Abbotsford; in taking it to have that sense, we regard it as the combination of the same Logical Element we can see in "Scott kept a cow at Abbotsford" with the Logical Element "runcible" to which a meaning was assigned by the new rule.

The situation is only slightly different with "Caesar is a prime number." Suppose we accept that this makes no sense, because only of a number can it truly or falsely be said that it is a prime number. In that case it would follow, on the view of nonsense I am explaining, that one kind of Logical Element is: term-for-a-number. That sort of Logical Element can be combined with the predicate of "53 is a prime number." If "Caesar" is defined as a number term, the sentence "Caesar is a prime number" can be regarded as a logical combination of that number term and the predicate term we have in "53 is a prime number" understood as it normally is. But unless "Caesar" is defined in such a way, the last four words of "Caesar is a prime number" do not mean what they do in "53 is a prime number"; we do not have that numerical predicate, that Logical Element, any more than we have the proper name "Parkinson" in "Smith has Parkinson's disease." We could proceed from the opposite direction. We could assign a new meaning to "number" (that of "minister" or "idiot," for example); "prime" is already ambiguous and will do perfectly well without further change. "Caesar is a prime number" can now be read as containing "Caesar," the same Logical Element as in "When did Caesar cross the Rubicon?" and the whole sentence will make perfectly good sense, saying of Caesar something it makes sense to say of a person. In summary, then, "Caesar is a prime number" can be made sense of in two ways: it can be taken as saying of Caesar something it makes sense to say about a person—in which case it contains the proper name of a person but not a numerical predicate; or it can be taken as saying of a number something it makes sense to say about a number—in which case it contains a numerical predicate but not the proper name of a person. If we make no such new assignments of meaning, the sentence is simply one which has some superficial resemblance to sentences of two distinct logical patterns; it has a word but no Logical Element in common with some sentences about Caesar, sentences of the pattern: proper name of a person combined with personal predicate, and it has words but no Logical Element in common with sentences like "53 is a prime number," combinations of number terms with numerical predicates. It fails to be of one pattern, because a meaning of a certain sort has *not* been determined for "is a prime number"; it fails to be of the other, because a meaning of a certain sort has *not* been given to "Caesar." Being of neither pattern (nor of any other), it is nonsense. It is our not having made certain determinations of meaning that we could make that is responsible for its being nonsense. And in this respect it is fundamentally like "Scott kept a runcible at Abbotsford." Let "runcible" mean *cow* and "Caesar" mean *20*, and both are cured of nonsensicality.

On this view, then, there is a significant similarity between (C) and (M). There are indeed differences, but they are less important. One difference, of course, is that we can make sense of (C) in more than one way. Or rather, more than one way may readily suggest itself, but this does not mark a logical distinction between (C) and (M). The logical point is that to make sense of either, we must be able to take that sentence as a combination of Logical Elements to which meaning has been assigned. It is *natural* to do it with (C), if we do it at all, either in such a way that the meaning of "Caesar" is what it is in

"Caesar crossed the Rubicon" or in such a way that the rest of the sentence means what it does in sentences about numbers; it is *natural* to do it with (M), if we do it at all, so that the whole sentence will say of whatever runcibles are what "Scott kept a cow at Abbotsford" says of cows. So there are two natural routes in one case and only one in the other. But logic issues no requirement that we take a natural route if we wish to make sense of the entire sentence; as far as logic is concerned, we might perfectly well have "Caesar is a prime number" express the sense, by appropriate assignments of meaning, that clematis is a fast grower.

There are several other related differences between (C) and (M). Sentences in the fifth category of nonsense, like (M), contain nonsense words, whatever exactly we mean by that. They contain words in some sense excluded from the vocabulary of English (or German or whatever), while sentences in category (3), like our (C), contain no word not part of the vocabulary of the language in which the sentence is constructed. Further, as an obvious consequence, assigning the meaning *cow* to "runcible" does not result in any word in English having two meanings, whereas if "Caesar" is defined so that it stands for some number in certain sentences, then the word "Caesar" can now occur in English sentences with two quite different sorts of meaning. But as I mentioned earlier, there is no law against this sort of thing, and it occurs all the time. Another difference is that of the psychological associations. Whatever the psychological associations may be of uttering the word "Caesar" in those contexts in which it is doing the work of standing for a person, they may be found when it is not doing any work, or when it is doing another sort of work in a sentence. And so on a purely psychological level there will be differences between type (3) nonsense and type (5) nonsense.

The various differences between type (3) nonsense and type (5) nonsense are on a relatively superficial level; the similarity is much more significant. Both arise from absence of meaning of some definite sort in one or several words, and both can be cured by assigning meanings of the relevant sort. There is in neither case any impediment of any non-psychological sort to such an assignment of meaning. You cannot give a word a *wrong* sort of sense; you cannot give it a sense which interferes or clashes (except psychologically) with what is already established in the language. A language without a multiplicity of *kinds* of use of individual words may be preferable, but only because it will then be easier to see what kind of work a term is doing; there is no logical mistake in the use of a single word in a variety of roles.

I have now brought out one central point of contrast between the natural view of nonsense and the Frege–Wittgenstein view, namely that the idea of a significant difference between type (3) and type (5) nonsense disappears. Another point of contrast, or (you could say) the same one put differently, is that on the natural view there is and on the Frege–Wittgenstein view there is not what you might call a functional account of nonsense. Now on any plausible view you can say that the sense of a sentence depends on the meanings of the words of which it is composed. How exactly that functional relationship should be expressed is a problem, but there is some such functional relationship. What the natural view holds, though, is something beyond this: that whether a sentence makes sense or not is functionally dependent on its parts, on their logical category. This is reflected in the idea of expressions that can be substituted for each other in some or all contexts *salva congruitate*, as they say. More particularly, the idea is that nonsense of type (3) is functionally explicable. Obviously, part of the point of an example like Carnap's is precisely that you can substitute the name "Russell" for "Caesar" in "Caesar is a prime number" *salva incongruitate*, as it were. So *whether* you get sense or type (3) nonsense when you put a word where "Caesar" is depends on the category of the word put there. Nonsense comes out given certain category combinations, sense comes out given others. There is also a certain amount of imagery that may go with this view of nonsense as functionally dependent on how categories are combined: the imagery of what the thing that you say would have to mean if it meant anything. The idea is that if you say "Caesar is a prime number" and you mean "Caesar" as a person's name and you mean the last four words in exactly the sense they have in "53 is a prime number" then the reason what you say is nonsense is that *the person* Caesar *having the property* you said 53 had—*that* is impossible, *that* makes no sense. This view is clearly expressed by Arthur Pap, for example, who thought that the meaninglessness of a sentence may *result from* non-linguistic relations between the designata of its constituent terms.[8]

The Frege–Wittgenstein view does not take any kind of nonsense to be functionally dependent on the categories of the terms combined in a sentence. If we are not now talking of the category of the thing you psychologically associate with the word, then to give the category of a word in a sentence is to give the kind of work it is doing there. The word does not have a category assigned to it which it brings with it into *whatever* context. This is not to say that words are not assigned to categories, but that the identification of a word in a particular sentence as playing a certain role there, as meaning a certain kind of thing, cannot be read directly off the rules. Sentences are not made up of ingredients, words-assigned-to-certain-categories, but are constructed on patterns, where the category of a word in a sentence depends upon the pattern (or patterns) in accordance with which the whole sentence may be taken to be constructed; and non-sense sentences of the third type have only superficial resemblance to the patterns we at first discern in them, and in accordance with which we try to construe them. In this view, then, there is no such thing as putting words of such-and-such categories together so that *that* is how you get nonsense. Wittgenstein expressed this at one point in the pre-*Tractatus* writings, when he said that an illogical language could not be constructed, where "an illogical language would be one in which, e.g., you could put an *event* into a hole."[9] An illog-ical language would precisely be one in which you could do what the natural view says we *do* do in making category errors.

What then is supposed to happen if we try to put an event into a hole?

> The event: the execution of Charles I in 1649, is in the crater of Vesuvius.

An "illogical language" would be one in which such a sentence would say of an event that it was in a crater. But there is no such saying as that, and no such thought as that: there is only a string of words imitating the expression of thought. Only a sentence which *did* say it would have the structure which we think we can see in that sentence; only a sentence which *did* say it would really be composed of expressions of those categories which, on the natural view, are illegitimately combined in it. That is, the idea that the sentence is nonsense because of the categories of the expressions illegitimately combined in it is implicitly (this is the diagnosis of the natural view from the Frege–Wittgenstein position) the idea of their forming a sen-tence which *does* say something—something which the holder of the natural view regards as an impossibility and which he denies is really sayable at all: this is the incoherence of the natural view, as seen from the Frege–Wittgenstein position. The contrasting view expressed by Wittgenstein in the passage quoted is not that there is an impossibil-ity of putting events into holes, which language conveniently pre-cludes our expressing; there is nothing at all but a confusion of words which has the appearance of expressing something or trying to ex-press something that we then say cannot be.

Someone might indeed claim that he uttered "The *event*: the exe-cution of Charles I in 1649, *is in the crater of Vesuvius*" meaning of an *event* that *it was in a crater*. He knows what it is to speak of events and of things in craters, and can he not tell us what he meant? If he says such things, one might well doubt that he does, as he says, know what it is to be speaking of an event; but in any case his reports of his intentions are here irrelevant. "Meaning an event" seems here to be no more than thinking of it; but what one is thinking of is not relevant to the work done by parts of a sentence. But if it is called into question whether the words he uses are doing the work they do in ordinary contexts, the natural view of type (3) nonsense is also called into question.

In Wittgenstein this view of nonsense is in fact developed much more than it is in Frege, and you could put it this way: for Wittgenstein there is *no* kind of nonsense which is nonsense on account of what the terms composing it mean—there is as it were no 'positive' nonsense. *Anything* that is nonsense is so merely because some determination of meaning has *not* been made; it is not nonsense as a logical result of determinations that *have* been made. I believe the roots of this idea are in Frege, but before explaining that claim, I shall give three quotations from Wittgenstein illustrating his view.

First, from *Philosophical Investigations*, §500:

> When a sentence is called senseless it is not as it were its sense that is senseless. But a combination of words is being excluded from the language, withdrawn from circulation.

An earlier version of that remark, in *Philosophical Grammar*, is also significant (p. 130):

> How strange that one should be able to say that such and such a state of affairs is inconceivable! If we regard thought as essentially an accompaniment going with an expression, the words in the statement that specify the inconceivable state of affairs must be unaccompanied. So what sort of sense is it to have? Unless it says these words are senseless. But it isn't as it were their sense that is senseless; they are excluded from our language like some arbitrary noise, and the reason for their *explicit* exclusion can only be that *we are tempted* to confuse them with a sentence of our language.

The third quotation is from a lecture in 1935.

> Though it is nonsense to say "I feel his pain," this is different from inserting into an English sentence a meaningless word, say "abracadabra" . . . and from saying a string of nonsense words. Every word in this sentence is English, and we shall be inclined to say that the sentence has a meaning. The sentence with the nonsense word or the string of nonsense words can be discarded

from our language, but if we discard from our language "I feel Smith's toothache" that is quite different. The second seems nonsense, we are tempted to say, because of some truth about the nature of things or the nature of the world. We have discovered in some way that pains and personality do not fit together in such a way that I can feel his pain. The task will be to show that there is in fact no difference between these two cases of nonsense, though there is a psychological distinction in that we are inclined to say the one and be puzzled by it and not the other. We constantly hover between regarding it as sense and nonsense, and hence the trouble arises.[10]

I should claim that the view of nonsense expressed in those three quotations is one that was consistently held to by Wittgenstein throughout his writings, from the period before the *Tractatus* was written and onwards. There is no 'positive' nonsense, no such thing as nonsense that is nonsense on account of what it would have to mean, given the meanings already fixed for the terms it contains. This applies even to Wittgenstein's discussions of privacy. It is very easy to take Wittgenstein to have meant that if you combine:

	rule
impossible to communicate	language
to another person	definition
	map

the *result* is something incoherent. What I am suggesting is that for Wittgenstein the sentence "Smith is following a rule that no one but Smith could conceivably understand" is discardable from the language, but not because of what it would have to mean if we were to stick to the meanings determined independently for its parts. It is, on Wittgenstein's view, in the same position as the sentence "Smith is following an abracadabra," though here too it can be said "there is a psychological distinction in that we are inclined to say the one and be puzzled by it and not the other."

I am not at all concerned to discuss whether Wittgenstein was right about private language (and the related cases). I simply want to include it as an example of how Wittgenstein's view of nonsense applies, because I think we often interpret Wittgenstein as saying things about private language which he could say only if he held the natural view of nonsense, which he did not.

The last thing I want to turn to is the root of this view of nonsense in Frege. As I have already indicated, I think it has important connections with Frege's principle in the *Grundlagen* that we should ask for the meaning of a word only in the context of a sentence, and it is these connections which I want now to explore further.

I shall start from a remark of Quine's about Frege: for Frege, Quine says, the primary vehicle of meaning is not the term but the statement.[11] Michael Dummett takes the ascription of such a view to Frege to be very misleading. I think Quine was right and Dummett wrong—and that it will be useful for us to look at the dispute. Dummett claims that the thesis that the unit of significance is the sentence not the word (this is how he puts the view Quine ascribes to Frege; cf. note 11) is either false or truistic, and that in neither case does it represent any thesis stressed by Frege. Either it means (1) that the words composing a sentence no more have a meaning on their own than do letters of a word, which is absurd, or the thesis put by Quine into the mouth of Frege means (2) that we cannot *say anything* with a sequence of words shorter than a sentence; and this is truistic, for what a sentence is is precisely an expression by which we can perform a linguistic act, or make a move in the language-game.[12]

There is obviously a question one might ask here whether it was not some thesis distinct from either of these two that Quine thought he was ascribing to Frege, and that *he* thought constituted a significant reorientation in semantics. That there is such a thesis is certainly suggested if we look at the passage in Frege that Quine actually refers to, which contains a very striking and puzzling remark.

In *Grundlagen*, §60, Frege is arguing that failure to be able to form a mental picture corresponding to a word is no reason to deny the word a content. We are imposed on by the opposite view only because we ask for the meaning of a word in isolation. But we ought, he says, always to keep before our eyes a complete sentence. Only in it have the words really a meaning. Mental pictures may float before us when we consider the sentence, but these need not correspond to the logical elements of the judgment. It is enough, he says, if the sentence as a whole has a sense; it is through this that the parts also get their content. (*Es genügt, wenn der Satz als Ganzes einen Sinn hat; dadurch erhalten auch seine Theile ihren Inhalt.*)

This is an extremely striking remark, and Dummett simply does not refer to the passage at all. I think it requires that something be made of the idea that the sentence is the primary vehicle of meaning, other than the two possibilities, one absurd and the other truistic, offered us by Dummett. Since Frege asserts in the passage that a complete sentence has got parts which do have content in the way the letters of a word plainly do not, he is clearly not asserting but implicitly denying the false thesis (thesis (1)). But equally clearly Frege is making a far stronger assertion than merely the truistic alternative Dummett proposes: that a sequence of words is not a saying of anything unless some complete linguistic act is being performed. If that were all he meant, the last sentence of the passage would be extraordinarily misleading.

Frege is not denying that we understand a sentence only because we know the language—know, that is, the general rules fixing the content of expressions in the language. What then can he mean when he says that the parts get their content through the sentence's as a whole having a sense? If he means that the sense of the whole sentence fixes what the parts mean, how could we ever understand new sentences? On the other hand, he does not merely mean that a word has meaning if it contributes to the sense of any sentence in which it occurs, in accordance with general rules; that is, he is not saying that it is the *general* possibility a word has of contributing to sense that confers meaning on it. That would allow for the possibility of a senseless sentence composed of words which had had content conferred on them by general rules. But what he actually says in the passage Quine refers to is that it is through the sense of the whole that the parts get their content, and if this means anything at all, it must rule out the combination: senseless whole and parts with content.

We need to see how Frege can do both: can mean what he says about the parts getting their content through the sentence's having sense, and can recognize that we grasp what a sentence says via our grasp of general rules determining the meaning of expressions in the language. We can do this by going back to the statement that words really have a meaning only in the context of a sentence, and taking it in a Fregean spirit, this way: we cannot speak about the meaning of expressions unless we know how to tell when two expressions *have the same meaning;* and they do not have the same meaning unless the sentence in which the first occurs expresses a thought (the possible content of a judgment) which has an element in common with the thought expressed by the sentence in which the other occurs. Identity of meaning applies, properly speaking, to *expressions in sentences* (the identity of meaning of two sentences will be a limiting case); that is why we cannot properly ask for the meaning of a word except in the context of a sentence.

We can now formulate an account of the way our grasp of the meanings fixed for expressions by the general rules of the language plays a role in our understanding of particular sentences. I assume there are two kinds of general rule, one kind enabling us to break down whole sentences into elements with a syntactic characterization, and another sort fixing the meanings of proper names, concept expressions and relational expressions of various sorts; neither kind of rule will apply unconditionally to a given sentence. Take as an example a sentence like one Frege uses: "Venus is more massive than Mercury." We can, using the general rules of English, characterize the structure of the sentence, but any such characterization will apply to the sentence only conditionally. Thus the sentence may be taken to be a two-term relational expression completed by the proper name "Venus" in the left-hand place and the proper name "Mercury" in the right-hand place, *but only if* the thought expressed by the whole sentence is that the object "Venus" stands for, whatever that is, has whatever relation it is the relational expression stands for to whatever object it is "Mercury" stands for. We may know that the proper name "Venus" stands for Venus; our knowledge may now be conditionally applied: the sentence is the proper name "Venus" *standing for Venus*, in the left-hand place of the relational expression, with the proper name "Mercury" in the right-hand place, only if the thought expressed by the whole sentence is that *Venus* has whatever relation "more massive than" stands for to whatever object "Mercury" means. If I know the rules determining the meaning of those expressions, I get such a reading of the whole sentence; it can be taken as the proper name "Venus" standing for Venus and the proper name "Mercury" standing for Mercury in the left- and right-hand places of the expression for the relation *more massive than*, only if the whole sentence is taken to have the content: *Venus is more massive than Mercury*. That is to say, the proper names "Venus" and "Mercury" (standing for the things they stand for) in the two argument places of the expression meaning *more massive than* make a sentence saying Venus is more massive than Mercury, but this is a calculation which so far tells us nothing of what a particular perceptible sentence says. The perceptible sentence *is* those two proper names in the two argument places of that relational expression—it is that logical combination of elements—only if it says Venus is more massive than Mercury. Taking the rules which fix the meaning of expressions in the language to apply to the particular sentence is not separable from making sense of the whole sentence (what Wittgenstein called *das Denken des Satz-Sinnes*). Of course it need not be done in the piecemeal way I have just described, though such an approach is not uncommon with unfamiliar sorts of sentence, like the headline "Forest Euro-kings." A non-reader of sports news might take a moment to work out which bit of that might be a predicate, and then to work out what "Forest" might be the proper name of, thus making it possible to take the whole sentence as saying of the team named that they have won the European championship.

On this account, then, the rules of the language enable us to determine the meaning of a sentence this way. They enable us to arrive at a way of taking the whole sentence as saying such-and-such; and that is the meaning of the sentence if the sentence is unambiguous, which it will be if there is only one possible reading that can be arrived at without adding new rules (definitions or syntactical rules) to the language. It would be correct to say that the rules of the language are in a sense permissions, though conditional ones: to make sense of a sentence is to apply such rules, but it is still a *making* sense, and not a mere recognition of what the pieces are and how they are combined, plus a following of the directions-for-use that have been determined for the individual pieces and their mode of combination. We do not just arrive at a result—the meaning—by following such directions, and to make sense of a sentence is not to correlate something with it but to make it make the sense. The hearer's activity in understanding is close to the speaker's in constructing the sentence—the hearer has in a sense to make the sentence *his,* but using *the* rules. The user of language—speaker or hearer—is a thinker of senses according to the rules.

This account of how our grasp of the general rules determining the meaning of expressions in the language enables us to understand a new sentence meets the requirement that if an expression can be said, properly speaking, to mean the same as some other, the one occurs in a sentence expressing a thought with an element common to that expressed by the sentence in which the other occurs. The requirement applies to different uses of the same word, or to different words: the word may be said to be used in the two contexts with the same meaning, or the two words may be said to have the same meaning in their respective contexts, only if the whole sentences in which the words occur express thoughts which have an element in common. It follows that a sentence which does not make sense does not contain words which can be said to mean what they do elsewhere. If this is Frege's view, then indeed he can hold both that it is through the whole sentence's having its sense that the parts get their content, and that our understanding of a sentence depends on our grasp of general rules determining meaning.[13] *That* such-and-such a word is a working part of a sentence and that it is *its* content we must grasp to understand the sentence is quite another matter, and cannot be told by observation.

If this is Frege's view, it does indeed represent, as Quine said, a reorientation in semantics. Its application to the question of what nonsense is is simple. It allows for two sorts of 'negative' nonsense—

that is, nonsense resulting from our *not* having made certain determinations of meaning, determinations which there is no logical impediment to making. A sentence may be nonsense because we have not made some rule of the first sort, enabling us to decompose the sentence syntactically. Alternatively, we may be able to assign a structure to it at least conditionally, but one of the parts thus picked out may have had no meaning of the relevant sort determined for it. ("Forest Euro-kings" would be nonsense of this sort if the proper name "Forest" had no meaning.) There is clearly no place, on this view, for 'positive' nonsense, for nonsense got by combining terms whose meaning is such that nonsense results from putting them together.

I have ascribed this view to Frege on the basis of the passage in the *Grundlagen* referred to by Quine, and other passages in the *Grundlagen;* and I have expounded the view without availing myself of the distinctions or the terminology Frege developed later. The view itself was not abandoned by Frege in his later work but generalized. The role of the sentence is taken by that of the completed function expression: *any* proper name, including sentences, can be taken as a completed function expression. (In fact, they can all be taken as the completion of function expressions of a special sort: those the expression for which consists *entirely* of indications of argument places.) I have ascribed to Frege the view that it is impossible to put a sentence together out of expressions whose meaning is such that they are illegitimately combined; the more general form of the doctrine is that it is impossible to put into *any* argument place an expression unsuitable for that place because of the kind of meaning it has. This I cannot go into.[14] My point in this last part of the paper has been to show how the general view of nonsense I have been talking about is connected with the *Grundlagen* principle that only words in a complete sentence can be said properly speaking to have a meaning. I should be disingenuous, though, in not adding that the last part of the paper had a further aim. There are parallels between the view I have ascribed to Frege and some central passages in the *Tractatus*, especially in the 3s, and most especially in the connection between 3.3 and the remarks that follow it. I have wanted these parallels to be suggested. I have also wanted to suggest, and again without argument, a *distance* between Frege's view and what might be called a Tarskian view. That is, there may at first appear to be parallels between a Tarskian theory of truth and a Fregean account of the relation between the sense (= truth-conditions) of whole sentences and the sense of the constituents (putting this now in the vocabulary of the *Grundgesetze*).[15] But if I am right in what I have said about Frege, this appearance of parallel is delusive.

Notes

1. Moore is said to have used this example in Margaret Macdonald's notes to Wittgenstein's lectures, in the passage part of which is quoted on pp. 106–7. The reference to Moore's example is parenthetical, and may have been added by Miss Macdonald.

2. Prior defends such a view in "Entities," *Australasian Journal of Philosophy* **32** (1954), reprinted in his *Papers in Logic and Ethics* (Duckworth, 1976). Quine takes a similar position in *Word and Object*, p. 229. See also Robin Haack, "No Need for Nonsense," *Australasian Journal of Philosophy* **49** (1971), and Michael Bradley, "On the Alleged Need for Nonsense," *Australasian Journal of Philosophy* **56** (1978).

3. I have heard it objected that this cannot be done, for example because Edward Lear introduced the word as an adjective. Lear's use of the word in adjectival position may indeed make Moore's use of it grate on the ears of purists, but the word is still a nonsense word, and Moore's use of it involves no logical error.

4. *Encyclopedia of Philosophy* **5**, p. 520.

5. *Frege: Philosophy of Language* (Duckworth, 1973), p. 62. Cf. also p. 32.

6. *Grundlagen*, p. x.

7. How exactly that sense of "meaning" should be explained is a matter treated in one way by Frege in the *Grundlagen*, in another by him in his later writings, and in yet another by Wittgenstein in the *Tractatus*. I am concerned with features of the account common to the *Grundlagen* and the *Tractatus*, some of which are also present in Frege's later writings despite the identification of sentences with proper names. Throughout this paper I also assume that there is no problem about the kind of meaning which proper names have.

8. Arthur Pap, "Types and Meaninglessness," *Mind* **69** (1960), p. 47.

9. "Notes Dictated to G. E. Moore," in *Notebooks, 1914–1916*, p. 107.

10. Unpublished notes taken by Margaret Macdonald of lectures on 'Personal Experience', Michaelmas, 1935. The quoted passage is from the lecture of 24 October, 1935; I have altered the punctuation and omitted a parenthetical remark (see note 1 above) which I believe is Miss Macdonald's.

11. "Two Dogmas of Empiricism," in *From a Logical Point of View* (Harvard University Press, 1953), p. 39. Later in the same article, Quine says that with Frege the statement rather than the term came to be recognized as the unit accountable to an empiricist critique—as the unit of empirical significance in that sense in which, for Quine himself, the unit is the whole of science.

12. Dummett, op. cit., p. 3.

13. P. M. S. Hacker, in "Semantic Holism" (in *Wittgenstein: Sources and Perspectives*, C. G. Luckhardt (ed.) (Cornell University Press, 1979), pp. 213–42), interprets Frege in an entirely different way. On his view, (1) Frege's remark about its being through the sense of the whole that the parts get their content renders it prima facie unintelligible that we should understand new sentences composed of known expressions (p. 221), and (2) the difficulty for Frege is resolved only when he later effectively replaced the doctrine that a word has meaning only in the context of a sentence by the idea that the sense of a sentence is made up of the senses of its constituent parts and is given by its truth-conditions (pp. 221, 225). While Hacker himself would reject a psychological account of meaning, his

interpretation in fact rests on just such an account. He misses Frege's own reasons for thinking that one will identify the meanings of words with *ideas* if one takes the view that they have meaning outside the context of sentences, and he takes the reasons to depend on peculiarities of Frege's early theory of meaning (p. 218). This leaves him unable to see how Frege's argument applies to the account he himself gives.

14. I have discussed Frege's view in more detail in "Frege and Nonsense" and in "What Does a Concept-Script Do?"

15. See John McDowell, "On the Sense and Reference of a Proper Name," *Mind* **86** (1977), especially p. 159, and Donald Davidson, "Truth and Meaning," *Synthese* **17** (1967).

Chapter 4

What Does a Concept-Script Do?

I

Two remarks made me wonder what a concept-script does. The first was Hans Sluga's, in this summary of Frege's claims for his concept-script:

> (1) Meaningful statements possess an objective conceptual content.
> (2) That content is only inadequately represented in ordinary language.
> (3) It is possible to design a system of notation in which the conceptual content of any statement can be given an adequate and clear expression.
>
> Implicit in this program is a threefold philosophical methodology. The task of philosophy is seen as *the determination of the objective content* of philosophically interesting statements, a *critique* of their expression in ordinary language, and their *translation* into an adequate language. It is a methodology which the analytic tradition has endeavored to carry out. It has done so by adopting the outline of Frege's program but modifying the details.[1]

Sluga then sees later analytical philosophy as the natural development of what Frege was at in his concept script. That line of development, I thought, could be contrasted with the line going to the *Tractatus*. Putting things crudely, on the *Tractatus* view there is no such thing as a translation of "philosophically interesting statements" into an adequate language; one point of developing such a language would be to enable us to see that there are no such translations, and thus to help us overcome our tendency to put together such statements. If the methodology of the analytical tradition is the natural development of Frege's philosophy, then the methodological pronouncements of the *Tractatus*, it would seem, are not. Well, which is? Or is there something the matter with that question? That then was one thing troubling me. The other remark that made me think that I had some problems about concept-scripts was Peter Geach's, in his very illuminating piece on saying and showing in Frege and Wittgenstein. The first of the four theses he defends is:

> Frege already held, and his philosophy of logic would oblige him to hold, that there are logical category-distinctions which will clearly show themselves in a well-constructed formalized language, but which cannot properly be asserted in language: the sentences in which we seek to convey them in the vernacular are logically improper and admit of no translation into well-formed formulas of symbolic logic. All the same, there is a test for these sentences having conveyed the intended distinctions—namely, that by their aid mastery of the formalized language is attainable.[2]

What puzzled me here was Geach's claim that we show our understanding of the logically ill-formed sentences which seek to convey these category distinctions in our mastery of a well-constructed formalized language. Is this meant to be consistent with the idea that a well-constructed formalized language can itself help us avoid the misunderstandings against which those logically improper sentences in the vernacular were addressed? That problem is closely related to the first, the one that arose in connection with Sluga's remarks. The central question from which I started was really: what is the relation between the idea a philosopher like Frege or Wittgenstein has of a concept-script and his view (implicit or explicit) of what methods are appropriate in philosophy? In Wittgenstein there is a tight connection between the two. The development of a concept-script is connected with the disappearance of philosophy as it has been practised. Are there any such links implicit in Frege's thought about a concept-script? Geach's article, showing the roots of Wittgenstein's doctrines about saying and showing in Frege's work, suggests that the roots of Wittgenstein's view of philosophy itself may be looked for in Frege, and that was what I proposed to do.

II

The natural place to start is with Frege's own summary of the route he had taken.

> I started out from mathematics. The most pressing need, it seemed to me, was to provide this science with a better foundation . . .

The logical imperfections of language stood in the way of such investigations. I tried to overcome these obstacles with my concept-script. In this way I was led from mathematics to logic. What is distinctive about my conception of logic is that I begin by giving pride of place to the content of the word "true," and then immediately go on to introduce a thought as that to which the question "Is it true?" is in principle applicable. So I do not begin with concepts and put them together to form a thought or judgement; I come by the parts of a thought by analysing the thought (*PW*, p. 253.)[3]

There is an awful lot in those few sentences. The important thing is the relation between Frege's notion of a concept-script and his use of the word "thought." He recognised that people might object that he was using the word "thought" in a sense different from the ordinary one. In fact, we should see him as laying out, in large part through the development of what he called a concept-script, the notion of thought that he refers to.

A concept-script is a mode of expression of thoughts so that what it is for them to be true is clear from how they are written, and, at the same time, the logical relations of different thoughts expressed in the notation are clear in the expressions of those thoughts. The difference between a concept-script and ordinary language is, Frege tells us, that in the latter there is only an imperfect correspondence between the structure of the perceptible sentence and the structure of what is expressed by it. Similarity of construction in the expressions may hide total logical dissimilarity in the structure of what is expressed; the genuine logical relations of the constituents are a matter left for one to guess at (*PW*, pp. 12–13).

I said that a concept-script is a mode of expression of thoughts, but I now want not exactly to go back on that but to qualify it: thoughts are what the concept-script shows them to be. What I am denying could be put in terms of a crude picture, roughly this: we are told that thoughts are what can be true or false, and so we can then look around and find *which* among all the things that we can think of— sentences, propositions, thoughts, what not—have the property we are after, of being true or false. Having found what we are looking for, we could then investigate its nature. Lo and behold, it can be analyzed, has such-and-such sorts of parts, or whatever. No. That with which logic is concerned has its nature made clear (or, if you like, its nature-as-far-as-logic-is-concerned) through a kind of writing of sentences in which everything of interest to logic is made clear.

Making *that* clear is going to take some doing. But I can start by showing what it is to miss altogether what Frege is aiming at.

I have seen a criticism of Frege for having identified properties with concepts in his sense. Frege had said "I call the concepts under which an object falls its properties," and the comment of the critic was that that identification would not do. Since *having a heart* and *having a kidney* count for Frege as one and the same concept, but are not what we should count as the same property (because their having the same extension is accidental), we should not (according to the critic) accept Frege's use of his term "concept" in explicating the idea of a property.[4] But when Frege says that he calls the concepts under which an object falls its properties, he does not mean to be giving an explication of the idea of a property. The point is not the idea of a property but what a property-as-far-as-logic-is-concerned is. The Fregean identification may or may not actually do what Frege wants it to do, but what he wants to do is precisely ignore everything that belongs to our ordinary idea of a property *except* what is of interest to logic. And logic has very narrow interests. If you and I fall under all the same Fregean concepts, than as far as logic is concerned you and I are one and the same thing. Substitute a reference to you for a reference to me in any context, and truth value will never be affected. Why should properties be any better off than you and me? *Logic* will treat their identity as it treats ours, ignoring what is not of interest to it. In the *concept*, we can see—this is Frege's claim—exactly what interests logic in what we ordinarily think of as a property. The critic's mistake was to think that *properties* have certain characteristics and a philosophy of logic ought to do justice to those characteristics. But that is not philosophy of logic for Frege.

Given, then, the specialized interests of logic, how exactly does a concept-script further them? In Frege we can see the beginnings of something which is fully developed in the *Tractatus:* what thought is is made clear not so much in sentences *about* thought but in the clear expression of thoughts in a concept-script.

Before explaining that, I need to mention an important difference between Frege and Wittgenstein, so that it can be kept separate from a different difference between them. Within any sphere of scientific investigation, as Frege sees it, we can distinguish between two things, the making clear of the subject matter of that activity and the establishing of the laws governing that subject matter. In gravitational mechanics, for example, we are not concerned with the chemical properties of bodies, and a notation for mechanics in which we did distinguish between bodies according to their chemical properties would mark something totally irrelevant to the science; it would to that extent be a misleading notation. The same general point applies to logic as Frege sees it: it is for him a science with a realm, a subject matter, of its own. There is on the one hand the business of making clear what is of interest to it, the character of its subject matter, and on the other there is the establishing of the laws governing that subject matter. (See, e.g., *FG*, pp. 107–10). If a concept-script does what it is meant to do, it shows the character of thought by the systematic marking in the script of everything with which logic is concerned. The logical laws then contain thought about thought, and their content is something that goes beyond what is shown of the nature of thoughts in a concept-script. (That is the view Frege takes most of the time. In one very late passage, he suggests that, if we had a logically perfect language, there would be nothing that logic itself, the discipline, could tell us that went beyond what was already clear to us in the way things were written in that language. But this late view would still be compatible with the idea that logical laws were themselves thoughts about thought.)

Wittgenstein rejects the analogy between logic and other sciences and the idea that there is on the one hand the making clear in a concept-script of that with which logic is concerned, and on the other the establishing of the laws about the subject matter, the laws being then thoughts about thought. There is no 'on the other hand' here, and logic is no *science*. When you have, in the concept-script, made clear the character of thought, nothing more remains to be said—or so he thought. That, then is one point on which Frege and Wittgenstein differ. It should be distinguished from another: can what is made clear of the character of thought in the way sentences are written in a concept-script *also* be put directly, in sentences *about* the character of thought?

In discussing that, I am going to use, instead of the word "thought," the expression for which it should be regarded as an abbreviation: "that to which the question 'Is it true?' is in principle applicable." A that-to-which-that-question-applies is expressed in a sentence. It gets expressed clearly, and with all the frills irrelevant to logic, irrelevant to the applicability to it of the question of truth or falsity, left off, in a concept-script. When one is struggling to grasp a thought, one may come out first with half-sentences, stammerings, vague jumbles, and only in the end get to a proper sentence. While one is struggling to get straight something about the internal character of *thought*, of that-to-which-the-question-of-truth-applies, one's stammerings and gropings, one's beginnings to get what glimmers, take the form of sentences in ordinary language *about* thought, about the relation between thought and its expression, about the elements of a thought, and so on. But just as we may say that that-to-which-the-question-of-truth-applies has its expression in a *sentence*, thought about the nature of that-to-which-the-question-of-truth-applies gets put clearly in a *concept-script*, a way of writing sentences. The word "thought" which I have allowed to stand in the last sentence: can *that* be taken to mean that-to-which-the-question-of-truth-applies? Can such thought, or 'thought', also be put in sentences? These questions get unambiguous answers from Wittgenstein. Frege treats them differently; he does not hold that in general what can be shown cannot be said. (I cannot discuss in detail this difference between their views; I touch on it briefly again in §III.)[5]

Let me give a simple example (and then a more complicated one) of how the character of thought may be made clear in a concept-script. We may start thinking about the dependence of the truth or falsity of a thought on what the thought is *about*, and we may put together thousands of philosophical sentences in such gropings. Frege leads us to a better kind of groping, making use of the notions of argument, function and value, terms of not-so-ordinary language, supplemented with metaphors of completeness and incompleteness. But thinking in terms of *arguments* and so on is itself a move, the crucial move, towards a notation, his concept-script, in which the character of the dependence is plain. I am suggesting that we see Frege's concept-script and notations derived from it as standing to the previous attempts to put our thought about the dependence in something like the way a clearly put sentence stands to the half-formed thoughts that preceded it.

Another example worth looking at briefly is the dispute between Wittgenstein and Frege about the kind of articulation necessary to anything that can express a thought. In the *Tractatus*, Wittgenstein held that anything capable of having the sense that a sentence has must be logically articulated. He took himself to be disagreeing in this with Frege, and I am sure that he was right. What I take to be Frege's view (in his later writings) is that (a) the expression of thought, a sentence, has the same kind of articulation as there is in complex designations like "Frege's birthplace," but (b) a complex designation has a sense of a sort which it is possible for an unarticulated proper name to have, which together imply that (c) the kind of sense a sentence has does not *require* that *whatever* has that sense be articulated. The sense that a sentence has could be the sense of an unarticulated proper name. (Since I want to treat this view purely as an example, I shall not discuss the grounds for ascribing it to Frege.) What is it then to take that dispute as an example of what I was talking about? Viewed as I suggest, to dispute about what articulation the expression of a thought must have is to dispute about the specifications for a concept-script. Wittgenstein's 'view about thoughts' gets its proper expression in a concept-script, in the exclusion from places where sentences can occur of any logically unarticulated expressions, in the exclusion from places where simple and undefined expressions can occur of any logically complex expression or any sign defined via others, and so on. In a concept-script of the sort Frege uses in the *Grundgesetze*, any argument place open to sentences is open to any simple or complex proper names, and vice versa. This openness of argument places is what it comes to to say, as he did, that sentences *are* proper names: logic does not need a kind of writing that marks a distinction between them by opening argument places to one but not the other.

Let me imagine, at this point, two sorts of comments.

(1) "You have been altogether too free with expressions like 'what logic needs', 'what logic is interested in'. Is it not time you were more forthcoming about what they are supposed to mean?"
(2) "You have not made very clear what is involved in the dispute between Frege and Wittgenstein about logical articulation—not, that is, made clear what kind of dispute it is. For, as you have explained the difference between them, it is a difference between two sets of specifications for a concept-script, and any further point of view on the dispute would get expressed in yet another set of specifications for a concept-script. That means that we cannot criticize a concept-script by *stepping outside* the business of the making of concept-scripts, of working out how to write sentences so that relations of interest to logic are marked in a systematic and thoroughly consistent way. To step outside would be to say: 'What we are expressing in a concept-script is *thoughts*. They have a logical structure, and once we find out what *that* is, we shall be able to see what logical structure to build into a concept-script the better to reflect the structure thoughts have. We should be able to judge between Frege's and Wittgenstein's concept-scripts by determining which has a logical structure corresponding to that of thoughts.' But if we reject that view, what exactly *is* involved in criticizing or evaluating a concept-script? If it is true that thoughts are in essence what they are shown to be in a concept-script, how is it *not* the case that Frege's concept-script embodies one notion of thought and Wittgenstein's another, and that no question of which is a better embodiment of what *thought* is can arise? If it is not a substantial *thesis* about something, *thoughts*, that they are expressed in sentences which are logically

speaking indistinguishable from proper names, how does Wittgenstein think that Frege is *wrong* in taking sentences to be proper names?"

To begin with, the second comment is confused. It is not the case, on the view I have been expounding, that what counts as *thought* is different in differently designed concept-scripts; nor is it the case that the only way to criticize a concept-script is to come up with another one. For help with both comments, we need to get back to the remarks of Frege's which I quoted earlier, which I said had so much in them. What they have in them is his conception of logic, in which, he said, he gave pride of place to the content of the word "true."

What made it possible for Frege to use the word "true" to "indicate the essence of logic" was its peculiar character. If we attach the predicate "is true" to a sentence, the sense of the sentence does not change, but the predicate is not on that account senseless. It is for this reason, Frege says, "that the word 'true' seems to make the impossible possible: it allows what corresponds to the assertoric force to assume the form of a contribution to the thought" (*PW*, pp. 251–2). We cannot, though, bring out what is peculiar to "true" unless we can make clear the difference between it and some other expressions whose sense, in certain circumstances, similarly collapses, as it were, into the sense of what they have been attached to. What "is true" does with *sentences*, these other expressions will do with some other groups of completed function expressions.

I can explain this in two ways, corresponding to two uses of "true" as a predicate:

(1) "p is true" = "The thought-that-p is true" = "The thought-that-p is a sense of the True."
(2) "p is true" = "p is one and the same as the True" = "The truth value p is one and the same as the True."

In the first case, what is meant by "true" is ascribed to a thought; in the second case, something else is meant by "true" and *that* is ascribed to a truth value. But the thought that [the thought-that-p is a sense of the True] is the same as the thought that [the truth value p is one and the same as the True], and that thought is the same as the thought that p. The two differing uses of "true" simply chop it up differently. I want to show what is peculiar to "true" by contrasting it with other function expressions whose sense collapses in certain circumstances; and I can do that either by sticking with the first type of use of "true" or by sticking with the second. I can get a class of peculiar function expressions in either case—a class of expressions whose sense collapses in the same way that of "true" does. It would be more complicated, though in some ways more Fregean, to use the first kind of case; but if I stick to the second, anyone can make the moves to the more complicated case for himself. Sticking to the less complicated case will enable me to make clear what I need to; so that is what I shall do.

We can start with any group of functions whose value is always one or other of two objects, for example, with functions whose value is always Wismar or Frankfurt. Call these B-functions and expressions for them B-expressions. We can define a particular B-expression, say "W( )," by specifying that the value of the function W( ) is Wismar whenever the argument is Wismar and is otherwise Frankfurt. "W( )" acts with completed B-expressions in just the way "( ) is true" acts with sentences. Whatever the peculiarity is that suits "true" for indicating the essence of logic, it is not *merely* the kind of collapsibility of sense it shares with "W( )," for "W( )" cannot be used to indicate the essence of logic.

How then are we to get at the significant difference between "true" and such expressions as "W( )," which we may call 'collapsing' expressions? Let me put this in a slightly different way. "W( )," as I have defined it, and "( ) is true," so far as that is what Frege would regard as a predicate with a properly determinate sense, can each take *any* complete expression in its argument place. The characteristic collapse of sense occurs, for each, only in certain cases; that is one reason I have avoided calling them identity operators. But we may call the class of argument expressions for which there is the collapse the 'preferred' kind of expression. We cannot bring out the peculiar character of "true" unless we can make clear the difference between it and collapsing function expressions whose preferred kind of argument is *not sentences*. It is the difference between a collapsing expression which is a *predicate* and others which are not. But the difference between a predicate and these other expressions is the difference between an expression for a function whose value is a truth value and expressions for functions whose value is not. The fundamental difference between the two types of expression is that the sense of a completed expression of the first sort (one for a function whose value is a truth value) is something *judgeable*; the sense of no other sort of completed function expression is. Other sorts of completed expression name this or that or the other depending on certain conditions, but their sense is never *that* any such condition is fulfilled. Thus "Frege's birthplace" names Wismar if he was born there, but its sense is not that the Wismar conditions are fulfilled, or that the Frankfurt conditions are, or *that* anything at all. The peculiar character of "true" does not lie in its being collapsible, but in that feature, combined with its preferred class's being sentences, and its being itself a predicate. Because it does not add anything to the sense of an expression of its preferred sort, what it seems to do when it has such an expression in its argument place is itself to express the "these conditions are fulfilled," the characteristic of thought itself. A thought is something distinguished from other senses-of-complete-expressions in being *judgeable;* but the grammatical indicators of judgeable sense normally function also, or can do so, as indicators of assertoric force. That is why Frege repeatedly warns us to dissociate assertoric force from predication. "True," in seeming to have as its sense the general form of thoughtish sense, the "the truth-conditions are fulfilled" that all thoughts have in common, can *also* seem to express the *recognition* of the truth of a thought. This then is why it can seem that what it contributes to the thought as a predicate is actually the assertoric force.

The business of *recognizing thoughts as true*, and the using of sentences uttered with assertoric force in expressing this recognition—that is the peculiar business indicated by the peculiar character of "true." What has it to do with *logic?* The general form of this peculiar business is: a thought is recognized to be true without being logically inferred from other thoughts recognized to be true, *or* it is logically inferred from others. Suppose, for example, I recognize the truth of a thought expressed by a sentence, and I take another sentence to be a material conditional whose consequent I take to express the same thought as the one whose truth I have recognized. I must then be able to infer the truth of the thought expressed by the conditional sentence as a whole. That rule belongs to the business of recognizing thoughts to be true; it is a 'law of thought,' or, as Frege says it would better be put, a 'law of judgment'. What underlies it is nothing psychological but merely the relations of the truth conditions of the two thoughts. A thought being essentially that such-and-such truth conditions are fulfilled, its identity is inseparable from the logical relations it stands in to other thoughts; its inferential relations cannot change while the thought remains unchanged. The wholly non-psychological character of the rules governing judgment is thus inseparable from what judgment is. There is no room for essentially different sets of rules governing how the activity of judging should be carried on. There can be variants of chess, with variants of what is allowed. But there cannot in that sense be variants of the prescriptions to be followed in recognizing thoughts to be true; there cannot be what used to be a valid inference (was a valid inference by the then laws of logic) but is no longer one. "True" is suited to indicate the essence of logic by indicating the tie between its complete unarbitrariness and what judgment itself is.

Frege did allow that there might be beings capable of grasping thoughts without having to use perceptible expressions of thought. But given that we human beings do have to use language in the expression of thoughts, something of central importance follows from the peculiar character of logic. Or, rather, it does not, properly speaking, follow from the peculiar character of logic; it *is* the peculiar character of logic reflected in the character of language, considering language as capable of expressing thoughts. The principles through which the laws of logic bear on thought expressed in language must be the same for any language. Frege puts the point this way: the logical component of the grammar of every language (i.e., that part of the grammar that does not reflect the psychological capacities, interests and so on of the speakers) is the same in all languages (*PW*, pp. 6, 142). It cannot, for example, be the case that in one language you *cannot* predicate the same thing of a concept as of an object and in some other language you *can*. In the development of language many human instincts and dispositions, including the logical disposition, were at work (*PW*, p. 269). If there had been at work *only* the logical disposition, language would be far better adapted to the expression of thoughts, and we should be able to see clearly in it what is there but as it were overlaid in the grammar of our actual languages, the logical features shared with all languages. Talk which uses "true" and takes advantage of its peculiar character is one way to get at something, 'the essence of logic'; and the same thing is being got at if we talk about what in a sense corresponds to the peculiar character of "true": the single logical-grammatical structure found in every language in so far as thoughts can be expressed in it at all. Corresponds: i.e., the logical component of grammar is what corresponds in the structure of language to the judgeability belonging to every thought in the stock of human thoughts, each of which (or at any rate its logical core) is expressible in every language, according to Frege. The impossibility of different logical-components-of-grammar in different languages corresponds to the impossibility of different prescriptions governing the peculiar activity of recognition of the truth of thoughts. I said that we have, in Frege's use of "true" and in talk like his of the identity of logical grammar in all languages, two ways of getting at something. Both would be unnecessary if we had a logically perfect language, in which the essence of thought and hence the essence of logic lay open to view.

I have ignored a complication in Frege's view. Thoughts may be communicated in ordinary language without the speakers' actually relying on the logical articulation of the sentences they utter and hear. The hearers use cues to guess at what thought the sentence as a whole expresses. But Frege combined that idea with a view of the structure of natural language on which it is possible for the sense of a sentence to be constructed from that of its logical components, and not just guessed at as he thinks we often do. The possibility of constructing the sense in that way is essential for inference.

The grammar of English does not allow us to put together sentences like "Five is greater than three is greater than three," in which a whole sentence has been put where only expressions of some other sorts may go. Frege came to believe that, in a correct notation, anywhere "five" could go, "Five is greater than three" could equally go. Now, given his view that the logical element of the grammar of all languages is the same, English and his concept-script must share that universal logical grammar. So *if* his concept-script is actually correct in allowing what corresponds in it to "Five is greater than three is greater than three," the exclusion of such sentences from English is not done by universal logical grammar but by the 'psychological' component of English grammar. (We can see that the Fregean claim I mentioned earlier, that any thought can be expressed in every language, is true only in a thin sense of "can." It can, i.e., the logical component of the grammar allows it to be expressed; but the non-logical component of the grammar may prevent its expression in any sentence that *it* will allow.) Just as the non-logical component of English grammar may exclude from English what logical grammar would not exclude, it may also allow combinations which logical grammar would exclude, like the putting of what *it* counts as a proper name where logical grammar cannot recognise a genuine proper name.

We are now in a position to get back to the dispute between Frege and Wittgenstein, about the character of a concept-script. If a language is capable of expressing thoughts at all, it must (here Frege and Wittgenstein agree) have as the logical component of its grammar what every language has. The point about *the* logical grammar applies not only to any natural language but also to a concept-script designed with the intention that the logical characteristics of the thoughts expressed in its sentences should be shown clearly in the perceptible structure of those sentences. A concept-script is unsatisfactory when it treats in the same way what is logically different (what *the* logical grammar treats as different) or treats in different ways what is logically similar. Let us stick with our example and ask what it would mean for Wittgenstein to be *right* in excluding sentences from argument places where expressions for numbers can go. If Wittgenstein is right, *and* if we assume as correct the view Frege and Wittgenstein both held about language, what follows is that there is a divergence in Frege's concept-script between the logical grammar it shares with all languages and the rules fixing which combinations of expressions are well-formed sentences of the concept-script. The upshot of the divergence is that, contrary to Frege's intentions and to his beliefs about what he had succeeded in doing, nonsensical combinations will be allowed. The situation is analogous to ones that arise in ordinary language, as in the example I mentioned, in which the non-logical component of grammar allows what it regards as a proper name where the logical component refuses to recognize one. If, instead, we assume Frege right and Wittgenstein wrong about the articulation of sentences, there will again be a divergence between what the rules of a concept-script (one meeting Wittgenstein's specifications) allow and what its own logical grammar, *the* logical grammar, allows. In this case, the upshot of the divergence would be the exclusion from the concept-script of combinations which would be allowed by the logical component of grammar; again, the situation is analogous to one which can obtain in ordinary language.

What then does all this come to as a reply to the second comment? There is, on the view I have been expounding, a right and wrong in disputes like that between Wittgenstein and Frege. When the design of a concept-script goes wrong, it is not that the structure of the script fails to match something external to it, but that the concept-script has structural features which diverge from its own, as it were, inevitable inner structure, which is thus not revealed clearly.

Later on, Wittgenstein came to say that, when we think that there is something queer or unique about thought, we are the victims of illusion. But at this point I am trying to make clear what it is we may thus seem to see; for it is not *all* illusion. Taking a view about the nature of thoughts is not quite like taking a view about the nature of whales, and we misread Frege and Wittgenstein both, if we forget that they themselves are concerned with the character of that difference, and thus concerned to 'place' what they themselves say. I mean "place" in the sense in which we can see Frege himself 'placing' his own remarks about concepts and their incompleteness, or about "true" and its relation to the essence of logic. In §III, I shall show the relation between this 'placing' and an understanding of what a concept-script is supposed to do.

III

In §II I did not draw attention to the issue of realism. It was there, all right; and in §III I shall be concerned with it. I shall describe a kind of realist view in order to ask what we should make of it if we took Frege seriously. Here is the view.

Among the kinds of things there are, are concepts and objects. *That* something—say, the number 4—is an object, is why it is appropriate for a term for it to have the logical character of a proper name, i.e., what Frege calls completeness or saturatedness; *that* something is a concept is why it is appropriate for a term for it to have the logical character of a predicate, i.e., to be 'incomplete', to have one or more gaps for argument expressions of the appropriate sort, the sort that stand for things of the kind that complete the concept for which it is an expression. Our linguistic expressions thus properly have a character which matches the independently fixed logical character of the things they stand for. The logical character of those things is prior, and belongs to them on their own; and we can in the use we fix for our signs get it right or wrong.

Well, what is to be made of that, if we take Frege seriously? Wittgenstein did, and it shows, for example, in the remarks following 5.47 in the *Tractatus*, where he is discussing the relation between logic and what all sentences share simply in being sentences. Language itself, he says (at 5.4731) prevents every logical mistake. Because it does so, we cannot give a sign the wrong sense. We cannot, he means, give a sign a sense which is inappropriate to the logical character of what it stands for, cannot make a mistake about what the logical character is of the thing we want the sign to stand for, and then give the sign a kind of use appropriate to the logical character thus wrongly conceived. There is no such thing as allowing a sign to figure in a *wrong* combination with other signs, *unsuitable* given the possible combinations into which the thing meant can enter.

But why is that taking Frege seriously? I need now to show how Frege enables us to see what is wrong with the kind of realism I sketched, but not by providing as an alternative some kind of anti-realist view.

The heart of the realist view that I have sketched is that logical categories provide a kind of *classification* of things. What we can get hold of through the concept-script Frege developed is a notion of 'logical category', tied directly to *kinds of argument place*. (In his explanation of the concept-script, a first kind of argument place is characterized by the 'completeness' of the arguments, and others by the number and kinds of argument places in the arguments that they are themselves open to. I shall spell it out in more detail later.) If we grasp that notion, the question "Are logical categories a classification of things?" will simply not be askable; it will drop away as mere muddle.

In the kind of realism I sketched there might be some question whether one was correct in putting *Socrates* in the logical place for an object. One would have committed some kind of logical gaffe if one had got his logical character wrong in thinking that he was an object, and had got him in the wrong kind of place, given his logical character. But, for Frege, what is *in* the logical place of an object *is* an object. Take, for example, his well-known discussion, in "On Concept and Object" about the concept *horse* (*TWF*, pp. 45–8). It is true that what he says there can be criticized on quite distinct grounds and was not his own last word on the matter; it is important for me at this point, though, as an illustration of his method. He argues that when we say that the concept *horse* is a concept easily attained, "the concept *horse*" stands for an object. It is, logically speaking, the subject; what it refers to is thus in the logical place for an object and therefore is an object. He is not going on the fact that "the concept *horse*" is a *grammatical* subject; the grammatical subject of "A horse is what you probably were in your last incarnation" would not have been taken by Frege to be a logical subject. As Peter Geach has pointed out in discussing "On Concept and Object," Frege had not in it "deliberately adopted an 'ontology'" with "special classes of object that were surrogates for concepts and functions in case of need!"[6] There is no possibility of logical disaster in putting Socrates in the wrong place or in referring to the concept *horse* in the absence of an obliging ontological category of concept-surrogates.

Here is how the realist picture works. We think that there are things in reality, including, let us suppose, since our realist is reading Frege, objects and concepts, the concepts themselves being of various sorts. And, now, *of* any of these various things, we think that we can think: it goes into this one of the logical categories or some other. What we have got in mind, though, is the *intelligible* application of the category terms themselves to items in *different* categories. We think, that is, that we can think that Socrates is an object and have got something right. But how then are we thinking of the concept we thus take him to fall under? What is absolutely essential to the realist frame of mind is that "it is an object" *can* be falsely said of some things. Otherwise, we could not think that we could use it in classifying things in reality. The use of "object" as a classifying term requires that there be things which are not objects. Now Frege is unlike Wittgenstein in thinking that "object" is a respectable predicate and *object* a respectable concept. (Here I am ignoring two sorts of complication. First, Frege did, in his early "Dialogue with Pünjer," take views closer to Wittgenstein's about such concepts; I am ignoring that piece here. Secondly, I am, where I can, ignoring complications of the general "concept *horse* is not a concept" kind, in order not to have to say repeatedly that when I call something a concept, or, e.g., ask whether such-and-such is a respectable concept, I am unfortunately using a term with the logical character of a first-order predicate when I need to speak about a second-order concept, that I am using a term as a proper name when I cannot want that, and so on.) But, although it is for Frege a respectable concept, it is not the concept the realist wants to use (and it is going to turn out that there is no such thing as what he wants). Since ( ) *is an object* is a first order concept, what can occur as its argument *is an object*. That is, it is true, of anything that you say is an object, that it is an object. You could not have said or thought that it was and have been wrong. "Everything is an object" and "There is nothing that is not an object" are *true*. And so the concept ( ) *is an object* is useless for classifying (which is why Frege had earlier denied that such concepts have content).

What about something's being a concept? Can a corresponding point be made about that? If we complete with an appropriate argument the concept that we try to refer to by "( ) is a concept," we do not *always* get the truth value *true*. The second order concept we want *can* be used in classifying, but only (given Frege's views) in classifying first order functions with one argument. Concepts are not, in fact, a logical category in the sense in which I have been using that expression in discussing Frege. Concepts and first order functions are defined for the same arguments and can occur themselves as arguments of any second order functions.

What I have just said appears to clash with Frege's own statement that the concept *horse* is not a concept but an object. For I said that the only thing you could classify with the concept we try to refer to as "( ) is a concept" is first order functions with one argument; and if that is correct, it seems that the only thing we shall be able to say is *not* a concept is such a function. Frege himself was clear enough that the predicate of the sentence "The concept *horse* is not a concept" does not refer to the second order concept we want (any more than the five words I just used refer to it, any more than the pronoun I have just used does). Let us find a way to refer to it.

(*x*) (*x* is a dog is a truth value)
(*x*) (*x* is a tree is a truth value)
(*x*) (*x*'s birthplace is a truth value)

The common pattern of those three sentences is an expression for the second order concept we want: a concept that all and only first order concepts fall under, or, rather, do what is for them analogous to falling under (what Frege calls 'falling into'). The second order concept we try to refer to by "( ) is not a concept" we can refer to by using the same pattern with a negation at the beginning, to get a new sentence pattern. There is no such thing as completing *either* pattern with the subject of "The concept *horse* is easily attained," which has *no* argument places. And that is how we should understand Frege's point that "the concept *horse* is not a concept." The sentence looks as if it says of something that it is not a concept, but if we think about what we try to say with "( ) is not a concept," we can see that there is no such thing as saying, or thinking, what the sentence looks as if it says.

Let me turn to the second order concept we try to refer to by "( ) is a first order function with one argument." Frege gives us one expression for this concept: "$\hat{\varepsilon}\phi(\varepsilon)$." So "$\hat{\varepsilon}(\varepsilon\cdot3 + 4)$" is a way of saying properly what we try to say by "$\zeta\cdot3 + 4$ is a function" (*PMC*, p. 136). Frege's point is that *any* expression for the second order concept we want will have to contain an indication that its arguments are first order functions with one argument place of their own. One can make the same point by using the common pattern of the pair

(x) (x is a dog is an object)
(x) (x's birthplace is an object)

or (given a Fregean definition of the conditional for all proper names) of the pair

(x) (x is a dog ⊃ x is a dog)
(x) (x's birthplace ⊃ x's birthplace)

In the case of each pair, the common pattern serves to stand for the second order concept we want. Each pattern is completed into a sentence only by expressions for first order functions with one argument.

We can now get to the central point here. *Every* thought that something is an object is true; *every* thought got by completing the concept we misrefer to as "( ) is a first order function with one argument" is true, and correspondingly for functions of higher orders and with different numbers of arguments. The whole idea of classifying anything using these notions breaks down, since it is impossible to think truly of anything that it does not belong to a given category. It is impossible—in a sense—to make a mistake about the logical category of anything, since what we call 'making a mistake' (e.g., thinking that the concept *horse*, of which we say that it is easily attained, is a concept) will turn out not to be the thinking of the thought we thought it was. There will be no such thing as that. A good concept-script will make clear to us that we were in a muddle in thinking that we had got something in mind, that we were expressing a thought at all.

We use the English word "category" as if logical categories were pigeonholes for a kind of classification, a logical classification, of things. As if there were some kind of class that logical categories all were, and as if *belonging in* such-and-such a category were some one thing, and some items belonged in one and others in another and others in yet others; as if, that is, to be a member of a logical category were something that went across the whole lot of categories. The language of *putting things into categories* misleads us into thinking the business is like recognizing that a plant goes into this or the other genus; it is the language, grammatically, of putting *objects* into classes depending on the first order concepts they fall under. We speak of grasping that *something* belongs in such-and-such a category or that an *item* does; that is, we use what ordinary language provides as variables indicating objects, in constructions which call for precisely such variables. And now what I am saying, speaking (inevitably) in that way, is that to put something into a category is not to classify it. There is no kind of class that logical categories all are.

There is an important kind of objection that people make. The things I have been saying about logical categories, that they are no kind of class, and that that way of putting the point is itself something that does not work—these are entirely dependent on one feature of Frege's concept-script (duplicated in the specifications for a concept-script in the *Tractatus*). That feature is that every argument place in a predicate or other function expression takes arguments of only one logical category. If we have a concept-script which meets that specification, and if the concept-script allows the predication of category terms at all, we shall then be able to say only of the things that actually are in the category in question that they are. Whenever we say that something is *not* in a category we shall be wrong, because only of what is in a particular category shall we be able to say that it is not in that category, and category predicates will not have a genuine classifying use. That will be the conclusion, whether we accept Frege's view that we *can* say of an object (e.g.) that it is an object or Wittgenstein's view that that is actually nonsense. In *neither* case is there any possibility of genuine classification using category predicates. So— the objection runs—what we need to do is call into question the Fregean and Wittgensteinian commitment to having *no* argument places open to more than one category. Frege himself, the objector might point out, was willing to question the commitment when he was worrying about Russell's paradox. He toyed with the idea of allowing some argument places open to proper names of one logical kind of object, some open to another, and a third sort open to both (*TWF*, pp. 235–6). And, the objector might continue, even if we could not point to Frege's own willingness to consider the move, there are good reasons for it. We must allow that there are genuine questions of the sort Frege's original view rules out. Take the question we may wish to ask about "The concept *horse* is easily attained," whether the concept *horse* that we are speaking about there is something which it is possible for Bucephalus and other things to fall under. Is there not something we are saying if we should want to say that it is *not?* Or indeed if we should want to say that it *is?* Can we not be right or wrong about this? Is there not a genuine thinking of two possible thoughts here, thoughts which contradict each other?

Let me look further at the objection. The idea of argument places open to more than one kind of thing is absolutely necessary (the objector may claim), since (he says) there are things that can be said truly of items of different logical kinds. It may even seem that Frege himself is committed to the idea that there are some things we can say of items in different categories. After all, it might be asked, does he not think that both first order concepts and first order relations are *first order*, i.e., take the same kind of argument?; that they are *incomplete*, though not in the same way?; that they have as their values only the two truth values?; that neither of them can fall under a first order concept? But the appearance of his saying the same thing of concepts and relations is itself created by what he would take to be an imprecision in ordinary language. There is no concept that both first order concepts and first order relations fall under (properly, none that they fall into), and in an adequate concept-script there is nothing that even looks like an expression for such a concept.

Very well; we stop trying to get Frege himself on the side of saying that some things can be truly said of items in different categories. Is it not nevertheless true? An example that was offered me in discussion was self-identity: surely (it was said), it is correct to say both of any object and of any concept that it is identical with itself.

Suppose we look at this first in a Fregean frame of mind. How close we can get to saying of a concept that it is self-identical can be seen if we consider what it is to say of a concept picked out one way that it is the same as a concept picked out another way. Given Frege's view of what we may loosely call conceptual identity, what it is for something to be f is the same as what it is for something to be g if and only if whatever is f is g, and conversely (*PW*, p. 120). Applying Frege's view, then, what it is to ascribe self-identity to a concept, or, rather, the nearest we can come to doing that, is to say that whatever falls under it falls under it, "(x) (x is bald ≡ x is bald)" expresses properly what someone is trying to say if he says that *bald*, the concept, is self-identical. (Since for Frege a sentence refers to a truth value, we can also write it this way: "(x) (x is bald = x is bald).")

If we follow Frege, then, we shall say that ordinary language gives us a false impression that we are saying the same thing of the concept *bald* and of Socrates when we say of them that they are self-identical. If we have a notation in which we say of Socrates that he is self-identical *this* way: "Socrates = Socrates," and if we say what we were trying to say about the concept *bald this* way: "(x) (x is bald ≡ x is bald)," it would not so much as occur to us that self-identity is something ascribable to objects and concepts both. The objection that it is possible for there to be things like self-identity ascribable both to concepts and to objects, and that we therefore *need* expressions with argument places open to expressions of different logical kinds rests (at least as it was originally stated) on simply assuming what was at issue. That is what the case of self-identity shows.

We need, though, to see more clearly where the difference between the objector's view and Frege's lies. I said that what Frege's concept-script gives us is a notion of category tied to *kinds of argument place*. But what counts as a *kind of argument place* depends on the needs of logic, given the way we analyze a sentence containing such-and-such terms that can be taken as logically significant. The difference between what identity comes to for objects and what it comes to for concepts (central in our example) is a reflection of the need logic has to allow for different kinds of substitution *salva veritate*.

To analyze a sentence is to take it as containing one or more expressions for arguments (each of which may occur in more than one place) and to take the rest of the sentence as having a different sort of logical role. For *that* part of the sentence (which I shall call the leftover part) to have a determinate meaning is for the truth value of the sentence as a whole to be fixed for each meaningful argument expression that can be substituted for the argument expression in our sentence (if we are construing our sentence to have only one argument expression), for each *pair* of argument expressions (if we are construing our sentence to have two argument expressions) and so on. There is a fundamental kind of analysis, available only in the case of some sentences: we *can* construe these sentences to have, as the only argument expression they contain, a proper name. Frege uses metaphor to explain what his terms "proper name" and "object" mean, the metaphor of 'completeness' or 'saturation'. We can see something of what is being got at by these metaphorical expressions if we recall that all analysis reflects the interests of logic: how the truth value of the sentence as a whole may be construed in terms of function and argument. We have to look at the way logic treats the use of one expression as leftover in some contexts and as argument in others, and at the way it tells, in certain circumstances, whether we have defined one leftover expression or two.

If what we view as the leftover expression in one sentence can be taken to be an argument expression in another (or in the same one, otherwise construed)—if, that is, logic will allow such an identification—logic will insist that the expression now viewed as leftover, now viewed as argument, make the same contribution to the truth or falsity of what is said. Logic will thus insist that it carry with it in the two cases the same rules for substitution *salva veritate* in sentences. When it is a leftover expression, what can be substituted for it *salva veritate* is any other expression which fixes in the same way as ours the truth or falsity of sentences as a whole for each meaningful argument expression (or set of argument expressions) by which it can be completed. If a leftover expression is to be viewed as occurring also as an argument expression, it must carry with it in the latter use exactly the same rules for substitution *salva veritate* as it had as leftover, or it would not be making the same contribution to truth value as in its use as leftover. That is, what can be substituted for it in contexts in which we are viewing it as an argument expression can be specified only in terms of the truth or falsity for sentences as a whole determined for every meaningful argument expression (or set of argument expressions) that *our* argument expression can itself be completed by in its use as leftover. Hence we write it in a concept-script *with* argument places, whether it occurs as leftover or as argument expression, since these places are essential to its identity as far as logic is concerned, its identity (that is) as an expression with such-and-such reference, making the same contribution to the reference of whole sentences in which it occurs. (It thus belongs to its identity that it can only be used predicatively.)

Let us now try supposing that we had a leftover expression with one argument place, and that the truth or falsity for sentences as a whole was fixed for it, for all argument expressions with no argument places of their own (proper names) *and* for argument expressions with one argument place of their own of some determinate sort. What logic would see is that we had defined *two* equiform leftover expressions which made entirely different kinds of contribution to the whole sentences in which they were leftovers. The expression would sometimes stand for one kind of function and sometimes for another; in its two uses it would have two entirely different referents. One of

Frege's criticisms of Hilbert is that he defines "point" so that it has two meanings related to each other in that way (*PMC*, pp. 93–4). We do not make the issues here clear if we say that for Frege and Wittgenstein no argument place can be open to more than one kind of argument expression. If it were open to more than one, logic would note that the leftover expression was being used in different contexts to make two different kinds of contribution to truth value; logic would thus count it as *two* leftover expressions with different kinds of reference. Given an expression which makes a determinate kind of contribution to truth value wherever it occurs, *there is no such thing* as putting two different kinds of argument expression into any of its argument places. A concept-script does not, therefore, rule out doing *that*, for there is no such thing. What it does rule out is the use of one sign in two logically different ways. And it can do this by a mode of writing leftover expressions so that the kind of argument expression for each argument place is clearly indicated.

For there to be logical analysis of any sentence, i.e., for there to be the construal of it as argument expressions and leftover part, logic will need rules of at least two different sorts for substitution *salva veritate* of the expressions picked out by the analysis as logically significant: one sort for the leftover part and at least one other sort for the argument expressions. (The rules for substitution characterizing the argument expressions in fact fix the kind of rule characterizing the leftover part.) I argued earlier that, if there is any possibility of construing what was leftover in one sentence as argument expression in another, we must use the same rules for substitution *salva veritate* in both cases. These two requirements generate a structure of kinds of rule for substitution *salva veritate* of expressions. In a concept-script, the structure will be clear; and any argument expression which can occur as leftover will be written with an indication of its own argument places and of the kind of substitution rule to which the expressions in them are subject. In a concept-script in which the indication of argument places is thus carried out systematically, there will be argument expressions properly written with *no* argument places. Writing them that way indicates the kind of substitutability *salva veritate* they have: that of *proper names*. The substitutability rules for proper names are what correspond on the linguistic side to *identity* in the proper limited sense. (Any other kind of substitutability *salva veritate* for expressions corresponds not to identity but to a relation analogous to it, on Frege's view.) An object, Frege says, is anything the expression for which does not contain any empty place (*TWF*, p. 32). Such an expression can never be identifiable as the same expression as one which in some analysis of some sentence is a leftover expression. It is *impossible* for a proper name to be a predicate; there is, in the eyes of logic, no such thing as that. The very close connection between *being an object* and being capable of standing in the relation of *identity* properly speaking is extremely important for Frege. When he considered avoiding Russell's paradox by splitting the logical category of objects into proper and improper objects, he thought that he would nevertheless have to have *one* relation of identity which could take as its arguments both proper and improper objects. That course makes the mess generated by the proposed solution worse than it would otherwise be; and Frege in fact rejected that solution. What is interesting is the way his description of the proposal illustrates how he saw logical categories: one thing he thought he had to leave in place in any acceptable solution was the connection between being an object and being able to stand in the relation of identity, "a relation given to us in such a specific form that it is inconceivable that various kinds of it should occur" (*TWF*, p. 235). There may be relations analogous to it, but for anything which is *not* a function there is, as far as logic is concerned, only *it*.

The upshot of all this is that you cannot be referring to the same thing twice (cannot be ascribing first this and then that to it) if the expression you use to refer to it makes two entirely different kinds of contribution to the truth or falsity of the sentences in which it occurs. You can refer to the same thing twice by expressions with different senses, but not by the same expression twice over when the rules for substitution *salva veritate* that it carries with it are different in the two cases. It would then refer to two different things. What kind of thing you are referring to, talking about, thinking about, is not separable from the kind of contribution to truth or falsity made by the expression for it. If we say that Socrates falls under the concept *bald* and that the concept *bald* is self-identical, we can take ourselves to be speaking about the same thing, the concept *bald*, twice, *only if* we do not take ourselves to be saying of the concept *bald* what we say of Socrates when we say that *he* is self-identical.

I went into all this to show what is involved in the dispute between Frege and the objector. The disagreement naturally expresses itself in one way, but it goes with a much more fundamental disagreement. The relatively misleading way of putting the disagreement is: it is about whether there are concepts, like *self-identity*, under which things in different logical types can fall.

What is at the heart of the disagreement is *logical analysis*. To show what I mean by that, I need briefly to set alongside *self-identity* another candidate that philosophers come up with when they look for concepts applicable to *anything* at all: being an *object of thought*. The idea is that whatever kind of thing the concept *bald* is, we can at any rate think about it, so it and Socrates share this: they are *objects of thought*.

Against this, we have Frege's remark that I quoted earlier: "I do not begin with concepts and put them together to form a thought or judgment; I come by the parts of a thought by analyzing the thought." If you take the judgment itself as primary, as Frege does, what you find is that you can indeed take *bald*—the concept—as an object of thought only by its not being an *object* of thought at all. That is, in the sense in which you think about an object by having a thought in which it figures as object (expressed in a sentence in which a proper name referring to it occurs), you think about a concept by having a thought in which it occurs as a concept, i.e., a thought expressed by a sentence containing an expression used predicatively, referring to it. There is no category-unambiguous thing, *being an object of thought*, and you only think that there is if you think you find the concept *bald* on its own, when you start looking for objects of thought on their own. The concept *bald* (if we really mean the *concept*) is something you can think about, all right—only because it is not *something* you can think about. Unless we are very careful with "something we think about," we go wildly wrong. What thinking about something *is* belongs to *what it is*, what kind of thing, and that is shown in the use of a term in the expression of thoughts.

My objector differs from Frege fundamentally in thinking that one can separate what it is one is thinking about from the kind of use terms have in the expression of thoughts. That is why he believes that one can be thinking about one and the same thing, the concept *bald*, when one says that Socrates falls under it and that it is also what Socrates himself is, namely, self-identical.

There is a sense in which the disputants pass each other by. The objector ascribes to Frege a view of a certain kind, a substantial thesis that Frege has (the objector thinks) built into his concept-script, but which can be discussed independently. The supposed Fregean thesis is that nothing can be thought of things of more than one logical kind, and the objector believes that it has been built into the concept-script in the rules governing what can go into argument places. He thinks that a *better* concept-script would allow Socrates and the concept *bald* into the same place in some thoughts (e.g., ascriptions of self-identity) and would allow Socrates but not the concept *bald* into a place in *other* thoughts, e.g., those ascribing baldness. One could disagree with Frege about what a good concept-script would allow without disagreeing in the fundamental way our objector does. He does not so much reject a view of Frege's as not see what kind of view it is. He does not see the possibility of letting the use teach you what you are talking about, where logical analysis is what shows you how a term is being used, what kind of contribution it makes (what kind of contribution logic sees it making) to the sentences in which it occurs.

Some years ago Hidé Ishiguro said that we should give up the misunderstanding of Wittgenstein, that he went from a 'naming' theory of meaning in the *Tractatus* to a 'use' theory of meaning in his later work.[7] She argues that in an important sense he *always* held a use theory. He never thought, as Russell did, that the meaning of a name can be settled independently of its use in propositions; in the *Tractatus* he held that the identity of the object referred to by a name is settled only by the use of the name in propositions. She traces this view back to Frege and extends it to the use of terms for things in logical categories other than that of objects. What I have been trying to make clear is that at the root of the disagreement between my objector and Frege is a disagreement about the relation between the way we use terms and what it is we are talking about. The 'use' theory which Hidé Ishiguro ascribes to Frege is a mode of thinking about that relation utterly alien to my objector. In his position *vis-à-vis* Frege's we can see something that recurs in later philosophy. The objector (so it seems, from Frege's side) looks resolutely in the wrong direction to tell what his own terms refer to. The metaphor is Professor Ishiguro's, from her description of the form of the disagreement between Wittgenstein (in his later works) and those who claim to know from their own awareness of their mental processes *what* they are thinking or talking about.

The dispute between Frege and the objector shows us something of what it means to speak of philosophy as a battle against the bewitchment of our intelligence (*PI*, §109), shows us something of what *kind* of difficulty there can be in philosophy. That battle against the bewitchment of the intelligence changed its form as the role in it of logical analysis changed. But what remains is the idea of it as a battle against something that turns us away from the direction in which what needs to be seen is open to view, and also the idea that what we need to see—if only we could see that that is what we need to see!—is how our terms themselves are used.

What it was our objector was originally objecting to may have sunk from view. I had described a kind of realism about the logical character of what there is, a realism that goes with the idea that we can do a logical classification of things, put them into the logical categories in which they belong, where logical categories are thought of as themselves some kind of class, and we can supposedly get such a classification right or wrong. I argued that if we understand what is shown in Frege's concept-script, that kind of realism drops away, sentences expressing it being recognized as so much muddle. The objector claimed in the first place that there *is* room for a logical classification of things and, to back that up, he claimed also that in general there is no good reason to proscribe all ascriptions of a concept to items in different logical categories. I want now to turn back to a question about realism and what a concept-script does, which I shall get to from two different directions.

First, imagine someone complaining that what I have said is all very interesting but it is not *Frege*. For Frege actually says that the difference between first and second level functions is not made arbitrarily but is founded deep in the nature of things (*TWF*, p. 41). He would say exactly the same about the distinctions between function and object, between relation and concept and so on. But have I not been denying that he believes in any such relation between logical structures and the nature of things? Have I not been suggesting that logic can do what it likes and pretty much ignore *the nature of things*?

Secondly, imagine someone ascribing to Frege the view that there are thoughts which cannot be expressed in language, but which are nevertheless thoughts. Thus, if we say that objects and functions are totally different from each other, that is a logically improper use of language, and there is in such a case no way of getting rid of the linguistic impropriety, and of saying what we are trying to say in logically decent language. On the view we are imagining (we are imagining it ascribed to Frege), although we cannot *say* the thing we are trying to say, what we are struggling with is nevertheless a true but inexpressible thought.

We shall come round to the first point if we start with the second. I find it difficult to be tolerant about the ascription of such nonsense to Frege (or about the same ascription in the case of Wittgenstein). When there is no way of saying properly what we are trying to say, what we come out with is in fact a kind of nonsense and corresponds to no ineffable truth. What Frege thinks is that through an inadequacy of ordinary language, we can form sentences in it which are acceptable according to its rules but which are not the expression of any thought. It is possible to become clear about what has happened, if we are led to see how thoughts are expressed in a language more nearly adequate by the standards of logic. In grasping the significance of the distinctions embodied in that language, we do not grasp any ineffable truths. A truth is a truth about something; a true thought (that is) is about whatever logic may construe it as being about. But the distinctions embodied in the concept-script are not what any thought can be about.

The reasons have already been touched on. A concept-script, I said in §II, does not get something external to itself right; if it is not an adequate concept-script, it is not through getting something external to itself wrong. On the other hand, it is not the case that just anything goes in constructing a concept-script. As Frege himself says, the distinctions embodied in it are not arbitrary but are founded deep in the nature of things. We should not ignore that remark of Frege's; we should give it the importance he attached to such points—but we have to be particularly careful not to misunderstand it. We need to ask: *what* nature of things? For, as I have just said, the distinctions which the concept-script must have in it are not fixed by anything external to it. Nothing external to it fixes its logical structure; but it is not arbitrary. *Where* then is the reality that fixes what distinctions must be embodied in it? That reality lies *in it*. There is an order, a logical order, *in* thought and *in* language. Thought's being about things, its having logical order, its being that about which the question of truth can arise, its being expressible in language—language, which itself has a single logical grammar so far as it is capable of expressing thoughts—all these come to the same. Thought is about things, but the logical order which is part of what it is for there to be any *aboutness* is not itself one of the things thought can be about. The distinctions between functions and objects, between first and second order functions and so on—those distinctions are indeed founded deep in the nature of things. But to understand someone who says *that* is to have understood the kind of 'placing' such a sentence requires. To take it to be an 'ineffable' truth is a truly perverse misreading, an attempt to represent to oneself a state of affairs while pretending that no representing to oneself is going on. Putting the matter another way: the distinctions in question come out clearly in a language which marks them systematically, by having expressions which make plain the logical character of what they stand for. But in such a language there is no expression which refers to any of these logical distinctions. Ordinary language enables us to form apparently referring expressions, like "the distinction between first and second order functions." But now the hard thing is to learn, from the fact that there are no corresponding expressions in a logically adequate language, that the distinctions are not objects of any thoughts. And whatever is *correct* in saying that these distinctions are founded deep in the nature of things, its correctness will not lie in the imagery that accompanies it, of functions with their functionhood, objects with their objecthood, lying there with their distinct natures in the nature of things.

Now once more about realism. Wittgenstein's later work has a significance for questions about realism and anti-realism which can be seen only through its relation to the body of ideas I have been talking about. And what characterizes that body of ideas is its style of answer to questions of the general type: *Where is* the reality which must guide us here? Where is the reality to which our mode of thought must be responsible?

I described a kind of realism in §III, a realism which depends on the idea of an external relation between the logical characteristics of things and the logical features built into our modes of expression. The kind of realist I imagined thought that the logical characteristics of things and the logical structures of our mode of expression *ought* to match but that they might not do so. It is actually part of such a view that the only alternative to it which can be conceived by someone who holds it is: in our modes of expression *anything* goes. The alternatives, that is, are conceived this way: *either* there is something external to the mode of expression (the independently fixed logical character of things) which is a measure of the logical adequacy of the mode of expression, *or* there is no measure of adequacy which is in a hard logical sense *unarbitrary*. There is also an anti-realist view characterized by the acceptance of precisely the same pair of alternatives. Both views then conceive the situation this way: *there is* a logical reality independent of and external to our modes of thought and expression, *or there is not* and the logical structures of our thought and expression are fundamentally arbitrary.

Frege, in the development of a concept-script as a tool for philosophical thought, allows us to get clear of the two alternatives, to leave them behind. He allows us to think about language, *any* language in which thoughts can be expressed, as having something in it, which may or may not be *clearly* there for us to see. A language is more nearly adequate by the wholly unarbitrary standards of logic so far as it makes systematically clear what is there in it, what it shares with all languages. The standard of logical adequacy is no external one, but that does not imply any arbitrariness in the measure. He lets us see that the reality by which the adequacy of a concept-script is measured is not external to it. In that way he shows us a *general* possibility of answering questions *where the reality is* to which in doing such-and-such we are responsible. By letting us see a reality somewhere else than where we were looking, he teaches us a new way to understand such questions. The realist I imagined, and the person who takes the opposite view to his, share a conception: either there is something where we are both looking for a reality, or there is not, and we are without objective standards; that is what they both think.

Look somewhere *else:* that is what we can hear in Wittgenstein's later philosophy; look where you do not think there can be any reason for looking. That is there to be heard in the *Tractatus,* and *it* simply makes clearer a message already to be heard in Frege's work. For him, the concept-script was a tool of intellectual liberation. A good concept-script would lay before us clearly what we need to look at, and thus help break the domination of words over the human mind; it would help free our thought from the trammels placed upon it by language inattentive to the promptings of logic (*Bs*, p. 7; cf. *Tractatus* 3.325).

It is a mistake to tie Frege's use of the concept-script too closely to the use, in the analytic tradition, of techniques of *translation* of philosophically interesting claims into an adequate language. One point of looking at the example "logical categories are a kind of class" was to see the significance of the fact that there is *no* translation of it into an adequate language. We need still to get clear about what is radical in Frege's vision; we can do that only by getting clear the relation between the dropping away of some philosophical views as mere muddle and the idea of the truth of logic as not something set over against what it measures but internal to it.

Notes

1. H. Sluga, *Gottlob Frege* (London, 1980), p. 67.
2. P. T. Geach, "Saying and Showing in Frege and Wittgenstein," in J. Hintikka, ed., *Essays on Wittgenstein in Honour of G. H. von Wright, Acta Philosophica Fennica* **28** (1976), pp. 54–70, at p. 55.
3. In addition to the abbreviations used throughout this volume, the following abbreviations are used in this essay:

    PW   G. Frege, *Posthumous Writings,* ed. Hans Hermes et al. (Oxford and Chicago, 1979)

    FG   G. Frege, *On the Foundations of Geometry and Formal Theories of Arithmetic,* ed. E-H. Kluge (London and New Haven, 1971)

    TWF   *Translations from the Philosophical Writings of Gottlob Frege,* ed. P. T. Geach and Max Black (Oxford, 1966)

    PMC   G. Frege, *Philosophical and Mathematical Correspondence,* ed. Gottfried Gabriel et al. (Oxford, 1980)

    Bs   G. Frege, *Begriffsschrift,* in J. van Heijenoort, ed. *From Frege to Gödel* (Cambridge, Massachusetts, 1967).

4. G. Currie, *Frege, an Introduction to his Philosophy* (Brighton, Sussex and Totowa, New Jersey, 1982), p. 94.
5. See also "Throwing Away the Ladder."
6. Geach, op. cit., p. 56.
7. H. Ishiguro, "Use and Reference of Names," in P. Winch, ed., *Studies in the Philosophy of Wittgenstein* (London, 1969), pp. 20–50.

Chapter 5

Frege Against Fuzz[1]

Anyone reading Frege is bound to be struck by his repeated and extremely strong claims about the significance of the *full* determinacy of concepts and relations. He says over and over that every concept must have a value for every object, because otherwise it would be impossible to set forth logical laws about concepts.[2] There are many other places where he repeats the demand for full determinacy without adding explicitly that what it is required for is the formulation of logical laws. In this paper I try to make clear the relation between the possibility of logical laws and the determinacy of concepts. But I do not actually get to that until Part II. I found, in thinking about the relation, that I did not understand what Frege thought went wrong with inadequately defined predicates. Did they have sense but not reference, like empty proper names? Part I explains how I found myself led into a morass by that question, and what the way out is.

I

There is a somewhat puzzling discussion of inadequately defined predicates in Michael Dummett's book *Frege: Philosophy of Language*. Dummett has a section (in the second of his chapters on sense and reference) about the Fregean thesis that an expression can have sense but lack reference. As he points out, the most obvious kind of case is that of complex proper names, like "the capital of Antarctica"; a simple proper name can equally have sense but lack reference. The puzzling thing happens when Dummett turns to the case of predicates and other incomplete expressions. Is there any analogue in their case to that of proper names with sense and no reference? After pointing out that there is an obvious analogy in the case of predicates which contain proper names lacking reference, he adds that Frege himself "singles out a different and less trivial case, that in which the predicate is not defined for every argument." He then argues against Frege that the analogy is not a good one and that a better one in Frege's own terms can be found.[3] What puzzled me was the initial implausibility of ascribing to Frege the view that such predicates *have sense* but lack reference, that they are in that respect analogous to empty proper names. That is, it is perfectly plain from the contexts in which Frege discusses the issue that he takes the predicates in question to lack reference. It is not at all clear what his view about their sense is. In fact, as soon as one asks what Frege thinks about the sense of these predicates, one finds oneself in something of a morass.

I shall leave aside for a moment the reasons for ascribing to Frege the view Dummett takes him to have.[4] Anyone coming to the issue after reading *Grundgesetze* §56 will, I think, look at things as I initially did and be baffled by Dummett's treatment. If we properly fix the concept for which a predicate stands, Frege says, any object that you choose to take will either fall under it or not, *tertium non datur*. He then goes on, "E.g., would the sentence 'any square root of 9 is odd' have a comprehensible sense at all if *square root of 9* were not a concept with a sharp boundary? Has the question 'Are we still Christians?' really got a sense, if it is indeterminate whom the predicate 'Christian' can truly be asserted of, and who must be refused it?"[5]

Those remarks plainly suggest that the ill-defined predicates about which Frege is concerned do not merely lack reference. Something is clearly amiss with their sense as well. And it is natural to read Frege that way, i.e., as *not* taking the ill-defined predicates to have sense but no reference, if we go on to the following section in *Grundgesetze*. There he criticizes the 'piecemeal definitions' given by the mathematicians of his day. If they define "sum of x and y," for example, for integers only, it will then not be fixed what the reference is of "the sum of the Moon and the Moon"; but it is surely natural to think that such piecemeal definition leaves the sense of "the sum of the Moon and the Moon" unsettled too. It would thus follow that the relation-term "the sum of x and y is less than ten" has neither a reference nor a sense.

As one considers these ill-defined incomplete terms, one may think of taking as a properly analogous case involving complete terms not empty proper names but what one might call woolly or fuzzy proper names. The very language in which Frege discusses the ill-defined predicates—they fail to stand for concepts with *sharp boundaries*—suggests that we consider a proper name of something with no sharp boundary, say "Paradise Wood," which I am taking to be the name of a wood near Monymusk in Aberdeenshire. (I am ignoring the fact that there are woods elsewhere with the same name.) We may take it that the boundaries of Paradise Wood are not precisely fixed. There are some sentences about the wood to which we may want to assign some determinate truth-value, despite the absence of sharp boundaries. We may, for example, want to say that "Paradise Wood is in Aberdeenshire" is true and that "Paradise Wood contains palm trees" is false. But there will also be some sentences containing the name of the wood to which we cannot assign a determinate truth-value. If there were not such sentences, "Paradise Wood" *would* refer in a decent Fregean way to a single object and not a logical fuzz.

We can now take such ill-defined proper names together with the ill-defined incomplete terms we considered earlier and make the puzzle arising from Dummett's discussion more puzzling. Later on in that very chapter he provides exactly what appears to be necessary to make clear the logically central feature of ill-defined predicates (and other incomplete terms) and fuzzy proper names. "The sense of a proper name fixes the criterion of identity for the object named." That is the sixth of Dummett's theses-of-Frege's-on-sense-and-reference.[6] There is no criterion of identity for the object named by "Paradise Wood" fixed by the sense of that name. To have a criterion of identity for the object named by "a" is to have a way of deciding, in all cases, whether b is the same as a.[7] There are many woods with precisely drawn boundaries such that it is not fixed whether they are or are not the same as the object meant by "Paradise Wood"; of no wood with precisely drawn boundaries is it fixed that it is the same as the object named by "Paradise Wood." That is really to say that there is no determinate object, no *object*, named by "Paradise Wood." (There are no fuzzy objects, only fuzzy ways of speaking, including fuzzy ways of speaking of identity.) The absence of a criterion of identity is one way of putting the sickness (from a Fregean point of view) of "Paradise Wood"; and Dummett's sixth thesis implies that the sickness is a sickness of *sense*.

There is an analogous point to be made about predicates and other incomplete terms. Suppose that an attempt is made to define a predicate "fx," but it is not determined for every object whether it falls under the concept *fx*. It will not then be possible to say, in the case of every concept *gx*, whether *gx* holds of an object if and only if *fx* does. That is, although it will be possible to say of *some* concepts that they fail to coincide with *fx*, there will be other concepts for which it is not determinate whether *fx* coincides with them or not. Of no fully determinate concept (i.e., of no concept) will it be possible to say that it coincides with *fx* in all cases. Frege believed that a concept *fx* cannot strictly speaking be said to be identical with a concept *gx*. But what is analogous to identity in the case of concepts *fx* and *gx* is its holding of every object that *fx* holds of it if and only if *gx* does. So, if, in fixing the meaning of a predicate "fx," we do not fix for every object whether it falls under the concept fx, what we lack is a way of deciding in all cases, i.e., for every concept gx, whether fx and gx stand in the relation analogous, for concepts, to identity. Dummett's sixth thesis about sense was that the sense of a proper name fixes the criterion of identity for the object named, where that is a way of telling, in the case of every object, whether it is the same as the named object. If a way of determining the identity of the object named belongs to the sense of a proper name, it would seem reasonable to conclude that a way of determining what, for concepts, is analogous to identity belongs to the sense of a predicate. Since the *complete* definition of a predicate "fx" is essential to its being determinate, for every concept gx, whether fx and gx stand in the relation analogous to identity, it seems that the complete definition of a predicate is essential to the predicate's having a *sense*. Let me emphasize that this is the way my argument originally pushed me; I am not saying that we should take this account of sense as true to Frege. The crucial premise of the argument is Dummett's sixth thesis, taken to mean that it is part of the sense of a name what is to count, in all cases, as *being the same as* what the name names. My puzzlement then arose from the apparent incompatibility of the argument I have just sketched with Dummett's suggestion elsewhere in the book that, on Frege's view, incompletely defined predicates do have sense but no reference.

Rereading Dummett on the various cases of expressions with sense but no reference made the puzzle worse yet. When Dummett discusses proper names which have sense but lack reference, he criticizes Frege for taking proper names occurring in fiction as cases of proper names with sense but no reference. Such proper names, he says, have only a *partial* sense, "since there is no saying what would warrant identifying actual people as their bearers."[8] We should take instead, as examples of names with sense but no reference, proper names used "with a serious, though unsuccessful, intention to refer", and he mentions here the use of "Vulcan" for the planet once supposed to lie closer to the sun than Mercury. In such a case, but not in fictional cases, the proper name has determinate sense because we have a criterion for an object's being recognized as the referent of the name, but it lacks a reference, because "there is no object which satisfies the condition determined by the sense for being its referent."[9]

What is interesting there is the distinction between partial and complete determination of sense. What makes it deepen the puzzle is that when Dummett goes on to raise the question how good the analogy is between proper names with sense and no reference and inadequately defined predicates (and other incomplete expressions) the contrast between partial and complete determination of sense does not come into his discussion, though it appears to be directly relevant. That is, there *appears* to be something wrong with the sense and not just the reference of these incomplete terms. In his interpretation of Frege on sense, Dummett has tied the notion of sense to two notions closely related to each other: criterion of identity and the condition for something's being the referent of a name. He has tied them to *sense* in such a way that he seems bound to say that all is not well with the *sense* of the inadequately defined incomplete terms. But he nevertheless ascribes to Frege the view that the terms have sense but no reference, a view which seems to have against it three things:

(1) Frege's own remarks (not just in *Grundgesetze*) about trouble with sense in these cases.

(2) One's natural understanding of what is involved in piecemeal definition, taking for granted a Fregean distinction between sense and reference.

(3) Dummett's own account of Frege on sense: on the relation between the sense of a name and what it is for something to be what the name names. His explicit remark that "to know the sense of a predicate is to have a criterion for deciding, for any given object, whether or not the predicate applies to that object"[10] seems totally inconsistent with allowing that an incompletely defined predicate may have a fully determinate sense.

What is there to be said in favor of ascribing to Frege the idea that incompletely defined predicates have sense but no reference, and in that respect resemble proper names with sense but no reference? The puzzle about all this is made still worse by the fact that one of the good indications that this is Frege's view follows almost immediately after one of the good indications that it is not. In the *Grundgesetze* discussion of inadequate definitions of incomplete terms, we have Frege explicitly making an analogy between "The sum of the Moon and the Moon is not one" (in the case in which "the sum of x and y" is defined only for numbers) and "Scylla has six dragon necks." "Scylla has six dragon necks," Frege says, is neither true nor false but fiction, because "Scylla" designates nothing. And the case with "The sum of the Moon and the Moon is not one" is, he says, similar. It too lacks a truth-value, because "the sum of the Moon and the Moon" does not stand for anything. It thus has the same logical effect on the sentence in which it occurs as "Scylla" does on the other sentence.[11] Frege does not actually say in this passage that "the sum of the Moon and the Moon" *has* sense; but since he does elsewhere explicitly say that sentences containing fictional names have sense and do express thoughts although they lack truth-values, the passage does suggest extremely strongly that he is ascribing a sense to the sentence "The sum of the Moon and the Moon is not one." In the face of what he had said earlier in the same discussion of definition, the implication is little short of baffling.

It may seem that we can get rid of the bafflement if we do not take the analogy with "Scylla has six dragon necks" to be more than a very limited one. Frege does not actually explicitly *say* that "The sum of the Moon and the Moon is not one" expresses a thought; surely (we may think) he cannot have believed that it did, given the supposition that "sum of x and y" was defined only for numbers. Ascribing to Frege the view, then, that I have suggested is initially plausible (that an ill-defined predicate has something wrong with its sense and does not merely lack reference), and holding on to Dummett's connection (in his reading of Frege) between a determination of sense and a criterion of identity for the referent of expressions which have that sense, one can piece together a not altogether implausible account. The trouble with it is that it is wrong; it is not Frege's view. What gives the show away is an extremely interesting passage, which has to be set alongside the baffling comparison with "Scylla has six dragon necks." (I quote from the *Posthumous Writings*, where "*Bedeutung*" is translated as "meaning.")

> [The intensionalist logicians] forget that the laws of logic are first and foremost laws in the realm of meanings and only relate indirectly to sense. If it is a question of the truth of something— and truth is the goal of logic—we also have to inquire after meanings; we have to throw aside proper names that do not designate or name an object, though they may have a sense; we have to throw aside concept-words that do not have a meaning. These are not such as, say, contain a contradiction—for there is nothing at all wrong in a concept's being empty—but such as have vague boundaries. It must be determinate for every object whether it falls under a concept or not; a concept word which does not meet this requirement on its meaning is meaningless. E.g. the word "*moly*" (Homer, *Odyssey* X, 305) belongs to this class, although it is true that certain characteristic marks are supplied. For this reason the context cited need not lack a sense, any more than other contexts in which the name "Nausicaa," which probably does not mean or name anything, occurs. But it behaves as if it names a girl, and it is thus assured of a sense. And for fiction the sense is enough. The thought, though it is devoid of meaning, of truth-value, is enough, but not for science.[12]

That passage does two things. First of all it makes clear that the analogy between "The sum of the Moon and the Moon is not one" and "Scylla has six dragon necks" is meant to be a far-reaching one. Frege is here saying that the occurrence of poorly defined concepts like Homer's *moly* ("*moly*" apparently means some kind of herb but it is not clear which) need not deprive the contexts in which they occur of *sense*. As with fictional proper names, the problems created for logic lie in the absence of reference. The second thing the passage does is make one reconsider the connection between the sense of a name and its capacity to pick out a single thing of the appropriate logical category. By doing so, one can find one's way out of the morass. But there is still one problem, a problem in part of exposition. There is no way of avoiding the conclusion that Frege speaks of sense in different ways. There are contexts in which he is apparently willing to ascribe a sense to proper names and incomplete terms lacking reference—to ascribe sense unqualifiedly—and there are others in which although a sense is to be ascribed to such expressions it is only of some attenuated or derivative sort. I believe that significant features of his view of sense are independent of *which* way of speaking of sense one ascribes to him. It was my blindness to these features which led me into the morass; to get out of it one has to drop one characteristic feature of Dummett's interpretation of Frege.

We should turn first to Frege's remarks about "Nausicaa" in the passage quoted. Imagine circumstances very different from ours, circumstances in which there is only one girl. Suppose that in these circumstances the name "Nausicaa" were to be introduced in this way: "Nausicaa is a girl." Its sense and its reference would be fixed by that mode of introduction in those circumstances. (At this point I want to leave undiscussed what is supposed to happen in *other* circumstances. In particular, I am not suggesting here that the name would have a different sense in different circumstances.)

The view I want to ascribe to Frege can be put in general terms. The general description is intended to cover both successful and unsuccessful introductions, in order to make plain how they differ. It is meant to cover ordinary introductions of terms and those of interest to Frege; they will be a special case. (It is not meant to cover Frege's views about primitive names and the ways in which their meaning is communicated.) A proper name may be introduced by a sentence of the form "N is a thing which ϕs", or, what comes to the same, "'N' stands for a thing which ϕs." (There are slight complications, which I shall ignore, about the latter kind of case. Another kind of complication arises about introductions involving more than one sentence;

I have a few remarks below about those cases.) The name is given both sense and reference by such an introduction if there is exactly one thing that falls under the concept φ, or *thing that φs*, which I call the introducing concept. The sense of the introduced proper name is fixed in part by the predicate used in the introduction, which I call the introducing predicate. That predicate fixes what in the sense of the introduced proper name is distinct from the sense of *other* proper names; the rest of the sense of the introduced name (its formal character) is fixed by the form of the introduction as that of a proper name. A demonstration that an introduction of a proper name fixes its reference is distinct from the introduction itself. (Such a demonstration is necessary, Frege thinks, if we are to be justified in using the introduced proper name in science.) A special case of an introduction is " 'N' stands for A" or "N is A," where "A" is another proper name in Frege's sense; that is, it may be a definite description or other complex name, or a logically simple proper name. Here the introducing concept, the concept under which exactly one thing must fall if the introduced name is to have reference, is: *is identical with A*. But the use of an *identity predicate* (a predicate formed by a sign for identity with one of its argument places filled by a Fregean proper name) in an introduction of a name is, as I read Frege, a characteristic merely of one type of introduction of a proper name. It is a type of introduction which allows us to substitute the introduced term for the possibly complex proper name which is part of the introducing predicate; and *that* will normally be the point of such an introduction. This type of introduction is what Frege usually means by the term "definition." He has reasons for requiring that all definitions in a rigorous development of a science be of this type; he wants us to be able to avoid the kind of investigation necessary to prove the adequacy of any other kind of introduction.[13] But his very reasons for preferring introductions of this type make it plain that they are not the only ones which can be adequate. Introductions which do not use identity predicates may be entirely adequate from a logical point of view, in that reference is secured; those using identity predicates may fail in that reference is *not* secured. About adequacy of sense I shall have more to say below; at this stage all I need is that if we allow any talk of sense at all as being secured by the introduction of a term independently of whether it has reference, then either sort of introduction— using an identity predicate or not—will secure sense. If we use "sense" narrowly, so that we speak of sense as belonging properly or unqualifiedly only to expressions which have reference, either sort of introduction may fix sense unqualifiedly or may fail to. A passage which supports the account I have given may be found in Frege's *Posthumous Writings* on p. 249. There Frege claims that the reason "$a^2 = 4$" does not fix the reference of the previously undefined proper name "a" is that two distinct numbers fall under the concept $x^2 = 4$. The suggestion would appear to be that the reference of "a" would be fixed by, e.g., "$a - 6 = 8$".

On Frege's view as I see it, if we substitute, in the sentence introducing a proper name, *any* expression which has the same referent as that of the expression for which it is substituted, we cannot affect the capacity of that sentence to determine the reference of the proper name, though such a substitution can affect the suitability of the definition for science. "$a - 6 = 8$" and "$a = 8 + 6$" must both or neither be capable of fixing the reference of "a," since the predicates "$x - 6 = 8$" and "$x = 8 + 6$" have the same referent. Similarly (on the assumption that there is only one girl) with "Nausicaa is a girl" and "Nausicaa is the unique girl." Another essential feature of the view I am ascribing to Frege is the distinction between our being *justified* in using a name as a proper name and its having a reference. On Frege's view, so long as it has not been shown that there is exactly one girl, I am not properly justified in using "Nausicaa" as a proper name, just as I should not be justified, on Frege's view, in using the expression "*the* girl" unless I had shown that there was exactly one girl. But, just as "the girl" would refer to the unique girl if there were exactly one girl, whether or not I had shown that there was exactly one, so "Nausicaa" does refer to the unique girl, if there is exactly one girl, whether or not I have shown that there is exactly one.

In several places, Frege discusses the introduction of terms by a *set* of sentences. The point in all cases is, not that such sets of sentences cannot succeed in fixing the reference of the previously undefined term or terms they contain, but that the kind of investigation to show that such an introduction is successful may be impracticable and is in any case best avoided. Further, the definitions cannot serve the purpose which definitions have in science unless such sets of definition-sentences are "solved for the unknowns." I shall ignore the complexity introduced by such cases; the fundamental issues are not affected. The important thing here is to distinguish carefully between what it is for the introduction of a term to be logically adequate (to fix reference unambiguously), and what rules there should be for the introduction of terms in a rigorous science to make it possible to ascertain logical adequacy and to allow definitions to serve the role they have in science. Frege's practice, often, is to bring out the evils of definitions which violate the principles of definition by examining particular cases of definitions which not only fail to adhere to those principles but *also* fail to secure reference for the term or terms defined. But he does not say or suggest that definitions which violate the principles can never secure reference.

I can now contrast the view I have begun to sketch (as Frege's) with Dummett's. Dummett has a distinction, as we have seen, between the relatively unspecific determination of the sense of a proper name (exemplified by fictional names) and full specific determination of the sense of proper names (determination which fixes a criterion for an object's being recognized as the referent of the name). A proper name has reference, on his view, only if two conditions are met: it has a specific enough sense to determine a criterion for an object's being recognizable as the referent of the name (that is what names in fiction supposedly lack), and there is exactly one thing which satisfies the criterion determined by the sense for being recognizable as the referent. On my view, there is no internal condition of specificity which a sense needs to meet. The difference between my view and Dummett's comes out if we look at the general form of introduction of proper names. On Dummett's account, a proper introduction of a proper name, one which will specify its sense fully enough to supply a criterion of identity for the object named, goes something like this: "'N' stands for A" or "N is A," where A is a Fregean proper name. Putting the matter in terms of the vocabulary I used earlier, on Dummett's view the introducing predicate must be an identity predicate. In contrast, I think that the requirement on a name, that it carry with it a way of distinguishing what it names from other objects, is associated with the form of proper namehood and is not a requirement imposed on the sense of the introducing predicate, considered independently of the concept it stands for. Frege says, on my view, that an introduced proper name refers if exactly one thing falls under the concept that the introducing predicate stands for: uniqueness is a matter of the predicate's *reference*, not its sense; it is a requirement essentially on the introducing concept. There need be no way of telling from the introducing predicate *alone* whether the name introduced by it carries with it a way of distinguishing what it names from other objects. Dummett's view implies that if a proper name is to have an adequately specified sense, the introducing predicate must have built into its sense a way of distinguishing the referent of the introduced name from all other objects. What fixes the sense of the introduced proper name is, then, the sense of the proper name forming part of the introducing predicate (partially completing the identity sign which the predicate contains, and standing for, or intended to stand for, the referent of the name). On my view, the sense of the introducing predicate determines the sense of the introduced proper name only taken together with the form of the introduction. The predicate itself need not contain a proper name and its sense is not the sense of the introduced name. It should be noted that there is no significant epistemological difference between the two views: to know that an object is the referent of a proper name you must on either view know that only one object falls under the introducing concept. The fact that sense is introduced by Frege in connection with epistemological issues is irrelevant to the question whether "Nausicaa is a girl" is from the point of view of *sense* an adequate, a specific enough, introduction of a proper name. I think it is clear that from a Fregean point of view, that introduction would be logically adequate if the realm of reference were rather different from what it is.

I mentioned that there are problems arising on any account of Frege's views because he speaks of sense in different ways. One difference between my account and Dummett's is that mine is entirely independent of which way of speaking of sense one chooses; Dummett's is not. On Dummett's view, it is through your knowledge of the sense of an expression that you can establish what its referent is, or indeed that it has a referent. Its having a sense must then be independent of whether it has a referent. My account leaves the matter open. It provides two descriptions of how one may determine what the referent of an expression is. These are equivalent if one is willing to speak unqualifiedly of an expression lacking reference as having sense. If one is not, there is a description of how we can establish what the referent is which does not suppose anything about whether the expression has sense. To find that something is the referent one needs to find out whether the introducing concept is uniquely instantiated and by what; one thus needs to grasp the sense of the introducing predicate. No mention need be made of the sense of the introduced term; it is not necessary to take any view about its having sense. A modification of Dummett's account could be constructed which did not commit one to allowing sense unqualifiedly to expressions without reference. Such a modified account would still have the central feature which I think it is a mistake to ascribe to Frege: that it is *internal* to an adequate determination of the sense of a proper name that the name carry with it a way of distinguishing what it names from other things.

For Frege, identity is tied directly to the realm of reference and not the realm of sense through the principle of the identity of indiscernibles; and that supports the idea that we should not ascribe to him any *internal* connection between a properly fixed proper name sense and a way of distinguishing the object named from other things. Whether we have a way of picking out what a name names from other things depends on what other things the object needs to be picked out from. Whether the identity of the object named is fixed depends on whether we can tell, of every object, whether it is the same as the object named. Success in that task depends on what distinguishable objects there are, which is itself inseparable from what falls under what concepts. The principle of the identity of indiscernibles obviates the need for any connection (of the sort Dummett thinks Frege makes) between the sense of a name and a way of picking out what it names from all other things. Given the introducing *concept*, whatever it is, we need only know whether exactly one thing falls under it to determine whether the name has reference. If we take the identity of indiscernibles seriously, we see that we should drop any idea that it should be internal to a sense that it is suited through its specificity to be the sense of a seriously intended proper name. Another way of putting the fundamental point is this. If we call a concept under which exactly one object falls an identity concept, then in a successful introduction of a proper name the essential thing is that the introducing concept be an identity concept. Such a concept has belonging to it *many* senses; *any* of them may be the sense of the introducing predicate. Some of those senses will be senses of identity predicates, some will not. An identity concept need not be named by an identity predicate. Dummett thinks that if one knows the sense of a proper name (a proper name which does not have merely partial sense), one knows that no more than one thing can fall under it. That does not fit well with what Frege says about names like "Nausicaa" (as Dummett recognizes), and should not be taken to be (even implicitly) Frege's view of sense. There is no distinction between "partial" and "complete" sense of proper names in Frege, and the addition of such a distinction makes trouble.

We are now in a position to turn back to ill-defined predicates. We may take as an example "x is evenly divisible by 41," which we may suppose to be defined only for numbers. However, we may now also suppose that, as it happens, the only objects that there are *are* numbers. In that case the predicate has completely determinate reference. The truth-value a name of which results from completing the predicate by a meaningful proper name is determinate in *all* cases, because the only meaningful proper names there are name numbers. If all objects are numbers, then the predicate has in fact got determinate sense and reference; there is nothing the matter with it.

Another simple kind of example to consider is suggested by Frege's remarks about the predicate "Christian." We might introduce the predicate this way: "x is a Christian is the true if x believes p and q" (p and q being two doctrines), "and x is a Christian is the false if x does not believe p and does not believe q." That is the whole definition. It is logically fine and dandy—that is, sense and reference are fixed as well as senses and references can be—if every object believes both p and q or neither.

An account parallel to the one I have given for proper names can be given for the introduction of non-primitive predicates. We specify the reference of a first-order predicate through what may be regarded as a second-order introducing predicate. That is, to determine the value of a concept for some or all objects is to fix that the concept falls within such-and-such a second-order concept; other kinds of specification of *which* concept our predicate stands for also place it within a second-order concept. Whether the introduction fixes completely the reference of a first order predicate depends on whether exactly one concept falls within the second-order introducing concept, and *that* depends on what distinguishable concepts (and objects) there are. Now about sense. If we say that an expression need not have reference to have sense fully or unqualifiedly, then the introduction of a predicate via a second-order introducing predicate will determine a sense, no matter how unspecific it is. Thus *"moly"* may be said to have sense. If we say that a predicate lacking reference can have sense only in some less than full-blooded way, then whether an introduction completely determines the sense of a predicate depends on the same thing exactly as determinacy of reference depends on; they both depend on whether exactly one concept falls within the introducing second-order concept. (*"Moly"* then may be said to have sense only qualifiedly.) In neither case is there any way of judging the sense of the introduced predicate to be inadequately specified merely by considering the *sense* of the introducing predicate. Either any sense will do (on the more generous Fregean view) or (on the stricter view) whether the sense of the introducing predicate will do is a matter of the realm of reference.

What my discussion of proper names and predicates was meant to bring out is then this. If we consider the introduction of a term, what in it goes to determine the sense of the introduced term is its form and the particular sense of the introducing predicate. There is no way to divide such introductions, going on what is internal to them, into some that are specific enough to fix the sense of the proper name or predicate that is being introduced and others that are not. *Either* we follow the lenient Frege in saying that expressions can have sense but no reference, and then *any* determination of sense is specific enough to fix sense, *or* we take the stricter line. In that case it is not internal to a particular determination of sense that it is specific enough to fix the sense of the proper name or predicate being introduced. Specificity *enough* is determined by what lies in the realm of reference. The crucial point I had not seen when I was lost in the original morass was that there is, on Frege's kind of view, no way to discriminate between senses on logical grounds without reference to the realm of reference. The idea that it is in part at least a matter internal to the unspecific sense of "Nausicaa," and not entirely a matter of an unobliging world, that makes the name lack reference—that is enormously plausible but false to Frege. And the same can be said of the idea I originally had that ill-defined predicates were more closely analogous to fuzzy proper names than to proper names with sense but no reference. That too depends on taking the fuzziness of the proper name as belonging to its sense independently of what is in the realm of reference. But there is no fuzziness in a fuzzy name if the realm of reference contains a few fewer items. Take a few well-chosen concepts away, remove them from the realm of reference, and the principle of the identity of indiscernibles does the rest: it will no longer allow you to distinguish several distinct objects falling under the concept (whatever it was) through which the fuzzy name was introduced, and it will be a perfectly precisely defined name. The *ill-definedness* of a predicate, like the *emptiness* or *fuzziness* of a proper name, is only made to be ill-definedness or fuzziness or emptiness through what there is in the realm of reference; remove some items, or add some, and all is well. The depth of the analogy Frege draws between fictional names and ill-defined predicates lies in this: in *all* cases, all would be logically in order with these predicates and proper names if the realm of reference were different. That point stands firm, regardless of what one wants to say about whether terms which lack reference can strictly speaking have sense. A change in the realm of reference cannot alone make a definition which is unsuitable for science suitable for it; but suitability for science is distinct from logical adequacy, where logical adequacy is a matter of the fixing of fully determinate reference. I should point out that what I have said about predicates can readily be applied to other incomplete terms; and I should repeat that I have excluded all along any consideration of primitive terms.

Before I try to apply all this to Frege's views about logical laws, I need to turn briefly to the issue I have repeatedly touched on, of Frege's ways of talking about sense. One way of handling the problems here may at first appear attractive. Take Homer's "*moly*" and the passage I quoted about whether we are all Christians. Homer's "*moly*" is taken by Frege to be a predicate with sense but no reference, and sentences containing it have sense but no truth-value. How, we may want to know, can that fit with his saying that "Are we still Christians?" has really no sense? For "Christian," it would seem, has sense if "*moly*" does, given the justification Frege offers for saying that "*moly*" does not deprive sentences in which it occurs of sense. Gareth Evans has said that those of Frege's statements in which he allows that terms with no reference can have sense are far more equivocal that at first appears.[14] That is very important, and applies fairly clearly to the "*moly*" passage. It can be read, and I think should be, to allow sense to "*moly*" only in an attenuated way. The passage about "*moly*" is actually consistent with ascribing to Frege the principle that *strictly* speaking what has sense is not an expression considered merely as an expression (introduced somehow or other), but rather an expression *standing for such-and-such*. Many passages in Frege support ascribing that principle to him or are more consistent with it than at first appear—Evans's point. We can then read Frege as saying that in fiction we set aside the realm of reference as it is, and treat expressions which lack sense as having sense, and sentences which express no thoughts as expressing thoughts: the senses, the thoughts, they would express if they (and the way they were introduced) were no different but the realm of reference *were*. In general, a sense sufficient for fiction, a courtesy sense, is what would, in certain fictional circumstances, *be* a sense, i.e., would (in those circumstances) be the way an expression presented what it stands for. So long as we keep the contexts of fiction apart from serious ones, it does not matter that we speak of what lacks reference as having sense; and so Frege can say that "*moly*" has sense. But if someone were to ask seriously whether we are all Christians, we must say that the question has no sense—although looked at from a strictly logical point of view, there is no significant difference between "*moly*" and "Christian": both are predicates the result of the completion of which by meaningful proper names is fixed in some but not all cases.

I said that that way of handling the problem may appear attractive; I meant that one cannot really get away with saying that Frege accepts the principle that strictly speaking only an expression which stands for something has a sense, and its consequence that strictly speaking only a sentence with a truth-value expresses a thought. It is unfortunately not the case that all passages in which he appears to be taking the opposite view are equivocal or qualified in the way some more or less plainly are. He is not in all such cases allowing sense to such expressions in a mere courtesy all-right-for-fiction-but-keep-it-away-from-science way. Evans apparently thinks that even the clear statements, towards the beginning of "Sense and Reference," that proper names without reference can have sense are, taken in context, more qualified and equivocal than they seem.[15] I should like to think that that was so, but find it too hard.

My concern then is whether the lenient Frege we find in "Sense and Reference" and elsewhere leads me back into the morass. I got into the morass through not grasping how far it was possible to push the analogy between empty proper names and ill-defined predicates. The analogy lies in what adequate and inadequate introduction is for any term, whether it is a proper name or an expression for some kind of function. The logical adequacy of the introduction of a term depends only on there being exactly one object or function falling under or falling within the introducing first or higher order concept. I do not have to get back into the morass if there is a way of keeping hold of the analogy, whichever Frege we follow, lenient or strict (the strict one keeping to the line Gareth Evans thinks he takes). I shall not go into the details; the analogy does I think survive. Taking the lenient view of sense strictly enough produces some extremely odd results, including that "The sum of the Moon and the Moon is one" does express a thought, even if "the sum of x and y" is defined only for numbers. But there are strong arguments against it independent of the queer results it produces in such cases as these.[16]

The lenient talk about sense treats sense purely from the internal side; the stricter way of talking allows us to speak of sense only when we connect a sense with something in the realm of reference. It thus takes sense externally, as it were. Given the way sense is introduced by Frege, the notion *has* the two sides; one side, the internal, is clearly adequate for some purposes. Since Frege was uninterested in those purposes, he never bothered to sort them out; he simply labelled them all fiction. The critical question in discussing Frege is not what the problems are if we speak one way rather than the other, but what if anything is the matter with a notion of sense which has such a split between its external and internal character, and which is connected with truth and falsity only through what is external to it. I shall not here consider that question. Part II is concerned with the split itself, or, rather, with one of its manifestations: external features of the mode of introduction of the words we use are what determine the applicability of logic to what we say in those words.

II

In reading Frege on sense we need to bear in mind the two sources of what he thinks. There are in the first place the considerations at the beginning of "Sense and Reference": the need for an account of identity statements and for a solution to closely related problems. But

Frege on sense cannot be understood if we forget the other source, forget that what Frege wanted the notion of *thought* for was its connection with inference. The passage I quoted in Part I about "Nausicaa" and "*moly*" says that logical laws relate only indirectly to sense; the fact that their direct bearing is not on sense is extremely important. But the indirect connection is still a vital one. It is after all thoughts which stand in logical relations to each other, thoughts which the laws of logic are in a sense laws of, thoughts which are the premises and conclusions of inferences. Thoughts visible to the logician's eye are always true or false; the fixed stock of thoughts, of thoughts properly so called, is tied to the unchanging realm of reference.[17]

In discussing Frege on definitions, I have kept separate two questions: How does an introducing predicate (first order or higher order) determine the reference of an expression introduced by it? If the expression being introduced lacks reference, can it nevertheless have sense? My argument has been that there is in Frege's discussions of many cases a discoverable answer to the first question that is consistent with his better and his worse answers to the second. The better, the strict, answer has its source in Frege's views about inference; the answer I have given as Frege's to the first has, I think, the same source. On Frege's view, inference goes, properly speaking, from premises which are true thoughts to a conclusion which is a true thought. But we apply the laws of logic to thoughts expressed by sentences. Such an application depends on the sentences' having parts which themselves have reference independent of the context. What counts as an adequate introduction of an expression is determined by the theory of inference. What exactly then is the tie between the full determinacy of the sense and reference of predicates and the application of logic? I can now try to answer that question.

My answer has two parts, one very short and the other as short as I could make it, but still very long. The argument of the two parts together is intended to make clear the contrast, on Frege's view, between proper logical inference and an ersatz sort of inference, the best we can have if any of our terms are incompletely defined. The short part of the answer is a sketch of the place of thoughts in Frege's view of inference. The longer part explains the logically repulsive imitation of inference we inevitably wind up with if we use inadequately defined terms. My aim, I should emphasize, is not to show why inadequately defined terms are bad for logic, or even whether they are, but how *Frege's* conception of the nature of logic reveals itself in his repeated remarks about the full determinacy of concepts.

A thought is the sense of a complex name of a truth-value, a sentence, and may be said to belong to that truth-value. The sentence whose sense it is may be regarded as a map of the thought.[18] That is, to divisions of the sentence into parts there correspond divisions of the thought. In such a division or analysis of a thought, it is construed as consisting of parts, the senses of expressions occurring in the sentence. The expressions stand for functions and objects; the sense of an expression may be said to belong to the function or object denoted by the expression. In an analysis of a thought, the truth-value to which it belongs is shown as the value of a function for such-and-such arguments. To show the truth-value as the value of the function, we divide the sentence expressing the thought this way: we treat the sentence as an expression (perhaps a very complex one) standing for the function (a concept or relation) completed by expressions standing for its arguments (functions or objects); the senses of these expressions are what, in this analysis, we are taking to be parts of the thought. The senses, that is, belonging to the function and its arguments (that function whose value for those arguments is the truth-value to which the thought belongs) are the parts of the thought. I shall speak of the functions and objects to which the parts of a thought belong as the functions and objects of the thought. Since a thought can be analyzed in different ways, we can pick out the parts of a particular thought and, correspondingly, the functions and objects of a particular thought, in different ways. What I have just said about thoughts depends on the 'strict' Fregean way of talking of sense. When I speak of 'genuine thoughts' in the rest of this paper I mean thoughts in the sense just spelled out. In an inference we derive the judgment that a thought is true from judgments that thoughts—premises—are true, relying only on the fact that the functions and objects of the premise-thoughts are functions and objects. Laws of logic are thus laws of what is true of functions and objects as such; *that* is how they are laws of judgment. They bear on thoughts expressed in sentences through the sentences' containing expressions standing for the objects and functions of the thoughts which those sentences express. That is, it is our sentences' being genuinely maps of thoughts, containing terms standing for functions and objects to which the parts of the thoughts belong, that makes it possible to apply the laws of inference to thoughts through the sentences expressing them. To say that sentences are maps of thoughts is not itself to say anything about what differently structured maps of the same thought there may be. When I spoke of "the functions and objects of the premise-thoughts" I meant what we construe to be its functions and objects on some one of the possible analyses of the thought. The bearing of logical laws on a set of premise-thoughts depends then on *some* construal of each of the premise-thoughts as a thought with such-and-such functions and objects.

I need now to make clear what kind of inference or 'inference' we get if we use incompletely defined terms, and here I shall develop the points in Part I about how expressions are introduced.

We may divide introductions of expressions into three. The descriptions that I shall give are not meant as proper definitions.

(1) An introduction of a proper name is empty if through it the truth-value of no sentence in which the proper name completes a meaningful predicate is fixed. An introduction of a predicate is empty if through it the truth-value of no sentence in which the predicate is completed by a meaningful proper name or completes a meaningful second-order predicate is fixed.

(2) An introduction of a proper name is complete if through it the truth-value of all sentences in which the proper name completes a meaningful predicate is fixed. An introduction of a predicate is complete if through it the truth-value of all sentences in which the predicate is completed by a meaningful proper name is fixed.

(3) An introduction of a proper name is partial if through it the truth-value of some but not all sentences in which it is completed by a meaningful proper name or in which it completes a meaningful second-order predicate is fixed.

A question that needs asking is: What justifies the idea that there is a third type of introduction, and that the first two between them do not include all cases? The idea seems to involve a breach of the Fregean principle that a sentence containing a part with no reference has no reference. (One might also ask whether the second and third types do not between them include all cases. I shall not discuss that question, although a complex answer to it follows from the rest of what I say.)

Take the introduction of "Christian" as before: "x is a Christian is the true if x believes both p and q, and x is a Christian is the false if x does not believe either." There are, we suppose, people who believe one but not the other; A believes both. So "A is a Christian" contains a predicate with no determinate truth-value for the names of some objects, completed by the name of an object for which the predicate is defined. What then is Frege's view about such sentences? (In giving his view, I am going to use "meaning" rather than "reference" or "referent"; I shall explain why at the end.) When we define a concept incompletely, we fix for some objects but not all whether they fall under the concept we are defining. The result of such a procedure is what Frege calls a "quasi-conceptual construction."[19] There is no concept, or anything else, which the predicate in "A is a Christian" means. But Frege does allow that such incomplete definitions are consistent with the predicate's having meaning (of sorts) when it occurs in certain contexts, i.e., completed by proper names of certain objects. This, however, is not an *independent* meaning: the predicate has no proper meaning of its own even in such contexts. (See Frege's criticisms of Peano's definition of identity: "*sie gibt also dem Gleichheitszeichen nicht unabhängig von a und b Bedeutung; d.h., sie gibt ihm überhaupt keine eigne Bedeutung.*")[20] In discussing a related kind of case, Frege says that when an ill-defined function expression is completed by the names of a pair of objects for which it is defined, meaning has been given by the definition not to the function expression itself but to the complex sign within which it occurs.[21] He holds that incompletely defined predicates are "to be regarded as meaningless from a logical point of view,"[22] meaningless because there is no concept they mean, and logic must treat as meaningless any predicate which lacks independent meaning. If the truth-value of a sentence does not depend on the independent meaning of its parts, logical laws cannot be brought to bear on the sentence. He is not inconsistent when he allows meaning to some sentences containing such predicates and to the predicates themselves in those sentences. But various things must be kept in mind about such cases.

(1) *This* allowance of meaning to such sentences does not extend to contexts involving inference.
(2) The meaning in question attaches to the sentence as a whole and is not functionally dependent on the meaning of the parts; for one (at least) of the parts lacks any independent meaning. If we speak of truth-*value* in such cases, we should recall that the truth-value is not a value of any function (any concept or relation) meant by a part of the sentence, as it is in the case of genuinely articulated sentences. It follows that if we are willing to speak of the sentence as expressing a thought, the thought is associated with the sentence as a whole. The sentence is not a map of the thought. Allowing a meaning to the sentence as a whole is not in breach of the Fregean principle that a logically complex name containing a meaningless part must be meaningless, since the sentence is not being treated as logically complex.
(3) Although Frege does allow that predicates like "Christian" may have context-bound meaning, this implies nothing more than that they occur in some sentences which are not meaningless. It would be unjustified to ascribe to him the view that, in

those sentences, they stand for something or other. For an expression to stand for something, in *any* context, it must have independent meaning or be a logically complex expression analyzable into parts with independent meaning. When meaning is independent, or a function of independent meaning, the translation of *"Bedeutung"* as "reference" or "referent", depending on context, is unproblematic; when meaning is dependent on context, such a translation would be, to say the least, tendentious. A comparison Frege does not use, but which may be helpful, is with the parts of "Parkinson's disease." It is determinate what object (i.e., what disease) is referred to by some expressions of the form "N's disease." But when they occur in "Parkinson's disease" or in "Bright's disease" neither "disease" nor "( )'s disease" is a properly defined Fregean function-name. Neither "disease" nor "( )'s disease" stands for anything in such contexts. But it would be wrong to call "disease," in those contexts, a meaningless word, using "meaningless" in the ordinary English sense, in which it does not mean "lacks Fregean reference" or "is logically meaningless." The whole of my argument here with respect to Frege's view of sentences like "A is a Christian" is that they are analogous to proper names like "Bright's disease": (a) they look as if they contain a function-name, but (b) they do not contain any properly defined function-name, and (c) there are some proper names such that, when they are inserted into the apparent 'argument place' of the seeming 'function-name', the expression as a whole is not meaningless, and the seeming function-name which is a part of the expression, while it has no 'logically admissible meaning' is, in an ordinary sense, not a meaningless word.

One point on which I have been relying is that, for Frege, to give an incomplete determination of what concept a predicate is to mean is to fix the result of completing the predicate with the names of some objects, and that is to fix the truth-value of some sentences. When Frege considers the predicate "3 + = 5," assuming a case in which addition has been defined only for positive integers, he says that 2 does fall under the concept in question, although it is undecided which other objects fall under the concept.[23] On his principles, it is not fixed *which* concept is meant, but that does not rule out saying that what *has* been specified is that such-and-such objects fall under the concept thus partially specified. There is nevertheless no implication that there are concepts which do not have a value for every object. It is clear that something has to give: you cannot, on Frege's view of what concepts and functions are (what constitutes what, for them, corresponds to identity), hold that an incompletely defined predicate or other function-name can *occur as a logical part* in a sentence with a truth-value. But we should not assume that he thinks it must be truth-value, rather than genuine logical complexity, which goes.

I have discussed the question whether a partial introduction of a predicate fixes the truth-value of any sentences in which the predicate occurs, and have given a very qualified Yes as answer. I know of no grounds for ascribing to Frege the view that there is such a thing as a partial introduction of a proper name, fixing even in a qualified sense the truth-value of some of the sentences in which the name completes a meaningful predicate. On the other hand, Frege's denials of meaning to sentences containing such proper names are in contexts in which what is at stake is whether the sentences may be taken as meaningful from a strict logical point of view. He does definitely suggest that ordinary language, of no concern to him, may allow proper names that do not designate an object determinately[24]; the suggestion appears to be that such names are not treated as mere empty names. Nothing that I know of would rule out treating "Paradise Wood contains no palm trees" entirely analogously to "A is a Christian" in the case I imagined. I am supposing, as before, that "Paradise Wood" is used to talk about what we in ordinary language call a particular wood, one near Monymusk in Aberdeenshire, but it is given no precise definition. There are (we may suppose) forty distinct woods, each of which could be named by a precisely defined name, sharing whatever the characteristics are through which "Paradise Wood" was introduced, but differing among themselves in others, such as precise area. I am also supposing that there are no palm trees anywhere in Aberdeenshire. Using what Frege says about predicates and making the necessary changes, we can construct an account on which "Paradise Wood has no palm trees" would count as true in a qualified sense. Its truth-value, though, would not depend on the independent meaning of its parts, and would not strictly be a *value*. The fuzzy name "Paradise Wood" could be said to have meaning in context. But to say such a thing would only be to say that it could occur in some sentences which were not meaningless. It would not be to say that when "Paradise Wood" occurred in such a context, there was something in the realm of reference for which it stood, that it there referred to a wood. To say of something that it is a *wood* may or may not be to use terms strictly: strictly speaking, anything that is a wood is an object, and there are no fuzzy objects, hence none for which "Paradise Wood," in any context, stands. In contrast with

"Paradise Wood," any name of a wood-in-the-strict-sense yields a determinate truth-value whenever it completes any independently meaningful predicate. If we speak of sentences containing names with context-bound meaning as true or false, such uses and such sentences must be kept away from logic. From the point of view of logic, they would be internally unarticulated proper names.

There is considerable logical symmetry between conditional definitions of predicates and partial introductions of proper names. A partial introduction of a proper name can be written as a definition fixing the truth-values of sentences in which the proper name completes predicates meeting a condition. That is, fuzzy proper names like "Paradise Wood," and any other proper names (like "Nausicaa") whose introducing concept is multiply instantiated, can be treated as if they were introduced by conditional definitions, analogous to the conditional definitions which Frege attacks in mathematics. The account of fuzziness can be extended to include multiply fuzzy sentences like "Paradise Wood is full of mushrooms." Much more could also be said about the fuzzy thoughts that fuzzy sentences, taken as wholes, express. But the theory of fuzz is not what I am after, except for one part of it: its bearing on Frege's views about inference. And to make that clear I shall need to spell out in slightly more detail what is involved in saying that a partial introduction of a proper name or predicate fixes the truth or falsity of some sentences containing the term. How does it do it?

We may call "Paradise Wood has no palm trees" true because *all* forty woods falling under the introducing concept of "Paradise Wood" lack palm trees. So we ignore the blur, as it were. *Whichever* precisely bounded wood we meant, the predicate applies, so why bother to mean one determinate wood? There is actually a general principle here: a sentence which is the completion of a meaningful predicate by a partially introduced proper name counts as true if the predicate stands for the introducing concept of the proper name or a concept to which the introducing concept is subordinate. It counts as false if its negation counts as true. Its truth-value is indeterminate in all cases in which the objects falling under the introducing concept (of which there must be *some* or the introduction would not be partial) do not *all* fall or *all* fail to fall under the concept referred to by the predicate which the partially introduced proper name completes. (I am not suggesting that the principle is trouble-free; it is not.) A corresponding account can be given for partially introduced predicates and incomplete terms in general, and the result of it will be, for example, that if arithmetical function terms are defined only for numbers, "82 is evenly divisible by 41" will count as true, and "2 + 2 =

5″ will count as false, and so on. Recall, though, that these are not, on the 'Fregean' fuzz theory, true or false in anything but a very qualified sense. The same general principle allowing us to speak of some sentences as true or false despite their containing partially introduced terms will allow us to speak of the thoughts associated with these sentences as themselves true or false in a similarly qualified sense. I shall in what follows speak of its being true that such-and-such if the thought that such-and-such is associated with a sentence which counts as true by the fuzz principle, and similarly for falsity.

I needed the contrast between complete and partial introductions of terms, and as much as I have spelled out of the theory of fuzz, in order to explain Frege's insistence on the need for *complete* introductions. We can, that is, now see what is wrong with the attempt to infer using terms introduced only partially. There is a wonderful image Frege uses in this connection: "Just as it would be impossible for geometry to set up precise laws if it tried to recognize threads as lines and knots in threads as points, so logic must demand sharp limits of what it will recognize as a concept unless it wants to renounce all precision and certainty."[25] What then would the absence of sharp limits do to logic? What would thread-and-knot logic be?

It becomes apparent fairly quickly that the principle of fuzzy truth and falsity gives trouble. Let us stick to Paradise Wood. We can say truly, according to the principle, that it is in Aberdeenshire; it will be false that bee-eaters nest in it; and such things are all very well. But now we may note that one thing true of the forty precisely bounded woods falling under the introducing concept of "Paradise Wood" is that each has a precisely fixed area. If we stick to the principle of fuzzy truth in the form I gave it, we can call true the sentence "Paradise Wood has a precisely defined area." However, if we take *any* precise area, there will be no determinately true or false sentence saying that Paradise Wood has *that* area. So although it will count as false that it has no precisely defined area, there is no precisely defined area that it is true that it has. There's trouble for you! What is coming to the surface here is that no sentence containing "Paradise Wood" has genuine logical complexity. If "PW1" is a precisely defined name of one of the woods falling under the introducing concept of "Paradise Wood," then any sentence "PW1 has area N," assigning to that wood a precise area, has a determinate truth value; the sentence "PW1 has a precise area" would not express a true thought unless there were some other sentence, assigning to PW1 a particular precise area, which *did* express a true thought. This logical relation of the thoughts can be shown perspicuously in Frege's concept-script or other notations sharing its features. But there is no such logical relationship between "Paradise Wood has some precisely defined area" and any sentence assigning an area to it; the sentence does not contain a reference to a wood, to an object, such that another sentence may stand in logical relations to it through containing a name standing for the same thing.

The fuzz principle has results which are as repulsive in the case of predicates as those it has for proper names. I did not actually state it for predicates; here is a way of putting it. A sentence containing a predicate given only a partial introduction counts as true if the result of replacing that predicate by a well-defined predicate standing for a concept falling within its introducing second-order concept is always a true sentence; it counts as false if the result is always a false sentence; its truth-value is undetermined in all other cases. (There must be some concepts falling within the introducing concept or the introduction is not partial.) Take "x is a Christian," introduced as before. If A believes both p and q, B p but not q, and C neither, we get determinate truth values by the fuzz principle for "A is a Christian" and for "C is a Christian." Fine. But now the fuzz principle lets us count as true this sentence: "(x) (x is a Christian is the true or x is a Christian is the false)," since what it apparently says of the ill-defined concept *x is a Christian* holds of any concept and thus of any concept falling within the introducing second-order concept of "x is a Christian." By the fuzz principle we can also derive the truth of "A is a Christian is the true or A is a Christian is the false," "B is a Christian is the true or B is a Christian is the false," and "C is a Christian is the true or C is a Christian is the false," despite the fact that "B is a Christian" is not determinately either true or false. The disjunction about B (better: apparently about B) has no logical relation to the disjuncts.

Frege says that the paradox of the heap results from our treating as if it were a concept what logic cannot recognise as such. The inadequate definition of "x is a heap," i.e., its not having a truth-value for every object, means that logic cannot recognise it as meaningful.[26] He does not spell out what exactly he takes the paradox of the heap to be or how ill-defined predicates lead us to it. However, it is possible to derive contradictions using "x is a heap" and applying the fuzz principle to derive what look like instances of logical laws. (Frege had discussed the logical characteristics of heaps in *Begriffsschrift* §27;[27] what he there claims is that if the property of being a heap is hereditary in his sense, "we would arrive at the result that a single bean, or even none at all, is a heap." He adds that the property is not hereditary with complete generality, since there are certain z for which *z is a heap* cannot become a judgment on account of the indeterminateness of the notion "heap." In the *Begriffsschrift*, then, the indeterminacy of the concept of a heap is not said by Frege to lead to paradox.)

If we use partially defined predicates or proper names in our inferences, it is possible to avoid trouble, but at a cost. The cost is loss of rigor, the kind of loss Frege saw in any mathematics based on conditional or piecemeal definitions. The fundamental reason for the loss of rigor is that the fuzz principle infects whatever it touches, turns what appear to be sound inferences based on a priori principles into mere simulacra of genuine inference with nothing to be said for them except that in certain *particular* cases they will not lead to trouble. But to rely on principles which in particular cases may not lead you astray is to have given up the certainty of logic.

Take the definition of "x is a Christian" as before, and consider two cases. In the first, all objects believe both p and q or neither. "x is a Christian" is therefore adequately defined; independently of context, it stands for a sharply bounded concept, i.e., a concept with the true or the false as its value for every object. In the second case, all Lithuanians believe both p and q or neither, and some Germans believe one but not the other. "x is a Christian" is in the world thus imagined only partially defined.

In what follows, the fuzz principle is applied to sentences containing "not" and to the corresponding thoughts; it will be as well to make clear how the word is used by Frege in non-fuzzy contexts. "A is not φ" will have the same sense and reference as "A is φ is not the true." "S is not the true" is true if S is some object other than the true, and is false if S is some object other than *that* (if it is other than other than the true, i.e., if it is the true). So "A is not φ" means the same as "A is φ is some object other than the true." To say of a sentence that it is not true is to say of a name that it does not stand for a particular object. If we take any sentence "'N' does not stand for M," saying of a name that it does not stand for some particular thing, it will have the same truth-value as "N is not M" only if "N" does stand for something. Thus we cannot in general, in discussing Frege's views, make any move from a sentence saying that a sentence "φ (A)" is not determinately true to a sentence saying "φ (A) is not the true." What I have said about "not" in connection with sentences corresponds to points about "not" in connection with thoughts. The only thing that needs remembering when we use redundancy operators in connection with the truth and falsity of thoughts is that we must be consistent strict Fregeans or consistent lenient ones.

What then is the contrast between the case of the complete definition of "x is a Christian" and the incomplete case? In the first case, we shall never be able to infer of an object A that (for example) A is a Christian or is not unless the thoughts that A is a Christian and that A is not both have determinate truth-value (are thoughts in the narrower sense). Let us turn now to the second case, and suppose that from the thought associated with "(x)[x is a Lithuanian ⊃ (x is a Christian or x is not a Christian)]" (true by the fuzz principle) and the true thought that A is a Lithuanian we infer that A is a Christian or is not. *That* will count as true by the fuzz principle, and one or other of "A is a Christian" or "A is not a Christian" will in fact also count as true by the fuzz principle and the other will count as false. But all is nevertheless not well. For "(x)[x is a German ⊃ (x is a Christian or x is not a Christian)]" also counts as true by the fuzz principle. From the thought associated with that sentence and the true thought that B is a German, we shall be able to infer, as with our Lithuanian, the thought associated with the sentence "B is a Christian or is not." Unfortunately B believes p but not q, and neither "B is a Christian" nor "B is not a Christian" has a determinate truth-value; the corresponding thoughts lack truth-value, or can, on the strict view, be said not to be thoughts proper. Since the method of inference was exactly the same as with A the Lithuanian, what the result in the case of B shows is that the method itself is at fault. Since the inference involving B is a misleading simulacrum of an inference, we have no business—if we are going in for logical inference—allowing an exactly comparable case involving Lithuanians. The fact that the method will not lead us into trouble if we stick to Lithuanians is in no way internal to it as a method. We have here thread-and-knot logic: principles of 'inference' which work in *some* cases. We can, by attention to particular cases, show that these methods of inference can be treated as guides to thinking what is true in some cases. But that is exactly what logical laws are *not*.

What I am trying to show in all this is why Frege thought that if we define mathematical function terms for numbers only, and then go on to make inferences using such ill-defined expressions, mathematics will lose its rigor. But it may be helpful if I press on further with the Lithuanians. There is a sort of *illusion* of rigor that is possible in the mathematical case, an illusion Frege was trying to remove; we can see what is at stake if we subject ourselves to the corresponding illusion in the case of the Lithuanians. In discussing it, I shall answer a possible objection to what I have already said about them.

We may think that we can argue in this way: Lithuanians all believe both p and q or neither. Hence by the definition of "x is a Christian," it is determinately true or false of *every* Lithuanian that he or she is a Christian. Thus an inference from the thought associated with "(x)[x is a Lithuanian ⊃ (x is a Christian or x is not a Christian)]" and the thought that A is a Lithuanian to the thought associated with "A is a Christian or A is not" has a justification that the corresponding inference about a German would lack. We think then that there is a contrast between the status of "Every Lithuanian is a Christian or is not" and "Every German is a Christian or is not." The fuzz principle enables us to say that the latter is true despite the fact that in the case of some Germans the sentences ascribing Christianity to them are not determinately true or false—but, we think, we do not have that problem with the statement about the Lithuanians.

The illusion is that there is a genuine contrast here, that reasoning from the truth about Lithuanians, that each is or is not a Christian, is unproblematic, because it is an honest truth, as it were. But what is true by the fuzz principle *cannot* be made honest; there is only an illusion that the thought associated with "Every Lithuanian is a Christian or is not" rests on some firmer foundation than the thought associated with "Every German is a Christian or is not" and thus *can* support the weight of inference as the thought about Germans cannot. The fundamental illusion is that there is a logical relation between the sentence "A is a Christian" and the sentences "A is a Christian or A is not a Christian" and "(x)[x is a Lithuanian ⊃ (x is a Christian or x is not a Christian)]," dependent on the presence in all three of the same predicate. A logical relation between sentences depends on what their logical parts are. We *have* to use the fuzz principle (or some principle sharing its fundamental features, of which more below) to assign any truth-value to a sentence saying anything about what objects are or are not Christians. And once it is used, it eradicates the logical complexity of the sentences to which it is applied. "A is a Christian," "A is a Christian or A is not a Christian," and "(x)[x is a Lithuanian ⊃ (x is a Christian or x is not a Christian)]" do not—any of them—contain as logical parts the predicate "x is a Christian." A logical part has a role in sentences independent of particular contexts; "x is a Christian" does not. The fuzz principle, which must be used in order to assign a truth-value to "Every Lithuanian is a Christian or is not" prevents there being any more logical justification for it than for "Every German is a Christian or is not." The justification for calling each true is the *same:* all the concepts falling within the introducing concept of "x is a Christian" make both sentences come out true. The fact is that you will not get into trouble with the one and you will with the other, but we have ceased to infer by anything remotely resembling logical laws if we attend to which *particular* cases give trouble. "But every Lithuanian really and truly *is* a Christian or is not! and that is *not* really true of the Germans!" The illusion has great force. But as far as I can see, the recognition of it as an illusion is essential in grasping the force of Frege's thought about definition.

The relevant point about the Lithuanians has been merely that a certain partially defined predicate has a value whenever it is completed by the name of a Lithuanian—and so what I have said about Lithuanians can be said about numbers. There is only the illusion of mathematics as an a priori science if it is infested with partial definitions, definitions of function terms with values fixed only for numbers, or for some subclass or classes of numbers. No mathematical proof containing a partially defined function term can be rigorous. It will contain assertions of what are merely fuzzy truths, truths that can stand in no genuine logical relations with other truths. (There is a relatively unimportant exception to that point if we follow Frege in allowing logically simple proper names, which is what fuzzily true or false sentences are, to play the same role in inferences as genuinely complex sentences.) We shall have in mathematics the *imitation* of rigor and shall always be dependent on our good angel to avoid logical disaster.[28]

The fuzz principle creates logical havoc for what is essentially a simple reason. It lets us treat sentences containing a partially introduced proper name as having a truth-value when it does not matter to the truth-value of the whole sentence *which* object, of those falling under the introducing concept, we speak of. We go along with the fiction as it were, that we are speaking of *a particular object* in those cases in which our actually picking out one rather than another particular object, from those falling under the introducing concept, and meaning *it*, would make no difference to truth-value. And so one of the things the fuzz principle will allow us to do is to say that our pretend-object has whatever it belongs to objects as such to have. Similarly for partially defined predicates and other function terms. The fuzz principle allows us to go along with a fiction there too, as of there being some function we meant, in those cases in which it would not matter to the truth-value of our sentences *which* of the particular functions falling within the introducing second-order concept of our function term we decided to mean. And so, among the sentences we shall be allowed by the fuzz principle to treat as true are those sentences ascribing to our pretend-function what it belongs to functions as such to have. Because the fuzz principle allows us to treat pretend-objects and pretend-functions as if they had what characterizes objects and functions as such, it will let us call true sentences which look as if they are instances of logical laws; for what a genuine instance of a logical law does is ascribe to objects or functions of various sorts or both what it belongs to objects and functions as such to have (more precisely, in the case of functions, what it belongs to functions of whatever sort to have as functions of that sort). Exactly what our pseudo-objects and pseudo-functions do *not* genuinely have—the logical character of objects and functions—the fuzz principle will allow us to say that they *do* have.

In logical inference we derive the judgment that a thought is true from judgments that our premise-thoughts are true, relying only on the fact that the functions and objects of the premise-thoughts are functions (of such-and-such sorts) and objects. The thought which we associate as a whole with a sentence whose truth-value is derived through the fuzz principle has not got functions and objects, in the sense in which I spoke of the functions and objects of a thought. That is because the sentence with which it is associated has not got logical parts; it itself is not properly speaking *a* thought but a blur of thoughts. We may then, if we do not heed Frege's warnings, treat such a thought as a 'premise', with or without other premises. What encourages us in this is that the fuzz principle will allow us to treat as true sentences which appear to be instances of the logical laws, containing the ill-defined proper names or function terms of our original sentence; such apparent instances-of-logical-laws provide us with further blurry thoughts to use in carrying out inferences from our premises. These will enable us to bring to bear on our premises logical characteristics which thoughts have as thoughts, dependent on their functions and objects being functions and objects. We shall, in our imitation instances-of-logical-laws be bringing to bear on our imitation thoughts principles of logical relationship characteristic of genuine thoughts. A proper inference draws, as I said, only on the character of the premise-thoughts as genuine thoughts, thoughts proper; the fundamental thing that the fuzz principle does is to allow us to ignore the fact that the 'thought' associated with a sentence is not a genuine thought. Since inference is nothing but a procedure dependent on the character of our thoughts as genuine particular thoughts, it lies in the nature of the fuzz principle that we can use it to create a repulsive simulacrum of logical inference. The particular kind of fuzz principle we use is irrelevant. There can be principles assigning truth and falsity to sentences with partially defined terms differing from our fuzz principle, but they must share the fundamental character with which it destroys the certainty of inference. A fuzz principle by its nature must treat what are not references to functions and objects as if they were, while the applicability of the laws of inference to what we say depends on our terms referring to functions and objects.

Conclusions

I have tried to show in some detail what Frege's views on inadequate definitions are and how they are related to his theory of inference. I have expounded the views on definition in such a way as to make plain that they are not dependent on allowing "sense" to be used generously, i.e., on allowing that terms with no reference may *unqualifiedly* be said to have sense. The integration of the views on definition with those on inference makes it natural to stick to a strict use of "sense," allowing only that there are second-class and derivative ways of speaking of sense in general and thoughts in particular, to be kept miles away from the serious business of science.

I have, in expounding Frege's views, stuck to the language and ideas of Frege-of-the-1890s. But Frege-of-the-1880s is as keen on the full definition of concepts as he was later: "All that can be demanded of a concept from the point of view of logic and with an eye to rigor of proof is only that the limits to its application should be sharp, that we should be able to decide definitely about every object whether it falls under that concept or not."[29] The demand for full definition is not dependent on the distinction between sense and reference nor on the treatment of sentences as names of truth-values. The demand for full definition is a demand for identity of content in the different occurrences of an expression (of an expression of a sort to have content), an identity dependent in the case of a predicate on the full definition of the concept which the predicate has as its *content* in the 1880s and as its *referent* in the 1890s. (It is more precisely a matter not of identity but of what is analogous to it, in the case of the content or referent of a predicate.) So, although I have used the 1890s language, much of the discussion can be carried on in the language of the 1880s.

I have had in mind several points of relation to the work of Wittgenstein. Two should be mentioned. First, in the sections of *Philosophical Investigations* leading up to §71, we find Wittgenstein rejecting his own earlier view and Frege's about the need for sharply defined terms. What is going on in those sections cannot be clear unless we fully grasp the force of the earlier position, fully understand why Frege nags and nags at the mathematicians, why he harps on the need for sharply bounded concepts and fully defined functions. The matter goes to the heart of our understanding of what logic is.

Secondly, I have tried to bring out features of Frege's view which are of direct concern to Wittgenstein in the *Tractatus*. I have had that especially in mind in showing the two sides, external and internal, of the introduction of expressions. It is *external* to the introduction of an expression not only that it fixes its reference but also that it fixes full-blooded sense, sense which is a mode of presentation of something (so that if the something is missing, what is left is only a mock-presentation). If the expression is to occur in sentences serving to express the premises or conclusions of inferences, it must have reference. In whatever way our terms have been introduced, something *else* is necessary—the realm of reference must have certain characteristics—if logic can be brought to bear on sentences containing those terms. If our sentences are to express thoughts proper, certain things must be the case: there must be in the realm of reference such-and-such objects, concepts, and so on. And it is not internal to the way terms are introduced that these things should be the case. For everything internal to the fixing of our terms might be the same, but if the realm of reference were different, logic and language might be unglued from each other. It has been one of my aims to bring out this externality of the application of logic to language on Frege's view, for the sake of making clearer the connections with the *Tractatus.*

Notes

1. I have benefited greatly from comments by Michael Resnik and Thomas Ricketts.
2. *Translations from the Philosophical Writings of Gottlob Frege,* ed. P. T. Geach and Max Black (Oxford, 1966), pp. 33, 159, 170; G. Frege, *Posthumous Writings,* ed. Hans Hermes et al. (Oxford and Chicago, 1979), p. 155; G. Frege, *Philosophical and Mathematical Correspondence,* ed. Gottfried Gabriel et al. (Oxford, 1980), pp. 114–5, 125. All references in the text to Frege's *Grundgesetze* are to the selections in *Translations from the Philosophical Writings.*
3. M. Dummett, *Frege: Philosophy of Language* (London, 1973), pp. 160–71.
4. Or, rather, took him to have. Dummett may have changed his mind: see M. Dummett, *The Interpretation of Frege's Philosophy* (London 1981), p. 34, but also p. 134.
5. *Translations from the Philosophical Writings,* p. 159.
6. M. Dummett, *Frege: Philosophy of Language,* p. 179.
7. G. Frege, *The Foundations of Arithmetic,* trans. J. L. Austin (Oxford, 1974), p. 73.
8. M. Dummett, op. cit., p. 160.
9. ibid.
10. op. cit., p. 229.
11. *Translations from the Philosophical Writings,* p. 167.
12. G. Frege, *Posthumous Writings,* p. 122.
13. *Translations from the Philosophical Writings,* pp. 170–1.
14. G. Evans, *Varieties of Reference* (Oxford and New York, 1982), pp. 14, 28–30.
15. Evans refers (p. 14) to "Sense and Reference," pp. 62–3 (in *Translations*) and to Frege's *Posthumous Writings,* pp. 191, 225. Cf. also further references in Evans, p. 28.
16. For some of the arguments, see Evans, pp. 22–30.
17. See especially Frege, *Posthumous Writings,* p. 130.
18. op. cit., p. 255; *Translations,* p. 123.
19. *Translations,* p. 159.

20. G. Frege, *Wißenschaftliche Briefwechsel*, ed. Gottfried Gabriel et al. (Hamburg, 1976), p. 236. The English version (*Philosophical and Mathematical Correspondence*, p. 115) is slightly altered in sense.

21. *Translations*, p. 169.

22. *Philosophical and Mathematical Correspondence*, p. 115.

23. *Posthumous Writings*, pp. 242–3; cf. also *Philosophical and Mathematical Correspondence*, p. 114.

24. *Posthumous Writings*, pp. 178–9.

25. *Philosophical and Mathematical Correspondence*, pp. 114–15.

26. *Posthumous Writings*, p. 155; *Philosophical and Mathematical Correspondence*, pp. 114–5.

27. In J. van Heijenoort, ed. *From Frege to Gödel* (Cambridge, Massachusetts, 1967), p. 62.

28. Cf. Wittgenstein, *Remarks on the Foundations of Mathematics*, ed. G. H. von Wright et al. (Oxford, 1956), p. 171.

29. *Foundations of Arithmetic*, p. 79.

Chapter 6

Throwing Away the Ladder: How to Read the *Tractatus*

Whether one is reading Wittgenstein's *Tractatus* or his later writings, one must be struck by his insistence that he is not putting forward philosophical doctrines or theses; or by his suggestion that it cannot be done, that it is only through some confusion one is in about what one is doing that one could take oneself to be putting forward philosophical doctrines or theses at all. I think that there is almost nothing in Wittgenstein which is of value and which can be grasped if it is pulled away from that view of philosophy. But that view of philosophy is itself something that has to be seen first in the *Tractatus* if it is to be understood in its later forms, and in the *Tractatus* it is inseparable from what is central there, the distinction between what can be said and what can only be shown.

Now what about that distinction? Peter Geach has written that it has its source in "the great works of Frege," in Frege's discussion of contrasts like that between function and object. The difference between function and object comes out in language, but Frege, as is well known, held that there are insuperable problems in any attempt to put that difference properly into words. We cannot properly speaking say what the difference is, but it is reflected in features of language; and what holds of the difference between function and object holds too of other distinctions of logical category. Geach is right that we can best understand what the *Tractatus* holds about saying and showing if we go back to Frege and think about what the saying/showing distinction in its origin looks like there. Geach actually makes a stronger claim: he says that "a great deal of the *Tractatus* is best understood as a refashioning of Frege's function-and-argument analysis in order to remove [from it the] mistaken treatment of sentences as complex names."[1]

That last point of Geach's, about how to understand the *Tractatus*, splits into two points if you think about it. Wittgenstein is trying to hold on to Frege's insight that there are distinctions of logical category, like that between functions and objects, or between first and second level functions, which cannot be put into words but which are reflected in distinctions between the signs for what is in one category and the signs for what is in the other. He wants to hold on to that, and at the same time to get rid of the assimilation of sentences to proper names. So for Wittgenstein a sentence will count as a wholly different sort of linguistic item from a proper name or any other kind of name. But if you are holding on to Frege's insight that fundamental differences in kinds of linguistic expression are the way fundamental differences in reality show themselves, differences in reality that cannot be put into words—and if you are also saying, against Frege, that sentences are a wholly different linguistic category from any kind of name, that will make sense if you are also saying that there are features of reality that can come out only in sentences, in their being the particular kind of sign they are, in contrast with names.

Here, then, is how Geach's point splits into two:

(1) In the *Tractatus* treatment of Frege's insight, sentences are no longer assimilated to complex names.
(2) Making that break, separating sentences off that way from names, is linked with the possibility of treating the distinctive features of sentences as reflections of features of reality, features that can only be reflected in sentences and that cannot themselves be *said* to be features of reality. Such a treatment of sentences would then be radically different from Frege's, but could nevertheless be said to be deeply Fregean in spirit and inspired by Frege.

Geach himself gives some detail of what is involved in Wittgenstein's getting rid of the assimilation of sentences to names; but he has rather less on what I have just been talking about: the applying of Frege's insight to sentences by taking their distinctive and essential characteristics to be the reflection of something in the nature of things that cannot be put into words.[2] But now to get back to where I was at the beginning: if we want to know why Wittgenstein thinks that there cannot (in some sense) be philosophical doctrines, we need to see the apparent doctrines of the *Tractatus* as they will look if we go further down the road that Geach points out as a road. That is, we need to see what kind of sign Wittgenstein took a sentence to be and how, by being that kind of sign, it can show things that cannot be said. But there is something that has to be done first. And one convenient way of doing it is to go back to Geach.

I have so far followed Geach in his way of putting the Frege insight. As he puts it, various *features of reality* come out in language but it cannot be said in language that reality has those features. Geach is here following both Frege and Wittgenstein in an important respect. Wittgenstein, throughout the *Tractatus*. when he speaks about what shows itself but cannot be said, speaks of these things as features of reality. *There is*, he says, what cannot be put into words. Propositions and reality have something in common that cannot be put into words. Even the linguistic form *"what* cannot be put into words," the words *"das Unsagbare," "das Undenkbare"*—such ways of talking refer, or must seem to, to features of reality that cannot be put in words or captured in thought. Frege, in speaking of the distinction between first and second level functions, describes it as founded deep in the nature of things;[3] and it is evident that he would say exactly the same about the distinction between function and object. There is a question how to take this sort of talk: the use of words like "reality," "the nature of things," "what there is," and so on, in specifying what cannot be put into words. The problem is particularly acute in Wittgenstein, given the passage at the end of the *Tractatus* (6.54): "whoever understands me eventually recognizes [my propositions] as nonsensical, when he has used them—as steps—to climb up beyond them. (He must, so to speak, throw away the ladder after he has climbed up it.)" The problem is how seriously we can take that remark, and in particular whether it can be applied to the point (in whatever way it is put) that some *features of reality* cannot be put into words.

Let me illustrate the problem this way. One thing which according to the *Tractatus* shows itself but cannot be expressed in language is what Wittgenstein speaks of as *the logical form of reality.* So it looks as if there is this whatever-it-is, the logical form of reality, some essential feature of reality, which reality has all right, but which we cannot say or think that it has. What exactly is supposed to be left of that, after we have thrown away the ladder? Are we going to keep the idea that there is something or other in reality that we gesture at, however badly, when we speak of 'the logical form of reality', so that *it, what* we were gesturing at, is there but cannot be expressed in words?

That is what I want to call chickening out. What counts as not chickening out is then this, roughly: to throw the ladder away is, among other things, to throw away in the end the attempt to take seriously the language of 'features of reality'. To read Wittgenstein himself as not chickening out is to say that it is not, not really, his view that there are features of reality that cannot be put into words but show themselves. What *is* his view is that that way of talking may be useful or even for a time essential, but it is in the end to be let go of and honestly taken to be real nonsense, plain nonsense, which we are not in the end to think of as corresponding to an ineffable truth. To speak of features of reality in connection with what shows itself in language is to use a very odd kind of figurative language. That goes also for "*what* shows itself."

This last point is extremely important for the issue what it is for there supposedly not to be philosophical doctrines. That is, I am contrasting two ways of taking the idea that there are no philosophical doctrines, as that idea appears in the *Tractatus*. You can read the *Tractatus* as containing numerous doctrines which Wittgenstein holds cannot be put into words, so they do not really count as doctrines: they do not have what counts as sense according to the doctrines in the *Tractatus* about what has sense. If you read the *Tractatus* this way, you think that, after the ladder is thrown away, you are left holding on to some truths about reality, while at the same time denying that you are actually *saying* anything about reality. Or, in contrast, you can say that the notion of something true of reality but not sayably true is to be used only with the awareness that it itself belongs to what has to be thrown away. One is not left with it at the end, after recognizing what the *Tractatus* has aimed at getting one to recognize.

That is very abstract and in need of some kind of illustration. Let me take the case that Geach was concerned with: the distinction between function and object. The case is from Frege but it is useful as an example of the general point. We can indeed say that for Frege it is a fundamental feature of reality that there is that distinction; it is founded in the nature of things. But is there a way of getting beyond that way of talking? Of using it as a ladder and then throwing it away? That distinction between function and object is reflected in language in what Frege speaks of as the *in*completeness of the sign for a function and the completeness of a proper name, which is the sign for an object. A proper name has no gap for an expression for an argument, whereas a sign for a function has gaps for one or more expressions for arguments of one or more kinds, one kind of argument-expression per argument place. It is not up to us to choose whether we shall have a language in which whenever there is a function-expression it will be incomplete. A language may be badly designed from the logical point of view, in which case the distinction between the signs for functions and the proper names will not be marked in a way that is easy to see. Suppose, though, that we become familiar with a well-designed language, in which the distinction between the signs is clearly visible. We may come to say, in grasping the logical point of the general distinction in that language between proper names and (for example) signs for first-level functions of one argument, that there is a distinction between such functions and objects and *it* is what comes out in that difference in the signs; and yet we shall recognize at the same time that we cannot go on thinking of it as a fundamental distinction between functions and objects. Seeing what it is for that notation to be well designed is seeing what it is to talk about a function or functions; it is to *use* expressions in a certain way. To refer to a function, that is, is to *use* a sign with a characteristic kind of incompleteness, and to predicate something of a function is to use a sign with its own further kind of incompleteness. And when we try to say *that* there is a distinction between functions and objects, we see that we are not *there using* language to talk about functions at all, because we are not there using signs of the distinctive sorts through which functions are spoken about and characterized. "There is a distinction between functions and objects, and it comes out in the clear difference between signs for functions and those for objects in a well-designed notation": that is what you could call a 'transitional' remark. There is a transition to be made, after which the word "function" will have no place in the philosophical vocabulary because it is not needed: there is no work it is needed for. Something else does whatever job there genuinely is for a predicate like "function" to do, the something else being the general logical features of signs standing for functions. A remark like "There is a fundamental distinction between functions and objects" is thrown out once we get the predicate "function" out of the cleaned up philosophical vocabulary. We are left after the transition with a logical notation that in a sense has to speak for itself. If we try afterwards to say why it is a good notation, we know that we shall find ourselves saying things which may help our listeners, but which we ourselves cannot regard as the expression of any true thought, speakable or unspeakable. When we say why the notation is a good one, when we explain what logical distinctions and similarities it makes perspicuous, we are in a sense going backwards, back to the stage at which we had been when grasping the point of the transition.

We can then look at some of Frege's logical work as providing replacements for certain parts of the philosophical vocabulary, in particular, predicates like "function," "concept," "relation." These are replaced by features of a notation designed to make logical similarities and differences clear. For Wittgenstein the provision of replacements for terms in the philosophical vocabulary is not an incidental achievement but a principal aim, and, more important, it is the *whole* philosophical vocabulary which is to be replaced, including that of the *Tractatus* itself.

Let me say more about this difference between Frege and Wittgenstein. Frege thought that a contemporary of his, Benno Kerry, was confused. Kerry had said that there were concepts that can also be objects, and that when, for example, we say that the concept *horse* is a concept easily attained, the concept *horse* is an object, one which falls under the concept *concept easily attained*. On Frege's view, the idea that we can say of a concept that it is a concept easily attained, or that it is a concept at all, just reflects confusion. The predicate "concept" cannot be predicated of any concept: we think we want it in order to say things about concepts, but to think that it will enable us to do so is confusion, confusion about what a concept is.[4] Wittgenstein thought that the *whole* philosophical vocabulary reflected confusion. We are all Benno Kerrys through and through. It is not that we are confused about what a concept is and what it is for us to be referring to a concept; it is that we are confused about what saying something is, what thinking something is. We are confused about the relation between logic and what we say and think; we are confused about what it is for some of what we say to be possible and some necessary and some impossible. The very words "possible" and "necessary" and "impossible" themselves are characteristic indications of lack of clarity, in just the way any attempt to use "concept" seriously as a first order predicate, as Benno Kerry did, is an indication of lack of clarity. What Wittgenstein wants to do is then to describe a way of writing sentences, a way of translating ordinary sentences into a completely perspicuous form. As part of the transition to grasping what is thus made clear, we may say such things as that the possibility of a state of affairs is not something that you can say but that it shows itself in signs with such-and-such general characteristics. But once the transition is made, the analyzed sentences must in a sense speak for themselves, and we should not any longer be telling ourselves that *now* we grasp what possibility is, it is *what* shows itself, *what* comes out, in a sentence's having a sense. We are left using ordinary sentences, and we shall genuinely have got past the attempt to represent to ourselves something in reality, the possibility of what a sentence says being so, as not sayable but shown by the sentence. We shall genuinely have thrown the ladder away.

The whole of Wittgenstein's philosophy, from before the *Tractatus* to his later work, contains different workings out of the kind of view of philosophy itself that I have just sketched. I do not want to play down the differences between early and later work. It obviously marks a great change in Wittgenstein's views that he got rid of the idea that you can replace philosophical thinking by carrying out a kind of complete analysis of sentences in which the essential features of sentence sense as such are totally visible. But what does remain intact after that idea goes is the conviction that philosophy involves illusion of a particular kind. John McDowell, in speaking of the kind of philosophical illusion from which Wittgenstein in his later work tries to free us, uses the phrase "the view from sideways on" to characterize what we aim for, or think we need to aim for, in philosophy. We have, for example, the idea of ourselves as looking, from sideways on, at the human activity of following a rule, and as asking from that position whether there is or is not something *objectively* determined as what the rule requires to be done at the next application. To think of the question in that way is to try to step outside our ordinary saying what a rule requires, our ordinary criticisms of steps taken by others, our ordinary ways of judging whether someone has grasped what a rule requires. We do not want to ask and answer those ordinary questions, but to ask what in reality there is to justify the answers we give when we are unselfconsciously inside the ordinary practice. McDowell takes Wittgenstein to have tried to show us how to come out of the intellectual illusion that we are thus asking anything.[5] My point now is that that image of McDowell's is useful in characterizing Wittgenstein's early view of philosophy as well. And I want to trace it back even further to how Frege leads us to see poor old Benno Kerry, who only wanted to look at concepts sideways on. In the *Tractatus*, the idea of the illusory view from sideways on has a very particular form. When we philosophize we try as it were to occupy a position in which we are outside logic, where logic is that through which we say all the things we ordinarily say, all the things that can be said.

That brings me back to Geach's original point, that we should see a great deal of the *Tractatus* as a refashioning of Frege's insight to avoid Frege's assimilation of sentences to complex names. I said that that point itself splits into two, and I now want to modify it; I shall have to use the 'transitional' vocabulary, the before-you-throw-away-the-ladder mode of speaking, to do so. Wittgenstein departs from Frege not only in treating sentences as a distinct linguistic category from names; he not only applies Frege's insight in an un-Fregean way by claiming that it is in the distinctive essential features of sentences as signs that certain essential features of reality show themselves; he *also* tries to make clear in his account of the kind of sign a sentence is a characteristic and un-Fregean view of logic. Logic will belong to the kind of sign ordinary sentences are, and if that can really be made clear, it will be clear also that in speaking philosophically, we are confusedly trying to station ourselves outside our normal practice of saying how things are, trying to station ourselves "outside the world, outside logic." So what Wittgenstein is doing in the *Tractatus* should be seen this way: he is holding on to Frege's insight, but, against Frege, taking it that sentence signs as distinct from other signs reflect certain features of reality; he is treating an account of the kind of sign ordinary sentences are as including an account of logic very different in important respects from Frege's, deeply critical of Frege's, and capable of being used as a footing for a fundamental criticism of all philosophical thinking.

II

What kind of sign, then, is a sentence? Wittgenstein says that a sentence is a fact, not a name. As it stands, that is a dark saying: dark, because by calling a sentence a fact, Wittgenstein meant that it was logically articulated. But for Frege, too, a sentence, and any complex name, is logically articulated. Since Wittgenstein plainly intends a contrast with Frege's view, what exactly is the contrast?

Let me put that question alongside some others. I have so far given a version of Geach's recipe for understanding the *Tractatus*. Read Frege, and read more Frege. And reflect on Frege. Then take sentences out of the category of complex names, make further changes to accommodate that fundamental shift, and you will thus get a great many of the characteristic *Tractatus* views. Where, it might be asked, does Russell come in? Or is his influence to be regarded as so secondary that the *Tractatus* can be understood without one's having to grasp the relation of any of its main points to Russell's work? Again, the theory of descriptions seems to play a significant role in Wittgenstein's thought. But *what* role? It is hardly as if commentators on Wittgenstein agree on the answer to that.

Here is a separate question. Wittgenstein says that all philosophy is a 'critique of language', and adds that the credit is due to Russell for having shown that the apparent logical form of a sentence need not be its real form. This should seem a slightly odd remark, given that Wittgenstein had a higher opinion of Frege's works than of Russell's, and it would surely seem that Frege should be given the credit for making clear the distinction between apparent logical form and real logical form. Had that not been one main purpose of Frege's *Begriffsschrift*? The question could also be put this way. In his remark giving credit to Russell, Wittgenstein is partially specifying what it means to call philosophy a critique of language. But, given what Frege had accomplished as a critique of language, why does Wittgenstein explain what kind of critique of language he has in mind by appeal to Russell?

My three questions have to be answered together. To see what is meant by calling a sentence a fact and not a name, we have to see what Wittgenstein got from Russell. To answer the question what

Wittgenstein got from the theory of descriptions, we have to see how, as Wittgenstein understood it, it involved a sharp logical distinction between a sentence on the one hand, and a sign that could stand for something in a sentence on the other. And, finally, the reason Wittgenstein gives *Russell* the credit for showing that the apparent logical form of a sentence need not be its real form is that in the theory of descriptions, the revealing of logical form is tied to the logical form of sentences as such, or what Wittgenstein saw as that form. Frege may indeed have shown that ordinary language conceals the logical characteristics of the thoughts expressed in it. But, as Wittgenstein saw Frege's accomplishment in contrast to Russell's, Frege's clarifications of logical form left in the dark the logical features distinctive of the expression of thought as such, the logical features of *sentences*. Putting this last point another way: you can look for the real logical form of a sentence only if you are clear what kind of sign a sentence is. You can look for the real logical form of a particular sentence or group of sentences only by exercising your grasp of what the general form of sentence is. As Wittgenstein read Russell, Russell had an implicit grasp of what was crucial; and Frege, for all his colossal accomplishments, did not.

Wittgenstein said that he, like Frege and Russell, regarded a sentence as a function of the expressions in it—and that point helps me draw my three questions closer still. To see what is meant by calling a sentence a fact and not a name will be to see what *kind* of function a sentence is of the expressions contained in it. But how do you make clear what kind of function it is? You provide a method of analysis of sentences, a way of rewriting them. As Wittgenstein sees it, what it is for Frege and Russell respectively to regard sentences as functions of the expressions in them is shown in the different ways in which they rewrite sentences in logical notation. What Wittgenstein saw in the theory of descriptions, then, was a method of analysis of sentences, a way of rewriting them, which made their kind of functionality clear. And because Frege's logical notation, although it is intended to show the real logical form of the sentences written in it, reflects what Wittgenstein takes to be a wrong view of the kind of function a sentence is, he gives Russell the credit for distinguishing the real from the apparent logical form of sentences. In what follows I shall not discuss so much what it is for a sentence to be a fact as what kind of function it is in contrast with the kind of function it is for Frege. A full account of why Wittgenstein says that sentences are facts would take me too far out of the way. And when I talk about the theory of descriptions, I mean it as looked at by Wittgenstein, not as understood by Russell.

What Russell actually does with sentences containing definite descriptions can be said to be the reverse of what Frege does. Frege looks at such sentences and regards them functionally. The definite description itself has no argument place within it and is thus suited to be in the argument place of first order predicates and relation terms. The truth or falsity of the whole sentences in which it occurs must then depend on what holds of the object satisfying the description. The functional analysis of sentences, in Frege's hands, is totally incompatible with allowing truth or falsity, or even some invented third truth value, to sentences which contain an empty definite description.[6] Russell goes in the opposite direction. Instead of moving *from* the functional analysis of the sentence *to* its necessarily not having a truth value if it contains an empty definite description, he goes—or so it seems—*from* the truth value the sentence has in those circumstances *to* a more complex functional analysis in which the definite description itself disappears, does not have the role of standing for an argument, or picking out that thing on whose properties the truth or falsity of the sentence depends. So he treats the question what the right functional analysis of the sentence is as in an important sense secondary. You cannot, if you are Russell, answer the question whether the definite description genuinely has the role of providing an argument, unless you are able to answer the *prior* question whether the sentence has a truth value when the definite description is empty. Russell's procedure is clearest in a striking passage in *Principia Mathematica*. He there claims that the sentence "The round square does not exist" is true, despite the fact that the grammatical subject does not exist. He goes on: "Whenever the grammatical subject of a proposition can be supposed not to exist without rendering the proposition meaningless, it is plain that the grammatical subject is not a proper name, *i.e.* not a name directly representing some object. Thus in all such cases, the proposition must be capable of being so analysed that what was the grammatical subject shall have disappeared."[7]

What I am interested in, then, is the contrast with Frege's procedure. That is, it is true that Frege and Russell have different views about what the right analysis is of sentences with definite descriptions, but I am focusing on a different disagreement: their different mode of arriving at their answers. Thinking about that difference made me see that Part I of this paper contains something misleading. I said there, following Geach, that we should see as the big change Wittgenstein made in what he took over from Frege that he gave up the idea of sentences as complex names. That is an idea of Frege's that you do not get in his early work. You get it after 1890; you do not get it in *The Foundations of Arithmetic,* in 1884. But, and this is what I realized, although Frege's views changed a great deal in that period, they did not change in their fundamental difference from Russell's. The kind of function Frege thought a sentence was does not change in one fundamental respect over that period, and it is *that,* and not whether or not the sentence is explicitly regarded as a complex name, that Wittgenstein rejects. He rejects a kind of functional view of a sentence when he says that sentences are not names, but the kind of functional view in question is present in Frege prior to his idea that sentences are names and goes deeper down in the Fregean structure of views. The view I mean is present in *The Foundations of Arithmetic,* in Frege's taking it that a complex designation appearing on one side of the equal sign in a mathematical equation has the role of designating an object, an argument, and that therefore we cannot put into such a place a sign which we have not shown *does* stand for something.[8] Here we see the procedure which goes in the opposite direction from Russell's. Frege starts with the equal sign and its argument-places, as determining the logical role of the complex name; Russell argues on other grounds that the complex name has no logical role of its own, and thus concludes that even when it looks as if it must designate an object, it need not do so for the equation or identity in which it appears to have a truth value.

Wittgenstein then sees Russell's treatment of sentences in the theory of descriptions this way: if they are going to say something true or false, their doing so is not dependent on whether any definite description they may contain is satisfied. The sentence's having a truth value at all is not the kind of thing that the satisfaction or emptiness of definite descriptions can affect. That then is putting into words what is better looked at as built into what Russell actually does. He *treats* sentences as having a kind of functionality different from that of complex names. That is, suppose that there is no such person as Beethoven's only half-sister, then there is no one who is the *father* of Beethoven's only half-sister. And that is reflected in language. If the description "Beethoven's only half-sister" is empty, then complex names in which *it* occurs are also empty and do not denote anyone. So that is the kind of functionality a complex name has. And Russell treats sentences as having a kind of functionality unlike that: their capacity to say what is true or false he treats as unlike the capacity of a complex name to denote something: he treats it as independent of the satisfaction of definite descriptions in it.

I need now to turn to one further feature of Russell's analysis of sentences with definite descriptions. Russell takes a sentence containing a definite description, say "the present king of France," and shows us how to rewrite it. The rewritten sentence does two things. Its having a truth value is clearly independent of the truth or falsity of the sentences saying that there is a present king of France and that there is no more than one present king of France. And at the same time the rewritten sentence clarifies the real functional character of the original sentence. The original sentence says whatever it does say in virtue of its functional character, which is shown to us through its logical relation to the analyzed sentence. Its functional character can thus be seen to leave it having a truth value independently of the truth value of two other sentences, those saying that there is at least one king of France, and that there is no more than one. What sign the original sentence is—what function of what parts—is inseparable from the capacity it has (shown clearly when it is analyzed) to keep its truth-valuedness independently of the truth or falsity of those two sentences.

Further, Wittgenstein accepted a version of Russell's account of the quantifiers.[9] He read it as enabling us to go on with a sort of analysis that shares the essential feature of the Russellian analysis of definite descriptions. In such an analysis we make clear at one and the same time two things: first, how our sentence is constructed, as what function of what expressions, and, secondly, that our sentence is a sign that maintains truth-valuedness over the range of truth *or* falsity of some set of sentences. If we take the sentence "The present king of France is bald" in its analyzed version, including quantifiers, we can go on to analyze it. We shall see it as containing sentences saying of this individual and that one . . . that it is a king of France, and at the same time we shall see that the quantified sentence retains truth-valuedness whatever the truth or falsity may be of any sentence saying of an individual that it is a king of France. This further step then deepens our understanding of the *original* sentence's functionality: it shows us more clearly *what* sentence it is at the same time as it shows us that the sentence maintains truth-valuedness independently of what the truth value is of any of a range (now enlarged) of sentences.

What is coming out here, as seen by Wittgenstein, is that a sentence is a sort of sign such that *which* sign it is of that general sort is tied to its maintaining truth-valuedness throughout any variation in truth values of some range of sentences.

Let me put that slightly differently. Russell's original sort of analysis goes *some way* to letting us see what sign a sentence is, of the general sort to which sentences as such belong, by showing how it maintains truth-valuedness throughout variations in truth value of a particular range of sentences, whose falsity we might have thought deprived it of any truth value. We get still clearer what sign a sentence is, what function of what expressions, if we are able to write it so that its truth-valuedness is shown to be independent of variations in truth value of some enlarged range of sentences. We should make *entirely* clear what sentence a sentence was, what its functionality was, if we were able to write it so that its truth-valuedness could be seen to be independent of the truth or falsity of any other sentence.

But that, as it stands, will not quite do. We need to see Russellian analysis, or its basic principle, extended in a different direction. The principle of Russellian analysis, as seen by Wittgenstein, is that the functional character of a sentence is grasped at the same time as it is seen how it maintains truth-valuedness whatever the truth or falsity is of some sentence or range of sentences. Besides thinking of Russellian analysis as going on and on to some final analysis, we need to think of it as beginning at as it were a zero stage; we need to think of it as using a general principle for reading sentences, which is actually applied at one stage earlier than the one we see in the theory of descriptions itself. Our preliminary grasp of what function of what expressions a sentence is involves seeing how by being that function of those expressions it is truth-valued, regardless of whether it itself is true or false. There will be no such thing as a syntactic characterization of a sentence, such that by fixing the meaning of the sentence's elements, it will turn out that only if the sentence is true does it have any truth value at all; nor will there be such a thing as a syntactic characterization of a sentence, such that it can turn out that, given a certain meaning of some of the sentence's elements, only if the sentence is false does it have a determinate truth value. There will therefore be no such thing as a reading of the syntactic structure of a sentence like "A is an object" such that, if A were not an object (whatever it may be that "object" means), the sentence itself would be deprived of truth value. A sentence cannot require its own truth as a condition of its own having a determinate truth value: this is part of a description of the kind of sign sentences are, the kind of functionality they have.[10]

I can now give a revised version of what I said about analysis. We make entirely clear what sentence a sentence is, what its functionality is, if we are able to write it so that its truth-valuedness can be clearly seen to be independent of the truth or falsity of any other sentence *and* of its own truth or falsity: independent of the truth or falsity of *any* sentence. We should thus be clear how by being the particular sign it was, the capacity to be used to say something determinately true or false belongs to it, is internal to it. The kind of sign a sentence is can now be put two ways: if something is a sentence, it is capable of comparison with reality, yielding true or false, regardless of the truth or falsity of any sentence; and sentences in general are capable of comparison with reality regardless of whether *it* is true or false.

This idea of *the body* of sentences can be seen to need more clarification than I have given it, and to run into an immediate problem about logical truths and logical falsehoods. Let me take that problem first. It is overwhelmingly natural to say something like this: that, if we fix the meaning of the sentential connectives, and if we stick to what we have fixed, and do not equivocate, then a sentence of the form "p and not p" says something which would be true if both p and its negation were true. Because it would be true only in circumstances which cannot be, it is therefore always false, necessarily false. Its truth conditions, which are perfectly determinate, are never met. And we shall want to say something roughly comparable about "p or not p." A sentence of that form has truth conditions which are in all possible circumstances fulfilled.

I hope that it is clear why I say that that presents a problem for Wittgenstein. No sentence in the body of sentences would have a single determinate truth value unless the truth value of contradiction is false; no sentence in the body of sentences would have a single determinate truth value if the tautology's truth conditions are not fulfilled. If tautologies and contradictions are genuine sentences, the idea of sentences as, by the signs they are, capable of truth or falsity regardless of the truth or falsity of any sentence—that idea has to go. And yet it seems that the overwhelmingly natural account forces us to say that if the logical signs are to be used consistently, we can form, using them, tautologies and contradictions: sentences with truth conditions fulfilled in all possible or no possible circumstances.

Wittgenstein's solution is that there is no such thing as consistent use of the logical signs: consistent use *of the kind we imagine*. There is no explanation of conjunction, for example, or negation, independent of the character of sentences as such. The fundamental idea is that sentences in the strict sense (signs so formed as to be comparable with reality regardless of the truth or falsity of any sentence) can be formed from other sentences, but that the rules for fixing the comparison with reality of sentences so formed from other sentences *also* fix the construction in the symbolism of sentence-like structures which merely reflect the logical character of their component sentences, and which themselves have *no* comparison with reality.

On this view, then, the rule fixing the place in the language of the logical constants (so called) is a rule determining the logical features of the comparison with reality of sentences, genuine sentences formed from genuine sentences. That fundamental rule will really be the meaning, all rolled up into one, as it were, of all the logical constants. And if we grasp that, we shall not be tempted to think of tautologies and contradictions as saying that something or other is the case. We shall not be tempted really to think of them as sentences.

I can now finish what I need to say about *the body of sentences*. The idea as Wittgenstein works it out requires that there be some sentences which can be seen directly to have the logical characteristic of sentence signs as such: the possibility of comparison to reality, comparison which yields true or false, belongs to the signs themselves and is independent of the truth value of any sentence. The idea of the body of sentences then requires, besides such base sentences, a method of construction of sentences from sentences, such that if the base sentences have seeably got the logical characteristic of sentences, the results will be sentences seeably sharing the characteristic or will seeably be merely sentence-like constructions never comparable with reality.

Let me put this conception slightly differently, using a term I have avoided: "entail." I have kept clear of it because its meaning depends on whether you treat logical relations as Frege does or as Wittgenstein does. What entailment is and which sentences entail which depend on whether a sentence is syntactically a sort of sign that cannot lose truth-valuedness by the truth or falsity of any sentence.

Suppose it is said that Wittgenstein and everyone else believes that to understand a sentence, you have to know what sentence it is. If my account is correct, it looks as if we could never know what sentence a sentence was except by carrying out its complete analysis, which of course we in practice never do. So if my account of Wittgenstein is correct, his is a lunatic account.

The reply is that we should think of two things as the same. On the one hand there is the fully analyzed sentence, which would lay out clearly in front of us what function of what expressions a sentence really is. To get what is going to be on the other hand we have to think of lifting up an ordinary sentence, and noticing, attached to it, like little wires, all the sentences which entail that it is true or that it is not. The ordinary sentence, together with *all* its little wires, is the same sentence as the fully analyzed one. So we can understand the ordinary sentence even though we do not know how to carry out its full analysis. The little wires are all there, all fixed by the logical structure of the language. As Wittgenstein puts it in §102 of the *Philosophical Investigations:* "The strict and clear rules of the logical structure of sentences appear to us as something in the background—hidden in the medium of the understanding. I already see them (even though through the medium of the understanding) for I understand the sign, I use it to say something."

III

More could be said about what kind of sign a sentence is, and what it means to call a sentence a fact. But I need now to get back to the questions I began with, about Wittgenstein's view of philosophy. I spoke of an interpretation of the *Tractatus*, which I called chickening out. Wittgenstein says, at the end of the book, that anyone who understands him will recognize his sentences as nonsensical after he has used them to get where they take you. He must throw away the ladder after he has climbed up it. To chicken out is to pretend to throw away the ladder while standing firmly, or as firmly as one can, on it.

P. M. S. Hacker is an example. He ascribes to Wittgenstein what you might call a realism of possibility. Each thing has, internal to it and independently of language, fixed possibilities of occurrence in kinds of fact, possibilities shared by all members of the category to which the things belongs. What we can say, what we can think, is that a thing has (or that it has not) one of the properties that, as a member of its logical category, it can have; or that several things stand (or that they do not stand) in one of the relations that as members of their logical categories they can stand in. What we cannot say or think is that the thing belongs to such-and-such a logical category, that it has this or the other logical properties of possibly being combinable in such-and-such ways. Language mirrors these internal logical characteristics of things. They are represented in language by variables, not by predicates or relational terms. Thus, for example, being an object is such a logical or formal property; and, in English, if we say "An object fell," the word "object" is really being used as a variable, and the sentence might be rewritten in logical notation as "$(\exists x)$ (x fell)." We violate the principles of logical syntax when we use a term like "object," a term for a formal concept, as a genuine predicate, as when we say "A is an object." Here we are trying to put into words something that shows itself in language but cannot be said.[11]

I call that chickening out. It involves holding that the things we speak about are members of this or that logical category, really and truly, only we cannot say so. *That* they are is represented in language in another way. The sentences of the *Tractatus* itself are taken to convey this form of realism, although the doctrine itself requires that any attempt to state it as a doctrine must fail. There are several characteristic signs of this chickening out. The first is the idea of a realm of necessities underlying our capacity to make sense as we do. Hacker explicitly ascribes to Wittgenstein the view that there are ontological categories, objectively fixed and independent of language, which the logical syntax of language is then required to mirror.[12] The second is the idea of there being such a thing as violating the principles of logical syntax by using a term in what, given its syntax, goes against what can be said with it. The two characteristic features are then combined in the idea that we violate the laws of logical syntax when we try to state those necessary features of reality that properly speaking show themselves in language. There is a very clear conception here of *something* you cannot do. Or rather, perhaps it is not all that clear, since it dissolves into incoherence when pushed slightly. Call it then a seemingly clear picture of something you cannot do: namely, put these perfectly genuine logical features of reality into words. There they are, though, underlying our use of words.

Wittgenstein's philosophy, throughout his life, is directed against certain ways of imagining necessity. Throughout his life, his treatment of logic aims at letting us see necessity where it does lie, in the use of ordinary sentences. The trouble with chickening out, or one trouble with it, is that it holds on to exactly the kind of imagination of necessity, necessity imaged as fact, that Wittgenstein aimed to free us from.

Take a sentence like "A is an object." If we think of it as stating a necessary condition for ordinary sentences using the name "A" to have a truth value, we are (it would seem) in immediate trouble. "A is an object" cannot be a member of the body of sentences—or so it seems, since all members of the body remain truth-valued irrespective of the truth or falsity of any sentence. So there are not, within that body, any sentences giving the necessary conditions of truth-valuedness of sentences within the body. But, now, if we think of this sentence "A is an object," withdrawn as it were from the body of ordinary sentences, and as stating something underlying the truth-valuedness of some of them (and hence the inferential relations of all of them), we are thinking of it as itself saying what it does on account of the expressions in it. We understand *it* (so we think)—but what sentence *it* is, what expressions how combined, is not separable from its capacity to say something truth-valued irrespective of the truth values of the—which?—body of sentences, standing in logical relations to each other, to which it belongs, and including its own negation. In so far as we take ourselves to understand it, we take its truth and its falsity *both* to be graspable. Even in thinking of it as true in all possible worlds, in thinking of it as something whose truth underlies ordinary being so and not being so, we think of it as itself *the case*; our thought contrasts it with as it were a different set of necessities. Our ordinary possibilities have the character of possibility, given that these underlying necessities are as they are, not some other way. This way of taking our sentence "A is an object" has got built into it a way of thinking of what is necessary, where what is necessary has got its own logic distinct from the logic of our ordinary descriptions of what is the case. From the perspective we now seem to ourselves to occupy, the logical rules governing ordinary sentences, the logical 'scaffolding' internal to the original body of sentences, will be thought of as needing to match, to be determined by, which necessities *do* hold.—From the perspective we now seem to occupy; but Wittgenstein's aim is to let us recognize it to be only the illusion of a perspective.

The contrast I want is the contrast between saying that that is the illusion of a perspective and saying that it is the correct philosophical perspective, only you cannot put into words what is seen from there. The philosophical perspective is fine, but you just need to shut up. On that second, chickening out, interpretation, Wittgenstein's general account of sentencehood rules out the expression, by any sentence, of the view from the philosophical perspective. What is seen from there is representable only in internal features of *the* body of sentences itself. But if things were different as seen from that perspective, different necessities would thus be represented in internal features of language; the system of possibilities in language would be different. So we have two crucial features of (what I am suggesting is) the wrong interpretation of Wittgenstein. There is still insistence on viewing possibility and necessity as fixed some particular way rather than some other; they are still really being conceived *in* a space. What is possible in the contingent world, what is thinkable, what is sayable, is so because of the way ontological categories are fixed. And with this there is the idea that sentences attempting to express any of these things are illegitimate, count as nonsense by the doctrines of the *Tractatus*.

We need to go back to the apparently innocent way I led us into all this: by showing, or seeming to, that, given Wittgenstein's view of what sentences are, there must be deep trouble with the sentence "A is an object." The argument was that no sentence giving necessary conditions for the truth-valuedness of a sentence can belong to the body of sentences. So "A is an object" was pushed outside, and then we had more trouble.

But what Wittgenstein *says* is that there is nothing wrong with *any* possible combination of signs into a sentence. He says at 5.4733 that *any* possible sentence is, as far as its construction goes, legitimately put together, and, if it has no sense, this can only be because we have failed to give a meaning to some of its constituents, even if we think that we have done so. Thus the reason why "Socrates is identical" says nothing is that we have not given any *adjectival* meaning to the word "identical." The word "identical" as it occurs in (e.g.) "The morning star is identical with the evening star" is, syntactically, a totally different symbol from what we have in "Socrates is identical." So the sentence "Socrates is identical" is legitimately put together, in the sense in which "Socrates is frabble" is, as far as its structure goes, legitimately put together. Both contain what are syntactically adjectives; all they need is for some adjectival meaning to be fixed for them. What I am emphasizing is that on Wittgenstein's view, the *only* thing wrong with "Socrates is identical" is the absence of an adjectival meaning for "identical," where the need for a meaning may be hidden from us by the fact that the *word* "identical" has other uses in which it is meaningful. A good logical notation would mark syntactical differences by the use of unconfusable signs, signs with visibly different structure. And then there would be no such thing as giving a word like "identical" a new syntactical role, where its already having a different role, in which it was meaningful, hid its meaninglessness in the new role.

We need to apply this to "A is an object." What is wrong with it, on the view of Wittgenstein which I am attacking, is that it is an attempt to put into words what really does underlie the intelligibility of what we say truly or falsely of A in ordinary sentences. That A is an object does underlie the intelligibility of ordinary sentences, but it is a violation of logical syntax to put *that* into words. Against this, here is how I am suggesting we interpret Wittgenstein. The very idea of the philosophical perspective from which we consider as sayable *or* as unsayable necessities that underlie ordinary being so, or possibilities as themselves objective features of reality, sayably *or* unsayably: that very perspective itself is the illusion, created by sentences like "A is an object," which we do not see to be simply nonsense, plain nonsense. "A is an object" is no more than an innocently meaningless sentence like "Socrates is frabble"; it *merely* contains a word to which, in its use as predicate noun, no meaning has been given. But we inflate it, we blow it up into something more, we think of ourselves as meaning by it something which lies beyond what Wittgenstein allows to be sayable. We think it has to be rejected by him because of that. We think of there being a content for it, which according to his doctrines, no sentence can have. But this conception of what we cannot say is an illusion created by our taking the word "object," which works in meaningful English sentences essentially as a variable, and putting it into other sentences where it has a wholly different grammatical function. When Wittgenstein says that we cannot say "There are objects," he does not mean "There are, all right, only *that there are* has to get expressed another way." That the sentence means nothing at all and is not illegitimate for any other reason, we do not see. We are so convinced that we understand what we are trying to say that we see only the two possibilities: *it* is sayable, *it* is not sayable. But Wittgenstein's aim is to allow us to see that there is no 'it'. The philosophical insight he wants to convey will come when you understand that you want to make use of a syntactical construction "A is a such-and-such," and that you are free to fix the meaning of the predicate noun in any way you choose, but that no assignment of meaning to it will satisfy you. There is not some meaning you cannot give it; but no meaning, of those without limit which you can give it, will do; and so you see that there is no coherent understanding to be reached of what you wanted to say. It dissolves: you are left with the sentence-structure "A is an object," standing there, as it were, innocently meaning nothing at all, not any longer thought of as illegitimate because of a violation of the principles of what can be put into words and what goes beyond them. Really to grasp that what you were trying to say shows itself in language is to cease to think of it as an inexpressible *content: that which* you were trying to say.

Take Wittgenstein's remark that there is only *logical* necessity (6.37 and 6.375). It is a wonderful remark. Logical necessity is that of tautologies. It is not that they are true because their truth conditions are met in all possible worlds, but because they have none. "True in all possible worlds" does not describe one special case of truth conditions being met but specifies the logical character of certain sentence-like constructions formulable from sentences. But the remark that there is only logical necessity is itself ironically self-destructive. It has the form, the syntactic form, of "There is only this sort of thing," i.e., it uses the linguistic forms in which we say that there are only thises rather than thises and thats. It belongs to its syntax that it itself says something the other side of which can be represented too. If there *is* only squiggledy wiggle, the language allows wiggles that are not squiggledy as well. But whatever the sentence aims to do for us, it is not to place the kind of necessity there is as this sort rather than that. It does not convey to us the philosophical but unsayable fact that there is only tautology not genuinely substantial necessity. In so far as we grasp what Wittgenstein aims at, we see that the sentence-form he uses comes apart from his philosophical aim. If he succeeds, we shall not imagine necessities as states of affairs at all. We throw away the sentences about necessity; they really are, at the end, entirely empty. But we shall be aware at the end that when we go in for philosophical thinking, the characteristic form of such thought is precisely that the sentence-forms we use come apart from what we have taken to be our aims. Not because we have chosen the wrong forms.

Back now at last to Wittgenstein's relation to Frege. The analogies could be spelt out in detail, and so could the differences. What I shall do instead is work through one particular analogy to make clear at the same time the deepest difference between them.

For Frege, you refer to a concept by using a term predicatively, that is, by using a term which makes a characteristic kind of contribution to the truth or falsity of the sentences in which it occurs. You cannot first predicate *horse* of Bucephalus, say, and then as it were turn round on yourself and grab hold of *what* you referred to by the predicative use of "horse" and catch *it* by using a term as a logical subject. It was Benno Kerry's idea that he could do just *that* that Frege criticized him for. Frege's criticism would also apply to Russell,[13] whose confusion (confusion, that is, as we may imagine it seen from Frege's point of view) is of a particularly helpful sort. Russell believes that the logical subject *humanity* is actually one and the same thing as the concept ascribed to Socrates when we say that he is human (they are "exactly and numerically" the same); and he adds that the difference between humanity when it is spoken of by a term with the logical features of a proper name and when it is predicated of something is in the *external* relations of the concept humanity and not in the intrinsic nature of the thing we are talking about. This idea that the logical character of the expressions you use in talking about something is irrelevant to what kind of thing *it* in itself is is then reflected in that 'rounding on oneself' that I spoke of, that attempt to *catch at* the very thing you had referred to by a predicative use of an expression, and to hold it up in front of you for philosophical consideration. I cannot here try to show what is involved in Frege's rejection of any view like Russell's as incoherent.[14] But it is important to see that Russell's view depends on a notion (or on imagining that he has a notion) of the identity of a thing, a notion of identity untied from the substitutability *salva veritate* of expressions referring to it. There is, he supposes, a position, a perspective, from which to think about things-with-their-intrinsic-nature, outside of the use of proper names and functional terms, with their *different* logical character, in sentences.

Just as, for Frege, you *refer to a concept* by using a term predicatively, and it is confused to think you can round on yourself and grab hold of *what* you thus referred to, so for Wittgenstein, *something that may be the case gets said to be the case* by a sentence, and it is confused to think you can round on yourself and grab hold of *what* you thus said to be so, and treat *it* as a logical subject. For Frege, the sign for a concept is an expression with the logical character of a predicate, with one or another kind of incompleteness internal to it, carrying with it a particular kind of rule for substitution *salva veritate*, different from the rule for substitution characteristic of proper names. So, for Wittgenstein, the sign for what is the case (*or* is not the case) is the sentence, a sign to whose functional character it belongs that no sentence's truth or falsity can rob it of its capacity for comparison with reality; and that logical character is tied to a particular kind of substitution rule, different from that for any referring sign. Possibility and necessity get expressed in the use of ordinary sentences, in inferences from these sentences to more of these sentences. It is a mistake to think that you can in thought catch hold of, mean, *that possibility* that is reflected in the ordinary sentence you use, and, for example, consider what underlies its being possible, as if that were a characteristic of *something*. The mistake is of the same general character as the attempt to ignore the way a concept is referred to, the attempt to mean *it*, bare of the logical accoutrements with which language covers it— which was what Russell explicitly says we can do.

I want now to say where my present argument will wind up, before I get it to go there. There is the Russell confusion, in which you think that you can grasp the identity of a thing abstracted from the use of a term for it in sentences, and against it there is the idea running through Frege's thought, that logical characteristics of the expressions that stand for a thing belong to *what it is* we were talking about. In Frege's hands, that principle is directed against Benno Kerry, and would have been directed against the remarks of Russell's I quoted. From Wittgenstein's point of view, that very confusion (the confusion of thinking that you can grasp what you are talking about, pulled away from the logical features of any expression for it) is present (without Frege's seeing it) in Frege himself, and in anyone who thinks of the laws of logic as true—true because their truth conditions are met. The turning of the Frege principle against Frege depends on this point: if Russell's confusion is the attempt to think of something, abstracting from the logical features of how we speak about it, then what you will take to be the same confusion as Russell's depends on what logical features you think there are, internal to how we refer to things. For Frege, the distinction between functions and objects, between functions of different logical levels, and between functions with different numbers of arguments: these distinctions all belong to the logical features of the referring expressions, the names, of *every* language. For Wittgenstein as for Frege, the logical characteristics of referring expressions are tied to the role of such expressions in sentences, where a sentence is a function of the expressions it contains.

But they disagree very deeply about what kind of function of the expressions in it a sentence is, and how you tell that an expression is one of those that a sentence is a function of. For Wittgenstein but not for Frege, you can tell what the sentence is, what expressions occur in it, only relative to the logical character of the sentence itself as a sign whose capacity for truth or falsity is independent of the truth or falsity of any sentence. The logical relations of sentences to each other enter the way we tell *what* sentence our sentence is, what expressions how combined. The whole of logic is internal to the logical character of every referring expression.

Here is a rough sketch of another way of making the contrast between Frege and Wittgenstein. For Frege the fundamental logical relation is that between concept and object; they are "made for each other."[15] That relation is reflected in language in the relation between predicate and proper name. Wittgenstein substitutes for Frege's fundamental logical relation between concept and object that between object and situation: they are made for each other. And that fundamental relation is reflected in language in the relation between two sorts of sign: one, that stands for something, and the other, that *in* which there is *standing for;* where the latter kind of sign, the sentence, has as its characteristic feature its capacity to occur as argument of truth-functional operations. The truth-functional calculus, within which sentences have their identity as signs, is what goes with any referring expression. (Frege and Wittgenstein could not differ about what sort of functions sentences are without differing about what sort of argument expressions in them are, without differing about the logical character of argumenthood.)

If you think that the whole of logic is internal to any referring expression, you will see the Russell confusion wherever anyone treats any part of logic as external to what we are talking about. Anyone who, like Frege, treats logical laws as holding of objects and functions will be imagining a kind of reference to objects and functions which (on your view) is an illusion: such a criticism is analogous to that which Frege could have directed at Russell. Given Wittgenstein's account of the character of sentences, it will appear that anyone who thinks of logical truths as genuinely true, anyone who thinks of logical truths as true because their truth conditions are met, will be in a confusion of the same essential character as Russell's: he will be supposing himself to have access to what he is talking about, even though he is abstracting from the logical character of the signs he uses to say anything. The idea of a science of logic is, on Wittgenstein's account, nothing but illusion.

Postscript, 1990

Consider this remark of Gilbert Harman's, made a few years ago:

> So, as far as I can see, no serious objections have ever been raised to the view that logic is a science, like physics or chemistry, a body of truths, with no special relevance to inference except for what follows from its abstractness and generality of subject matter.[16]

No serious objections have ever been raised to the view that logic is science; the history of this century's philosophy has had read out of it not only the *Tractatus*, its aims and accomplishments, but also Wittgenstein's later attempts to show how we may be misled by conceptions of logic as a kind of science, how we misunderstand 'the truth of logic'. Crispin Wright, in *Wittgenstein on the Foundations of Mathematics* (published four years before Harman's remark) tried to remedy the failure he saw in contemporary thinking about Wittgenstein: that Wittgenstein's ideas about logic and mathematics, expressed most fully in *Remarks on the Foundations of Mathematics*, are dismissed or ignored, even by those who treat seriously his philosophy of language and the philosophy of mind deriving from it. Wright tried to give systematic exposition and argument for Wittgenstein's views, although he saw himself as "[running] the risk of representing him as engaging in philosophical theorising of the kind he distinctively forswore."[17]

My account of Wittgenstein on 'the truth of logic' differs in several respects from Wright's. Some of those differences are explained in the introductory essays in this volume and in "Wright's Wittgenstein." Here I want to connect those differences more directly with "Throwing Away the Ladder" and the essays on Frege.

I see the *Tractatus* as a great first expression of an idea that is deepened in Wittgenstein's later work and never given up: of the link between misunderstandings of 'the truth of logic' and our attachment to philosophy thought of as doctrines and theses and theories. Wright believes that it is possible first to explain Wittgenstein's views about logic and mathematics (he argues that they are rooted in Wittgenstein's 'anti-realism'), and only *after* that to confront the question whether those views are compatible with Wittgenstein's conception of philosophy as not putting forward theses and therefore as not interfering with mathematical (or other) practice. I do not think that we can get clear what Wittgenstein's views about logic and mathematics are, and only after doing so examine their relation to his view of philosophy; the attempt thus to separate the ideas about logic and mathematics from the understanding of philosophy makes the former depend upon philosophical doctrines (in Wright's case, on anti-realism). "Throwing Away the Ladder" thus illustrates the way I differ from Wright on these issues; taking Wittgenstein's early writings, I focus on the link between his view of logic and a conception of philosophy radically at odds with philosophy-as-doctrines.[18]

Our missing of Wittgenstein's achievements—in philosophy of mind and in philosophy of logic and mathematics, in the *Tractatus* and in his later work—may go with our missing the significance of the encounter between Frege's understanding of logic and Wittgenstein's. We fail to see clearly the import of Frege's insights into the nature of logic and the tensions in Frege's views. Wittgenstein's work comes out of his profound interest in those tensions[19] and his own insight into what they mean for the character of philosophy, what it can do for us. So there is this further difference from Wright: I think it important to place Wittgenstein's ideas about 'the truth of logic' in relation to what he saw as Frege's accomplishments and their implications for Frege's own conception of logic.

Harman said that he could not see that any serious objections had ever been raised to the idea of logic as science. It was Frege who gave its most powerful expression to that idea. I believe that an understanding of Frege can help us to see our way past the false alternatives of realism and anti-realism in philosophy (that is what I argued at the end of "What Does a Concept-Script Do?") and to see the power of Wittgenstein's criticisms, in the *Tractatus* and later, of the conception of logic as science.

Notes

1. P. T. Geach, "Saying and Showing in Frege and Wittgenstein," in *Essays on Wittgenstein in Honour of G. H. von Wright*, ed. Jaakko Hintikka, *Acta Philosophica Fennica* **28** (Amsterdam: North-Holland, 1976), pp. 54–55, 64.
2. Hans Sluga also touches briefly on the point; see Sluga, *Gottlob Frege* (London: Routledge and Kegan Paul, 1980), p. 144.
3. Gottlob Frege, "Function and Concept," in *Translations from the Philosophical Writings of Gottlob Frege*, eds. P. T. Geach and Max Black (Oxford: Basil Blackwell, 1966), 41.
4. Gottlob Frege, "On Concept and Object," in *Translations from the Philosophical Writings of Gottlob Frege*, pp. 42–48. See also "What Does a Concept-Script Do?" §III.
5. John McDowell, "Non-Cognitivism and Rule-Following," in *Wittgenstein: To Follow a Rule*, eds. Steven H. Holtzman and Christoper M. Leich (London: Routledge and Kegan Paul, 1981), pp. 141–162 *passim*, but especially p. 150.
6. See Gareth Evans, *The Varieties of Reference*, ed. John McDowell (Oxford: Clarendon Press, 1982), p. 11; also P. T. Geach "Frege," in *Three Philosophers*, G. E. M. Anscombe and P. T. Geach (Oxford: Basil Blackwell, 1963), pp. 136–9.

7. Alfred North Whitehead and Bertrand Russell, *Principia Mathematica to *56* (Cambridge University Press, 1962), p. 66.

8. Gottlob Frege, *The Foundations of Arithmetic,* trans. J. L. Austin (Oxford: Basil Blackwell, 1974), p. 90.

9. Friedrich Waismann, *Wittgenstein and the Vienna Circle,* ed. Brian McGuinness (Oxford: Basil Blackwell, 1979), p. 39.

10. Frege, in *The Foundations of Arithmetic* (see pp. 40 and 62), is sometimes said to hold, like Wittgenstein, a 'contrast' theory of meaning. But I believe that Wittgenstein's view is not Frege's. There is no suggestion that Frege's view is a view about the logical structure of sentences.

11. P. M. S. Hacker, *Insight and Illusion* (Oxford: Clarendon Press, 1972), pp. 20–4.

12. Hacker, p. 23.

13. Bertrand Russell, *Principles of Mathematics* (London: Allen and Unwin, 1937), p. 46.

14. I discuss those arguments of Frege's in "What Does a Concept-Script Do?"

15. Gottlob Frege, *Posthumous Writings,* eds. Hans Hermes et al. (Oxford: Basil Blackwell, 1979), pp. 118, 178.

16. Harman, "Logic and Reasoning," *Synthese* **60** (1984), p. 111.

17. Wright, *Wittgenstein on the Foundations of Mathematics* (London, 1980), p. viii.

18. There is a very interesting discussion of that link in Thomas Ricketts's "Facts, Logic and the Criticism of Metaphysics in the *Tractatus*" (unpublished). Ricketts shows clearly the relation between Wittgenstein's criticisms of Russell's idea of logic as a science and his criticisms of metaphysics. On the related question of how the *Tractatus* itself is to be read, see also my "Ethics, Imagination and the Method of Wittgenstein's *Tractatus*," in R. Heinrich and H. Vetter, *Wiener Reihe* **5** (forthcoming).

19. On what we miss of Frege, on the tensions in his views and on Wittgenstein's interest in those tensions, see Joan Weiner, *Frege in Perspective* (Ithaca, 1990) and three essays of Thomas Ricketts's: "Frege, the *Tractatus* and the Logocentric Predicament," *Noûs* **15** (1985); "Generality, Meaning, and Sense in Frege" *Pacific Philosophical Quarterly* **67** (1986); "Objectivity and Objecthood: Frege's Metaphysics of Judgment," in L. Haaparanta and J. Hintikka, eds., *Frege Synthesized* (Dordrecht, 1986).

Chapter 7

Wright's Wittgenstein

[Note, 1990. In this critical notice of Crispin Wright's *Wittgenstein on the Foundations of Mathematics*,[1] I argue that (1) Wright pays too little attention to the *Tractatus;* (2) the book, though critical of Michael Dummett's views, stays too close to his conception of the nature of philosophical questions and of how they can be answered; (3) there is inadequate understanding of Wittgenstein's conception of grammar and its relation to philosophical method. As a result, Wright's Wittgenstein is too far from Wittgenstein. I have here omitted some introductory remarks and §I of the original review.]

II

Wright's book has a great cast of characters whose views are compared with Wittgenstein's, criticized in the light of his and used to explain and criticize his: we have the intuitionist, the strict finitist, various anti-realists, the platonist and quasi-platonist, the radical and modified conventionalists; Dummett, Davidson, and Quine appear, as do John Stuart Mill, Jonathan Bennett, A. J. Ayer, and A. C. Ewing. The author of the *Tractatus* is conspicuously absent: he makes two brief appearances in footnotes. It is puzzling that he gets so little attention when so much is given to so many other views of mathematics, logic, and language. Various things go wrong because of his absence and others not so well as they might. Here are three examples:

> (a) The essential thing in conventionalism, as characterized (several times) by Wright, is the denial that "necessary statements state a priori *facts* whose acknowledgment constitutes our recognition of necessity, and failure to acknowledge which is a kind of worldly ignorance" (p. 365). With conventionalism so characterized, the *Tractatus* counts as conventionalist. Wright recognizes that in the *Tractatus* necessary statements are not significantly true, but perhaps the recognition was simply an

afterthought. At any rate, unless he counts the *Tractatus* as conventionalist, he needs an alternative account of conventionalism. (b) Wright devotes a chapter to the relation between Davidson's program and Wittgenstein's views, focusing on the question whether the validity of principles of inference can be explained in terms of a theory of meaning. The *Tractatus* is not mentioned—although it bears directly on the question: what kind of explanation—if explanation is possible at all, in any sense—of principles of inference can be given? If one wants to know what Wittgenstein would have questioned in Davidson's program, one might investigate how it would be criticized from the *Tractatus* point of view—which he never entirely repudiated. Wright regards it as something of a scandal that Davidsonians never discuss how "their program complements, supersedes, advances, or undermines the ideas of the most original philosophical thinker of the twentieth century" (p. 279), and tries to show that the undermining may go the other way. Indeed, but how much of that undermining was well under way in 1919?

(c) Wright often touches on Wittgenstein's later view of internal relations. But that view can hardly be made clear without consideration of the *Tractatus* and of the respects in which the views in it were modified later and those in which they were not. Wright's discussion of following a rule—perhaps the most important single theme of the book—suffers from his neglect of these matters, running into difficulties that might have been avoided by attention to the *Tractatus* (and to such passages as *Philosophical Remarks* III, which help one trace the path from the *Tractatus* views to the later discussions of following a rule, intention and expectation). What goes wrong in Wright's account is that he misdescribes the significance of 'agreement in judgment'. To explain this, I shall summarize and examine part of Wright's 'rehearsal and elaboration' of Wittgenstein on following rules. Here is the summary:

Prior to our verdicts, it is not determined—not objectively—what counts as, e.g., *red* in as yet unconsidered cases. If I call some previously unexamined thing red, I can be said to recognize what application of "red" continues the familiar pattern of use; but the word "recognize" is appropriate only because there is the possibility of my agreeing or disagreeing with the communal verdict on the case, and thus the possibility of significantly judging my response correct or incorrect. If there is no communal verdict on that case, I nevertheless have standard inductive grounds for supposing that there *would be* agreement with my judgment, and may thus justifiably claim to have *recognized* what it is to continue in the same way. "Correct" and "incorrect," which thus have significant application to the responses of individuals (because there is "the authority of securable communal assent on the matter") have no real content applied to the communal verdict itself (because there is no comparably available standard). (See pp. 216–20.)—That account of Wittgenstein's view is directly connected with Wright's claim that the rule-following considerations rest on an anti-realist argument. I shall return to that matter, but shall first explain—differently—the role 'agreement in judgment' has for Wittgenstein, making use of three points: to say that someone has applied a word consistently with past practice is to describe what he did via an internal relation with past practice; one major difference between Wittgenstein's earlier and later work concerns *where to look for* internal relations; one major similarity is that when a description is given via internal relations, the relations in question are not hypothetical.

Instead of considering what it is for me, in my verdict on some hitherto unconsidered thing, to use "red" as it has been used, let us consider what it is for me to have given a verdict—at all—on the color of something, or to have described something, or even to have spoken English. No such description needs to be justified in terms of what a solicitable communal verdict on my activity *would be.* It is not, e.g., a well-grounded hypothesis that I was speaking English. What makes something I do a giving of a verdict or of a description is largely a matter of its place and mine in a life of, among other things, description-giving, verdict-making. One feature of that life (one of the things giving it its characteristic physiognomy) is 'agreement in judgment' on many matters, including the kind of agreement there is (and the extent of it, its limits) in the application of color terms. In certain circumstances, of which an important one is one's having learned to participate in linguistic activities with the feature of agreement, one's saying certain words may be the giving of a description.

Suppose that I come back from the garden and tell you that the tomatoes are still green. What is it for me to have used the words in accordance with our past practice? The words "in accordance with" mark a connection, an internal relation, which on Wright's account is still to be made, still only hypothetical: for the communal verdict is, when I tell you about the tomatoes, something we could only hypothesize about. On Wittgenstein's view, though, a claim that someone has adhered to a past practice needs the *general* background of shared responses (the "peaceful agreement" which is "the characteristic surrounding of the use of the word 'same' ")[2] but does not need justification in terms of an actual or hypothetical communal verdict on the particular case.

But—it may be said—the background of peaceful agreement, and the fact that someone has learned English, do not alone mean that he *has* adhered to past practice. Indeed; but if you want to know what it is to have done so, ask how you would put someone in a position to judge. You would teach him English—including those modes of criticism and evaluation which are part of speaking the language. Although it is possible to question whether someone has used a word in accordance with a practice, such questions are settled without giving to 'securable communal assent' the determinative role Wright thinks it must have.

> If when a language is first learnt, speech, as it were, is connected up to action . . . then the question arises, can these connections possibly break down? If they can't, then I have to accept any action as the right one; on the other hand if they can, what criterion have I for their having broken down? For what means have I for *comparing* the original arrangement with the subsequent action?[3]

Wright thinks that Wittgenstein's answer is that an individual's action can be compared with the original arrangement only because what is involved in the original arrangement is settled by what the community agrees is involved in it, for any application of the rule. And my action can be compared with *that*. But what makes comparison with the original arrangement possible is not that *there is* something, the communal verdict on what that arrangement involved in *this* case, with which my action can be compared, but that *we do* something, criticize ("You can't be sticking to your own definitions; look. . . .") without running into unsettleable disputes; in that context, a judgment can be a comparison with what was originally arranged, and I may be justly criticized for departing from it.

I have gone over this partly because of its connection with the matter of anti-realism. Wright takes Wittgenstein's views about following rules to rest on "the fundamental anti-realist thesis that we have understanding only of concepts of which we can distinctively manifest our understanding" (p. 221). That thesis enables one to reject as empty the idea that the communal verdict (on what is in accord with past practice) is correct or incorrect in virtue of its relation to an objective standard. If *that* is empty, then the communal verdict alone can provide a standard against which an individual's response may be compared; and we can thus explain (what otherwise is inexplicable) why a 'community of assent' is a necessary part of the background against which an individual's response may be judged correct or incorrect.—But the anti-realist underpinnings are necessary only if 'agreement in judgment' plays the role for Wittgenstein that Wright thinks it does. But an account of that role should cohere with a story about how Wittgenstein's earlier views changed; Wright's does not.

Wright asks in passing (p. 400) which doctrines from the *Tractatus* survive to explain the continuity throughout Wittgenstein's life of his view of necessary statements as not significantly true. If Wright was trying to find those strands in Wittgenstein's thought which make intelligible and perhaps defensible his view of necessity, why was that question asked only to be dropped? The point applies not only to continuities in Wittgenstein's view of necessity but to the other important continuities in his views of logic and mathematics and of the possibility of philosophical discoveries about their nature.

III

In the Preface, Wright says of Dummett's ideas about realism that they "have enormously influenced my approach to these questions and constitute, indeed, almost as much as Wittgenstein's own ideas the subject matter of this book" (p. ix).—The presence of Dummett's ideas in the book is no weakness; the effect of Dummett's approach on Wright's is, because it is not made clear how very different that approach is from Wittgenstein's.

Dummett has introduced us to the realist and anti-realist, who turn up in any number of philosophical disputes. The realist in them is characterized by his insistence that the meaning of the statements in dispute is explained by an explanation of their truth-conditions; understanding such a statement is knowing what must hold for it to be true and need not include knowing how we should establish whether it is. We can indeed understand such a statement independently of whether its truth or falsity can be established. Dummett's anti-realist will insist that the general form of explanation of meaning is explanation not of truth-conditions but of asssertibility-conditions. We are trained in the use of statements of the sort in dispute by being taught to assert them in certain conditions; this training does not fix what it is for such statements to be true or false independently of the obtaining of conditions which we could take to establish their truth. Hence the anti-realist may dispute the principle of bivalence or that of excluded middle or both for statements of the disputed class.

To make clear the problem created by using Dummett's approach in discussing Wittgenstein, I shall look further at a particular dispute important for both Wright and Dummett, that concerning statements about the past. Here the realist holds that such statements are true or false independently of there being memories or evidence that would enable us to assert or deny them, and the anti-realist denies that. Let me use a picture to make the dispute clear.

The box on the left represents a past state of affairs—say, using Dummett's example, it is Dummett's being in his college room at 2:45 on February 12, 1969. The vertical line separates the person considering some present traces of that past state of affairs from it itself. The past state of affairs is not itself accessible to him; the line between him and it is as it were the wall behind which the past lies. All he has accessible to him is whatever evidence of that state of affairs there now remains (represented by the dotted box). We could add to the picture a representation of later stages, in which different, or no, traces of the original state of affairs are accessible to an investigator.

The realist takes the picture as showing what it is to grasp the meaning of "Dummett *was* in his college room at 2:45 on February 12, 1969." One has to grasp what it is for Dummett to be in his college room; one thus grasps what has to lie on the far side of the line for the sentence stating that Dummett was in his room to be true. We can *go by* only what is on the other side of the line, but even if there is nothing on that side, the truth-conditions of the past tense sentence are clear and are either met or not.

The anti-realist rejects the picture as incorporating an illegitimate point of view above or outside of time. It misleads us about the possibility of explaining the meaning of past tense statements, misleads us into thinking that we have some grasp of what it would be for such a statement to be true independently of any situation which would any longer enable us to assert it. How, he asks, in the nature of the case, could we have come to understand what that is? We could hardly have been shown circumstances in which a past tense sentence could be seen to be true, entirely independently of there being anything which made it any longer possible to tell that it was.[4]

While this is hardly the whole dispute, the central issue is clear: namely, whether we *can have a conception* of what it would be for a statement about the past to be true independently of any situation which would justify its being asserted now or in the future. A feature of much of Wright's book is that it is similarly concerned with arguments about whether we *can have certain conceptions*, and Wittgenstein is read as implying that we *cannot*. Wright claims, e.g., that we "cannot give content" to the idea that meanings "can be determinate in such a way as to settle that some statements are incapable of conflict with contingent fact, irrespective of whether we ever appreciate as much" (p. 389). This claim is used in explaining what we grasp from Wittgenstein's discussions of following a rule. Again, on p. 340, we are told that we must drop the picture of objective constraints, imposed by our prior understanding of concepts, which make it the case that an untried calculation has a unique proper outcome. We must drop it because there are no investigation-independent facts about how our concepts must be applied if we are to be faithful to them; as a result there is no sense in the idea that rules of inference "already determine certain connections which proof and calculation can draw to our attention, but whose status does not depend on that event." That argument is said to be explicit in Wittgenstein's discussion of 'the mathematical machine' in *Remarks on the Foundations of Mathematics*, III (Wright refers to II) §§47–8.

The realist takes it that we logically cannot be in the position which we ideally (so it seems) should want to be in to explain the truth-conditions of sentences about the past. That is, the past fact that I should ideally like to point to for you in explaining some past tense sentence is necessarily *not* here for me to point to. So if you ask me to explain what would make that sentence true, this may appear like asking me whom I meant in a case in which I have to answer: unfortunately he has gone and will never come back, so I cannot put you into the *best* position to grasp who it is, i.e., by *showing* him to you; all I can do is a sad second best, giving you a description or a picture.

My last paragraph is based on Wittgenstein's discussion in the *Blue Book* (pp. 37–8) of the relation between a wish and the wished-for fact (which is—unfortunately—not here for me to point to in explaining my wish to you). In another discussion of similar cases (beginning at *Philosophical Investigations*, §§425–6) he draws attention to a symptom of confusion: its seeming to us that in *our* use of some expression we go by indirection, we make detours: "we see the straight highway before us, but of course we cannot use it, because it is permanently closed." Applying this to the dispute about the past: the 'straight highway' that is permanently closed (the closure marked by the line in the picture) would give access to the *past event itself*. As we know, Wittgenstein believes that in such cases we are confused by a picture; and this may seem to put him with Dummett's anti-realist. But the important thing to get clear is how Wittgenstein differs from the anti-realist, despite the inclination he had towards such a view. (In discussing whether it is the foot or the sense datum of it which is real, he said: "I have never experienced the temptation to realism. I have never said 'What exists is the foot', but I have been strongly tempted to idealism."[5] That temptation to a kind of anti-realist view is visible in many places in his work, but usually with criticism of it, as, e.g., in the discussion of 'logical machinery' in his 1939 lectures.)[6]

The trouble with the anti-realist is that he thinks that he can see— well enough—what it would be for the realist's picture to be correct, and differs in that he thinks we *cannot have* a conception representable in that way. Against realist and anti-realist, Wittgenstein's point is that the picture does not at all make clear what is involved in having such a conception. The case of talk of the past is like others which Wittgenstein discusses in many places. We learn the use of certain sentences; we then learn to use others constructed from these: for example, we teach someone who knows how to use "p" the phrases "A wishes that p" or "A expects that p" or "It is not the case that p." Wittgenstein once described such sentences as composed of "p" with an 'index'; we can then ask what the relation is between the use of "p" and that of "p" with the index. For "p" and "p"-with-index are *used* in utterly dissimilar circumstances; what role then does the understanding of "p" itself play in our understanding of the new sentence?[7]

In the case of talk of the past, we may note such things as:

> (a) One can show someone *what* it is that one said *was* so (when one said that Dummett *was* in his college room) by showing him something that *is* so (Dummett now in his college room), just as one can show someone what one wants him *not* to do by doing just that.
>
> (b) If someone has not yet learned to talk of the past, we can teach him to say that p *was* so only if (in general) he is already capable of using "p" or is learning to do so. While there are cases in which this is not so, in general if he were taught to assert "p was the case" in those circumstances in which we do, and was hesitant or doubtful just when we were, but had not been taught to use "p" or similar sentences, then whatever capacity he acquired it would not be the capacity we exercise when we say that p was the case. To learn to talk about the past is to learn a new way of using things we have already learned or are learning. Just as expectation can only be expressed in a language that can express the present state of affairs,[8] what can be said about the past in a language depends on what can be said about the present.

Just as expectation of a future state of affairs is represented by a sentence constructed in a characteristic way from a present tense sentence ("It is raining," "A expects that it will rain"), a past state of affairs is represented by a sentence constructed in a characteristic way from a present tense sentence ("It is raining," "It rained"). What is thus shown in the structure of the new sentence is a relation between its truth-conditions and those of the old. The concept of expectation is so made that what is describable as a present state of affairs (expecting . . .) can be 'fulfilled' by a future state of affairs, and will be fulfilled or not (compare *PI*, §§438, 445, 461); the concept of the past is so made that a present tense sentence transformed in certain ways is made true ('satisfied') by what may have been the case, and will in any case be made true or not by what was the case (in the same grammatical sense as that in which order, wish or expectation are fulfilled *or not* by what turns out; again see *PI*, §461). It is perfectly true that these features of the grammar of expectation and of the past do not show us at all how to *apply* the concepts with these features; we are as yet told nothing about when we can say that someone expects that *p*, or what is evidence for Dummett's having been in that room in 1969. But an adequate description of the use of these concepts will not be a matter merely of giving the criteria used in applying them and indicating when they are defeasible; simply to have learned when to say "*p* was so" and when to doubt it will not in general be to have learned when to say that *p* was so. One's learning must embody connections between the practice of using "*p*" and that of using "*p* was so" or one will not have learned to speak of the past.

To return to the misleading picture. The realist's picture is, if understood properly, perfectly all right. The two elements on the left—the representation of some state of affairs and the vertical line marking it off as 'in the past'—correspond to elements of a past tense sentence, constructed from a present tense sentence with an 'index'. The vertical line in the picture serves as index. A representation of a state of affairs, together with the past index, has a use different from that of the sentence without the index. It is used on the basis of present criteria; and that is represented on the right hand side of the picture.

The picture shows that the truth-conditions of the past tense sentence are 'in the past'. It is what Wittgenstein calls a "pictorial representation of our grammar" (*PI*, §295). This means in part that the picture may be wrongly taken to show more than that, to show how concepts with that grammar would 'ideally' be used.

In the disputes between realist and anti-realist, we should see Wittgenstein as critical of both. (Compare *PI*, §402). Failure to grasp how he differs from the anti-realist in particular will leave us without an understanding of his approach to many issues. Further, whenever we find ourselves thinking that there cannot be a conception of a certain character, we are slipping into just the sort of position that the anti-realist takes up against the realist about the past.

IV

Wright does not see the force of Wittgenstein's notion of grammar nor its relation to his philosophical method. Let me take objectivity, a central notion of the book, as illustration. Wright's idea is that we have certain ordinary beliefs about objectivity which are called into question by Wittgenstein. For example, we normally believe that the truth or falsity of ordinary decidable statements is an objective matter. Thus, e.g., we believe that an object whose shape we have not yet observed has got a determinate shape irrespective of whether we actually ever do inspect it. That is a belief in what Wright calls the 'investigation-independence' of decidable statements; he argues that it requires there to be objective patterns in our use of concepts. That is, the belief that a thing has an objectively determinate shape depends on the belief that "there are facts about how we will, or would, assess its shape if we did so correctly, in accordance with the meaning of the expressions in our vocabulary of shapes." That itself is a belief that the pattern of our use of expressions for shapes "extends of itself to cases we have yet to confront" (p. 216)—and we do, he thinks, ordinarily suppose that our use of language conforms to such objective patterns. These ideas of ours about objectivity Wright thinks are called into question by Wittgenstein, in particular by his arguments about following rules.

Wright denies that it need be possible to formulate these ideas about objectivity clearly or coherently in order to attack them; a philosopher may reject a notion precisely because he believes that no coherent account of it can be given. What sort of understanding of it must he have if he is going to reject it? In the case of investigation-independence, Wright says that "the Wittgensteinian" opposing that idea may "contend that we have a sufficient grasp of the essential spirit of this conception to evaluate its short-comings, and that our possession of that degree of grasp is quite consistent with an irremediable unclarity concerning what a belief in the investigation-independence of a particular class of statements really consists in" (p. 206). Some such claim as that ascribed to 'the Wittgensteinian' is, it seems, one Wright must make *in propria persona* and ascribe to Wittgenstein as well at many other points in the book, where he discusses whether an idea or notion should be rejected for philosophical reasons. Thus, e.g., in summarizing the bearing of Wittgenstein's discussion of rule-following on the objectivity of necessary truths, Wright gives as one point in the argument this: "We cannot give sense to the idea that our communal speech habits pursue objective tracks which we laid it down as our intention to follow" (p. 390). But what does it mean to say that we cannot give sense to some idea? We should take Wright as claiming, *in propria persona* here, that we have sufficient grasp of the essential spirit of the idea to evaluate its short-comings. For Wright does not want to say that we cannot give sense to the *sentence* "Our communal speech habits pursue objective tracks." Throughout the book he takes it that such sentences may be merely 'embroidery' on the facts of our continued agreement in use. There is, however, on his view a distinct and objectionable sense we can grasp clearly enough to criticize.

Wittgenstein's remarks that philosophy leaves everything as it is appear puzzling—as Wright recognizes—if his arguments go against widely held ideas. But we can tell whether that *is* how to take the arguments only if we see how he saw the 'ideas' Wright thinks they undermine. I shall look at three cases.

(a) Wright thinks that we have a notion of the length of an object as an objective property which we can determine by accurate measurement. This conception imposes on us the principle that "accurate measurement of an object gives different readings on different occasions if and only if the object has changed" (p. 106).—What is wrong here is that grammar is being represented as an idea about the relation between measurements and reality. To say "Length is an objective property" would on Wittgenstein's view be to characterize the grammar of length; part of this grammar is that we say that an object has changed its length if, from what we take to be accurate measurements of an object's length, we get divergent results.

(b) Wright thinks that most people accept the 'investigation-independence' of statements about shape, and that it is undermined by Wittgenstein's arguments. There are (this is what those arguments establish) no investigation-independent facts of the shapes of as yet unexamined things.—But that is not Wittgenstein's view; for him the question "Are there or aren't there such facts?" would itself be confused: it makes it seem that there is something which we do not know and which philosophy can find out; it makes grammar look like facts. For "Things have determinate shapes independent of our investigations" and "Nothing has a determinate shape until it is examined" are grammatical statements. The latter gives part of a different grammar of "shape" from ours, one in which it would be nonsense to speak of the shape of an unexamined object.

(c) Wright discusses whether philosophical considerations should lead us "to think of ourselves as bringing necessity *into being* when we judge a statement to have that status" (p. 391). But "We bring necessity into being when we judge a statement to have that status" would be a characterization of the grammar of necessity. It says that "*p* became necessary last Tuesday" makes sense; that is to say, it is a characterization of the grammar of a language we do not speak. In our language there is no question "When did the necessity of *p* come into being?"; and that grammatical point can also be put (more misleadingly) by saying that if *p* is necessary it was always necessary. The idea that we might critically evaluate the view that what is necessary was necessary independently of our judging it to be so rests on mistaking grammar for facts.

A philosopher may say "We bring necessity into being when we judge a statement to have that status" in a philosophical enquiry into the character of necessity. But what needs to be said about it then is like what Wittgenstein says (*PI*, §339) about "Thinking is not an incorporeal process." That is not the right way to reject "Thinking is an incorporeal process." The latter makes a grammatical distinction (between "thinking" and, e.g., "eating") in a way "that makes the difference . . . look *too slight*." If we say that "thinking is not an incorporeal process" we are still in the unclarity shown in "Thinking is an incorporeal process."

Wright thinks that philosophical insight (e.g., getting straight whether necessity is brought into being by our judgments) might properly lead us to want to 'straighten out' our grammar if it is misleading. But Wright and Wittgenstein have different notions of what it is for grammar to be misleading. For Wright, there is a getting straight whether necessity *is* brought into being by our judgments, and the misleadingness of our grammar would lie in its suggesting the wrong answer; for Wittgenstein, the misleadingness of our grammar lies in part in its suggestion of question and answer. No 'straightenings out' of grammar will remove the tendency to take grammar as fact; Wright's idea of attempting to 'straighten out' grammar itself suggests a possible comparison between what grammar suggests and what philosophy shows us is so.

Wright touches on the problems here when, towards the end of the book, he sketches an argument showing that philosophical reasoning does not lead to *discoveries* (in at least some cases in which we might have thought it did). But this is merely noted in passing (p. 441), not developed or connected with his earlier and inconclusive discussions of the nature and limits of philosophical enquiry.

I have not tried to explain or defend Wittgenstein's use of the notion of grammar, but to show its bearing on Wright's presentation of the philosophical issues he is discussing and the views of Wittgenstein's he is expounding. In particular I have not tried to show *why* the things Wright takes as ideas or notions subject to philosophical evaluation would not be regarded by Wittgenstein in that way, nor why Wittgenstein would think that we are cheating ourselves if we believe we have a 'sufficient grasp of the essential spirit' of a notion—despite its incoherence—to judge its shortcomings.

Wittgenstein's later philosophy of logic and mathematics is continuous with that of the *Tractatus*, is distorted if seen in anti-realist terms, and does not involve the denials of objectivity Wright sees. So much for what I take to be major weaknesses of the book. I turn now to two of its strong points, illuminating in different ways of the real Wittgenstein.

V

The best thing in the book is the discussion of E. J. Craig's attempt (in "The Problem of Necessary Truth")[9] to show the inadequacy of conventionalist accounts of necessity. The conventionalism Craig attacks would not, Wright argues, be held by an astute conventionalist. Craig's conventionalist thinks it possible for it to seem (and to continue to seem) to all well-placed observers as if a count had been properly carried out in all respects, despite conflict between its results and our arithmetic (as in Dummett's case: the count first of 5 boys and 7 girls and then of 13 children altogether in an apparently unchanged group). This conventionalist thinks that we make arithmetical statements like "5 + 7 = 12" necessarily true (make it a convention that results like the Dummett one indicate a miscount) in the face of such possibilities. But a more astute conventionalist can claim that part of the convention that such-and-such results indicate a miscount is the convention that when we get such results *there is* independent perceptual evidence for the occurrence of some particular miscount, which we should uncover if we were able to investigate properly. But, as Wright shows, even the astute conventionalist is in for trouble from Craig's argument.

Such a conventionalist can regard our arithmetic as preferable to an alternative (say, in which $7 + 5 = 13$) on practical grounds: given the usual behavior of the things we count, we get into less trouble with our arithmetic than we should with another. But Craig shows that it is not a contingent matter: if a situation appears to support a deviant arithmetic and to conflict with ours, it *cannot* continue to do so if we carry out checks of a sort which he describes in detail. It is possible to go on holding an alternative arithmetic in the face of the absence of support from such perceptual checks (and to go on maintaining that *there is* independent evidence supporting the alternative arithmetic in the face of failure to find such evidence). But Craig's demonstration that alternative arithmetics necessarily run into a certain kind of trouble gives support to the idea that our arithmetic is superior to alternatives not merely on practical grounds, but because things *cannot* be as another arithmetic requires them to be. Whenever they appear so, Craig shows us *how* to find out that they really are not.

In the most important part of his discussion, Wright makes clear that Craig has not produced what he thinks he has. He thinks he has produced an argument about what in the nature of things *underlies* our arithmetic (its relation to the perceptual criteria for counting properly); Wright claims against this that what Craig has given is the most fundamental sort of proof-strategy for elementary arithmetical statements. We are indeed, Wright points out, led by reasoning of the sort Craig gives to the conclusion that it is *unimaginable* that a situation should persistently appear to conform to an arithmetic in which, e.g., $1 + 1 = 3$. Any convincing proof of elementary arithmetical statements

> *must* seem to show something about the potentialities of the perceptual criteria for counting correctly, etc.; if no such proof could be given, their status really would be comparable to that of any (consequences of) explicit conventions. But it is not. The intuitively natural response to a query about one of them is not, for example: "That is simply what we *mean* by '5', '+', . . . ," but: "How could things possibly be *otherwise*?" (p. 438)

Thus what Craig provides is argument of precisely the kind that gives its characteristic physiognomy to our acceptance of elementary arithmetical statements. A conventionalist has no need to reject the claim that our arithmetic can be supported by such demonstrations—any more than he need deny the existence of mathematical proof.

Wright's discussion puts Craig's argument another way up, as it were; turns it in a direction we did not see that it could be turned.

Even on a second reading, the surprise, the drama here, remain intact. Without specifically appealing to Wittgenstein at any point in the crucial section, Wright provides one of the most elegant illustrations of what Wittgenstein tries to get us to do in philosophy.

Wright's treatment of Craig's argument should be connected with two remarks of Wittgenstein's:

> When the proposition seems not to be right in application, the proof must surely shew me why and how it *must* be right; that is, *how* I must reconcile it with experience.[10]

Wright brings out that Craig's discussion shows us exactly how to do this in the case of elementary arithmetical propositions; that is, he shows us how Craig's proof-technique fits exactly what Wittgenstein thinks a proof should accomplish.

In discussing what it is to describe the function of language and of rules, Wittgenstein writes:

> The difficult thing here is not, to dig down to the ground; no, it is to recognize the ground that lies before us as the ground.
>
> For the ground keeps on giving us the illusory image of a greater depth, and when we seek to reach this, we keep on finding ourselves on the old level. (ibid., §31)

Craig tries to reach the level *below* that of our mathematical practice—the level of necessary relations between arithmetic and perceptual criteria for counting correctly; Wright shows that Craig gives a full, detailed, and illuminating description of the *old* level, of mathematical practice itself: in particular, the practice of giving certain sorts of convincing demonstrations that lead (on Wittgenstein's view) to the fixing of our concepts. Craig reminds us how utterly convincing such demonstrations are.

Immediately after those last remarks, Wittgenstein has "Our disease is one of wanting to explain." In this splendid section of the book, Wright does not try to explain why we cannot explain; he shows that Craig's attempt to give a certain sort of explanation is not what Craig thinks. The explanations of which the rest of the book is full try to take us to the underlying level even when they say that things are *not* there that we need for our (realist) attempts at explanation, or that there is no point of view from which we could tell anything about such a level. Wright keeps gesturing at it to tell us what we cannot do. And he does not do so in showing what is right and what is wrong with Craig's paper.

VI

Wright raises important questions for anyone seeking to understand Wittgenstein's philosophy of mathematics. Here are two of them.

(a) Wittgenstein holds that we could infer, calculate and measure in ways very different from the actual ones—just as we could have a different unit of length. That last part of the claim is important; the first part is not specifically characteristic of Wittgenstein but is accepted by, e.g., Frege (people could infer in ways which conflicted with ours; they would be not only mad but *wrong*). Dummett had complained that Wittgenstein's examples are thin and unconvincing; and Barry Stroud had attempted to show that the thinness of the examples does not indicate a weakness in Wittgenstein's approach. Wright makes clear why there really is a problem here.

Consider the case of measurement and Wittgenstein's example: the people who do something with elastic rulers that he refers to as measuring. But the criteria for an activity's being *measuring* are not that it *looks* like our measuring; for it to be measuring, its function in these people's lives must be analogous to that of measuring in ours. Wright's point is now this:

> Measurement with soft rulers will be useless if the results are applied for the kinds of purposes for which we measure; but if they are not, it is seriously unclear what good grounds there could be for saying that these people who, talking apparent English, solemnly lay floppy rulers alongside things and seem to record readings are doing anything that may informatively be described as 'measuring'. (p. 71)

Wright argues that Wittgenstein's examples, if looked into and developed, will 'destabilize': it will appear *either* that the activity described has an application so unlike that of measuring (inferring, calculating) as to make it unreasonable to describe it as such; *or* the application, the purposes, of the activity will be like enough to ours to make it clear that these people are using procedures inferior to ours: if it is really measurement that they are using these soft rulers for, they would be well advised to change over to more rigid ones. One unit of measurement may be superior to another in certain circumstances and inferior to it in others; but if Wright is correct that is not how it is with the choice of rigid rather than soft rulers. If your purposes allow the description of what you are doing as *measurement*, you must be better off with rigid ones.

This is surely a problem that needs raising. A useful approach might be to examine the range of purposes and applications which enable us to identify a people as measuring something, say, but in a different way, to see whether Wright's claim that such cases will destabilize in one of the two directions is sound. That it may not be is suggested by the case of measuring time. What people do is identifiable as reckoning time if the reckoning is used, e.g., to coordinate activities and to keep track of their history and relationships. Time has been reckoned by 'soft rulers'—in the middle ages.

> Reckoning ordinarily . . . twelve hours of day and twelve of night, whatever the season, people of the highest education became used to seeing each of these fractions, taken one by one, grow and diminish incessantly according to the annual revolution of the sun.[11]

Is this clearly inferior to the use of a more uniform measure? A more uniform measure (the burning of candles of uniform length) was known but was not generally used because it was not wanted; people were generally indifferent about what would be marked by less 'elastic' measures. Given *their* purposes, 'elastic' measurement is not inferior.

In this case and others (the Nuer system of time reckoning described by Evans-Pritchard is a good example[12]), we can see people who reckon differently from the way we do, whose purposes are close enough to ours for there to be no problem in describing them as reckoning time but far enough away for it to be most unclear whether they should achieve *their* purposes any better by going over to our methods. I do not know how far attention to such cases can help resolve the issue Wright raises; but he has done a service by raising it.

(b) When Wittgenstein discusses necessity and related subjects, he often points out that a sentence which has been used so that it is experimentally verifiable may be given a *new* use, as a rule. It is thus made 'aloof' from experience, withdrawn from doubt; it is now non-temporal, a standard or norm by which we can describe what happens. With the aid of such notions, Wittgenstein tries to characterize the sorts of use distinctive of necessary statements. Wright emphasizes that Wittgenstein does not intend the contrast between rules of description and descriptive propositions as a sharp one: he quotes *Remarks on the Foundations of Mathematics*, V §5, where Wittgenstein first says of the contrast that it shades off in all directions and then adds that "*that* in turn is not to say that the contrast is not of the greatest importance."

The problem Wright raises concerns this contrast. He points out that a deeply held conviction of the truth of some statement may be reflected in the way apparently conflicting evidence is treated. The hypothesis that all such evidence can—somehow—be explained away may be held to, even when all ordinary standards for rejecting it have been met. The willingess to treat apparently conflicting evidence this way is itself a "measure of the depth, or stubbornness, of a conviction" (p. 412). If we want to draw a contrast, even one that is not sharp, between descriptive propositions and rules of description, how should we distinguish between that 'aloofness' from experience characteristic of rules of description and that 'aloofness' showing the depth of the conviction that some descriptive proposition is true?

Wittgenstein does not discuss this problem in his writings on mathematics, though, as Wright mentions, there are remarks touching on it in *On Certainty*. The questions Wright raises are of great importance, bearing not just on the nature of mathematics but in general on what it is for some characteristic of the use of an expression to belong to its grammar. Obscurity about this matter affects the question too how Wittgenstein's philosophical methods are to be applied; it leaves unclear the force of "This is what we do," said of our treating some kinds of claim as indefeasible, some kinds of doubt as not to be raised.

The strong points of the book are what leave one disappointed with the rest of it, and with the book as a whole. The last third of it is the best: more assured, more consistently interesting and less cluttered. It is indeed a very valuable book for anyone concerned with the main problems of philosophy—but how many "but"s one wants to add!

Notes

1. All page references are to *Wittgenstein on the Foundations of Mathematics* (London, 1980), unless otherwise specified.
2. Ludwig Wittgenstein, *Remarks on the Foundations of Mathematics* (third edition: Oxford, 1978), VI §21. References not specifying the third edition of this book are to the second (Oxford, 1967).
3. Wittgenstein, *Philosophical Remarks* (Oxford, 1975), §23.
4. See Michael Dummett, "The Reality of the Past," in *Truth and Other Enigmas* (London, 1978), pp. 358–74, especially pp. 362 and 369.
5. Margaret Macdonald, unpublished notes on Wittgenstein's Lectures on "Personal Experience," 1935–36, lecture of 19 February 1936.

6. *Wittgenstein's Lectures on the Foundations of Mathematics, Cambridge 1939*, ed. Cora Diamond (Ithaca, 1976; Chicago, 1989), pp. 194–9.

7. See *Wittgenstein's Lectures, Cambridge 1932–1935*, ed. Alice Ambrose (Totowa, N.J., 1979), p. 113.

8. *Wittgenstein's Lectures, Cambridge 1930–1932*, ed. Desmond Lee (Totowa, N.J., 1980), p. 6.

9. In *Meaning, Reference, and Necessity*, ed. Simon Blackburn (Cambridge, 1975), pp. 1–31.

10. *Remarks on the Foundations of Mathematics* (third edition), VI §3.

11. Marc Bloch, *Feudal Society*, vol. I (London, 1965), pp. 73–4.

12. E. E. Evans-Pritchard, *The Nuer* (New York and Oxford, 1974), chapter III.

Chapter 8
Secondary Sense

I want to suggest that what Wittgenstein called the use of certain expressions in an absolute sense in ethical and religious discourse has certain logical resemblances to what he later called the use of an expression in a secondary sense. I shall first note a few points from the Ethics Lecture,[1] but I shall not expound the arguments. I shall then explain what I take to be his conception of secondary sense, and lastly I shall try to show the connection between secondary sense and some of the problems raised in the Ethics Lecture. Here I shall not be trying to expound Wittgenstein's views.

At the beginning of the Ethics Lecture, Wittgenstein notes that words like "right," "good," "important" are used in a trivial or relative sense, as well as an ethical or absolute sense; later on in the Lecture he makes a similar distinction with "safe" and "miracle." We have, for example, the use of "this is the right way to Grantchester," where its being the right way is simply a matter of fact. With this, we may contrast speaking of *"the* absolutely right road." This "would be the road which *everybody* on seeing it would, *with logical necessity,* have to go, or be ashamed for not going." The tendency to speak in such ways was a tendency to try to go beyond what could be said: ". . . our words will only express facts" and facts are all as it were *on a level.* We are trying to say that something stands out above the level of the facts. No fact has absolute value: that is to say, any fact is just—a fact, on the dead level of all facts. And it cannot be a fact that something has absolute value: it cannot, that is, be a fact that something stands out from the facts.

Wittgenstein refers to three experiences to explain what he is trying to express when he is tempted to use expressions like "absolute good." In describing these experiences, he says, one is tempted to "misuse language." They are the experiences of wonder at the existence of the world, absolute safety, and guilt. He thinks they are the experiences meant when people say that God created the world, that they feel safe in the hands of God, and that God disapproves of their conduct. These experiences seem themselves to have 'absolute value'. But he finds this extremely paradoxical. If they are experiences "they are facts; they have taken place then and there, lasted a certain definite time and consequently are describable." Suppose then that someone suggests: "If we say our experience has a quality, which we call 'absolute value', what we mean must be a fact like other facts; we just do not yet know the correct logical analysis of the expressions we use." Wittgenstein's reply to such a suggestion would be that he can see clearly that no significant description could be an analysis of what he was saying. At about the same time as the Lecture, he said that it was important to end all the 'chatter' about ethics: whether the Good can be defined, etc. In ethics, you *cannot* say what you are trying to say. "But the tendency, the thrust, points to something."[2] This, it seems to me obvious, is an attempt to say it again; "points to something" is here as much (or as little) a misuse as any of those mentioned in the Lecture.

He denies in the Lecture, and again in a conversation with Waismann in 1930 (ibid), that ethical and religious expressions are similes, although they do seem to be.

The three points to which I am drawing attention are then (1) in ethics expressions which have a straightforward fact-stating sense are used in another, 'absolute' sense; (2) these ethical uses are connected with experiences which cannot be described without misusing language; (3) these uses appear to be similes, but what they say cannot be put 'in prose', as they might be if there were a straightforward resemblance.

I shall turn now to explaining what Wittgenstein meant by secondary sense.

In both the *Brown Book* and the *Philosophical Investigations*, Wittgenstein notes such facts as that when we ask people who know the use of the words "darker" and "lighter" to arrange the vowels in the order of their darkness, some people will just be puzzled, but others will arrange the vowels in some order. If we ask someone what color he is inclined to say the vowel *e* is, he may reply that for him it is yellow. If we ask someone whether he thinks Tuesday is lean and Wednesday fat, or the other way round, he may tell us which view he takes.[3] (Some people who take a view on this associate with the week a picture which allows a more or less literal application of "fat" and "lean," e.g., picturing the week as a spectrum, the Tuesday band being narrow, the Wednesday band broad. But someone may take a view here without thinking of it in any such way. See Wittgenstein's comment on vowel-darkness, *BB*, p. 136.) Have these words "darker," "yellow," "fat," "lean" different meanings here from their usual ones? Wittgenstein says that they have a different *use*. But he says, first, that it is *these* words with their familiar meanings which he wants to use *here* (it is just like the wish to use about Wednesday *exactly* the gesture one would use in describing someone with a pot belly), and later, that it is not a matter of giving a word like "yellow" a 'metaphorical' sense—"for I could not express what I want to say in any other way than by means of the idea 'yellow'" (*PI*, p. 216). This is what he would call using a word in a secondary sense.

What is being excluded when he says that the secondary sense is not a metaphorical sense? Certain sorts of explanation. This does not mean that I cannot say what I said in other words: if someone asks me what I mean when I say Wednesday is fat, I might reply that I meant *corpulent*. What *is* being excluded is the sort of explanation we can give of dead or deadish metaphors like "they were deluged with applications" and the rather different sort of explanation we can give of live ones like "man is the cancer of the planet." We can, for example, explain such a metaphorical use of "cancer" by drawing attention to the features of cancer which are important in the work the metaphor does, and the features of men which are thus emphasized. The speaker might say he meant the way the natural balance of species on the planet (cell types in the organism) is totally destroyed by the reproduction without limit of one species. The other species are crowded out, destroyed. The process, once started, seems impossible to stop. And so on. Such explanation is impossible when an expression is used in a secondary sense. It is not simply that words are lacking for a feature which I see in Tuesday, and to which I want to draw attention. It is not that I am aware of something in Tuesday, and then I see that the metaphorical use of "lean" is appropriate—unless this simply means that I see speaking of leanness as appropriate. If I use the metaphor "man is a cancer" I think that what is happening to the planet can perhaps best be put this way, but what I think is happening is independent of there being such a thing as cancer. There is no harm in saying that a secondary use (I use this as an abbreviation of "use in a secondary sense"; see *PI*, §282) is *in a sense* metaphorical, provided we are aware of the differences, but to avoid confusion, I shall not use this way of speaking.

In the case of both secondary uses and metaphors, the words are often used of something outside the range of things to which the word might be applied in teaching its use.[4] If there is some word which is taught by examples of colored things and vowels, that would not mean the same as "yellow." Similarly, one thing said when one says that calling a man a cesspool is metaphorical is that a word applied as a matter of course to some men and cesspools does not mean the same as "cesspool." (So it is a mistake to say that the application of "cesspool" to a man *must* be a metaphor. A word applied as a matter of course to both is not metaphorical in its application to either; it just is not equivalent to any word of ours. The application of "cesspool" to men *is not* literal; this characterizes the use of the word and does not follow from it.)

In the case of metaphorical uses (as opposed to secondary uses) the shift from the range usable in teaching is accompanied by a shift in meaning; the expression is given what William Empson calls a pregnant use.[5] We may, for example, be able to pick out features "which are treated as 'typical or essential' for the case in hand" (e.g., ferocity rather than furriness in calling man a wolf). In the case of a secondary use, we may feel like saying that the meaning has been changed, but it is puzzling to say that the shift from the usual range is *accompanied by* a shift in what we meant. If we say the meaning is not the same, it cannot be said what different meaning the expression has. Wittgenstein writes that if he were asked what he really meant by speaking of 'fat' and 'lean' days of the week, he "could only explain the meanings in the perfectly ordinary way" (*PI*, p. 216). In the case of some secondary uses, one can put what one means in other words, but this way of speaking will involve the same, or a similar, shift from the primary use ("Wednesday is corpulent"), or the use of expressions themselves explicable only in terms of expressions shifted from a primary use. One can sometimes also explain by putting someone in a position in which he may be inclined to express himself in words given a secondary use; in what sense this is a matter of giving him an experience will be discussed below. It is characteristic then, that if I think of the shift from the usual range, I may be inclined to say that the meaning must be different; while if I recognize that there is no question of giving you an explanation of how I meant the words, different from the 'perfectly ordinary' one, I may say that the words mean what they always mean.

B. F. McGuinness has suggested that an expression used in a secondary sense (in Wittgenstein's sense) has the sort of ambiguity "healthy" has.[6] There are resemblances, but more significant differences. I shall contrast "healthy diet" with "sad music" and "timid face."[7] There is this similarity between "healthy diet" and "sad music": someone must have the capacity to use "healthy" of living beings, and "sad" of men, before we can teach him the use of "healthy" for diets, "sad" for music. But healthy diet is just diet conducive to health, and sad music is not music conducive to sadness in the listener, nor music which sounds as if it had been written by a sad man, nor music which is nice to hear when you are sad, nor . . .

(The only reason for thinking it is something like that is the idea that it *must* be, that if it is not meaningless, *some* such account must be given. But to recognize that expressions may be used in a secondary sense is to see that they are not meaningless in these secondary uses even if we cannot give an account of what they mean in words used in their primary senses. If you know what it is to be sad, and you call some music sad, you mean precisely that.) There is no question of seeing health in a diet, but if you know what it is to be sad, you may be able to hear sadness in music. There can be no question of only sometimes being able to see health in the diet, nor of someone's helping you to see it, in the way you can be helped to hear the sadness in some music, or courage in a picture-face ("'the face as it were shows indifference to the outer world'," *PI*, §537).

(Wittgenstein likens this latter case to that of a German who explains to himself the agreement of the French predicative adjective by saying "they mean the man is *a good one.*" The connection can, I think, be shown by the relation between what the German says to himself and a secondary use of "meaning." Someone who is familiar with the primary language-game with "meaning," in which there is no question of *feeling* a meaning, may say things like "I can *feel* the same meaning in 'fast'—not eating and 'fast'—firm if I tell myself it's a matter of *holding fast*, but I just can't *feel* it in 'fast'—quickly." The German who tells himself that the French mean 'a good one' might similarly say that only if he does that can he *mean* the feminine ending when he says a French sentence. Compare a feeling that the French cannot possibly *mean* both "*ne*" and "*pas*" when they negate a sentence.)

Wittgenstein writes that only those for whom the word has the primary sense use it in the secondary one. He compares this relation between use in the primary and secondary sense with the relation between calculating on paper or aloud and calculating in one's head; earlier he makes essentially the same comparison with the relation between acquaintance with trains and playing at trains (*PI*, p. 216, and §282). I find a useful example here is that of playing certain games with oneself. I shall consider Hearts, a card game for three or four players; but there being a game with such-and-such features is unimportant. The rules for playing with three are slightly different from those for playing with four, but this difference does not give the game a different feel. It is possible to set oneself the problem of inventing rules for playing the game with two players; there might be several solutions, but the structure of the game is such that any solution, however interesting a game in its own right, will have to some extent a different feel. There is no problem of inventing rules for playing the game with oneself: the rules are the rules for playing with three or four. (There is in this situation the problem of discerning the aims of the 'players'. The way in which the lone player does this helps to determine whether he is pretending to be several people playing the game or is simply playing by himself. Both are what I would call secondary activities.) Wittgenstein imagines children who know nothing of trains picking up the game of trains from others, and playing it without realizing that the game is copied from something. He says "We might say that the game does not have the same *sense* for them" (*PI*, §282). We can also imagine that people unacquainted with Hearts should pick up the activity of playing Hearts by oneself without realizing that the game is based on an activity for several people. And here too we might say that the game did not have the same sense for them. But I would not say of someone who had picked up the two-person game from those who knew the three- and four-person game, that it could not have the same sense for him if he did not see it as a two-person version of the other game—even though they would, and he would not, always think of the game as a two-person version of Hearts.

The 2-person version of Hearts is just a game that *resembles* Hearts. We can justify calling it "2-person Hearts" by saying "After all, the rules are similar, you have the same aims . . ." But there is no *similarity* between the rules for playing by yourself and playing with three or four. There are no further rules which are alike *or* different. This does not make playing by yourself more—or less—like the standard version than is the 2-person version. The difference between the relation of the standard version and playing by yourself, and the relation of the standard version and the 2-person game is, I want to say, not in the *dimension* of more or less likeness. I might say that the activity of playing by oneself, as engaged in by those who play with others, is not self-contained.

Is playing by yourself *really* playing Hearts? If people played a game apparently like Hearts but seemed to see no more difference between playing with three or four and playing by yourself than we see between playing with three and playing with four, we might say "They only play to see how it will come out, and not really to *win*." If they are doing what we are doing when we play Hearts, their dictionary of games will not read "Hearts: a game for one or more." That playing Hearts by oneself is not just one case of *plain* playing Hearts goes to characterize the game. But this is not to say you can't really be playing *Hearts* by yourself (see *PI*, §364).

What makes the case of playing Hearts by oneself analogous to a secondary use of an expression is the following: (1) We would be puzzled by someone's regarding Hearts by oneself as merely a matter of playing a game for one or more with one player, and might be inclined to say that he didn't really understand the point of the game or at any rate had quite a different understanding. We should say that someone who regarded his talk of the darkness of vowels as a matter-of-course application of "darker" understood the word "darker" differently from the normal person.[8] (2) We might say of someone who seemed to be playing Hearts by himself but did not realize that he was playing a game for several people by himself, something like Wittgenstein's "It hasn't the same *sense* for him." Someone might recognize the music people called 'sad' and might use the word of it himself, but we would not say that he could hear the sadness or that he meant what we meant by calling it sad, unless he were able to use the word of men and their feelings. (3) Hearts by oneself does not have rules *like* those of Hearts. The rules are the familiar rules. But the activity is very different! "I don't know whether to call it like" (*PI*, §364). The words I give a secondary use I want to use "with their familiar meanings." (4) Someone who knows that Hearts is a game for three or four may be extremely puzzled when told that someone is playing Hearts by himself. It may sound as if it *must* be some other activity than the one he knows. He might be quite unable to see how it could make sense to say of Hearts—the game he knows is for three or four—that a man is playing *it* by himself. He will say that what must be meant is some distinct game with a degree of resemblance to Hearts. On the other hand, some people who have been taught the game, if told "Go and play Hearts by yourself," will do so. It may be completely natural for them to react so, even if they have no inclination to think of Hearts as a game for any number from one up. A secondary use, similarly, may just sound puzzling to some. And sometimes, when such a use comes natural, it may seem that if it is not nonsense, it *must* be a non-literal application of a word, such that some alternative account of what is being said must be possible in literal language, and the use of this non-literal language will be explained by the existence of a certain degree of resemblance. (There are many examples of this tendency in the philosophical literature concerning reflexive applications of expressions completed by two names in their primary use, e.g., "—— deceives ——," "—— has a duty to ——," " —— does not know what —— wants," "—— commands ——.") It is important that even if a secondary use is natural, this does not imply that it is what I should call a matter-of-course application of the expression.

I have compared secondary uses of expressions with secondary activities. But in a sense this is an attempt to lift myself by my own bootstraps; for the linguistic activity of talking about a secondary activity, e.g., playing Hearts by oneself, will involve the use of expressions in a secondary sense, or of expressions which can only be explained in terms of them. Thus I have used the expression "playing Hearts by oneself"; this is a secondary use of "playing Hearts." This means, for example, that someone taught to describe those who were playing Hearts by themselves by using the expression "playing Hearts by oneself" would not use it in the same sense I did, if he had no grasp of the use of "playing Hearts." (It would make no difference if we had a word for playing Hearts by oneself which had no visible connection with "Hearts." If it *is* a word for playing Hearts by oneself, its sense would not be grasped by someone who has no grasp of the use of "Hearts.") Where I want to speak of an activity as not being 'self-contained', I will use an expression, the activity of using which will not be 'self-contained'. This is not a point limited to talk of activities; it is in fact the application of a more general point. Wittgenstein says of the experience of seeing *this* as apex that it is an experience whose substratum is the mastery of a technique. We might say that this experience is not 'self-contained'. But how is it an *experience*? "It is a different though related concept" (of experience)[9]—and not a 'self-contained' one.

I have mentioned that expressions are sometimes used in secondary senses in giving one's feelings or experiences, such as hearing the sadness of the music, experiencing a meaning. It is important to note the variety of examples of such uses (which the following examples hardly begin to indicate). (1) Wittgenstein discusses this case in one of his aesthetics lectures: "All have learnt the use of ' = '. And suddenly they use it in a peculiar way. They say: 'This is Lloyd George,' (of an actor) although in another sense there is no similarity. . . . The most exact description of my feelings would be that I say: 'Oh, that's Lloyd George!' "[10] (2) G. E. M. Anscombe gives as an example of one type of internal description of sensations "a sensation of flying" where this is not meant to suggest that it is like the sensation one would get in flying: "the special thing about *this* kind of internal description is that it uses a word taken from elsewhere; it is as it were a metaphor—only *that* this metaphor strikes one is part of the experience it expresses."[11] (Note that it follows that only someone who can speak of flying in ordinary circumstances can have this experience.) (3) Stanley Cavell discusses the use by poets of such language as "the mind is brushed by sparrow wings" in expressing a feeling. This sort of language resists paraphrase in a way that poetical use of metaphor does not. Some people will not get it; if someone does not, we may perhaps be able to evoke place and atmosphere which help him to see the line in question as "a natural expression, the only expression."[12]

The use of certain expressions in a secondary sense in describing or expressing feelings or experiences has considerable importance in philosophy, where the danger is of mistaking such an expression for something else. Wittgenstein actually introduces the subject of secondary sense in connection with his discussion of the temptation to regard meaning as an experience. This is a temptation which gains part of its strength from the fact that there are experiences which may be ascribed only to those familiar with the ordinary language-game with "meaning", experiences whose content we naturally describe in terms of meaning a word in such-and-such a way. Such experiences are in fact especially likely to occur when we philosophize. That there are experiences of meaning a word in such-and-such a way is consistent with the fact that in the primary sense of the word "meaning," meaning a word is not an experience. ("Chess is a game for two" is consistent with "He's playing chess by himself.")

There is a closely related secondary use of "meaning" to express experiences, which could in some cases give rise to philosophical difficulties. This is "coming to know the real meaning of the word ———." I once stood on a ledge behind a waterfall, where all I could hear was the water thundering *down,* all I could see in front of me was thousands of gallons hurtling *down.* The experience I had I could describe only by saying something like "Now I know what 'down' means!" A much more striking example is provided by Ruskin, who describes in detail the place and events by which he was moved to say "And then I learned—what till then I had not known— the real meaning of the word Beautiful."[13] It is obvious that there is nothing wrong with speaking of the 'real meanings' of words in describing this feeling; it would be absurd to *complain* that Ruskin knew perfectly well what "beautiful" meant beforehand, absurd to say that he could have said anything he wanted to say without using language in such a misleading way, absurd to say that he was either using his words in a new and unexplained sense or with merely 'emotive' meaning. It is characteristic of such an experience that certain expressions, with their familiar meanings, should be forced on one, as a piece of music played in a certain way, or a picture, might seem the only way one could express what one felt. Although I felt forced to use the expression "Now I know what 'down' means!" I did not take this for an "immediate perception or knowledge of a state of affairs" (*PI,* §299), but the situation is close enough to philosophical ones for us to see how the temptation here is possible and yet not to feel it. (We can see the possibility of a range of cases leading from Ruskin's to knowledge of Beauty Itself.)

When Wittgenstein says that in doing philosophy we misunderstand grammar, what he sometimes means is that we mistake a secondary use of language in expressing an experience for the statement of a special sort of fact. This comes out particularly clearly in his discussion of the 'visual room' (see *Remarks on the Foundations of Mathematics*, I, §8, for a very different example.) What the discoverer of the visual room found "might even be called a new sensation" (*PI*, §400). But such a 'sensation' is one you can have only if you are capable of applying certain words in the ordinary ways. Thus the concept of sensation here differs from the concept used when we speak of a sensation of intense pain. (Compare *PI*, p. 208.)

When I help someone to hear the sadness in the music, there is no difference in the sounds he hears. If I say "He hears it differently now," Wittgenstein would say that there is a modified concept of *sensation* here (*PI*, p. 209). If we try to account for this sort of fact without noting the modification in the concepts of sensation and experience, we are likely to make one of several errors. We may say that the experience of hearing the sadness is an experience like any other, and we may even try to identify it with certain bodily reactions (for this and the following, see especially *PI*, p. 209; compare also *Lectures and Conversations*, "Lectures on Aesthetics"). Or we may say "If it's not *just* something going on in us, it must be either heard—the way the notes are—or something *sensed* but not actually *heard*, as it were alongside the notes." Such reactions reflect a failure to see the significance of the fact that the understanding of what it is to be a sad person is necessary for someone to recognize music as sad ('in the *full* sense of the word') and this characterizes the concept of hearing as it is used in "hearing the sadness." Suppose a philosopher to have a conception of language as usable to describe experiences and what is experienced only if these are facts—which "took place then and there, lasted a certain definite time," that is, only if the experiences are experiences logically like hearing such-and-such a note. Such a philosopher might recognize that on such a view of language, it would be a mistake to treat hearing the sadness in the music as a describable experience. He might then say that "sad music" and "hearing the sadness in the music" are misuses some find tempting. He might say that the very fact that someone is prepared to give a theory of any kind about 'sadness in music' in words which make sense is enough to show that that theory will not do. What I have just said about sadness in music I have said with Wittgenstein's remarks about 'ending the chatter about ethics' particularly in mind. I am not suggesting that he took such a view about sadness in music.[14]

From this point on, I shall no longer be primarily concerned to expound what I believe to be Wittgenstein's views. I shall be applying his account of secondary sense, and I just do not know whether he would have applied it in this way himself. The application will be a sketch of one way of looking at the sort of ethics he discussed in the Ethics Lecture. I do not know whether this is the best way of looking at this sort of ethics, but I do not know what is wrong with it.

Mistakes one can make in giving an account of sadness in music are paralleled by ethical theories. The 'chatter about ethics' arises from failure to see that what we say in ethics (not *all* of what is said in ethics, but all that is said in ethics characterized by 'the tendency, the thrust' Wittgenstein spoke of to Waismann) cannot be said in words given their primary sense, nor are we expressing an 'emotion' which could be identified without reference to the expression of it in words given secondary uses. If there is some experience we are expressing when we say "That is absolutely the right way" (and we are not using the words in the relative 'right-way-to-Grantchester' sense) it is an experience characterized by one's being impelled to use the expression taken over from the other language-game (taken over from *PI*, p. 216). In any case, to say that it is an experience characterized by one's being impelled to use a certain expression does not imply that the expression of it is not an assertion. I shall return to this below. I do not want to suggest that the use of an expression like "right way" in a secondary sense is all that characterizes ethical discourse of the sort Wittgenstein meant, although it is important that one be struck by the frequency with which such a pattern appears, in both philosophical and non-philosophical talk in ethics. I may know the use of "X wants me to ———" and then I speak of what is wanted of me, but not *by* anyone, what just *is* wanted of me. Rush Rhees contrasts Wittgenstein's claim that "absolutely safe" is a misuse with Wittgenstein's claim that the absolute "ought" is a misuse. To say to a man who has behaved badly and does not want to behave better that he *ought* to want to behave better, Rhees says, is, in such circumstances, a natural remark, the only remark you *could* make, in fact. It is not a misuse, while "absolutely safe" is.[15] But speaking of 'absolute safety' can *equally* be a natural way of speaking, the only way to express oneself (compare Cavell's remark, quoted above). The parallel between "absolute safety" and "absolute ought" was, in Wittgenstein's view, the relation both have to the respective relative uses. That this relation holds is not an empirical claim (compare especially *PI*, p. 208). Thus it would be confused to object to the view I have been expounding that the question which use of "ought" a child learns first, the absolute or the relative, is to be settled empirically. No use of "ought" *is* the absolute use if it is the only use a person grasps. A child might be taught to use "ought" in such-and-such ways in such-and-such circumstances, to respond to its use in such-and-such ways, just as a child might learn to say "My doll is in pain" independently of the ability to use "pain" of people. But such a child does not mean what a child would who makes believe that his doll has a pain; and empirical data about the learning of different uses of "ought" would be irrelevant to the question of the logical relation between absolute and relative sense. The tendency to see "absolute safety" and "absolute ought" as misuses was a result of being struck by logical features of both which could not be handled on the view of language Wittgenstein had when he wrote the Ethics Lecture. (Compare the necessity, in Kant's account, to ask how a categorical imperative is *possible*.) One source of difficulty with "ought" is, I think, removed if we look at its relation to the more obviously secondary uses in ethics, such as talk of what is wanted, when there is no one (in a plain sense) who wants (plain sense); of what matters, when there is no one (plain sense) to whom it matters, no observable result which will be different; of *the* way, which is not the way to some place (plain sense) someone wants (plain sense) to go; and so on.

When Wittgenstein denied that ethical and religious uses of language involved the use of similes, this was because with a simile it is possible to explain what you are using the words to mean without going beyond what he then called 'significant language.' He does, later, call such uses figurative. He says of "In my heart I understood when you said that," "It is not a figure that we choose, not a simile, yet it is a figurative expression." (*PI*, p. 178) To understand is *not* to be able to give a paraphrase in words used in their primary sense; nor is it to see what is said as *merely* the expression of an emotion. This is brought out most clearly in the following exchange from a lecture on religion.

> *Wittgenstein:* Suppose someone, before going to China, when he might never see me again, said to me "We might see one another after death"—would I necessarily say that I don't understand him? I might say simply, "Yes. I *understand* him entirely."
> *Lewy:* In this case, you might only mean that he expressed a certain attitude.
> *Wittgenstein:* I would say "No, it isn't the same as saying 'I'm very fond of you'"—and it may not be the same as saying any-

thing else. It says what it says. Why should you be able to substitute anything else?[16]

Wittgenstein suggests the man is using a picture, but a picture which *he does not choose.* I have emphasized this idea of a figurative use of words which is forced on us partly because it helps to show the difference between this view of ethical statements and any view of them as expression of will. Of course there is no denying that someone might use moral language to express his decisions; but there is no reason to think we *must* be doing this if we are not describing the world we observe. We may—*some* of us, *sometimes*—speak as if we were giving a description of another world, of superfacts, or very queer facts. To understand this activity is not to be able to paraphrase, in words given their primary sense. To say "One ought absolutely" is not the same as saying "I declare myself for this" and "It may not be the same as saying anything else. It says what it says." (Not that *that* means it always, in any circumstances, makes sense to speak this way. See Rhees, op. cit.)

Professor Anscombe has objected to the views of contemporary moral philosophers that while they recognize that expressions like "moral obligation" can have, on their own views, no content, they are not willing to give up these expressions, but try to give them an "alternative (very fishy) content."[17] On the view I have been expounding, if "morally ought" and the like are not merely phrases which get me to do things, or with which I express my own decisions in a strangely misleading way; this is because we are here taking "ought" over from its relative use and giving it a very different absolute one. (Its being a secondary use leaves it unsettled, however, whether it is of great importance or of no more than "Tuesday is lean.") We need not and cannot anyway give an alternative definition in words given their primary use; and we have not done so if we speak of God's law. I cannot, of course, begin to discuss religious language as such, here: I should say only that talk of God's law and God's power remains at the same distance from our primary use of "law" and "power" and so on as the absolute use of "ought" does from the primary use.[18] This is not to say that the absolute use of "ought" *can* stand on its own, outside a divine-law context. Consider Professor Anscombe's argument against Kant: the idea of 'legislating for oneself' is nonsense because "the concept of legislation requires superior power in the legislator" (op. cit., p. 2). Now, "legislating for oneself" is, I think, a secondary use of "legislating"; and it is not in general true that a secondary use carries the same implications as a primary use. (If a particular use does carry the same implications, they are often given a secondary sense. An example of what I mean is the use of "knowing in the heart" in talk of 'self-deception': the implication of the primary use is that the deceiver knows the falsity of what he gets the other to believe. For an example from ethics, see *Tractatus* 6.422.) But suppose that talk of legislation without superior power in the legislator sounds to most of us like grammatical nonsense; suppose that to say "Legislation to oneself is just like ordinary legislation—only without superior power" sounds like the answer to the riddle "Why is the elephant like the mouse?" "They both have tusks, except the mouse." Kant did in fact, at one time at least, take such a view. He wrote that when a man sees himself as accused by conscience, it would be absurd for him to think of the accused and the judge as the same person. "Hence for every duty man's conscience will have to conceive someone *other* than himself (*i.e.*, other than man as such) as the judge of his actions . . . Such an ideal person must be a scrutinizer of hearts . . . But at the same time he must *impose all obligation* . . . he must be, or be conceived as, a person in relation to whom all our duties are to be regarded as also his commands.—Now since such a moral being must also have all power (in heaven and on earth) in order to be able to give his law its due effect, and since such an omnipotent moral being is called God, conscience must be conceived as a subjective principle of responsibility before God for our deeds."[19] So the difference between Professor Anscombe's view and what Kant, at one time, held is not about the absurdity of talk of 'moral obligation' without God, but about the character of our knowledge of God and his laws. But what would it show if there were indeed general agreement that moral obligation without God is absurd?[20]

Kant speaks, in the paragraph after the one quoted, of the Idea of a Supreme Being as given subjectively, not objectively. The words "subjective" and "objective," Wittgenstein remarks, "betoken a difference between language-games" (*PI*, p. 225). But, we may wish to say, it is not simply a matter of a difference of language-games, but of whether there can be truth and falsity in a particular language-game. And we might feel that there was such a question about secondary uses in general. It is obvious that the truth-status of what is said in a primary linguistic activity does not settle the question of the truth-status of what is said in linguistic activities secondary to it, any more than knowing about what winning is in playing Hearts settles the question of what winning might be in playing Hearts by oneself.

Wittgenstein said in 1945, "Someone may say 'There is still the difference between truth and falsity. Any ethical judgment in whatever system may be true or false.' Remember that '*p* is true' means simply '*p*'. If I say: 'Although I believe that so and so is good, I may be wrong': this says no more than that what I assert may be denied" ("Some Developments," op. cit., p. 24). This suggests that if one wants to know about the truth-status of a secondary use, what one must do is look and see whether there is assertion and denial within the linguistic activity with which one is concerned, and if so, what forms it takes. I mean this: we can note such things as that we do say "I know that the music is sad, but to-day I just can't hear it" but not "I know that Tuesday is lean, but to-day I just don't see it that way." In some cases what we have to note will be much more complicated things. For example, we can imagine the unspoken dying thoughts of various historical characters; Geach mentions that Wittgenstein spoke of this activity in one of his lectures, and of its connection with such activities as telling someone your thoughts (*Mental Acts*, p. 3). It is clear that some 'dying thoughts' can be fitted easily onto some people's lives, and others cannot, and others can but only with a stretch of the imagination. This activity has consequences of a different sort from the consequences of the activity of fitting colors onto vowels. Thus, to see such-and-such dying thoughts as capable of being fitted onto Hitler's life might change one's attitude to him and to others. I might speak of such a game as capable of revealing a kind of moral truth; if I were asked to explain what it was for a piece of fiction to contain such truths I might compare it with this case among others. One central point about such games is the possibility of someone's just not seeing what you see. (For an illuminating discussion of a similar feature in both aesthetic and philosophical discussions, see Cavell, op. cit., second section.) And it may also be impossible for someone to see the *sort* of thing which is being said clearly enough to contradict it. Now we may say that if it cannot be contradicted, it is not an assertion, even if it looks like one. Indeed; but it does not follow that if *I* cannot contradict something, it cannot be contradicted. However, there is a serious problem here, which I can only mention. It may be that there is a primary use of "assertion," "I believe," "is true," "is a property," and so on, such that, e.g., an assertion is something *anyone* can make; an assertion about the facts is about the facts which confront us all. And it may be characteristic of certain language-games that we use expressions indicating that we are making such statements of fact, but that *these* expressions are given a secondary use. We may, for example, want to speak of *properties*, and yet recognize that we do not have in mind *just plain* properties. (See, for example, Moore, and Cavell, op. cit., p. 90n.) So it will not be enough to see whether there is assertion and denial in a linguistic activity, if one asks whether there is truth and falsity in it. There may be many activities secondary to what we elsewhere call assertion and denial. To recognize that they are secondary assertion-activities is to see the mistake in analyzing what is said as *merely* disguised expressions of will or feeling; so to speak analyzing away the assertion-character. Moreover, to recognize that they are not just plain assertions is not to be committed to saying they are merely fictional or make-believe assertions—as if that were the only sort of secondary assertion-activity there might be[21] (and as if *that* made it clear what was going on). There may be certainty in these secondary language-games; but "the kind of certainty is the kind of language-game" (*PI*, p. 224).

In conclusion I shall mention some points I am conscious of having ignored. Central to the idea of a secondary use is the distinction between a matter-of-course use of an expression and one which may be natural enough yet not just a matter-of-course use. I have left this pretty much in the dark. Secondly, I haven't said anything about the way in which what Wittgenstein says about secondary use is connected with other things in the *Investigations*, in particular, with the attack on private ostensive definition. The connection can be seen in Geach's discussion of irreducible analogies (*Mental Acts*, chapter 17). Thirdly, I have not considered the differences between ethical uses of expressions taken over from their primary use, and more down-to-earth cases of secondary use, like that of "sad music" and "experiencing the meaning," and, for that matter, "Tuesday is lean." I do not want to say (obviously) that there are no differences, but that there are considerations about meaning relevant to all such cases, principally these: when we talk about meaning, we do not always mean use (see, e.g., *PI*, §§43 and 561); the meaning of an expression given a secondary use cannot be understood by considering *that* use alone. The fact that the secondary use is different from the primary need not lead us to think that the meaning must be different and *then* to cast about for what that different meaning might be.

Notes

1. *Philosophical Review*, 1965, pp. 3–12.
2. F. Waismann, "Notes on Talks with Wittgenstein," *Philosophical Review*, 1965, pp. 12–16.
3. *The Blue and Brown Book*, pp. 136–9, *Philosophical Investigations*, p. 216.
4. They *need* not be. For simplicity I shall here ignore the special problems raised by the cases in which the range is the same.
5. *The Structure of Complex Words*, chapters 17 and 18. See especially pp. 333–4.
6. *Proc. Arist. Soc.*, 1956–1957, p. 311. McGuinness also regards the possibility of translation as consistent with a secondary use; he claims that at least some sec-

ondary uses rest on weak resemblances. These views seem to me wrong. He is right that "I don't know what I want" is a secondary use, however—but not in *his* sense.

7. Wittgenstein does not actually call them secondary uses, but they share important logical features of what he does call secondary uses, and if I understand his explanation of secondary use, they are secondary uses. Anyway, I shall treat them as such.

8. See *BB*, p. 139. Wittgenstein there discusses a tendency to say "he must have understood the word differently." For an example of a philosopher exhibiting this tendency, see *Philosophical Remarks*, §4.

9. *PI*, p. 208. See also §§370–3.

10. *Lectures and Conversations*, pp. 32–3.

11. "On Sensations of Position," in *Analysis*, 1961–1962, p. 56.

12. "Aesthetic Problems of Modern Philosophy," in *Philosophy in America*, ed. Max Black, pp. 81–2.

13. *Ruskin Today*, ed. Kenneth Clark, pp. 137–8.

14. The passage in the *Philosophical Remarks* referred to above suggests that in the case of some secondary uses at least he would have been inclined to make a move somewhat like the one he suggests 'many of you' would make, on p. 11 of the Ethics Lecture.

15. "Some Developments in Wittgenstein's View of Ethics," *Phil. Review*, 1965, p. 20.

16. *Lectures and Conversations*, pp. 70–1.

17. "Modern Moral Philosophy," in *Philosophy*, 1958, p. 8.

18. Compare Wittgenstein's remark in 1930 that if any sentence expresses exactly what he means, it is: Good is what God commands. At the time the sentence seemed suitable to him because it brought out the way in which absolute value was beyond the reach of descriptive language. (Waismann, "Notes on Talks with Wittgenstein," op cit.)

19. *Metaphysics of Morals* II, Acad. pp. 438–9. Translated by Mary Gregor as *The Doctrine of Virtue*, pp. 104–5.

20. Professor Anscombe has written on a related problem: "One can imagine the existence of a people whose language did not include the expression of a wish that things had been otherwise. It would be possible to formulate the wish in their language by using their expression for wishing and their past tense; yet it might be that to them this sounded incomprehensible, or like mere bad grammar." ("The Reality of the Past," in *Philosophical Analysis*, ed. Max Black, 1950, p. 55.) They say, e.g., "The concept of a wish requires the possibility of fulfilment." Professor Anscombe says that they would seem to be psychologically different from us.

21. Compare *PI*, pp. 228–9.

Chapter 9
The Face of Necessity[1]

When competent and careful readers of a philosopher come up, quite confidently, with accounts of what he says which are not merely wrong but obviously wrong, and obviously wrong about essentials, it may be important to see how this has happened. In the case of Wittgenstein, there is a group of obviously wrong accounts about essentials. Wittgenstein is said to hold such things as that we are free to infer as we like, that logical commitment is reducible to relations among noises, sensations to behavior, and that meaning is nothing but 'use'.[2] It is important to understand how it is that such obviously wrong accounts can be given, important to see what Wittgenstein *is* doing in those passages which certainly do seem to provide support for these accounts, if he is not taking those views. (In fact, what he is doing cannot be understood unless it is clear why it is easy to misunderstand those passages.) I shall consider one member of this group of wrong accounts, that of inference; and in order to make clear what Wittgenstein was trying to say, I shall use a comparison he suggests several times, that with our recognition of facial expressions.

Here is Michael Dummett's account of Wittgenstein's view.[3] Wittgenstein differed from the logical positivists, who held a modified conventionalist view of logical necessity, by going in for "a full-blooded conventionalism." On the logical positivists' account, the logical necessity of a theorem is derived from the conventions we accept for the use of certain terms. These are the conventions reflected in the axioms and rules of inference. Given our acceptance of these, we must accept the theorems, and this necessity is not a matter of any further convention. Wittgenstein on the other hand is said to hold that "the logical necessity of any statement is always the direct expression of a linguistic convention. That a given statement is necessary consists always in our having expressly decided to treat that very statement as unassailable; *it cannot rest on our having adopted certain other conventions which are found to involve our treating it so*" (pp. 328–9). The italics are mine. It is the italicized portion which is especially misleading. As I shall make clear, Wittgenstein is not, in Dummett's sense, a conventionalist, because he does not deny what conventionalists deny.[4]

Having foisted this infer-as-you-like account on Wittgenstein, Dummett makes the obvious objection to it, which I shall look at for two reasons. (1) An account of inference which was open to this objection would be a joke, would not come near being an account of anything we could *recognize* as inference at all. (2) I want to draw attention to a certain peculiarity in one of the formulations of the objection. A closer look at the kind of case Dummett is speaking about when he makes this objection will lead me into the central points I want to discuss.

Dummett proposes the following example of an application of Wittgenstein's supposed views. We first learned a criterion for saying that there were 12 things of a certain kind, namely, reaching 12 at the end of the procedure of counting. At a later time we choose to adopt a *new* criterion for saying there are 12; we say, e.g., when there are 7 boys and 5 girls in the room, that there are 12 children. There is no justification for this new criterion implicit in the original procedure. Can the old and new criteria clash? If we count 7 boys and 5 girls and 11 altogether, we say "there must have been a miscount." "The necessity of '$5 + 7 = 12$' consists just in this, that we do not count anything as a clash" (p. 329).

"This account," Dummett says, "is very difficult to accept, since it [ordinarily] appears that the mathematical proof drives us along willy-nilly until we arrive at the theorem" (p. 329). And again: "We naturally think that face to face with a proof, we have no alternative but to accept the proof if we are to remain faithful to the understanding we already had of the expressions contained in it" (pp. 332–3).

Dummett gives an argument in support of this natural objection (pp. 333–5). He considers in detail the decision to say that I must have miscounted whenever I reach such results as 7 boys, 5 girls, and 13 altogether. He points out that if I have miscounted, this means that there is some particular mistake I have made: I have either counted this child twice, or failed to count that one, or left out a number in the series, or. . . . And a disjunction is not true unless one at least of the disjuncts is. So "it cannot be right to count something as a criterion of the truth of the disjunction whose presence does not guarantee the existence of something which would show the truth of some one particular disjunct." Now, in this case, if one of the disjuncts *is* true, that means that there is something which anyone who could count would already have to take as showing he had miscounted. And so it seems that it is right to take the results "7 boys, 5 girls, 13 altogether" as a criterion of a miscount only if such results guarantee the existence of something which *would* have shown me I had miscounted by my earlier criteria. The necessity for a miscount when there are such results does not therefore depend entirely on our adopting some convention.

Dummett's "it cannot be right . . ." seems to be an example of "making the wrong, inappropriate gesture for a verbal expression in philosophizing."[5] For the verbal expression says that you have no business saying that the disjunction *must* be true, if p, unless p really *guarantees* that *one* of the disjuncts *is* true. You cannot say such-and-such must be the case unless such-and-such *must be the case.*[6]

This is the peculiarity to which I wanted to draw attention. I am not saying that there is no room for remarks like "You can't say it must unless it really must," but that, first, it is interesting that one can say just that without being aware that that is what one has said, that saying no more than that can, if it is decked out in enough words, have the appearance of being a justifying argument; and, secondly, that it is interesting that one can be under the impression that Wittgenstein has denied that one cannot say it must unless it really must. To take him to have denied it is in fact like taking the remark that what is shown cannot be said for a denial of what is shown. (Of course, if he had taken the view Dummett ascribes to him, that there is *nothing but* our inclinations to give this or that statement the place of a 'necessary truth', he would indeed have been attempting to deny that we cannot say it must unless it really must.)

To see what is right and what is wrong with Dummett's argument, I want to turn to a case like it but simpler, more primitive. My object is to show how Dummett's attempt to defend something Wittgenstein does not deny is a result of what Wittgenstein called being misled by a picture, in this case the picture involved in talk of necessary truth.

I shall first explain why I shall take a simpler example than Dummett's. Dummett's case was of a man who could count things but knew nothing of addition. Dummett says that before he is taught addition, he would say "I have miscounted" only when he noticed that he had, e.g., counted one of the children twice over; after being taught, he will say it on the basis of 'additively discordant results'. This account is queer in two ways; it is in part to avoid the problems thus caused that I shall consider a related but simpler case. First, it is surprising, to say the least, that a man should come to recognize the results "7 boys, 5 girls, 13 altogether" as a criterion for some mistake's having been made if he did not already accept *any* results like "7 boys first count, 8 boys second count" as a criterion for some mistake's having been made. One might say that you cannot hope to get the idea of *additively* discordant results over to someone who has no idea of *plain* discordant results. Secondly, some unclarity about his own example is reflected in Dummett's talk of mistakes and miscounts. "Mistake" is ambiguous here, "miscount" quite misleading. "A mistake has been made" leaves it open whether it is merely that a procedure has not been carried out properly, or rather that *the* result which the procedure would have in this case if carried out correctly has not been reached. (The first alternative does not imply that the procedure has such a result: one can, e.g., make a mistake when one's task is to count—merely to say the numbers in order—as fast as one can for five minutes.) Failure to notice the ambiguity of "mistake" is connected with failure to see that in the case as Dummett describes it, the man does not mean 'miscount' by "miscount"—and that is misleading. If he has the idea of a miscount, he has that of the correct result. But to have the idea of correct and incorrect results (as opposed to correctly and incorrectly carrying out the procedure), he must be able to recognize certain results as incompatible with each other, i.e. (in *this* case), as showing that *some* mistake has been made. If the man does not accept, e.g., the results "7 at the first count, 8 at the second" as showing some mistake, I do not see that the word "miscount" as he uses it has the force it has for us.[7]

These unclarities in Dummett's description can be avoided if we consider instead the case of a man who has yet to learn to recognize *any* results of counting things as discordant. He has been taught the following game (it could equally be part of another game, e.g., one kind of task in a game with a variety of tasks). Pencils are arranged in rows on a table. When you point to a row of pencils, he says the cardinal numbers in order from 1, one number for each pencil, as he touches them in order from the left. Then you say, "Outcome?" and he gives the last number. He has been taught that he must not count any pencil more than once, and he must not omit any, he must not count them in any order but one by one from the left, he must not leave out any numbers, or repeat any, or get them in the wrong order. He knows that all these are mistakes in the procedure he was taught, as is giving any number but the last when "Outcome?" is said. He is penalized for any such mistake. The pencils are quite open to view, and it is quite easy to see that no pencils are added to any of the rows or removed, nor do they seem to appear or disappear on their own.

Now I might well say that if the man carries out the procedure he was taught with the same row twice and says one number at "Outcome?" the first time and another the second, then he must have made a mistake.[8] Or I might say that there is a result which is *the* result if the procedure is carried out correctly. Let us try to see what it might be to get the man himself to recognize the necessity I just spoke of. Suppose that he has noted that usually when he gets two different results for the same row, he has made some mistake. But on some particular occasion, say, he gets two different results, we say, "You've made some mistake," and he denies this. Now suppose that what we *do* is this. We count a row together with him, emphasizing the way we *do* remain in step the whole time, bringing it out that we both say the same number for each pencil. Of course, this may not lead him to do or say or see anything.[9] But let us suppose that he says "Aha!" and now acts and speaks in such ways as to enable us to say that he sees that he must have made a mistake if he gets two such results.

In discussing this change, it will be useful to have some abbreviations. I shall refer to the game with the rules as I described them as activity A; the game like A but with the further rule that the penalty for mistakes is exacted whenever two different numbers are given at "Outcome?" for the same row, I shall call activity B. Before the change, the player said, "I've made a mistake" only when one of the mistakes listed in the description of A was drawn to his attention, and there was no conjunction of "I haven't made a mistake" with any number of statements giving the numbers he had reached which was ruled out; I shall call this activity C but what I have given is an incomplete account of it.[10] Afterwards he plays a game D in which one is entitled to say "I have made a mistake" in the old circumstances and also whenever two different numbers are reached in counting the same row; and "I have not made a mistake" is correspondingly limited.

It will be useful to ask what exactly is wrong with the following kind of account of the change (roughly the kind of account given by Dummett's Wittgenstein). What our 'proof' did was to get the man to switch from A to B and from C to D, where in both cases we have merely a pair of slightly different activities—the rules are slightly different—just as a game would be slightly different from chess if its rules differed in not permitting an option at the first move of a pawn. If the rules of C are different from those of D, "what we are talking about is something else."[11] And so, if we look at the matter this way, "There must be a mistake if I get first 7, then 8 for a row" would be *merely* a way of putting an arbitrary rule of a new game; and what the player goes on to say in this new game, D, has not the sense which "I made some mistake" has in the first game, game C. We may infer from this: if we say that "I made some mistake" *does* still mean the same when he says it on this new criterion, then we cannot accept that he has merely arbitrarily started playing a different game. So what I have to do is show how a description of what the man did in terms of an arbitrary switch from two games to two slightly different ones is inadequate, and this will have to account for "I am not saying something different now when I say 'I made some mistake' despite the fact that I use a new criterion." And similarly I must be able to account for such remarks as "The new rule in B is *right*"; for that would seem nonsensical if B is just a slightly different game. I want now to explain what more is involved than a mere switching from A to B in terms of a contrast between ways of seeing pairs of games. Someone might see activities A and B as related in the way chess and the variant I mentioned are related. But he might see the relation differently; perhaps he would say "A is really the same as B" or "I'm still doing the same thing, really." (Of course it is not enough that he says this.)

What sort of difference is this? In order to explain, I shall make use of a notion of Wittgenstein's which I discussed in "Secondary Sense."[12] Wittgenstein mentions the possibility that the children of a certain tribe unacquainted with trains might pick up the activity of playing at trains from children who were acquainted with trains. But "one could say that the game did not have the same *sense* for them as for us" (*PI*, §282). In "Secondary Sense" I gave a similar example: the sense which the activity of playing Hearts by oneself has for me depends on my understanding of it as playing by oneself a game for several players. To say that playing Hearts or chess or Monopoly by oneself has the sense it has for me only because I can play games for several people and know that these are among them is to give a merely necessary condition, not a sufficient one. Someone might play Hearts and also have picked up the activity of playing Hearts by himself, and yet the latter might not have the sense for him that it has for me. He does not see the game as I do, and this will come out in various ways in his mode of play. ("Fine shades of behavior. Why are they *important*? They have important consequences." *PI*, p. 204) Perhaps also the psychological accompaniments of playing in his case will be different. But this use of "sense" does not refer to any such psychological accompaniments of play: there is no accompaniment which one could rule out as a possible accompaniment in those for whom the game has a different sense. It is obvious that this use of "sense" cannot be identified with 'rules for the use', 'rules of a game', or anything like that; for two people may be playing a game with identical rules and yet the game have different sense for them. If the sense is not a matter of the rules for the activity or the psychological accompaniments of it, if it is not reducible to the behavior of those engaged in it, what is it? There is a kind of answer to this which I can give, but it may not be the kind which we feel we want. I can, for example, compare saying that two activities have the same sense to saying that two picture-faces have the same expression. This is not like saying that the mouths are the same length, the eyes the same distance apart: it is not that kind of description. But it is not a description of *something* else, the expression, distinct from that curved line, those two dots, and so on. Just as I can lead you to make comparisons of the expressions on picture-faces, I may be able to lead you to make comparisons of sense, e.g., by showing you obvious differences in sense. These comparisons are made in a different dimension from comparisons of rules for an activity, or psychological accompaniments of an activity, or behavioral dispositions. In the dimension in which games are compared by looking at their rules, there is no room for the comparison I am making. "If there is no room here, there *is* room in another dimension."[13] To go on then to ask "If a difference in sense is not a matter of different rules, *what* is it?" is like asking "If a description of the expression on a picture-face is not just a complicated method of describing lines and dots, *what is* being described?" It is not a shortcoming of philosophy that it should not be able to produce a something in reply, should not indeed have a reply beyond "Don't you know?" (a nudge, not an answer; it does not mean "We all know, of course, *what* it is, only it is impossible to say").[14]

The purpose of introducing the notion of sense was to explain the significance of, e.g., taking activity B as 'really the same as' activity A, and the player's doing just that, I should say, characterizes the sense engaging in B has for him. I am contrasting this player who engages in B seeing A in it, with, e.g., someone who was taught B without being given what we should regard as the explanation of the relation between the rules. The sense of activity B, as he engages in it, is different from what it is for the first player. And we can also imagine that someone who was taught A might just suddenly up and decide to play B instead, without seeing B as anything but a slightly different game. In such a case, too, I should say that it did not have the sense for him that it has for the first player.

One expression of taking activity B as really the same as A is the acceptance of the rule that different results for the same row be taken as a criterion for a mistake's having been made. But does this new rule mean that we are no longer talking about the same thing when we say "A mistake was made"? If one plays a language-game with rules different from the rules of another, but using the same 'pieces' (such as, in this case, "some" and "mistake"), there is a question whether this is merely a new language-game which just happens to involve the same pieces, or whether the identity of the pieces belongs to the game (*PI*, §566). And this is a question about the sense of the language-game.[15] Just as one can characterize the sense which B has for someone by saying that he sees it as already implicit in A, so one can characterize the sense that D has for someone by saying, e.g., that he sees the identity of the pieces with those of C as an essential characteristic of the game. But if he sees the face of C in D this will come out in the way he carries out the counting procedure. I mean that if, for example, someone were to *say* "I made a mistake" on the basis of having arrived at different results for the same row, but objected vigorously and did not at all appear to see the point when the ordinary penalty for mistakes was exacted in these circumstances, it would be quite obscure what he meant.

(I have been speaking of our taking a game as essentially the same as one with different rules, or our seeing the face of one game in another with different rules. In *Philosophical Investigations*, Part II, §xi, in dealing with related subjects, Wittgenstein points out that there are a number of related concepts which are important to us here. In particular, we may note a distinction between saying "Ah, it must be so!" when suddenly struck by a new physiognomy, and, e.g., "Of course it must come out the same whichever way you count," which might be said by someone who is not now struck by a physiognomy but rather takes it completely for granted. My references to taking one game as the same as another are meant then to refer to a variety of related possibilities.)[16]

I have tried to explain the inadequacy of describing the change brought about by the 'proof' in terms of a mere switch from A to B and from C to D. Such an account ignores differences of sense, where the sense of an activity is like the face it has. To avoid complexity, I have more or less ignored the fact that there are two closely related kinds of comparison of sense. There is the face the player sees in the activity and the face we see in what he does. "He sees a certain face in this game" is something which might be said by those who see a particular face in the way he plays it. (That a man sees the lion in a picture and does not merely 'read' the picture like a blueprint or know what is supposed to be there, is a description we may give when we see what he says and does, see in it the face of seeing the lion.)

I shall now try to show how the idea that we are forced to infer as we do is connected with what I have just said.

One of the important distinctions Wittgenstein discusses in §xi of Part II of the *Investigations* is the one I just mentioned, between a picture which conveys something to us immediately and a picture which we can recognize to be a representation of something or other by some method of projection, but which does not convey something immediately (see, e.g., pp. 203–4). Someone looking at a picture might see only curved lines here and yellow spots there, but he may know a way of telling that it represents a lion with a shaggy mane. On the other hand, the same picture may convey something to me immediately (what makes it do so will be partly a matter of "custom and upbringing"; *PI*, p. 201) so that I say with no hesitation or doubt at all—and not because I know or guess what it is supposed to be— "It's a lion charging right out at you." I have no choice here what I shall say. (If I had just decided to call it a lion, it simply would not be a case of seeing the lion.) But to say "It's *not just* lines and spots, it's a lion!" is not to say that there is *something* in addition to the lines, something which explains why I have no choice.[17] Even if the drawing conveys something to me in this immediate way, I cannot somehow rule out that someone else, or I myself later (perhaps seeing the picture against a different background) might see a zebra instead, in the same immediate way; nor can I rule out that it may convey nothing at all in this immediate way to someone else.[18]

We may compare my seeing activity B as essentially the same as A with seeing in a picture—no doubt about it, no ambiguity here—a charging lion. In such a case there is no choosing how I shall see it. I may choose to engage in an activity with such-and-such rules; I do not choose the sense the activity will have for me. If, for example, I am shown that in some game I have been playing, a trick allows the first player to win (*RFM*, p. 100), I "now see something different and can no longer naively go on playing"; of course in a sense the game consisted in the moves on the board, and "these I could perform as well now as before": I can decide to go through the moves as I did before, but not that the game shall still have the same sense. Similarly, if I have been shown a proof that 7 + 5 = 12, I might decide to go through the motions of the counting-game in just the way I did before, but that is not to say I can decide that the game will have the same sense it did. If I now go through the motions of counting all the children together when I am in no doubt that there are 7 boys and 5 girls, one might say that I cannot really mean it, that I cannot *think* "I wonder how many there are altogether." In *Remarks on the Foundations of Mathematics*, Wittgenstein compares this sort of "can't think" with "this sequence of notes makes no sense, I can't sing it with expression. I cannot *move* with it. Or what comes to the same here: I don't move with it." (I, §116) I do not choose to follow the tunes I do follow, nor the sentences I hear or read. If I decide to play a game in which one says "I have made a mistake" when one counts the same row twice and gets first 7 and then 7 again, I do not decide whether "mistake" will mean the same here as it did in the old game, or indeed whether the game will have the character of a language-game at all.

If we see that we are struck forcibly here, this may seem puzzling: we may ask, "*How* can I really be forced to see it as I do, unless there is *something* forcing me, something which would force anyone else as well?" This is one of the questions of which Wittgenstein says, referring to his own inclination to ask them, that they show that "something looks *paradoxical* to me; and so a picture is confusing me" (*RFM*, V, §45; compare also *BB*, p. 169). These questions are close to Dummett's remark that on Wittgenstein's view it would be quite unclear *how* the proof performs the remarkable feat of getting me to rule a form of words out of the language (p. 332). Now there are ways of answering such questions as "What kind of training do you have to give people if you want them to see game A and game B as in a sense identical or if you want them to follow this proof or grasp that calculation?" But this sort of question is not the kind we might want to ask, not the kind bothering Wittgenstein or Dummett, not the kind which supposedly shows that a picture is confusing us. The question "How can I really be forced to see it as I do unless there is something . . . ?" seems to arise only if we take the entirely natural use of "forced" here to be completely analogous to speaking of being forced by a threat, say, to do something unpleasant; in that sort of case, the force and what we are forced to do by it are distinct. And it thus seems that if the picture fits, there is *something* forcing us (the necessities which our rules reflect); if there is not something besides what we actually do, the picture does not fit, and we are not *really* forced. The point is, then, that we are misled into thinking that "forced" can be appropriately used only in certain ways and so do not look to see how it is used, how we would tell the difference between someone who merely makes it a rule to say such-and-such when so-and-so and someone who *infers*.[19] The man in Dummett's example, who accepts a new criterion for there being 12 children, is guided by the meanings of "5," "7," and "12" as he originally learned them. But it is just as confused to go from such facts to a philosophical theory to answer *how* this is possible as it would be to go from the fact that pictures do immediately convey lions to us to a philosophical theory concerning whether the lion is really there in addition to the lines before we see the picture, or whether we construct the lion ourselves, or whether perhaps it is really there but only comes into existence when we look. This is a picture of a lion—and that one there is not. I shall return to this matter of being misled by pictures.

Suppose then that we ask whether the sense of a term can be fully determined by the rules already given for its use, so that we can say of any suggested rule of inference that it is right or wrong, fits or fails to fit the sense already given. The argument Wittgenstein seemed to be committed to, on Dummett's view, was that the rules make the game, and different rules would not be wrong, but would just make the game a different one. Since no choice of rules is ever wrong, we are free to infer as we choose.[20] But consider the two rules: (1) you can say that a mistake has been made whenever you get first 7, then 8, for the same row; (2) you can say that a mistake has been made when you get first 7, then 7 again for the same row. We can indeed appeal to the meanings of the terms used in game C to distinguish between these rules: they are not merely two different rules, either of which we could just add to C. (We could merely go through the motions of the activity like C but with the second rule added; we would not be speaking of what would be spoken of by any beings for whom such a game made sense. The term they use when they catch a counting error and when they get the same result twice is not translatable into any term which has a place in our life or into a disjunction of such terms.) The appeal we can make to the meanings already determined is not an appeal to something which somehow makes it impossible for any beings, in any circumstances, to combine what we have done so far—the moves we have made, the explicit formulations of rules we have accepted—with a rule of inference different from ours, and still make sense. *Such* an impossibility simply does not come into an appeal to the meaning.[21] Of course, an activity might make no sense if played with different rules, but we are only too likely to mislead ourselves if we say, "It *has* something now, which it wouldn't have if we changed the rules"—and forget that it may *have* this in the way a face may have its particular expression.

I want to connect what I have already said with two points concerning the senseless and the nonsensical in the *Tractatus*. This is to make clear the ways in which we are 'misled by pictures'; and I shall also use it in trying to explain what has gone wrong when Wittgenstein is supposed to be denying just what he denied he was denying.

(1) Consider again the man who was brought to change from A to B. Originally, he gave the number which he reached in the series by doing something, as he might give the number he reached by counting as fast as he could for a minute; it is as yet no part of the game as he learned it and as he plays it that there is *the* number which the pencils have and which you necessarily reach if you carry out the method correctly (in the sense that when we are playing the game which can in fact be won by a trick, but do not yet know this, it is not part of the game as we play it that there is this possibility). While he is useful to us if we want to give descriptions, he himself does not

yet give any. What he says is not said in a game whose sense is such that something else is denied;[22] the game is not one of 'representation of a distribution in a space'.[23] I just said that there is some number which the pencils have: getting rid of the formal concept 'number' and replacing it (if we could!) with a disjunction of the possibilities in the players' space, we have an example of the kind of utterance which is senseless on the *Tractatus* account in the way "p v~p" is. What I said—"There is some number which they have"—was the expression of my taking activity B as I do, as I also expect others to do. It looks like the seeing of some sort of justification for engaging in B instead of simply playing A, like the grasp of a fact which makes the new rule in B correct. It is as if this 'fact' (there being some number which they have) made it possible for there to be truth *or* falsity in any sentence giving the number of pencils, gave sense to them all!

A concept, Wittgenstein said, is something like a picture with which one compares things (*RFM*, V, §50). What he means by a concept can have a place in a variety of language-games, but I shall consider simply telling someone that this thing is a such-and-such and that that one is not, and so on. We might teach someone to *say* "Yes it is like that" when the thing pointed to had some particular feature, and "No it's not" when it lacked it, and this procedure might be carried out correctly, without the person's having any concept of the feature in question, in Wittgenstein's sense. This can be seen in the way the pair of responses can be taught by the use of examples. "It's red" and "It's not red" can be taught in a way not unlike that in which we might teach the activity of sorting all red things into one pile, all square things into the other (and no square red things or other such awkward cases turn up).[24] No concept of red need be exercised in such a game. The ability to give the right response does not require any grasp of the sense of "not" (does not require that the presence of "it's red" in "it's not red" is not merely that of an index[25] in a complex word which has no more of an essential connection with "it's red" than there is between "red" and "square"). It is no part of the game as it was taught that in it there is comparison with a picture such that things must be *so or not so*. "It must either be red or not," like "There is some number which the pencils have," may be the expression of one kind of concept's being forced on us. We adopt a new instrument of language, a new language-game; but we speak as if the rules of this game were justified, as if there were in some sense a question whether the world in its essence were such as to permit this kind of comparison.

When a kind of description makes sense, it is natural to express this in a simile: we may speak of what *is*, independently of what is the case or not. (See, in addition to *PI*, *RFM*, I, §72, where Wittgenstein notes that "the proof has shown me that this is the case" involves the same simile. To speak of any statement as 'logically true' would involve this simile.) This connection which we make between making sense and something's existing of a certain sort can seem to be an insight into the relation between the nature of reality and the possibilities of making sense in general. And it can seem that if you do not take this form of expression at face value, you must, after all, be denying it, saying, "There is *nothing* in virtue of which this makes sense"; and so Wittgenstein has been taken to *deny* the view in the *Tractatus*.

(2) In thinking about what is said in the *Tractatus*, we may imagine a simple world, in which, say, there are 6 objects, which can be configured in such-and-such ways; and we imagine the language in which this world may be described. We imagine such worlds? Of course this is in an important sense quite impossible on the *Tractatus* view. To do so would be to imagine as not holding those 'facts' whose holding is a presupposition of the sense of all sentences, true or false, a presupposition of our *thinking* anything. These constructions of ours, whose comparatively easy intelligibility is supposed to help us understand the relation between language and the world, are in fact unintelligible (which is not to say they do not help), must be unintelligible, given the 'form' of the world (which determines what all propositions must have to be intelligible). Thus there is no possibility of comparing *different* ways of thinking and talking with what we do, if their being thinking and talking at all depends on their not being *really* different. If we do not make sense that way, we cannot, and there is really no sense in "we do not."

In the *Investigations*, on the other hand, Wittgenstein says that a language-game is to be regarded as an object of comparison (§§130–1). A way of thinking and talking can be compared with ours; we can ask how it is like some of ours, and how it is different. And the answer is not settled by its being a way of thinking, by its being possible to say something in this language. This, then, is a very important difference from the *Tractatus* view.

The fact that the language-games are then objects of comparison, and not descriptions to which reality *must* correspond, does not, however, mean that we might just up and engage in these language-games if we felt like it. We may compare the game which could be won by the first player by a simple trick. Wittgenstein wants to say of it: it stops being a game when this has been pointed out to us, but it is not as if it somehow was not a real game before this. It was a game all right, but all that we can do now is go through the motions of playing, we cannot *move* within the rules as we did before. Similarly, the player of A who is led to play B, to see in it the game he was playing before, can no longer go on playing A 'naively'; he cannot play as he did before. If, having come to see A in this new way, he consciously tries to play A as he did before, this will no longer be doing the same; he will be merely going through the motions, he will not mean what he says in giving discordant results as he did before (not because the psychological accompaniments are different). But this is as different from what it was before as was the wearing of togas in revolutionary France from wearing them in ancient Rome. That it is a matter of convention whether we wear togas or not is not to say whether, if we should decide to put them on, this would be a case of 'dressing up like a Roman' and not 'getting dressed'. I might say, "One can't any longer mean it, if one puts on a toga nowadays"—as I cannot mean what might be said in some language-games (See, e.g., *PI*, II, §xii; *Zettel*, §339).

If I find that I cannot do more than go through the motions of a game, or that a game with such-and-such in it has not for me the character of a language-game (or has it no longer) I may say that there is something which rules out the intelligibility of what is said there, that there are objective possibilities and impossibilities which determine that *this* can have no sense.

(It is partly this sort of point which accounts for the impression, given to Dummett and others, that Wittgenstein denies the *objectivity* of proof. It looks as if Wittgenstein is saying that it is all really subjective, after all, only what characterizes it is that we *say* it is not. But Wittgenstein is not denying that there is all the difference between what is really an objectively valid proof and one which only appears valid (Compare *PI*, §304). Misunderstanding of the use of "objectively valid" and of such natural philosophical responses as "By objective, I mean that it is not *just* a matter of our reactions, our feelings of conviction, but that these reactions are justified by facts independent of what we say or feel" can make it seem that what matters is a something which in fact could make no difference at all to us. Compare the idea that pain is like the beetle in the box with the idea that perhaps we have always gone wrong in multiplying 4 by 3. Just as it is what we call pain that makes all the difference between pain-behavior with and pain-behavior without pain, it is what we call a necessity that makes all the difference between objectively valid inference and invalid inference. When Wittgenstein says that a valid inference is one which follows a certain paradigm and whose validity is not dependent on anything else, it is the 'else' which is the point. It is not a matter of whether there is or is not really any necessity to infer as we do, but the *kind* of use "necessity" has.)

If one speaks of something, 'the form of the world' which rules out the intelligibility of a language-game with certain rules, one has not given an explanation, even though the language one uses is that of perceiving a profound truth about the world, may make it look as if one is explaining something in terms of something else underlying it (as if one had 'seen right through the phenomena'). Wittgenstein's idea is not to deny these 'profound truths'; he isn't trying to say that we are just mistaken if we think that it is the a priori order of possibilities that enables us to make sense with these sentences, if we think that the sense of a sentence 'points to a reality beyond it' (*BB*, p. 167), that certain rules of inference are right and others not merely mean we play a different game but a game which could not fit reality; but he is saying that such pictures and elaborations of pictures do not tell us what it means to say that something makes sense and something else does not, and they do stop us looking. They can, for example, stop us seeing that while it does matter what we call sense, while we cannot just say what we like, there are new possibilities here—and equally there is disappearance of old possibilities. If we express ourselves in the language of a guarantee of our rules by the underlying nature of the world, by a special sort of fact, it is easy to think that if someone were to play with somewhat different rules, he must be playing it wrong; if the timeless essence of the world guarantees the sense of what we say, guarantees that we are thinking something, what he says cannot really be thinkable at all. (See, e.g., *Zettel*, §§372–3.)

Now it might be asked: who except Wittgenstein himself ever got into these particular tangles? If I say that we are inclined to speak as if a profound truth about the world underlay the fact that such-and-such makes sense or does not, it may be certain, all right, that Wittgenstein once spoke this way, but why do I make it sound like something universal, or at any rate universal among philosophers?[26] Consider again part of Dummett's argument against the view that what does or does not follow, what does or does not make sense, is whatever we are pleased to decide. "It cannot be right to count something as a criterion for the truth of the disjunction whose presence does not guarantee the existence of something which would show the truth of some one particular disjunct"; in other words, if it is right to count the results "7 boys, 5 girls, 13 altogether" as such a criterion, it is because these results do really guarantee the presence of such a something. Dummett thus speaks as if there were facts of a special sort (guarantees given by the presence of some things and not by others) which made it right to accept certain rules, which explained why you could not just say what you liked. That is, he seems to be comparing two things of the same form: the rule that we are to infer this way, and the guarantee given by the presence of one thing that something else is present. If the rule is right—is not just something we have freely chosen, such that we could have chosen the opposite equally well—it has something behind it, namely the guarantee. This picture of what it is for a rule to be right, if its application is not examined, must make it appear as if there are two alternatives: *either* you accept that the rule is right only if there is something behind it, the guarantee; *or* you deny that there are any such guarantees setting limits to what we may say, and are thus committed to the view that we are free to infer as we like. ("We are free" would not imply that there is no psychological pressure to go one way rather than the other, but rather that there is *nothing but* our feeling inclined to do this rather than that.)[27]

(Here we might compare the sort of case discussed in Part II of the *Brown Book*: when we distinguish between a mere jumble of lines and a drawing of a face we may speak as if the latter were not a mere jumble because there was a particular expression-pattern which the lines of the drawing fitted, and as if the jumble were a mere jumble because there was none which it fitted. We use a form of expression which suggests a comparison of the lines on the paper with something else: a pattern in our minds. The point of bringing up this example here is that the denial that what we are doing is comparing two things with the multiplicity of a face (*BB*, p. 165) need not seem to involve the claim that there is really nothing but a jumble. It is easier here to recognize such a denial for what it is: it says that we can speak of a picture-face as having a particular expression when we are making a comparison of it with something else, say, another face, and also when that is not what we are doing; and so the use of a form of words which suggests a comparison—and the fact that we mean what we say—does not settle what we are doing.)

I shall now try to make clear the *kind* of mistake that is made when Wittgenstein is said to hold that we are free to infer as we like, or to give a behavioristic account of meaning, taking as an example the picture embodied in Dummett's remark about the guarantee. Suppose that someone takes this picture as making it clear (in essentials at any rate) what is required if we are properly to speak of a rule of inference as correct, and that it therefore does not occur to him that even given that we mean just exactly what we say, the use of the remark may be other than what one might think from the form of words used. If someone looks at the matter this way, the denial that what we are *doing* is comparing the rule with something else can only appear to him as an attempt to replace the picture of such a comparison with one supposedly more correct (thus a denial that the picture of the comparison fits in the way one might think is taken as the denial that it fits at all); it thus appears as the assertion that there is nothing but different rules of inference, to be chosen as we please.

Wittgenstein then *neither* accepts the second alternative *nor* offers us a third. But this is not to say he accepts the first alternative either. To think of the two as alternative accounts, to think that one must accept one or the other (or, if not, come up with a third, whatever that might be) is already to have been misled by the picture embodied in our talk of logical necessity. That it can be misleading is not to say that we should really give up using the picture, stop talking that way. It is no accident that we do; no mischievous demon has been at work in our language putting in misleading analogies which the philosopher can simply discard when he has seen through them. To give up thinking and talking in such terms would be to give up the life in which these figurative expressions do have an application (just as giving up the picture of our 'inner' mental life would be giving up the kind of life in which that picture is applied). To give up altogether the pictures that mislead us when we talk as philosophers about proof and reasoning would be to give up—not Platonist mathematics—but mathematics, reasoning, inference, what we recognize as making sense, as human thinking. The picture of a necessity behind what we do is not then to be rejected, but its application looked at. When Wittgenstein attacks a picture, it is the picture thought of as giving us an idea of the use, and elaborations of the picture which emphasize just what is misleading.

I took Dummett's remark about the guarantee as an example, but I should say much the same about our saying that we are forced to infer as we do by the meanings of the words we use, as these have *already* been determined. There is nothing wrong with the picture (again, of a comparison between the ways of inferring which are for us part of making sense, and something else which underlies them and makes them correct) provided we realize that it can mislead us about what it really is to distinguish sound from unsound inferences, the ways we do this and the ways we recognize what others are doing as the same. This does not mean that whatever we choose to say is right, is right; for if I merely chose to say "This conclusion follows" or if many of us merely chose to, it is obvious that whatever we were doing, it would not be inferring.[28] What we do when we infer is such that it makes sense to say that we are forced to do it that way, given the meanings of the words, but if you want to know what sense it makes, the pictures will not help you.

Appendix

I shall try to make clear what is shown by some of Dummett's objections. ". . . The mathematical proof drives us along willy-nilly until we arrive at the theorem" (p. 329). It drives us along because of the meaning already in the terms: that is the 'driver'. And this meaning, it seems, is such that, should we adopt some rule other than, incompatible with, the one we adopt in accepting the theorem, this could not make sense, could not, together with the original rules, determine concepts different from ours. It is not only that *we* should not find ourselves able to do more than go through the motions of a game with such rules. For it to seem that this is not all, for it to seem that there *could* be no meaning determined by such rules, no playing such a game and meaning it, for it to seem that the original rules *completed* a meaning, a fat balloon whose shape was now settled without any possibility of pumping more air into this corner or that—all this says something about what it is like for us to take the proof as proof. We may indeed express ourselves in terms of limits on what could have sense, limits fixed unalterably, independently of our lives ("Look here, you *can't* mean anything by that!"). And indeed, if we were confronted with a case of someone who, some time after looking at a proof, simply decided or felt suddenly impelled to play a game like one he had played before, only with a new rule that it was to be counted as a mistake if anyone reached a result expressed by a sentence adding the word "not" to the sentence at the end of the proof, he would obviously not be accepting the proof as proof. The game he plays would not be one in which the theorem had the place of a theorem, just because he had not seen the old use of the expressions contained in the theorem as essentially the same as the new: the rules of the game he goes on to play could not be said to determine a new concept *with* the old rules. Thus Dummett's objection that "we think that face to face with the proof we have no alternative but to accept it if we are to remain faithful to the understanding we already have of the expressions contained in it" is not something Wittgenstein would deny.

Consider also the argument Dummett gives against the view, supposedly Wittgenstein's, that "one has the right simply to *lay down* that the assertion of a statement of a given form is to be regarded as always justified,[29] without regard to the use that has already been given to the words contained in the statement" (p. 337). Dummett says that if Wittgenstein were right, communication would be in constant danger of breaking down. The point of his argument is essentially this: I cannot understand the new sentences you utter unless I know the sense of the words. If you have a right to accept any rules of inference you choose, without regard to the use you have already given a word, you will be unable to give me an explanation of the sense of your words without reference to the inference relations which you have elected to recognize between every sentence using any of the words and *all* other sentences. Any explanation you give me of the meaning of a word which falls short of this still leaves it open how you will exercise your right to recognize as valid whatever inference-patterns involving this word you choose; since these 'elections' of yours go to determine the sense of the word, I do not know what you mean. Compare the case of two people who would give the same explanation of the existential quantifier. They may, as we know, differ in the arguments which they accept as valid, at the end of which there is a sentence including the quantifier. So the original explanations of the meaning of the quantifier hid from me the difference in the meaning of those sentences which both would assert. In *this* case, I can learn about the difference in meaning; but if it is impossible for *any* explanations which do not refer explicitly to *all* sentences to shut off the possibility of further determinations of meaning, there is no way to avoid such possible failures of communication.[30]

The objections I discussed first reflected the fact that the account of inference ascribed by Dummett to Wittgenstein is not an account of something we could take to be *inference* at all; this last argument shows, not that if Wittgenstein were right, communication would be in danger of breaking down, but that the account ascribed to Wittgenstein is not an account of *communication* at all. If I have *simply* adopted a new rule governing my noise-productions, this will not *be* ruling a form of words out of the language; and even if everyone does it, it will not be ruling a form of words out of the language; for it will not be language. It is not that I shall not know what you mean, but that a game in which the players, having done some things, are not *in a sense* forced to do something else, is not one in which there is the face of meaning at all. "Language is a phenomenon which we know from our language" (*RFM*, p. 103). And we could even say, "Language *has* something—it's not just saying so-and-so in such-and-such circumstances." Its rules are akin both to what is arbitrary *and* to what is not. (See *Zettel*, §358.)

(To say that it would not be language if we could make new rules however we liked is not to say that we have a guarantee that there will be no breakdown of communication.)

Notes

1. I am indebted to many helpful comments from Dr. Aaron Sloman, who, however, disagrees with most of what I have to say.
2. The misunderstandings I have in mind in fact depend on misunderstandings of "use" which, for example, make wholly unintelligible Wittgenstein's view that use is difficult to look at. Knowing the use is not knowing when to come out with an expression; when, however, he is said to reduce meaning to use, it is use in this flat, dead sense which is often meant.
3. "Wittgenstein's Philosophy of Mathematics," *Philosophical Review*, 58 (1959), pp. 324–48. Reprinted in Dummett, *Truth and Other Enigmas* (London, 1978), pp. 166–85, and in *Philosophy of Mathematics*, ed. Benacerraf and Putnam (Englewood Cliffs, 1964), pp. 491–509.
4. In any case, his use of "convention" (like "use") is often misunderstood.
5. *Zettel* §450. It is not the sort of case mentioned in §451, though it is a related one.
6. That it is of this form comes out even more clearly if we consider taking the result "7 boys and 5 girls" as a criterion for there being 12 children. Dummett's argument, applied here, would amount to saying that it cannot be right to do this unless there being 7 boys and 5 girls does guarantee the existence of something which would show the truth of "there are 12 children" by the old criteria, namely, 12 children. Compare *PI*, p. 201, final paragraph, a very similar example of a literal repetition accompanied with the gesture of finding a justification for something. I'm not saying that Dummett's argument shows nothing. See Appendix.
7. This point is related to that made by Wittgenstein in *PI*, p. 187, about the difference between describing and doing something which, while it may be useful to others in giving a description, is not itself that. What I have said is that the question whether what one is doing at the end of a count-and-point procedure (I do not say a 1–1 correlation procedure) is *giving the number of ———s* depends partly on such things as whether one accepts any criteria for *some* mistake's having been made in carrying out the procedure, other than noticing some particular mistake. Dummett actually says that the person he describes could find out by counting that there were 5 boys in the room. This is not compatible with the rest of Dummett's description. *We* may find out how many by asking the person for his result, but *he* has not got a way of finding out how many there are (and cannot even ask) unless he has a grasp of the distinction between what he got and how many there are.

    On the same page of the *Investigations*, Wittgenstein says "A description is a representation of a distribution in a space." G.E.M. Anscombe comments that we can hear in this remark the voice of the author of the *Tractatus* "like that of the drowned ghost in the song." (*Introduction to Wittgenstein's Tractatus*, London 1959, p. 78) The difficulty with Wittgenstein's remark is knowing what to do with this *Tractatus*-like remark in its setting in Part II of the *Investigations*; one main difficulty with the *Investigations* as a whole is to see what exactly is happening to the *Tractatus*. What I have said about the person who does not as yet accept any results of repeated counts as showing that some mistake or other has been made (although he does speak of mistakes) is an application of this remark about description. Two points: (1) it is not relevant whether Wittgenstein's use is the 'ordinary use' of "description"; what he here calls descriptions are of central importance in our lives. (See also *RFM*, remarks on concepts on pp. 194–5.

Here and elsewhere in this essay, all references to *Remarks on the Foundations of Mathematics* are to the 1956 edition.) (2) It should not be imagined that recognition of the incompatibility of two results, in the sense of their showing that *some* mistake has been made, is anything like a 'necessary and sufficient condition' for description. To see that it is not sufficient, take the following case. If a rule required dance-step$_1$ when one sort of music is played, dance-step$_2$ for another kind, etc., one might recognize that *someone* at least must have made a mistake if not all are doing the same step. But even if one does realize that, one's own waltzing away, say, is not a description of the music. I shall not discuss the general issue of the necessity of this condition. But one of my reasons for taking a more primitive case than Dummett's is that in my example one can more easily see the connection between logical necessity and the idea of description as representation in a space.

8. I should also say that he has made one of a more limited list of mistakes, e.g., that it could not be that the only mistake was his counting from the right rather than from the left. I mention this to bring out further the distance between the capacity to go through a count-and-touch routine and a capacity to tell how many there are.

9. Is he then 'stupid'? The question is what we are calling stupidity here; it can be answered by trying to make clear what non-stupidity is; and this is what I shall be doing on pp. 247–50. Suppose he sees only the relation between two apparently properly conducted counts and does not see the necessity I wanted to show him. What phenomena would *have* to draw his attention to a necessity underlying phenomena? It is a mistake to think that I could avoid this problem by offering him a formal proof that, in such-and-such circumstances, a method with these features has a result which you must reach if you carry it out properly. Appeal to the notion of formal proof in fact increases the difficulty, for a number of reasons.

I have referred to *the* result of counting a row of pencils. To avoid a possible confusion here and elsewhere in this chapter, I should point out that there is an important distinction between this case and the case, e.g., of counting the cardinals greater than 17 and less than 62. In both cases one might say that there is *a* correct answer to the question "How many?" But the difference between the two cases comes out in, for example, the possibility of *calculating* the answer to "How many?" in the second case but not in the case of the pencils. I am indebted to Rush Rhees for drawing my attention to Wittgenstein's discussion of this point and to the significance of calculating the answer.

10. I have not indicated why it is a *language*-game nor why I identify what is said in it as something like our talk of mistakes. In particular I have not said what makes "I have not made a mistake" incompatible with "I have made a mistake." The question can be discussed in a way which is in part similar to my discussion of the incompatibility of "7" and "8" in certain circumstances.

11. *Zettel*, §320.

12. Chapter 8 of this volume.

13. *PI*, p. 200. In a related context (*Lectures and Conversations*, p. 32), Wittgenstein uses the metaphor of 'weighing in a different balance'. But a new balance here means something that gives you the possibility of a new kind of comparison, and that is a new dimension.

14. A first reaction might be that philosophy should if possible avoid any truck with such notions as this of sense. But is that reaction so natural? Our suspicions of such notions may themselves be the symptoms of philosophical disease. (It may

seem that I make the notion of sense sound 'mysterious and ineffable'. But that is because the claim that a term is used differently from the way we are inclined to think it *must* be used is not taken seriously, but is taken to mean that it is used in just the same way, only of *something* quite different, and of course this 'something' would have to be something quite mysterious and ineffable!)

A main concern of Wittgenstein's is to enable us to see how it is that there is no paradox in rejecting the demand to produce a something-besides in reply to these "*what* is it?" questions and at the same time *not* saying "There is really nothing here but. . . ." (See, e.g., *PI*, §304, *RFM*, Part I, app. II §18, Part II, §76, Part V, §45.) It is significant that such passages have been taken to express both acceptance of behaviorism (e.g., by P. Bernays in his review of *RFM*, *Ratio*, 2 [1959–60] pp. 1–22) and acceptance of the grammar suggested by "something besides" (e.g., by A. Donagan, "Wittgenstein on Sensation" in ed. G. Pitcher *Wittgenstein: The Philosophical Investigations* [Garden City, New York, 1966] pp. 324–51.)

15. That is, it cannot be settled by considering merely the moves so far made, together with explicit formulations of rules, if any (these being moves in a related game), as these alone do not settle the sense, do not even settle whether the game was a language-game.

16. If one were to speak of an *experience* of coming to see the face of one game in another, the 'substratum of this experience', would be 'the mastery of a technique', which means that this concept of experience is different from, though related to, that of having a toothache. See *PI*, p. 208.

17. The objection is thus not to "something besides" but to the grammar it suggests. That one is misled by the suggestion comes out in what one might call the 'something besides' tone of voice, characteristic of the step from, e.g., "not just a collection of words, it has a sense" to "there is something in addition to the words, their sense". Donagan (op. cit., p. 345) is a striking case of a philosopher who makes precisely this step in the course of expounding Wittgenstein's attempt, at *PI*, §304, to show us that we need not make it. Passages like §304 need to be *heard* in the mind's ear; one has to hear what they are directed against.

18. This does not, however, imply that it is just a 'psychological fact' about me that I see the lion, or that it is all merely a matter of my behavioral dispositions.

19. If Wittgenstein were, as Dummett suggests, substituting the picture of 'nothing there', or any other such picture, for the 'Platonist picture' of discovery within a world of peculiar objects, he could not have been serious in saying that we had to look and see what inferring was in actual cases (nor could he have been serious in saying that he was not advancing any debatable theses; *any* answer to such a question as "Well, *is* there something *or* nothing there?" would be just such a thesis). It is only if we look that we can see what it is we call inference, the variety of the cases we recognize as valid inference. When Wittgenstein speaks of the 'motley' of mathematics, he does not mean that we just choose to follow proofs, that proof is not objectively valid, but that objectively valid proofs are genuinely various, and so is what we call following a proof.

20. Compare *Zettel*, §320 ". . . if you follow other rules than those of chess you are *playing another game*; and if you follow grammatical rules other than such-and-such ones, that does not mean you say something wrong, no, you are speaking of something else." One difference between this and the view of Dummett's Wittgenstein is that in *Zettel* there is no implication that we can just simply choose the sorts of things we shall 'speak of'. What we are speaking of, and

indeed whether we are speaking of anything at all, is a matter of the sense of the game. Compare also Dummett's Wittgenstein, who "appears to hold that it is up to us to decide to regard any statement we happen to pick on as holding necessarily, if we choose to do so" (p. 336) with the actual remarks of Wittgenstein's which gave Dummett this impression (*RFM*, V, §23). The view can be read into these remarks only by assuming that Wittgenstein thinks we have "the right to attach what sense we choose to the words we employ" (Dummett, p. 336). But Wittgenstein does not take such a view; if he suggests that a technique of inference different from ours would not be wrong (in this sense, that the rules of inference are involved in the determination of the meaning of the signs), this must be taken with the view that "not every technique has an application in our life" (*PI*, §520).

21. See Rush Rhees, "The Philosophy of Wittgenstein," in Rhees, *Discussions of Wittgenstein* (London 1970) pp. 37–54. I am much indebted to this article and to Rhees's Preface to *The Blue and Brown Books*.

22. It is important that it is a matter of the sense of the activity that when something is said, something else is denied; this cannot be put into a description of what is to be done when. Compare the failure of Friedrich Waismann's attempt to build propositionhood into the structure of a game (*The Principles of Linguistic Philosophy*, chapter XIV, pp. 285–91). Compare also Dummett's view (p. 347) that someone has learned the meaning of the logical operators if he has been trained to produce complex statements in certain situations. (Dummett speaks of 'assertion' but leaves it obscure why it should be called that.)

23. I am not saying that there is 'representation of a distribution in a space' afterwards; for, on my description, as the player engages in B, it has not for him the sense of a *language*-game. We can say "As he sees it, there is *some* outcome uniquely determined by the row," but not that he tells us how many pencils he thinks there are.

24. This point is not altered by consideration of more complicated games with "not"; it is connected with Wittgenstein's criticisms of Frege in the *Tractatus* (see especially 5.02). See also *RFM*, V, §47.

25. In the sense of *Tractatus* 5.02, *BB*, p. 21. See also the first paragraph of *RFM*, V, §47.

26. [Note added in 1990] The reading of the *Tractatus* implicit in this paragraph is modified elsewhere in this volume; see the introductory essays and chapters 3 and 6.

27. Of course, one could object that this is not really being free to *infer*; to say something merely because you are psychologically impelled to is not to draw a conclusion. (This point is closely connected with the problem of whether reason alone can determine the will.)

28. This is part of what Dummett's argument *can* show. For a consideration of some of his arguments in the light of what I have been saying, see Appendix.

29. A queer view to ascribe to Wittgenstein, who tells us to look at the use. It is obscure, to say the least, what it would be for the rules of a language-game to say, e.g., "You may always write this down." What Wittgenstein says of logical truths is, for example, "It could very well be said that they were not propositions at all; and one's writing them down at all stands in need of justification" (*RFM*, pp. 53–4). "To accept a proposition as unshakably certain—I want to say—means to use it as a grammatical rule" (*RFM*, p. 81)—and Wittgenstein does not mean some rule running "You may always assert this." To take a proposition as nec-

essarily true may then be to give it a certain function, but it is a long story to say what makes it possible for what we do to *be* giving the proposition this function.

30. The situation is indeed worse than this, as even if you tell me all the inference relations you accept, sentence by sentence, still, on the view being attacked by Dummett, there would have to remain a question of what followed from what you had said. Dummett says that on the view he is attacking it is impossible to give an account of the use of our language. The sort of account he has in mind *is* impossible. He claims that "the general form of explanation of meaning, and hence of the logical operators in particular, is a statement not of the truth-conditions but of the assertibility conditions" (p. 347). No statement, either of truth-conditions or of assertibility conditions can, taken by itself, be an adequate explanation of the meaning of the logical operators or of anything else, either on the *Tractatus* view or on that of the *Investigations*. Dummett suggests that Wittgenstein went from one to the other of these views, but it is important that he took *neither*. On the *Tractatus* view, the truth-table for a complex proposition is itself a propositional sign; that is, it is merely an alternative notation; the truth-table for a connective is simply an alternative notation for the connective; and no notation can be understood unless the 'real signs' are *already* grasped. To speak as Dummett does in this context of a Frege-*Tractatus* view is to ignore the significance of the criticisms of Frege in the *Tractatus*, to ignore the remark that what can be shown cannot be said, to ignore Wittgenstein's 'fundamental idea', to ignore the significance of the 'real signs', to forget the relation between 4.024 and 3.42. Both *RFM* and the *Investigations* start from the problems raised bt this way of looking at things. (Compare *Tractatus* 5.552 and *RFM*, I, §8; and note the connection between the idea of a grasp of the 'real signs' as presupposed in any explanation of the terms in our spoken language, and the opening sections of the *Investigations*; the connection is particularly clear in §32.) Unless one is clear about these points in the *Tractatus*, it is impossible to follow what is said about 'use' in the *Investigations*, impossible to see the connection between what was said about 'showing' in the *Tractatus* and the idea of a 'form of life' in the *Investigations*. It is significant that the incoherence of Dummett's example (of the person who supposedly understands that there are 5 boys, although he does not grasp its incompatibility with anything else) is due to the same confusion I have just been talking about: the idea that what we understand can be made clear in a statement, either of truth-conditions or of assertibility conditions. "How words are understood is not told by words alone" (Zettel, §144).

Chapter 10
Riddles and Anselm's Riddle[1]

Where you can ask, you can look for an answer, and where you cannot look for an answer, you cannot ask either. Nor can you find an answer. (*PG*, p. 377)[2]

By "look," Wittgenstein meant "look with a systematic method." The interesting questions in mathematics don't have such methods of solution. Are they then not questions? They are spurs to mathematical activity, stimuli for the mathematical imagination. (*Z*, §§696–7). Trying to solve them is like trying to move one's ears when one has never done so, like trying to unravel a knot which one does not even know is actually a knot—and setting someone such a problem is like asking him how white can win in twenty moves in a game whose rules have still to be invented. (*PG*, pp. 363, 393; *PR*, pp. 182–5). One can, however, say "I shall know a good solution when I see it"—and in that respect these problems are like riddles. (*L*, p. 84). They are of an utterly different sort—problems in a different sense—from those one gives a child, and for which it gets an answer according to rules it has been taught. Again Wittgenstein used the comparison with a riddle to make this clear. The ones given to the mathematician without a method of solution are

> like the problem set by the king in the fairy tale who told the princess to come neither naked nor dressed, and she came wearing fishnet. That might have been called not naked and yet not dressed either. He didn't really know what he wanted her to do, but when she came thus he was forced to accept it. It was of the form "Do something which I shall be inclined to call 'neither naked nor dressed'." It's the same with the mathematical problem. "Do something which I shall be inclined to accept as a solution, though I don't know now what it will be like." (*MM*, 22.5.35).

I shall turn the comparison between such mathematical problems and riddles in the opposite direction and use it to cast light on riddles in Part I. My aim, though, is more general: the kind of groping search, of seeking for something not specifiable in advance, and which perhaps is not for anything that can intelligibly be described at all, includes searching for an answer to "the riddle of life in space and time," "the riddle *'par excellence'* " as Wittgenstein called it, and which he said was not a question. It includes seeking God, as Anselm described it—what we look for we do not know, and what we find is not what we looked for. The discussion of riddles is thus meant to bear on the great riddles, and on the notions of ignorance and mistake with which they are correlative. And so also on the related idea in such contexts of the *hidden*: the hiddenness of God is akin to the hiddenness of the solution to a riddle, to that of any object of the kind of groping search with which I am concerned.

I shall not take on these problems in general but shall instead, in Part II, look at "What is that than which no greater can be conceived?" which I shall treat as a great riddle. It is thus possible to see what Anselm's proof in *Proslogion* II–IV accomplishes, and where it leaves the fool. It is one thing for a riddle to have a solution, and quite another for us to be clear that if it does, the solution cannot be anything we take to be a figment of the imagination. In the case of that than which nothing greater can be conceived (hereafter "TTWNGCBC"), Anselm proves the latter; but the fool may deny that there is any solution. This is unlike saying that nothing falls under some concept. With any riddle, though, one may think there is no solution and be shown up—but not exactly by the facts. What shows there is a solution to the Sphinx's riddle is not the facts of human locomotion.

The fool may be shown up or not, but not by philosophy—it cannot lead to the conclusion that he is trying to say something that cannot meaningfully be said. The attempt to show the opposite by Wittgenstein's methods involves a failure to understand the nature and source of great riddles. I shall examine this question briefly in Part III.

I

If you want to know what is proved, look at the proof.
(*PG*, p. 369).

If it is only the proof which shows us what it means to say, e.g., "Every algebraic equation has a solution," what about "Does every algebraic equation have a solution?" It seems that it is only when we have the answer that we know how to understand the question. (*MM*, 10.6.35). Before the proof, "there was only a rough pattern of that sense in the verbal language"—and the idea that it might in some way be filled in, the expression given mathematical sense (*PG*, p. 374, *RFM*, p. 153). Similarly with a riddle: it is only when one has the solution that one knows how to take the question, what it is for it to have an answer. That is clear in the case of the Sphinx's riddle, or that of the king and the princess. But take "What has six legs, two heads and a tail?" (a horse and rider)—and contrast it with "What grows from a minute disc and has thin leafy fronds, bordered with a delicate fringe of pale brown hairs?" The sense of the predicate in the riddle is unclear, and the sort of value the variable can take in "x has 6 legs . . ." is completely undetermined; just the opposite is true of the honest question (compare *PR*, p. 145). If we rephrase the riddle "What *beast* has six legs . . . ?" the meaning of "beast" is left unclear. If I told you the riddle and explained what "beast" meant and "having six legs" etc., we could not say that *you* had solved it. Wittgenstein makes a parallel point about asking someone to construct a heptacaidecagon, before any method has been developed. To explain exactly what the request meant would be to give him the answer. (*L*, pp. 76, 85).

Suppose I demonstrate the solution to you by showing you the last horse-and-rider in the world, and counting its legs, heads and tail. If it were then swallowed up by an earthquake, you could not say "There is *no longer* a solution to the riddle, although there *was* one." (Compare *L*, p. 76.) Whether there is as solution does not depend on what exists, nor on the ways in which we can identify things falling under this or the other concept. *Having six legs, two heads and a tail* is not a way of identifying things falling under the concept 'horse and rider'; it is not a mark of any concept, in Frege's sense or taken more loosely. (A riddle-beast is not something to be looked for among the fabulous beasts.) Saying "There is no solution to this riddle" is thus very different from saying "There is no winged horse," and equally from "There is no plant such as you have described." Correspondingly, the occurrence in a proposition of "the solution to the riddle '——'" or of the riddle-phrase itself is very different from the occurrence of descriptions like "the winged horse." These are 'descriptions' in a different sense; "description" is like "question" or "discovery," which Wittgenstein says may be used for entirely different sorts of thing (*PG*, pp. 359, 380). In mathematics, he said, there is no such thing as a description and its result, or something named and something also described (*MM*, 3.6.35). Before we have a method of calculating it, "the first prime greater than 10^{10}" is not a phrase which refers to something we are not yet able to pick out in other ways—and "the trisection of the angle" should not be thought of as a description that *cannot* be satisfied. Wittgenstein's warnings about investigations of the mathematical realm—against thinking that we look for objects which satisfy a given description, or discern the properties of given objects—should be seen then with the remark about the princess, who does not find something satisfying a description, but a way of making the king's words into a description.

If I ask you "What has six legs . . . ?" and you give up, I might point down the road and say "There's one." That might help you to get the solution, but you might only gather that to solve the riddle you had to find a way of describing what I had pointed to, which you could connect to the riddle-phrase—and, knowing that, you would probably succeed. But if I had not led you to grasp *how* it is to be thought of as something with six legs, etc., I have not told you the solution or shown you it. Two general points come out here. First, that "I shall know a good solution when I see it" does not mean that the 'fit' between the riddle-phrase and a thing is as it were automatically given by the thing; far from it. There is not anything, present in our experience or thought of, which will of itself enable us to make the kind of connections we need to make to solve a riddle. Saying that you will know a good solution if you see one is not at all like saying you only know what love is when you have felt it. Further, to know the solution to a riddle is not merely to know of something that thought of in *some* way or other it is the solution: you have to know *how* it is the solution. If you are simply told that *man* is the solution to the Sphinx's riddle, but do not understand why—if, that is, you do not understand why man is supposed to have four legs in the morning and so on—you are in the position of someone who 'knows' that every equation has a solution without any idea of how that may be arrived at. In neither case does the proposition giving the solution stand on its own.

In the light of what I have said it may seem puzzling that we can guess at the solution to a riddle, and puzzling, too, that we can reject something as the solution without knowing what the solution is. For if it is the finding of something we are willing to recognize as the solution that fixes the sense of the riddle-question, how can we reject anything before we have the solution? I could put the problem this way. Whoever is asked the Sphinx's riddle has the answer before his eyes, as it were. But if the solution to a riddle can be something that is before your eyes and you still not recognize it, how are we able to say of anything that it *is not* the solution? If in a sense we do not know what we are looking for, how can we say "This isn't it"? And yet it is clear we can. If you were the princess and the king had set you the task, you might think "At any rate, I cannot come in my ordinary clothes." Or take the corresponding kind of question in mathematics. If I am asked "What fraction, squared, gives 2?" I can recognize, even before I have a system which gives me a way of deciding all such questions (and in that way fixes their sense), that 1.4 is *not* the answer. But *what* it is not, is only as yet a form of words. The rejection of an answer, like the question itself, seems not quite to grasp its own sense (see *PG*, p. 455), seems to exist, as it were, on borrowed sense, on an advance from the solution to the problem.

This capacity to reject candidate-solutions is really quite problematic. For suppose the Sphinx has asked you her riddle, and you are groping for a solution. As a centipede goes by, you think, "Well, it can't be him, he's got too many legs at every time of day." By the same reasoning, though: the solution to the riddle has to be something that at some time has more than two legs. Men have two legs or one or none, and never more; so—it seems—it cannot be *man* either. If the sort of reasoning by which you exclude *the centipede* would also exclude *man,* and if *man* is the solution,[3] then it seems you were correct in excluding *the centipede* only by accident, that you had no right to your certainty he was not it.

We have given a condition which the solution to the Sphinx's riddle must meet—and we can often give such conditions, just as we can for the solution to a mathematical problem. But what meeting the condition amounts to is clear only when we have the solution (compare *L,* p. 78). And so our difficulty is this: how can one say of something that it does not meet a necessary condition for being the solution if—it seems—by twisting meanings enough, anything can be the solution? Compare the expectation of a Messiah; for example, "In what manner should the Messiah come, since through him the scepter was to be eternally *in* Judah, and at his coming the scepter was to be taken away from Judah?" One might say, from the point of view of a first century Jew, "Herod clearly fulfils half the prophecy, since the scepter he holds is taken *away* from Judah—but not the other half. But as for Jesus, he fulfils neither, having *no* scepter." (*P,* p. 216). One can specify other necessary conditions too of being Messiah, which were apparently not met by Jesus. But the claim is then made that all of them are met, if understood properly—that he is not, as it had seemed, even more of a failure than Herod, but rather an exact fit, although this is only something that he himself is supposed to make clear after his death. (Compare a remark of Pascal's that we only understand the prophecies when we see their fulfilment; their obscurity is inseparable from the hiddenness of God; *P,* p. 180.)—What sort of game *is* it then, in which what seems to be a clear non-solution turns out to be the solution after all, if only you are ingenious enough in determining what is to count as fulfilling the conditions? There is a 'riddle' which itself comments on this feature of riddles:

A: What's green, hangs on the wall, and flies?
B: I don't know. What?
A: A herring.
B: But a herring's not green.
A: You can paint it green.
B: It doesn't hang on the wall.
A: You can hang it on the wall.
B: It doesn't fly.
A (shrugs): So it doesn't fly!

It may be laboring the point, but A's riddle is no riddle, not because *a herring* doesn't satisfy the conditions, but because A is only playing at the activity of making something out to be a riddle-solution.

I can bring out the philosophical difficulties here in another way. We are all reasonably confident that those who thought the world would end in the year 1000 were wrong. The end of the world did not come then. But what do we mean by that? *What* did not happen? If we are not clear about what the conditions would be in which we should say it *had* ended, we cannot say "It hasn't" and mean anything. The *sense* of a proposition cannot thus depend on its truth.— So what are we saying when we say the world did not end then? Something rather like this: that whatever, if anything, "end of the world" should be taken to mean, it is not going to be *this* that is referred to. But then we do not as it were state a fact when we say that the world did not end in 1000; we are doing something more like making a linguistic determination: *this* is not going to *count as* the end of the world.—But how then is the meaning of it *not* fixed already? And if it is not fixed, why should we not fix it as we choose? What stops us saying that the world ended in 1000, if the meaning of the words is not fixed?—Well, what stops us saying that *a herring* is the solution to A's riddle?

Within mathematics, the 'solution' of a problem by trial-and-error methods gives rise to the same difficulty. Take "What is the next prime after 47?" and suppose I have a calculation which, for any two cardinals, determines that the one is or is not the next prime after the other. Suppose, too, that I have as yet no method of answering the question; trying out the cardinals on the lookout for the next prime is not a method. (See *PR,* p. 175.) Using the calculation I already have,

I reach the result by trial and error that 53 is the next prime after 47. But this is *not* finding the answer to my question, which 'alludes' to a series for which I have as yet not got a general rule. Since no sense has yet been fixed for "next prime" *as it occurs in the question*, how can I say 53 is *it*? I can now say that I will not be satisfied with any general rule that does not give 53 as the next term in the series; but that is not a mathematical answer to the question. The mathematics necessary to answer it would remain to be done. (What obscures this point is the taking of "the next prime . . ." as a description in the ordinary sense.)

These points can be clarified by considering the following case. Suppose an infant has been taught what kissing is, and when told "Kiss your toe," kisses its toe, and so on. Now suppose it is told "Kiss your elbow." It will try and fail to kiss its elbow, but what it is trying to do, what would count as success, is clear enough. Now we say "Kiss your ear." The baby may do something, e.g., may kiss its arm and put the arm to the ear. But what is to count as kissing one's ear was not settled by anything the baby had been taught—and whatever is done is not an attempt of the same sort as the attempt to kiss the elbow. (I do not mean it thinks "What can I do that can be *called* 'kissing my ear'?") The task is of a particular form: a request is made by pursuing linguistic analogies; but the training in dealing with requests of this general pattern does not determine what is to count as fulfilling *this* request. Wittgenstein gives a parallel account of the mathematical problem "trisection of an angle". We have "I bisect this angle," "I quadrisect this angle," and so on, and we know how to use these expressions. We then make a new and purely linguistic construction, led to it by analogy with the sentences we have been using: "I trisect this angle" (*L*, p. 88). But all this is is a sentence formed by continuing certain linguistic patterns. We then decide—for excellent reasons—not to call anything we do "trisecting an angle," even if we were to find a procedure which gave a good empirical approximation to a trisection. And we might similarly decide there was nothing we wanted to call "kissing one's ear."

We may formulate similar claims for many riddles. Thus, e.g., "Come neither naked nor dressed" is formed on an already familiar pattern of commands we know how to obey, like "Come neither early nor late." And the phrase "Something than which nothing greater can be conceived" is again one we might construct from "Something (say, Jerry Ford) than which *something* greater can be conceived," substituting "nothing" for "something." What we have then in some riddles at any rate is: a linguistic expression put together by continuing familiar patterns, so the question or request looks like those we know how to use; to solve it, though, what we need is not something of which we have been given a description, but something which it will strike us as right to call by the phrase. And it is the familiarity of the pattern which makes it possible for us not to see the kind of quest we are engaged in.

We can now see what it is to give 'necessary conditions' for a solution, and to use them in rejecting possible solutions. This is essential to my understanding of Anselm's method. He gives us, I should say, necessary conditions for the riddle "What is the thing than which no greater can be conceived?" We may thus argue, e.g., that TTWNGCBC cannot have a beginning, and this condition may be used in rejecting possible solutions. But no such necessary condition, including *not* being a figment of the imagination, would guarantee that there is a solution.

It is clear from what I have said that to reject something as a solution is not a matter of some description's not fitting it. For in the riddle-phrase we have something that looks like a description, but what it is for that 'description' to fit something has not been settled. Similarly, to give necessary conditions for a solution is not to give characteristics which a thing must have if a given description is to fit.

Take the simple case of the Sphinx's riddle and the necessary condition mentioned earlier: "having at some time more than two legs." Here, clearly, the formulating of the condition is a purely verbal move. Whatever we will *call* "something which has four legs in the morning" must be something of which we can also say in some sense "it has more than two legs at some time"—but the meaning of the condition-phrase is no more settled before the solution than is the meaning of the riddle-phrase itself.

If a riddle-phrase is constructed by a sort of linguistic playing around—the forming of questions *like* questions we can answer, the making of requests *like* those we know how to satisfy—the formulating of necessary conditions is a closely related linguistic activity. Take as an example "the last day," and suppose that we come by this phrase in the following way. We have "last day of the year," "last day of February," "last day of his life," and so on. And we also have the possibility in our language of dropping phrases that give a merely relative sense to a superlative: if we have "strongest man in the city," we may also make sense of "strongest man." Using that operation we form "the last day"; not the last day of anything but the last day *simpliciter*. Now if a day is the last day of February, no day of February comes after it; if there is a day in the year after December 30th, December 30th is not the last day of the year. And so on. This then is a familiar pattern.—Suppose we take the phrase "the last day"—a phrase we may wish in the end to throw out as meaningless—and connect with it a phrase modelled on the pattern just described. Nothing is going to be called "the last day" unless we are willing to say of it "no day comes after it"; this pattern is one we don't want to abandon (see *RFM*, p. 147). We can formulate such connections perfectly well without any suggestion that either phrase—"the last day" or "no day comes after it"—need make sense. Rather, the working out of linguistic analogies in the formulating of such conditions gives these phrases whatever meaning we may wish—at this stage—to say they have.

A corresponding case from mathematics is "the rational number p/q which squared gives 2." If we construct this phrase, we may connect it with "$p^2 = 2q^2$" without supposing either to make sense, without taking either, that is, to be more than a pattern in the verbal language with no mathematical 'body' behind it (*PR*, p. 192). We continue in the same way: "p is not odd"; and this condition enables us to reject $p/q = 7/5$, without bothering to multiply. We can see the cost of not rejecting it: a system in which there was something called squaring an odd number which gave what we called a multiple of 2— and sight unseen, we do not want that. Such a solution would be like A's herring: that is not what we should call meeting the conditions.— What I have implied by taking as an example part of a *reductio* proof is that the derivation of riddle-conditions is the same sort of reasoning as that in a *reductio* proof. The relation between such proofs and riddles can be seen more clearly if we continue this one. By steps I shall not go over, we may arrive at "p is not even" and we may now abandon the initial phrase, and say that there is no solution. The cost of not abandoning it at this point would be a system in which something we call a finite cardinal may be neither odd nor even. We have gone the other way—sometimes—at such points. Pascal says of 'the number of numbers'—a phrase constructed on analogy with "the number of chairs in this room" (*L*, p. 253)—that it cannot be odd and cannot be even. ("The addition of a unit cannot change infinity.") This seemed almost to be a *reductio ad absurdum*: how could it be a number and not be odd or even? (*P*, p. 156). The cost of holding on to the phrase was calling something a cardinal number without saying it was odd or even—which he would not quite rule out. But if we can escape that near-*reductio* by coming up with things we are inclined to call cardinals, though neither odd nor even, we can equally escape the particular *reductio* proof of the irrationality of $\sqrt{2}$ by coming up with things we are inclined to call finite cardinals, though neither odd nor even. The princess's next task; but we may refuse to count anything as its fulfilment—that is what it is for the proof to be successful. What both *reductio* proofs do is persuade us to accept a task as inseparable from the one we started with, where both the old task and the new are of the form "Find me something I shall be inclined to call such-and-such." A 'reduction to a contradiction' shows us that unless we give up so many of the familiar patterns of connection that our 'solution' will seem totally pointless and artificial, our task is inseparable from finding something which would incline us to say something of the shape "*p* and not-*p*." This is not intended to be a general account of such proofs, but to illustrate a form of reasoning and make two points about it clear. First, if a *reductio* proof leads us to reject a phrase—"the greatest prime," say, or "the trisection of the angle," or again, "a private language"—this is not because the phrase expresses something which cannot be found or done. And—not really a distinct point—the proof does not start with any assumption that the phrase does express something that can be found or done. We do not assume it makes sense. (You could say we play at using a phrase of that shape as an assumption.)—If it worries us how there can be any necessary connections between phrases which may be discarded as meaningless, we may say that the 'necessary connections' used in such a proof, or in the working out of the conditions for applying a riddle-phrase to something, are as it were *promises* of necessary connections: "Something that looks like this will be a necessary connection if I get what I want."

Frege would say of the derivation of conditions, as I have described it, that it was not reasoning at all. He says of a comparable case "This looks as though what is proved is the wording alone, without the thought-content . . . Rubbish! A mere wording without a thought-content can never be proved" (*FG*, pp. 79n–80n). The important thing, however, is not whether it is called a proof, but how very different it is from other things we call proof, how very different such reasoning is from other things we call inference (*PG*, p. 380).—The difficulty about calling a *reductio* proof a proof is the same as the difficulty we have seen all along—about calling the interesting questions in mathematics *questions* and the discoveries that settle them *discoveries*, about calling a description like "the next prime" a *description* or a mathematical proposition detached from a proof a *proposition*— something which we may *know*, be *ignorant of, conjecture, assume, deny*. The differences in kind to which Wittgenstein draws attention are easily missed. What could look more like a question than the question whether Goldbach's conjecture is correct? Or like the discovery of an interesting property than the discovery of the irrationality of $\sqrt{2}$? And what could look more like a description than "TTWNGCBC"?

II

Anselm's proof can be understood properly only if we attend to just such differences.[4] Failure to attend to them has led to all the talk about whether existence is a property (or whether, if it is not, 'necessary existence' is). But that is all irrelevant; no perfection is. More accurately, the term "property" (or "predicate") is here used of something quite different from what we ordinarily mean. To see this, take the example mentioned earlier: TTWNGCBC *has no beginning*. The condition-phrase "has no beginning" can be connected with the phrase "TTWNGCBC" by an argument of the sort I described, based on the development of linguistic analogies. There are connections between having a beginning and being brought into existence, between being brought into existence and being dependent on something else, and between being dependent on something else and lacking something. These connections are found in ordinary language, which has been quarried to put together Anselm's phrase. In connecting that phrase with "having no beginning" we are saying that if we ever were inclined to call anything "TTWNGCBC," the language we spoke would be one in which we could also make sense of "has no beginning" and in which nothing could be the one that was not the other. "TTWNGCBC has no beginning" is as it were the outer shell of a necessary connection.

If we use this condition-phrase to rule out the idea that Zeus might be TTWNGCBC, it is not because we have a more adequate conception of the divine nature, one including the property of having no beginning, and compared with which our idea of Zeus falls short. Zeus is thought of as having a beginning—and anything we should call TTWNGCBC, we should say had no beginning. But *that* cannot itself rule out Zeus, since we do not yet know what we might call "having no beginning."[5] What is clear is that thinking of him as we do, we are not thinking of him as TTWNGCBC. That is, if he were the solution, it would be hidden from us—and to recognize him as the solution, we'd have to find a way of describing him as 'having no beginning'. The possibility of Zeus's being the solution, although he apparently fails to meet one of the conditions, is like the possibility mentioned earlier, of Jesus's being said to fulfil prophecies which at first he appears not to fulfil.—We might, though, reject altogether the possibility of Zeus's being the solution—and that would be a move like "The world did not end in 1000 AD": in advance, sight unseen, we might reject any solution which would allow Zeus to count as eternal. (Here "Zeus has a beginning and so is not TTWNGCBC" is the outer surface of a valid inference from a true premise, in a language we do not speak.)

We have then a use of "possible" and "impossible" ("conceivable," "imaginable") in connection with what we *might* be willing to accept as a solution. This use is extremely important in the proof. To see what it involves, we should think of Wittgenstein's remark about nonsense: "When a sentence is called senseless it is not as it were its sense that is senseless. But a combination of words is being excluded from the language" (*PI*, §500).—When we start talking about the imaginability of something's being conceivable (etc.), it is not as it were a matter of a sense that possibly makes sense. But a combination of words is being entertained by us; we do not rule out the possibility of a new language-game, in which that word-shape has a place, being one we should find ourselves at home in.—This use of modal terms is extremely common. "It is conceivable that we should come to have experiences belonging to a sense organ we don't yet possess" is a clear example. Wittgenstein says "Our being given a new sense I would call revelation" (*PR*, p. 172). "Revelation"—because it is not a discovery in a space, describable in advance, but a 'discovery' of a space.

All this is worlds away from Descartes's proof, from his spelling out of what is implicit in the idea of a perfect being, an idea present in our minds and supposed to have some definite content. Instead we have a procedure anyone can use whether or not he has an idea of a perfect being. And if he has one, the procedure can even be turned on it. "Is it conceivable that your idea of a perfect being should be shown—by something you haven't even dreamed of—to be straw?" One need not be able to understand the word "God," Anselm says, and one will still be able to make something of "TTWNGCBC"—here he is evidently thinking of it as a construction from familiar bits of ordinary language. The procedure is different not only from Descartes's but also from Norman Malcolm's.[6] For Malcolm, too, we start with a concept of God, not our own personal property, but a socially given concept—of a being absolutely without limitation. We can then work out—as with Descartes—what properties necessarily belong to God, given this conception of him. The language, the form of life, is already given; there is here nothing like looking for a language we do not have.—The contrast between any such procedure and Anselm's is emphasized by Karl Barth. Anselm's phrase does not, he says, tell us anything about what sort of being God is, and no statement about his nature can be extracted from it by analysis—that is, it lacks content. He calls it a rule for thinking about God—for telling that something is *not* being thought of as God (*A*, pp. 77–89, 128). What I have tried to show is how very unlike other things we call 'rules' it is.

The effect of my argument so far is to shift the weight of interest in Anselm's proof—from the question whether Anselm succeeds in proving that TTWNGCBC exists (or exists necessarily) to the question: What if he does? Where does such a proof take us? For if the phrase is regarded as a riddle-phrase, to say that TTWNGCBC exists leaves all the interesting questions open.

This should make us less terrified of proving that TTWNGCBC exists. I shall sketch a proof, but in doing so I shall not follow Anselm's. Anselm's proof as it stands, though, may be read much more easily if we clear our minds of the idea that "TTWNGCBC" is a description in the ordinary sense. We shall not then assume that conceiving it as not existing and conceiving it as existing are like thinking of a winged horse as not existing and then imagining it to exist. If the proof shows that there is a contradiction in denying the existence of TTWNGCBC, "contradiction" does not mean the sort of thing we usually mean, or that Kant meant. It is the sort of contradiction there is in saying of Zeus—who may be the solution to a thousand riddles—that in him we find the solution to the riddle of life, although unfortunately he does not exist.

Anselm's formulation of the proof depends on the idea that figments of the mind constitute a category of object. Professor Anscombe has, I think, shown that that is as absurd as thinking that direct objects are a type of entity. The proof I shall give stands to Descartes's *Meditations* III proof roughly as Anselm's stands to the *Meditations* V proof. The latter two depend on a principle which can be formulated in various ways, e.g., as "Existent things are better than figments of the imagination." *Something* can be said for the principle, but it is not worth saving. The *Meditations* III proof rests on the idea that something we may have in mind may be quite beyond the *inventive* capacities of human beings. It may be such that we could not have thought it up ourselves, just as an unintelligent person may have in his mind an idea of a machine so complex that we may say "He must have got the idea from someone else—it's quite beyond *him* to think that up." We might call it the Cleopatra principle, since she uses it to prove she did not just dream up Antony. Just as Anselm gives (I should suggest) a riddle use to the same principle Descartes uses in another way, I shall give a riddle use to the Cleopatra principle.

The argument might at first be put this way: that reality may surprise us, not only by showing us what *is* the case, when we had not suspected it was, but also by showing us something beyond what we had ever taken to be possible, beyond anything we had thought of at all. Our conception of what is possible might be altered by reality to include something not merely beyond anything we had imagined, but beyond anything we *could* imagine, given our finite capacity to imagine things. Consider then all gods, all the beings we have thought up, all the products of the religious imagination of mankind. Surely we cannot rule out that a being who really existed might show these up for what they were? Might make them—not least our 'adequate objects of worship'—appear a queer collection of bloodless abstractions, monsters, sentimental projections, and so on?—In that case, TTWNGCBC cannot be identified with anything we think of as merely a product of the human imagination. For something better than that—well, perhaps there is no such thing—but it *is* conceivable; and so there would be a contradiction in identifying TTWNGCBC with any figment of the mind.

That puts the argument in a naive form. We can see what is going on if we look at an apparent paradox: "The idea we have of a being we could not have thought up ourselves is an idea we have ourselves thought up." It is easily resolved. We can construct "something we could not think up ourselves," and may hold open the possibility of coming to do something with this phrase—we might even call that having an idea of such a being. But this is not to have anything in mind of which we want to say "*It* couldn't have been thought up," and we shall not say that of anything we take to be a human invention. The argument I have given makes a connection between the two phrases "TTWNGCBC" and "something we could not think up ourselves"; and so we shall not take anything to be the solution to Anselm's riddle if we think of it as a human invention. (What the proof relies on is naively expressed in terms of reality surpassing what we had taken to be possible. We may indeed come to grasp a new possibility in connection with a reality; but it is not a matter of finding something of a certain description and inferring that it is possible for there to be such things. I cannot discuss this matter further.)

Just as we may infer that TTWNGCBC has no beginning—i.e., that nothing is going to be recognized as a solution unless we think that "has no beginning" can be made to stick to it—we may infer, by Anselm's *Proslogion* II proof or mine or some other, that TTWNGCBC must exist. But something more can be said about what "exists" means here.

Imagine it argued that any such proof of the existence of TTWNGCBC constitutes part of a *reductio ad absurdum* of the whole business. For it may be said that whatever we can conceive to exist, might (we can conceive this) be conceived to be a mere figment of the imagination. We might at any rate conceive there to be beings with greater powers of imagination, who could conceive it to be such. But to conceive that it might be conceived to be such a figment is to conceive that something better than it could be conceived—and then we cannot conceive it to be TTWNGCBC.—The only way out is to show that the principle that everything that can be conceived to exist can be conceived not to does not apply to TTWNGCBC. (It would apply, Anselm suggests, if we put together corresponding phrases about islands or anything else.)

So what we have in *Proslogion* III is not a separate argument but an essential part of the proof, as Barth points out—and it is in fact quite closely related to the cosmological argument.[7] I shall explain, not what Anselm means by "cannot be conceived not to exist," but what is required by the proof. The idea is that if you think the thing away, its nature cannot be as it were left behind. It is not, that is, that we could not have thought it up, but now we have it, we can imagine that it might never have existed. To imagine it away is to imagine away even the hope of a concept of it. As we conceive it, all language about it is dependent on it. Less picturesquely, it is a matter of the absence of any description of the thing, in the ordinary sense. When Anselm speaks of things whose existence we *can* deny as existing here but not there, now but not then, or only in part here and now, what he is bringing out, I should say, is the possibility of referring to such things by descriptions. This only makes the matter darker. What sort of thing is it which cannot be referred to by a description in the ordinary sense?

Some light is cast on this if we look again at "What's the next prime after 47?" "53 is." If we have not yet got a system to which such questions and answers belong, the proposition giving the answer can be taken as an honest proposition giving the result of a calculation—but then it is not an answer to the question we asked, a question which 'alluded' to a series for which there is as yet no general rule. Taken as an answer to the question, as a proposition in the system we do not yet have, it is no more than the outer surface of what will be a true proposition. We might say it has meantime a sort of 'promissory meaning': its meaning has to come to it 'from without'. Any proposition incorporating a riddle-phrase before we have the solution may be thought of as having such meaning; and getting the solution then turns the phrase into something which can be used as a description.[8] If we are able to make statements about something, but they all have 'promissory meaning' *only*, and anything else is taken to be ruled out, we have something which cannot be referred to by an ordinary description. To speak of a being that cannot be conceived not to exist is to speak of a form of discourse all of which is like "53 is the next prime" before we have a general rule. This is a grammatical characterization of a special sort. It is not merely a matter of using the term "grammar" for something different in kind, which would stand to what Wittgenstein usually refers to as "grammar" roughly as "question" used of a riddle stands to "question" used of an ordinary question. It is the 'grammar' of a 'language' in which we could talk about what makes language possible. Looked at another way, it is the grammar which shows us what kind of question it is we are trying to answer. If something is spoken of, and, as we take it, perfectly well, in a language with a grammar in Wittgenstein's usual sense, then what is spoken of isn't spoken of *as* the answer to a great riddle. Just as "53 is the next prime," when we cut it down to size and treat it as an honest mathematical proposition giving the result of a familiar calculation, bypasses the question we asked, something which is spoken of in an honest language-game, whose grammar tells us what kind of thing is being spoken of, isn't the answer to a great riddle. The question "What is the next prime after 47?" 'alludes' to a rule we do not have; and to be a great riddle is to 'allude' to a language whose full transparency to us is ruled out. If it does not, it is a different kind of question.

I have spoken of such 'grammar' in general terms; but in fact many statements about God function (at least in part) as 'rules' of 'grammar' in the sense just given. For example, "We only know his nature in glory." Nature, or essence, is what is expressed by grammar, and we might as well say "We only know the grammar of talk about God in glory." Or again, "Strictly speaking, only God has a conception of God." "God is not distinct from the word by which he utters himself." "A proposition about God is an empty shell requiring to be filled from above."—So there can be all the language-games you like in which there is talk of God. But if we take them as honest language-games, they bypass the great riddle, and in that sense, we are not talking about God in them. "Talk about God" is as peculiar an expression as "God."—Putting the point another way: terms like "hidden" and "revelation" can be used *within* a language-game in which God is spoken of, but they can also be used as grammatical terms. Much confusion in philosophy of religion results from failing to distinguish these uses.

What Anselm needs for the proof is that we can conceive there to be a being whose non-existence cannot be conceived. He believes that there is a being which *must* be so conceived, and that neither the world nor anything in it *can* be so conceived. That belief is essential to the significance of the proof, but is in a sense external to it. After claiming that we can conceive there to be such a being, he argues that TTWNGCBC must be thought of as such a being. Otherwise we could conceive something greater. But to speak of such a being as greater than any being whose non-existence can be conceived, is like speaking of an infinite number as *much greater* than a huge finite one (compare *PG*, p. 464). It is here a question of an entirely new use of "greater." To ask a great riddle is to be prepared to use the word "greater" of something which has the 'grammar' of 'a being whose non-existence cannot be conceived'. To speak of something as the solution to a great riddle is, then, to take it as the unique case in which an argument of the *Proslogion* II type can succeed. Not to allow such an argument to go through characterizes what you are thinking of as something which the Anselm-worry can apparently catch hold of. Surely you can imagine coming to say "So something greater than that, that I couldn't have suspected, was possible after all!"

My account may seem inconsistent: how can I say something may be spoken of as the solution if I have said that to know the solution to a riddle is to have as it were a translation of the riddle-phrase into an honest bit of language, and that that is ruled out in the case of a great riddle? The resolution is straightforward: I can know *that* something is the solution but not *how* it is—just as I can be told what the solution is without being told how it is, in the case of an ordinary riddle. The identifying of something as the solution in this thin sense is itself a proposition with 'promissory meaning'.

What then has been proved? Barth claims that the proof needs an 'extra premise' if it is to prove anything positive. I shall put his point in language very different from his. Without the supposed extra premise, all that is proved is that you cannot identify anything as TTWNGCBC if you take it to be something we have thought up, where that implicitly depends upon taking the question "What is TTWNGCBC?" as a great riddle. The 'extra premise' needed for the proof to do anything more than make plain the grammar of great riddles is the identification of a solution in the thin sense just explained, which carries with it the implication that there is a solution in the full sense.—What this means for the proof can be seen by contrasting the truth of a proposition about TTWNGCBC with that of "53 is the next prime," taken as the answer to a question as yet without a place in any system. We can commit ourselves to rejecting any system which did not give 53 at that point: it *will* come out true in any system which we shall accept, and so its being taken as true in advance rests on what we shall do. What is it, though, to accept a proposition about TTWNGCBC 'in advance'? We are not here determining which solutions we shall accept, because there is no accepting any without changing the question. To accept it as true is not then a matter of our making such a commitment but is conceived as relying on one, as it were. Conceived in this way, it is more like taking "53 is the next prime" as true, when you have the word of someone who has a general rule for calculating the series. We can use this image to explain what difference it makes to the proof that Anselm thinks 'there is a solution'. (It is a bit much to call it an extra premise if its sense must be in dispute.) It means that the difference between Anselm and the fool is as it were like that between two people who follow a piece of mathematical reasoning which starts with a proposition-shape. The one does not know whether it is anything more than a shape which he may eventually consign to the dustbin and call nonsense. The other knows or takes himself to know that it has been proved, although he is not clear how. So whenever Anselm says to the fool that such-and-such is conceivable, he himself has two ways of taking what he says, the fool only one. You, he thinks, cannot rule it out as a shape which might be given a use; for him it is already the shape of a truth he has been given. If he says "This is something you'd have to call 'greater'," he means also that it is called "greater" *already*. From his point of view, then, the incoherence in attempting to deny God's existence once you have been given the solution— which he calls the absurdity of creature judging creator—is that of purporting to judge a thing that leaves you without the linguistic footing for any judgment of your own about it. (See also *Proslogion* XIV.) This means, however, that it is just as incoherent for you to take yourself to be judging of such a being that something greater *cannot* be conceived as it is for you to judge that something greater can be: God does not come up to scratch any more than he fails to. This is not to say that there cannot be something like a demonstration that such-and-such is TTWNGCBC—but a demonstration which cannot be separated from the authority or apparent authority of the being in question. Compare the passage in Luke in which it is Jesus after the resurrection who is supposed to show what otherwise would not have been visible: that he is what the Messianic passages of the *Old Testament* point to. Similarly with TTWNGCBC: we are not to expect to spot the solution ourselves. An identification of something as TTWNGCBC is a truth of faith or it is nothing; and the fool cannot coherently accept any such identification. When Anselm says of himself that even if he did not want to believe God's existence, he could not but know it, that is because for him the identification of something as TTWNGCBC cannot be questioned.

Is the proof, thought of as proof of the existence of God, and not just as an explanation of what is to think of something as God—is it then circular? Not strictly. In some respects it resembles the 'circle' of the *Grundlegung*. (No coincidence: for the good will—whose possibility is what is there in question—is something which has a "worth supposed to be so great there cannot be any interest which is higher." The sphere of revelation is now the moral, but its grammar is unchanged; we are still engaged with a great riddle.) It is not merely that the 'extra premise' Anselm uses is not something he can be said to know or even to think he knows, if "know" is here taken in a narrow sense: what we know we could have asked before we knew, and we could have understood the question. For the premise involves something he has in mind, an object of thought—but an 'object of thought' with a queer grammar. If the fool says "Anselm, what you have in mind, your God, isn't TTWNGCBC and doesn't exist," then for Anselm the fool's words are like those of someone who, groping for a solution to the Sphinx's riddle, thinks "What she means cannot be *man*." One can believe that of 'what she means' only because one does not yet understand her words at all, except as a riddle. Since one does not know how the words may be taken—what the *possibilities* are—"what she means" is itself opaque to one. Anselm's claim is that words in the fool's mouth which refer to what he—Anselm—has in mind (and which he refers to by the title 'Lord') are opaque to the fool in that way; there is a sense in which he does not understand his own words, and his belief depends on that failure of understanding. (See *Proslogion* IV.)

If there is no straightforward premise which the fool denies and Anselm asserts, how can the issue between them be expressed? What the fool can say is clear from the analogy with "53 is the next prime." That, we saw, may be thought of as an answer to a question which 'alludes' to a rule we do not have, or simply as giving the result of a straightforward calculation which can be carried out with any pair of cardinals. It is thus as it were 'deflated'. The fool can similarly 'deflate' propositions which for Anselm have 'promissory meaning'. He does not treat what is said of Anselm's God as if it were dependent for its sense on anything beyond the language-game; as he treats it, it bypasses the great riddle. And whatever interest it may still have would not be dependent on the connection with the language of great riddles.—He may then deny that Anselm's God is TTWNGCBC, and here he is not 'deflating' that phrase itself. He may leave it open whether there is anything else he might like to do with it, or he may reject it—not necessarily as a mere exalted bit of phrase-making.[9] (He may also 'deflate' *it*, which ignores the kind of interest it expresses.) To say that Anselm's God is not the solution to the great riddle is to say he does not exist—in an important sense. It is not a matter of the language-game's being without a foundation. Precisely in being taken as a language-game and nothing more, it does not need one. Rather, in a sense he does not exist as God: for being the solution to the great riddle is not distinct from 'necessary existence'. "If he isn't God, he doesn't exist" is condensed, but correct.

III

Arguments derived from Wittgenstein have been used to show that the fool's claim is incoherent. I do not think it can be done; and to show why not, I shall look briefly at Malcolm's argument. Malcolm argues that necessary existence can be ascribed to God, because that is how God is spoken of in the language-game in which the concept of God has its home. So the fool is trying to say something which simply cannot be said in the language-game. If Malcolm's procedure were sound, it would mean there is a *philosophical* confusion in regarding the God of the *Old Testament* as a genocidal maniac, a super-Hitler. For in the language-game in which this person is spoken of, one cannot say such things. Whatever is to be said to someone who says them, though, he is not to be shut up by "In this language-game he is *called* 'good'." Similarly, no appeal to the language-game is available as a reply to someone who says that the God portrayed in the Bible, far from existing from eternity to eternity as they said, does not exist at all, but is a mere figment of the religious imagination. What that means is: whether or not you can look anywhere for the answer, do not at any rate look here; just as the person who speaks of the acts of the *Old Testament* God as evil means: *here* we cannot see the goodness of God. Do not look here, or here we cannot see it—where this need not imply that we know what we are looking for; and in either case we might come to say we were wrong. The phrases used in the search and in the denial have not been taken out of the language-game which is their home. They have a life of their own, and in fact it is their place in the language-game which creates at least some of the interest in it. The situation is quite different from that of scepticism about other minds, where philosophical difficulties may arise when we ignore the use. In that sort of case it may indeed be helpful to say "This language-game is played."

What difference it makes, that "this language-game is played," depends on the game. Set theory is 'played', too. But Wittgenstein wanted to show that it was not what we had taken it for—and he thought that our interest in it would be very different once we saw that. I am not suggesting that that is what Anselm's talk of God is like, but that there is no support in Wittgenstein for the idea that if a form of words has a place in some activity, that form of words is not expressive of deep confusion. ("Mathematics is ridden through and through with the pernicious idioms of set theory."—*PR*, p. 211.) He spoke in connection with set theory of the *glitter* of the concepts. The 'glitter' of the concepts *here* is even more dazzling: what after all are we talking about but that than which nothing more dazzling can be conceived?

A religion may play an important part in someone's life, and he need not be concerned with it as providing an answer to the great riddle. Phrases which for others are connected with the great riddle do not have that significance for him. But their place in the activity cannot be understood merely by considering such 'deflated' uses. *One* expression of this is that it is not the fool but Anselm who may make trouble for such a 'form of life' by telling us it is conceivable that "judged and condemned by TTWNGCBC" might be something we could come to say of the form of life itself.

These phrases are not the inventions of theologians, something added onto the self-sufficient body of religious life—any more than the gleaming concept-formations of set theory are mere excrescences on an existing calculus. Set theory misinterprets its own idioms, Wittgenstein says, and it is that very misinterpretation which is responsible for the invention of the calculus itself—which is not thus shown to be *incorrect*, but at worst uninteresting (*PG*, pp. 469–70).—Arguments derived from Wittgenstein's later work have been used to show that religious forms of life are not *incorrect*, but these arguments have been misunderstood. If there is a language-game in which we use the phrase "the least integer not nameable in fewer than nineteen syllables," it is not right or wrong, even if in *this* game 42 is called that. That would merely be unnatural. And that's the sense in which a use of "TTWNGCBC" *within* the language-game may be shown to be 'not incorrect'. Whatever use it has is natural or unnatural, and that is all. If we hanker after something which is called that and has a right to be, the correctness of the language-game is uninteresting. The arguments showing that the language-game is not incorrect—that the answers given in it need no justification beyond what counts as justification in the game—do not touch the difficulties here. For we may feel that even if *all* the questions that can be asked in our language-games were answered, there would be something untouched by *all that*.—The questioning expressed in great riddles is *anyone's*; the possibility of such questions belongs to language itself and not to any particular language-game. The tendency to ask them does not depend on any form of life other than speech itself: it is as much something primitive, something given—as much a kind of behavior—as responding to other people (and is indeed found in small children). A language-game *begins* with behavior. If a language-game has its source or one of its sources in *this* kind of behavior—in the constructing of questions (or 'questions') which hold us as these do—we cannot give an adequate description of the game by looking at what goes on in it, or by looking at that together with the non-linguistic responses on which the game may also depend.

Postscript (1990)

Anselm's conception of talk about God as like riddles comes out clearly in the *Monologion*. That work shares with the *Proslogion* a riddle-style, which Anselm finds especially appropriate in talking of the triune character of God. His explicit references to riddles in the *Monologion* occur in his comments (chapter LXV) on the difficulty of talking about the Trinity, and are themselves couched in riddle-talk. We express and do not express a thing, see and do not see a thing, when we express it in riddles (which is how we express it when we are unable or unwilling to put it into straight plain words appropriate to it) and when we see not it itself but an image (as one might say of one's own eyes that one had seen but had not seen them, having seen only their image). Such expressing-and-not-expressing, seeing-and-not-seeing, characterizes the attempt to talk about God. We cannot properly speaking describe God, but when we reason about God, "as it were in riddles," what we say is not therefore *false*.—Much that has been written about Anselm's modal logic is incompatible with Anselm's own view of the riddle-character of what he says.

Notes

1. I am indebted to Hidé Ishiguro for her helpful comments on an earlier draft of this essay.
2. In addition to the abbreviations used throughout this volume, the following abbreviations are used in this chapter.

   PG   Wittgenstein, *Philosophical Grammar*
   Z   Wittgenstein, *Zettel*
   PR   Wittgenstein, *Philosophical Remarks*
   L   *Wittgenstein's Lectures on the Foundations of Mathematics*
   MM   Margaret Macdonald's notes (unpublished) to lectures in 1935 (References are to date of lecture).
   P   Pascal, *Pensées*, trans. J. M. Cohen, Penguin
   FG   Frege, *On the Foundations of Geometry and Formal Theories of Arithmetic*
   A   Barth, *Anselm: Fides Quaerens Intellectum*

   References to *Remarks on the Foundations of Mathematics* in this chapter are to the 1956 edition. At several places in Part I, I have tried to deal with questions raised by David Shwayder in "Wittgenstein on Mathematics" (in *Studies in the Philosophy of Wittgenstein*, ed. Peter Winch) and by R. L. Goodstein in "Proof by *Reductio Ad Absurdum*" (in his *Essays in the Philosophy of Mathematics*).

3. "Man" or "a man" *gives* the solution, in the sense explained by Professor Anscombe in "The Intentionality of Sensation" (in *Analytic Philosophy*, Second Series, ed. R. J. Butler).

4. Their significance is brought out in Karl Barth's *Anselm: Fides Quaerens Intellectum*, a work to which I am greatly indebted.

5. Compare *Proslogion* VIII. A condition-phrase "not merciful" is derived for God, who is nevertheless said to be merciful.

6. "Anselm's Ontological Arguments," *Philosophical Review*, 1960.

7. The relation has been obscured by Kant's description of the cosmological argument as an *a posteriori* argument. But God's existence may be said to be essential for the *possibility* of contingent beings.

8. In the case of mathematics, it turns the phrase into something which functions in some ways like a description.

9. An argument which, like that of *Proslogion* III, makes clear the 'grammar' of great riddles, may form part of a *reductio* argument of a special sort, which persuades us that there is nothing we should call a solution, and that that in a sense *is* the solution. *Tractatus* 6.41 is part of such an argument. What has value as nothing else *can*, must lie beyond everything that is accidental. This makes the same grammatical point as *Proslogion* III.

Chapter 11

Anything but Argument?

Yet if the appeal on behalf of animals is to convince those whose hearts do not already so incline them, it must, like appeals on behalf of dependent human beings, reach beyond assertion to argument.
Onora O'Neill[1]

I choose this sentence as exemplifying a view of how philosophical discussion in ethics can be carried on, and how it should be carried on—a view as common as it is confused. It rests on a conception of moral thought which is not merely false, but which also renders unaccountable and incomprehensible the moral force of many kinds of literature. That is not all it does, but it is enough to be getting on with.

I

Let me place the sentence in its context. It comes from Onora O'Neill's review of Stephen Clark's *The Moral Status of Animals*, a book whose aim is to change the way we think about animals. Professor Clark's book does, indeed, contain arguments, but these are for the most part directed *against* various claims that human beings have a special and unique moral status, that they—unlike animals—must be treated with respect. Professor O'Neill criticizes Clark not so much for the arguments that *are* there as for the ones which are not, ones which would show us the *grounds* for granting the moral status of animals. Clark suggests a way of looking at animals—as our kin; but we may find that our hearts are not touched by what Professor O'Neill refers to as Clark's "vision of the peaceable kingdom." And

> if we are not persuaded by the vision and ask for reasons for accepting his view that animals are kin, we find no arguments. He believes that animals have both varied sorts of sentience and

intelligence, and that this grounds at least a claim that unnecessary suffering is wrong. But he wants us to accept that animals have far more extensive moral claims. And here he appeals only to the heart.[2]

Professor O'Neill contrasts Clark's approach with that of those who have been engaged in recent philosophical debate on abortion and euthanasia and the like, and who have probed the grounds of moral obligations to those who do not have normal human capacities. She says of these debates that they scarcely stir the surface of Clark's book—and it is at this point that she makes the claim that I have started with: that a convincing appeal on behalf of animals must go beyond assertion to argument.

Let me go back to that original sentence: its precise wording is important. Here are some questions about it.

1. Yet if the appeal on behalf of animals is to *convince* . . . it must reach beyond assertion to argument.

When we engage in philosophical discussion about such a subject as abortion, or the moral status of animals, *whom* should we think of ourselves as trying to convince? For if we proceed by giving arguments, we presumably do not expect to be able to convince anyone who is incapable of following our arguments, or who is too prejudiced to consider them. And if we are talking about convincing *human beings*, surely it is a fact about many of them that one certain way of *not* convincing them is to try arguing the case. So we do recognize incapacities and attitudes of mind which would leave our arguments—however good as arguments they may be—simply passing by those with such incapacities or attitudes. No one who urges another philosopher to give arguments thinks of argument as capable of convincing *everybody*. When we put forward arguments, or urge someone else to do so, we have some conception of what it would be to succeed in giving genuinely *convincing* arguments, and also of those who would nevertheless not be convinced, even should they attend to the arguments. Now, argument is simply one way people approach moral questions, and there are other ways of trying to convince someone of one's view of animals or fetuses or slaves or children or whatever it may be. Suppose someone writes a novel (call it *Oliver Twist*, or *David Copperfield*) with the aim (among other aims perhaps) of leading people to share a concern for children. Suppose he succeeds in writing something which is genuinely convincing in its way. By that I do not mean that he succeeds in convincing people. Just as a convincing argument is not one which will succeed in convincing everyone who attends to it, a convincing novel-with-a-moral-aim is not one which will succeed in convincing everyone who reads it. If we judge such a work to be convincing, we may recognize nevertheless that there are certain kinds of incapacity which would leave someone unlikely to be convinced by reading the novel. Two examples of such incapacities: a very limited moral imagination; an intelligence inadequately trained and incapable of recognizing irony.

Now, given that there are various styles in which one may attempt to convince someone of some moral view, and given that any such attempt, even if it is convincing (in whatever way attempts in that style can be convincing), will not actually succeed in convincing people with various sorts of incapacities or prejudices, why should it be thought that when a philosopher tries to convince those who are not already convinced, he *should* aim at convincing by argument those who can be convinced by good arguments? It would not be enough to say: that is what philosophers do. It is indeed what *some* of them do, or perhaps, more accurately, what all of them do some or most of the time. What we have seen, though, is that when a philosopher aims to convince, as Clark does, and uses a style which—as he himself recognizes—will not succeed with those whose hearts cannot be moved at all by the vision he suggests, he is told he ought to use a method which is as it were heart-indifferent. But it is not at all obvious that the method is appropriate. I believe that underlying the idea that one *ought* to use such an approach is the idea that when someone is *reasonably* convinced of something, the convincing will have to have proceeded by arguments (or what could, at any rate, be set out as arguments), and the capacities of his head and not of his heart will be all that is involved. Part of this idea is that becoming convinced in any other way is merely a matter of the operation of *causes*. Alterations in someone's heart are carried out not by reasonable convincings but by—mere—persuadings. But this takes me to a second question.

2. If the appeal "is to convince *those whose hearts do not already so incline them*," the convincing must go on by arguments.

Why? The picture that is suggested is that we start with a person whose heart has some fixed inclination: towards animals, or indifferent to them, towards cats and against rats, towards whites and against blacks, or whatever. If a person's inclinations are (say) towards cats and against rats, the only way of leading him to take rats more seriously will be to give him *arguments* (e.g., that there are no grounds for concern for cats that are not equally grounds for concern for rats, rats and cats not differing in any morally relevant way). But is this supposed to be obvious? It seems not only not obvious but not even true. Let me take the case again of someone who writes a novel with the aim of convincing those whose hearts are not already inclined in some direction. Must we say: either he is not going in for convincing—not really—or he is producing arguments? Is there nothing that is an attempt to enlarge the moral imagination? It is Onora O'Neill who makes use of the comparison with appeals on behalf of dependent human beings: *like* such appeals, she says, those on behalf of animals must proceed by argument. Is *David Copperfield* not (among other things) an appeal on behalf of those who were locked up as madmen, like Mr. Dick? Is it not meant to convince those whose hearts were not already inclined in the same direction as the heart of Betsey Trotwood? Was it not meant to show them, and show them with imaginative force, a way of looking at the Mr. Dicks of the world? Some hearts are not 'already inclined' some ways because their possessors have not exercised their imaginations in certain directions, have not been led to do so. Is an attempt to widen the imagination something which it is all right for novelists to do, but not all right for philosophers? It does not seem as if *that* is Professor O'Neill's point; for she writes as if the heart as it were simply went whatever way it did, and that *serious thought,* directed at those whose hearts go initially in some direction which one thinks is the wrong direction, aims for the head and not the heart of its intended audience. But this *must* be a mistake. Dickens aims at the heart, and there is serious thought in what he does; he aims to convince and not simply to bring it about that the heart goes from bad state 1 to good state 2. He does not aim at *mere* conversion, if I may put it so. *If* the idea is that that is all right for novelists but not for philosophers, what is there to be said for it? Admittedly, the ways we can, as philosophers, *judge* some philosophical work which is directed at enlarging our imaginations— as Clark's is—will not be the same as the ways in which we judge sheer arguments; but the problems of exercising philosophical judgment of such works need not incline us to regard them as not—as such—philosophical works at all.

Professor O'Neill gives a slightly different version of the same point at the end of her paper, and I do not find that it makes things any clearer:

> It is because [Clark] seeks to do morality without metaphysics that his appeals can reach only the audience who share his commitment to animals.[3]

The idea is that through metaphysics one can make plain the *grounds* of moral standing. Again I want to ask: is the point that the appeals of *anyone* who 'does morality' without making plain the grounds of moral standing can reach only those who share his commitments? Does 'doing morality' include writing essays, poems and stories? If so, the claim is so obviously false as to make one think it cannot be meant; if not, if 'doing morality' is doing it in the context of philosophy, why is it that *philosophers* 'doing morality'—and they alone?— are in this pickle?

3. "reach beyond assertion to argument"

Is this *meant* to imply that the only way of going beyond assertion is going *to* argument? If Professor O'Neill's point is that one may reject anyone's unargued-for vision of things, that is correct but hardly interesting. One may also simply reject a claim for which sound argument has been offered. Someone who rejects a good argument does so at a cost: for example, at the cost of showing his own incapacity to think carefully. Someone who rejects some articulated ways of looking at things *may* show limitations of other sorts. To proceed beyond assertion in an attempt to convince others of a way of looking at animals, or dependent human beings, or trees or whatever is to produce something that makes plain *a* cost of rejecting the view in question; and there are costs of different kinds, depending on the style of the attempt to convince. But in any case there are *various* ways of proceeding beyond assertion; and in fact as far as I can see it is the conviction that beyond assertion there lies *only* argument that is the basis of Professor O'Neill's description of what Clark does *as* assertion.

I have raised these questions about a single sentence of Onora O'Neill's. Before I return to them, I need to cast a wider look around—first at some remarks earlier in her paper.

Professor O'Neill writes of a problem that she thinks arises, given Clark's views. For him the root of our moral response is in the affections; how then, she asks, can we not be landed with a 'particularistic, local morality'?—for that is what our affections tie us to. She recognizes that Clark thinks that our personal and particular affections can lead us to a more objective hierarchy of values, in which respect goes beyond personal kin and friends. But, she says, he does not make clear how this transition is brought about, and he indeed confesses (*her* word, and important) that

> my strongest temptation is to reckon the rational hierarchy . . .
> no more than a paranoid fantasy as soon as it takes on a life
> separate from the heart's affections and the plain evidence of
> sense . . .

Her comment is that if we follow this temptation, the moral claims of those for whom we care are stronger than those of distant strangers with whom we feel no bond, or than those of nearby human kin for whom we do not care, or than those of animals for whom we feel nothing warm.[4]

Now, why does she think that if we follow the temptation to regard a rational hierarchy *wholly independent* of the heart's affections as a paranoid fantasy, we must be landed with a hierarchy entirely *dependent* on unmodified personal affections? That we are thus stuck is a reasonable conclusion to draw only if one makes an unreasonable assumption, namely that the *only* way to lead someone from his initial personal affections to a recognition of moral status going beyond the things he initially cared for is by appeal to purely rational considerations.

But here we are back at points we have already considered. It is simply not true that someone who holds that moral thought must rest on the natural affections is committed to the idea that moral thought will, as a result, be as narrow as those affections initially are in all of us, unless something happens to happen to make the affections wider, a bolt from the causal blue, transforming the character of the person it hits. I leave open here the further question raised by this passage whether the moral claims of those who are near and dear to us are not (often enough) stronger than those of distant strangers with whom we feel no bond. Fortunately, we are not confronted by the simple pair of alternatives: all beings who have whatever it is that rationally grounds moral respect are morally at the same distance from us *or* only those we naturally care for have any moral claim on us. (I suspect Professor O'Neill of doing something like this: Clark wants to reject *both*, but what we have to take seriously is that he rejects the first; therefore he is—like anyone who rejects the first— landed, like it or not, with the second.)

Professor O'Neill claims, I said, that Clark tells us nothing about how the transition from particularistic affections to a more objective hierarchy of values is supposed to come about. But this is a revealing misreading on her part.

That is to say, Clark gives an answer to that question, but it is not visible to Professor O'Neill—because she does not see it as a *possible* answer; it is not an answer of the sort she is looking for. The answer he gives is that the transition depends on our coming to attend to the world and what is in it, in a way that will involve the exercise of all our faculties; and that religion, poetry, and science, if uncontaminated by self-indulgent fantasy, are the most important modes of thought leading to that kind of attentive imaginative response to the world. It may be that this answer itself needs explanation; but at any rate it is a summary of an answer, one that reflects a way of thinking about morality very different from Professor O'Neill's.

II

At the beginning of this paper, I said that Onora O'Neill's conception of moral thinking makes it impossible to account for the moral force of many kinds of literature. I want now to explain that.

Our—philosophers'—paradigm of moral thinking is just what Professor O'Neill suggests: that of an interweaving of fact and general principle. Thus, e.g.: if you recognise cats as having moral status, this must—we shall tell you—be grounded in their having something which on your principle counts as morally significant, say sentience or intelligence; and if as a matter of fact there are no differences of sentience or intelligence between cats and rats, and the only differences are these slight ones of physiology and behavior, which surely cannot be regarded as of moral relevance, then surely you must give up your idea that rats lack moral status *or* give up your idea that cats have it. (This conception is expressed in Professor O'Neill's repeated statements[5] that if Clark wants to ground the moral status of animals on their being our kin, he owes us an explanation of what he takes this kinship to consist in and of how it is supposed that kinship, consisting in whatever, makes respect for the needs and interests of animals their due.) It is possible to assimilate the moral thinking in some straightforwardly didactic literature to that model, but it will not fit most other cases.

Take, very briefly, three examples.

First, there are in Wordsworth's *Lyrical Ballads* several poems clearly meant to lead their audience to new moral responses. One would say that of the poems even without the description in the Preface of Wordsworth's intention: to enlarge the reader's moral and emotional sensibilities. "The Old Cumberland Beggar" is especially interesting as an example, because the moral aim is very clear, and because there is actually an argument (given in enthymematic form) in it, roughly this:

> None of the created forms can exist divorced from good;
> Therefore least of all can any human being be scorned without sin;
> Therefore the old beggar is not to be deemed useless.[6]

But it would be absurd to believe that that argument (or that argument more fully spelled out) is what is intended to do the work of convincing anyone who had been inclined to deem old beggars useless. We have not only the structure and content of the poem, but Wordsworth's Preface, to make clear that the moral force of the poem is created by the way objects are described and feelings given in connection with each other: *that* is how Wordsworth thinks to enlighten the understanding and ameliorate the affections of those readers who can respond to such poems.

It might be objected that Wordsworth's account is obscure and that, so far as anything can be made of it, it means only that a poem may lead us to accept a moral view by describing particular applications of it in language likely to engage our emotions—which no one, Onora O'Neill or anyone else, is likely to deny. What then is there supposed to be in Wordsworth's practice to clash with the philosophical model?

We may see how to answer that if we ask one question two ways: What moral view is centrally conveyed in such poems as "The Old Cumberland Beggar," "Simon Lee," "The Brothers," "The Idiot Boy," "Michael"? What view of human nature is reflected in Wordsworth's conception of his own practice? One expression of the moral view may be found in "The Old Cumberland Beggar," when the response of the villagers to the beggar is explained: we have all of us one human heart. But what is it to be convinced of that? What *sort* of conviction is it that such poems aim at? It cannot be separated from an understanding of oneself, from an acknowledgment of certain capacities of response in oneself as appropriate both to their object and to one's own nature. Rather a lot to expect! Wordsworth believes that we have a capacity to respond with deep sympathy to the feelings of other people—that is, when they are moved by the "great and simple affections of our nature," "the essential passions of the heart." The poet's representation of a person under the influence of such a feeling can excite in us a feeling appropriate both to what is described and to our own nature, the appropriateness being something we can come to recognize in part through the kind of pleasure such a poem gives. The "competence and confidence" with which we are able to judge that truth of the kind Wordsworth thought had been achieved is inseparable (he thought) from the strength with which the heart responds to the representation. We can come to recognize what is expressed in "we have all of us one human heart" through coming to feel the force of the heart's responses to such poems as the ones I mentioned. In *a* sense, someone who has not learned to respond with the heart in such ways has not learned to think ("thought with him/ Is in its infancy"); for thinking well involves thinking charged with appropriate feeling. Poetry then helps develop the heart's capacities that are the basis for the moral life by deepening our emotional life and our understanding of it.

The second example is one I have already mentioned: the attempts by Dickens to lead people to a sympathetic way of looking at children. Many features of many of his novels are relevant to this aim: I shall take only one. Dickens again and again shows us how the world looks to a small and helpless child. For example:

> I remember Mr. Hubble as a tough high-shouldered old man, of a sawdusty fragrance, with his legs extraordinarily wide apart: so that in my short days I always saw some miles of open country between them when I met him coming up the lane.[7]

My claim is that such sentences are part of the way Dickens attempts to realize a moral aim: that of getting the reader to attend to a child as a center of *a* view of the world, and, of what is particularly and in many ways peculiarly a *child's* view of the world. Orwell commented that no novelist has shown the same power of entering into the child's point of view, and that no one before Dickens had noticed what he did of how children perceive and think.[8] There are many passages in Dickens in which what we are shown from the child's view has obvious moral significance: being slighted, having one's privacy invaded, being unjustly treated—and it is easy to see how these are related to Dickens's moral aims. But my point now is that there is a moral aim even in passages which do not bear specifically on treating a child well or badly. Stephen Clark remarks on coming to experience, through affection, "the possibility of considering the object in its own right,"[9] and I suggest that such passages in Dickens show us what it is to attend to a child so; Dickens, that is, provides paradigms of a sort of attention. His aim, like Wordsworth's, is to enlighten the understanding and ameliorate the affections by providing descriptions which stimulate imagination and moral sensibility; like Wordsworth, he sees the achievement of such an aim as inseparable from writing something that will give pleasure.

I should say more about 'paradigms of a sort of attention', since it might be thought that the point of attending in a particular way was in what we could find out by such attention, and that whatever facts we reached, they could be fitted into the philosophical model of moral thought. If, that is, Dickens shows us a kind of attention, in this particular case to children, why then it surely is morally significant if it enables us to leave behind moral views resting on ignorance of what children are like, their needs and capacities.

The moral significance of the kind of attention given by Dickens to the things he writes about is not a matter of its leading us to grasp facts of which we had previously been unaware. The attention which we see directed towards the lives and thoughts of children has a characteristic emotional color, the result of its combining great warmth, concentration of energy, and humor; it expresses a particular style of affectionate interest in human things and imaginative engagement with them. Dickens does not say: "Look at this: children do this and that, see thus and so, feel such-and-such, and these facts must be taken to be morally relevant." Rather his descriptions (not only *what* is described but the language in which it is) show an attention which *engages* us—if he is successful, and does not fail by getting the emotional tone off through sentimentality. Where he is successful, the description is not only enjoyable but can contribute to our lasting sense of human life, of what is interesting and important.[10]

Dickens also presents many cases (Gradgrind's the best known) of a contrasting sort of attention, a kind of concentration on 'the facts' which is cold and even insolent. Far from its being the case—on Dickens's view—that the point of the kind of attention we give lies in what we find out, what we *can* find out by a coldly presumptuous approach to the world can feed no adequate moral thought.

My third example is the use of various sorts of 'warm' irony, especially characteristic of writers like Jane Austen and Henry James. As James himself points out, such irony may be combined with "that fine taste for the truth and the pity and the meaning of the matter which keeps the temper of observation both sharp and sweet."[11] Since one main use of such irony is in moral criticism of human character and forms of social life, we may think that the criticism, whatever it is, might be expressed straightforwardly, without irony, and that the moral interest of passages in which irony is so used depends on that extractible content. I do not care to argue whether the idea of the 'extractible content' makes sense; probably it does make some. The important point is rather the moral interest of the particular kind of irony exhibited in such works as James's and Jane Austen's. The reader of them is invited to share a way of viewing human nature and its failings, in which amusement, sympathy, critical intelligence, and delicacy of moral discrimination all play a role. Besides showing us the possibility and attractiveness of that view of human nature, such literature can lead us to a rejection of the heavy-handed, sententious, or solemn in moral thought; we see that the seriousness and depth of moral thinking is entirely independent of any earnest or moralizing tone—and indeed that such a tone is itself something for ironic treatment. The appeal of such a view is to the intelligence of the reader, inviting him, as it does, to give moral thought, moral criticism, a place in an ideal of civilized human life. The appeal is to the intelligence, but does not go via arguments—however hard *that* may be to fit into our philosophical schemes.

III

An attempt might be made to force the varieties of moral thought found in literature into our philosophical model this way: it might be said that a moral view can be presented in literature but its critical evaluation must be carried out through argument. How can we judge a view except by seeing what its grounds are and what we are committed to in accepting it? And how else can we see that, except by argument: argument for it, including argumentative elaboration of the view itself, and argument against it? How else can we judge the *strength* of a moral view?

How else indeed? It is not an unanswerable question—and argument does have some role in supporting the judgments, themselves more various in kind than the philosophical model allows, that need to be made.

In the case of an attitude like that Dickens shows us towards children, or of an ironic attitude towards—let us say—American life, the one thing we cannot do is ask, quite independently of the form the attitude is given in particular works, whether *that* sort of attitude towards such-and-such kind of thing is appropriate. How would that go? Are the facts about children such that the kind of interest Dickens takes is fitting? *What* facts? Are we to describe children, their perceptions, emotions and thoughts, and then find some principle for directing emotional attitudes towards things of any sort whatever (small sentient Martians included) having such-and-such properties? This is sheer comedy, and not the way to get at what is right (when it is right) or wrong with a presented attitude. As I mentioned, Dickens's own view is that the investigation of facts, facts, facts *cannot* show us what we need in order to respond well to the world. Or suppose we ask whether American life is such as to make an ironic attitude towards it appropriate. Someone might be inclined to say "Yes, yes!," sniffing in the unironic American consciousness a peculiarly fitting target for ironic criticism. Such a judgment, though, would be dependent on his having already grasped and enjoyed the pointedness of particular ironic treatments of if not American life itself sufficiently similar things; his intelligence has developed that way—and whether *that* is an appropriate development is not a question to be settled by general principles governing the suitability of ironic appreciation.

If we consider a particular ironic treatment of something, it may be judged to be unconvincing, and the judgment supported by argument. Thus, for example, F. R. Leavis argues (unconvincingly, as I should wish to say) that the ironic 'placing', in *Portrait of a Lady*, of Isabel Archer's illusion of free choice is unconvincing—because, supposedly, James has failed to put her character in a sharp enough critical light; she is insufficiently specified.[12] Again, James himself argues that the 'ironic idea' in de Maupassant's treatment of the blackguard in *Bel-Ami* is 'injured' by the depravity of all the characters over whom he is victorious.[13] If a work uses both irony and argument, as for example Hume's "Of Suicide," either—or both—may be judged unconvincing; the judgments are characteristically different and supported by different sorts of consideration. Thus one might argue that Hume's ironic treatment of the contemporary view of suicide is unconvincing because he has not got a 'civilized' alternative to the 'superstitious' view: "diverting a few ounces of blood from their natural channel" so obviously will not do. Like criticism of an argument as unconvincing, criticism of a use of irony as unconvincing is directed at the *thought* of the writer; it is not a matter of judging the work in question to be unpersuasive, or unlikely to be successful as propaganda. I have taken irony as an example; similar points could be made about criticism of other kinds of moral thought in literature—and out of it.

But it may be said that *that* sort of criticism is of limited interest. If a moral view is presented, by argument or otherwise, we may judge that the *presentation* fails (or is flawed as whatever kind of presentation it is), but that leaves open the question of evaluation of *what* is presented. And it is here (or so the suggestion would run) that we *must* come to something like *philosophical* criticism. Thus, e.g., in the case of Hume, it might be said that whether or not the irony works, what matters is to establish whether he is *right* that suicide "may be free from every imputation of guilt or blame." But we should note that Hume has *two* aims. Showing suicide to be morally permissible is the subordinate one; the more important one is to illustrate the superiority of the 'philosophical' over the 'superstitious' approach to things of importance in human life. (In fact, Hume loses interest in the subject of the permissibility of suicide as soon as he gets to questions irrelevant to his main aim, and the discussion then loses its intellectual distinction.) *Does* he show that the philosopher's way of thinking about a question like suicide is preferable to that of the 'superstitious'? He cannot do so if his view of suicide is shallow; and the philosopher's model of what it is to judge a moral view does not fit judgments of the sort we need to make about Hume.

We develop the capacity to make such judgments through habits of awareness, reflection, and discrimination.[14] That is, we come across all sorts of things which invite emotional response, or invite the taking up of an attitude or of a mode of thought—including here, as 'issuers' of such invitations, works of literature and philosophy. At first such responses will not be *considered* ones at all: we respond (let us say) with delighted amazement and wonder at fairy tales, in a wholly unreflective way. But we can come to be aware of what makes for deeper understanding and an enriching of our own thought and experience; we can come to have a sense of what is alive, and what is shallow, sentimental, cheap; as we make comparisons, we come to know what are the reasons for our interest in this, our feeling that that is important. We thus learn also to support our judgments with arguments, which will in many cases depend on the kinds of comparison we are able to make: the shoddy thought can be shown up by being placed alongside the genuine.

This is a kind of learning to think; it plays an essential role in the education of the emotions and in the development of moral sensibility. I have spoken of literary and non-literary works which invite us to respond emotionally or to take up some moral attitude or view of life; what I need to add is that such works may include in the 'invitation' an invitation to just the kind of awareness and critical reflection that I have described. We are familiar enough with the kind of critical attention invited by philosophical argument, the kind of work demanded by it of the reader; but critical attention to the character and quality of thought in a work may be asked of a reader in many other ways as well. Further, a work may invite the reader to elaborate and develop a way of looking at things and to respond critically to it then as a possibility, perhaps leaving open in various ways how it is to be elaborated, perhaps incorporating any number of suggestions. This is in fact what Stephen Clark does, and his book is indeed demanding of a reader in quite different ways from those of standard contemporary moral philosophy. For example, at the end of a discussion of the fantasies that distort our thought about the non-human world, Clark prints, without comment, Gerald Manley Hopkins's "God's Grandeur." He neither asserts nor argues that the poem is free of such fantasy; nor does he show us the bearing of the poem on what it is to think without fantasy about animals. What thought the placing of the poem there shows and what thought it asks of the reader is clear enough, if, that is, we read with habits other than those of philosophers trained to look *only* for assertion and argument. If Clark's aim is that his readers acknowledge something in themselves which habits of thought and response overlay and keep hidden, it is essential that he invite us to set our imagination and sensibility and intelligence to work; only that exercise can put us in a position properly to judge the view of animals he invites us to take up. Like any judgments worth bothering with, it will call on more than just the capacities of the head.

IV

Someone might conceivably agree with what I have said in Part III about the critical assessment of moral thought, and indeed use it to make a different objection from any I have considered. You may be right, he says, that presentations of moral thought invite critical reflection of *various* kinds, but a *philosophical* work invites a particular kind of assessment of any moral view it presents: it invites assessment of it by assessment of the arguments for it, the placing of it in an articulated body of moral thought.

Such a view reflects in some ways a shrinkage of the original claim made in Onora O'Neill's piece: that no one not already convinced of a view like Clark's could come to be convinced of it except by arguments. The idea is now that human beings, even including philosophers, might be convinced by such a work, but that without more in the way of argument and articulation than Clark provides, certain characteristically *philosophical* kinds of assessment of his view—implicitly invited by the presentation of the work as a work of philosophy—cannot be made.

What underlies the objection is, in part, the idea that philosophy, as contrasted with literature (or at any rate with literature not itself steeped in philosophy) presents us with views whose generality and systematic interrelations are important. We are not told, when a work of philosophy presents a moral view, that this is right and also that, but are shown that the thises and the thats are all consequences of some general propositions about what beings of such-and-such sorts ought to do, taken together with claims about the facts and perhaps some general points about human nature; at the very highest level there may also be statements linking various kinds of moral status of a very abstract sort ('moral agent', 'bearer of rights', and so on) with very general kinds of characterization, like sentience, rationality, and the capacity for free choice.—Thus when we come across such claims as that Individual A has a right at time t that state of affairs S obtain at time t^* only if Individual A is the type of object that is capable of desiring that state of affairs S should obtain at time t^* (etc.),[15] we should greet this not with blank unbelief that anyone should want to think such a thought but with the reassuring certainty that here at any rate is moral philosophy critically assessable as such.

What is wrong with the objection is not the idea that philosophy is characteristically more systematic than literature in its presentation of moral views; it is rather the implicit view of the *kind* of system that moral philosophers should aim at. But it is not merely a view about moral philosophy. If we think that philosophers should try to work out moral views with *that* kind of systematic generality, it is because we think that *people* should aim to order their own moral thought in something like that sort of way, even if we do not expect them to work out fully explicit systems. Even without such expectations, we think that they ought to be able to feel the force, or be able to be brought to, of objections and lines of argument which clearly depend on the idea that that kind of systematic order is desirable. One of our inheritances from the Great Age of Metaethics is that we take to be 'morally neutral' such ideas as that the body of someone's moral thought is improved when his principles are altered so that they no longer give counter-intuitive results in some case no matter how unlikely (is it permissible to destroy an acorn that has been treated so that it will become a rational being in two years' time?) or when they are formulated more clearly so that it can be determined what their consequences are for such cases, or when his underived principles no longer make use of allegedly 'morally irrelevant' distinctions like that between human beings and animals. But these ideas belong to a particular ideal of moral thought, the same one expressed in the current objection, in *its* idea of how moral philosophers should aim to present their moral views. Such an ideal of moral thought is far from being the only one and far from being some sort of obvious consequence of what morality is. It embodies a particular view of the relation between morality and human nature: a view of *which* human capacities are characteristically exercised in the development of someone's moral life, and more specifically of what it is for someone to exercise his capacities as a thinking being in that development. We take the explicit formulation and testing of principles, for example, as such an exercise, but not the bringing of imagination to bear on observation, or the recognition that that has been done. Too narrow a view of what is an exercise of one's capacities as a thinking being—the identification of those capacities with those of the 'head' in the sense in which I have been using that term—leads us to mistake what is merely *an* ideal of moral thought for something far more obvious than it is.

Whatever else may be wrong with the current objection, the attempt to draw back from Professor O'Neill's claims about how, how only, we can convince was a mistake. The ideal of moral thought that is expressed in that objection cannot be separated from her view of what is involved in convincing someone of a moral view, of what it *must* be like to do so. We could put it so: there is, after all, a distinction between *convincing* someone of a moral view he has hitherto been inclined to reject and simply *getting him to change* his moral views. At the very least, if he is to be convinced, he must be led, through the use of his capacities as a thinking being, to take a certain change in his moral outlook to be an improvement of some sort, a development for the better. But now what is to *count as* such a development? And what is to *count as* a use of one's capacities as a thinking being in taking a change in moral outlook so? Take as unproblematic the idea that it is always an improvement in the body of someone's moral thought when it comes closer to being a single coherent organized system of principles, whose application to particular cases can be fixed by adequate empirical data, take as unproblematic the identification of one's capacities as a thinking being with those of the head—and one has answered those questions, answered them in a way that makes clear, or seems to, that only argument can convince.

The conclusion is that the arguments I have given are in a sense quite useless. For if someone takes a view of the relation between human nature and morality from which it follows that only argument can convince, you cannot convince him by examples that convincing *does* not need to go by arguments, nor can you show such a person by examples that assessment of a moral view *does* not rest on its argumentative elaboration. Any case that might be brought will not or rather cannot count; what I have called cases of convincing must be relegated to the limbo of mere persuasion. But there is after all no compulsion on us to go that way, well trodden as it is. Stephen Clark is hardly alone in taking a very different view of how morality and human nature are related; nor do you have to go in for his brand of Aristotelianism laced with Pyrrhonic Scepticism, Neo-Platonism, and Episcopalianism on different days of the week to do so. You can be a Catholic, an Existentialist, or a Marxist, as Iris Murdoch once said,[16] or None of the Above, like Dickens, Wordsworth, Henry James, and a host of others. What is characteristic of some of these views, including Clark's, is that they take as the root of morality in human nature a capacity for attention to things imagined or perceived: what I think it would be fair to call a loving and respectful attention; W. H. Auden speaks of it (in describing the implicit morality of Walter de la Mare's verse) as a combination of wonder, awe and reverence, and another very characteristic expression of such a view may be found, in Wordsworth, in an early draft of *The Prelude*:

We live by admiration and by love,
And even as these are well and wisely fixed,
In dignity of being we ascend.[17]

It is easy to see that anyone who accepts such a view is likely to regard imaginative literature as of the greatest importance in developing and strengthening our moral capacities, and in turning them in new directions.

Such a view of the relation between morality and human nature is—not least because what one takes *morality* to be is not something given in advance and independently—highly disputable; and it is perfectly all right for philosophers to dispute it. But what is not all right is for philosophers to lay down exclusive ground rules for the discussion of moral issues in blithe unconsciousness that they are simply taking for granted and building into those rules a totally different view of morality and its relation to human nature. And that in a way makes it sound more of an impersonal matter than it is; for our views on this point show as nothing else in philosophy does so clearly how we see ourselves, what we take to be ourselves most truly and what we find it difficult to own.

I began this paper with three questions about the relation between giving arguments and convincing someone of one's moral views. We *can* hold the following: that a *convincing* appeal for a moral view is one which shows the view in question to be connected systematically with a rationally acceptable morality. *Argument* is the way in which we make such connections clear; to make a moral assertion rationally acceptable is to show such connections by argument. If we hold that view, the answers to the questions I asked at the beginning are indeed clear. But it is important to note that "if."[18]

Notes

1. Review of Stephen Clark, *The Moral Status of Animals*, in *The Journal of Philosophy*, LXXVII, 7 (July 1980), p. 445.
2. ibid.
3. op. cit., p. 446.
4. op. cit., p. 443.
5. op. cit., p. 442, pp. 445–6.
6. See lines 67–87.
7. *Great Expectations*, chapter 4.
8. "Charles Dickens," in George Orwell, *A Collection of Essays* (Garden City, New York, Doubleday, 1954), pp. 67–8.
9. Stephen Clark, *The Moral Status of Animals* (Oxford, Clarendon Press, 1977), p. 91.
10. "Life," "interest," "importance": cf. Henry James's much stronger remark about its being art that *makes* life, makes interest, makes importance (in *The Letters of*

Henry James, ed. Percy Lubbock (New York: Scribner's, 1920), volume II, p. 490).

11. *Letters*, op. cit., Vol II, p. 225.

12. F. R. Leavis, *The Great Tradition* (New York: New York University Press, 1964), p. 111.

13. "Guy de Maupassant" (1888), in Henry James, *Selected Literary Criticism*, ed. Morris Shapira (London: Heinemann, 1963), pp. 105–6.

14. Here, and elsewhere in this paragraph and the next, I am drawing from remarks of Henry James's, in the Preface to *The Portrait of a Lady* (New York: Scribner's, 1908) and in "The New Novel" (1914), in *Selected Literary Criticism*, op. cit.

15. Compare Michael Tooley, "A Defence of Abortion and Infanticide," in *The Problem of Abortion*, ed. Joel Feinberg (Belmont, California: Wadsworth, 1973), p. 61.

16. Iris Murdoch, "Vision and Choice in Morality," *Proceedings of the Aristotelian Society*, Supp. Vol. XXX (1956), especially pp. 46–7 and 54–6.

17. William Wordsworth, *The Prelude, 1799, 1805, 1850*, ed. Jonathan Wordsworth, M. H. Abrams, Stephen Gill (New York and London: W. W. Norton, 1979), p. 500.

18. An earlier version of this essay was read at a meeting of the American Philosophical Association. I have been helped by comments on that earlier essay and suggestions by Margaret Batten, Andrew Austin, Lawrence Becker, D. Z. Phillips, Martha Bolton, Robert Bolton, and A. D. Woozley. Some remarks of Onora O'Neill's in "The Power of Example" (*Philosophy* 61 [1986], 5–29) bear on this paper. See, on the issues raised by her discussion, §III of "Introduction II: Wittgenstein and Metaphysics" in this volume.

Chapter 12

Missing the Adventure:

Reply to Martha Nussbaum[1]

Moral attention is our topic: the other side of it is moral *inattention*, obtuseness, and denial. Professor Nussbaum began with a quotation from Henry James's Preface to *What Maisie Knew*: that "the effort really to see and really to represent is no idle business in face of the *constant* force that makes for muddlement."[2] James was speaking there of a particular kind of obtuseness: the moralistic dismissal of art, of the novelist's art, expressed in the criticisms of *What Maisie Knew* as a morally disgusting work. Just such 'lucidities', coming from such critics, he 'appreciates' for the vivid reminder they provide the painter of life, not just of the conditions in which he works but also of the rich opportunities he has. Professor Nussbaum mentions the significance of the analogy for James, between the *moral* imagination in a good life and the *creative* imagination of the novelist. James in fact uses the moralistic criticisms of *What Maisie Knew* to point that analogy: here suggesting that it lies between the monstrous circumstances in which Maisie's freshness must operate (the blunted moral perception, the dim moral lights, of those who surround her) and the circumstances of the artist in a social world in which perception of life is characterized by incapacity to see or to value Maisie's vivacity of intelligence.[3]

I want to look more at obtuseness, look at it in terms suggested by Professor Nussbaum. And I want to bring out some connections it has with two other terms important in her paper, *improvisation* and *adventure*.

I shall start with some obtuseness in philosophy: with a particular wild misunderstanding of a kind of moral activity. William Frankena, in a well-known introduction to moral philosophy, asks his readers, right at the beginning, to take as an example of ethical thinking Socrates's reasoning in the *Crito* about whether to escape from prison. According to Frankena, Socrates has three arguments to show that he ought not to break the laws by escaping. Each has two premises: a general moral rule or principle and a statement of fact. The three arguments are then: first, we ought never to harm anyone, and if Socrates escaped he would be harming the State; secondly, we ought to keep our promises, and if Socrates escapes he will be breaking a promise; and thirdly, we ought to obey or respect our parents and teachers, and if Socrates escapes he will be disobeying his parent and teacher. Frankena comments that Socrates's argument is instructive because it illustrates how a reflective and serious moral agent solves problems by the application of moral principles; and he goes on to raise questions about how a reflective moral agent can proceed to try to justify the principles themselves. Thus one sees what it is to be reflective about one's working ethics.[4]

Frankena's account may seem quite unextraordinary and indeed humdrum. But it is because we are so used to such talk that we do not see how very odd it is as an account of Socrates's thought. The oddness of it is most easily brought out if we consider the statement of fact in the third argument: that if Socrates escapes he will be disobeying his parent. *That* is not a fact unless it is a fact that the Laws of Athens are Socrates's parents. How is that a fact? If Socrates had said, "Crito, you don't know this, but I was brought up by wolves," there would certainly have been a fact about Socrates's upbringing of which Crito had previously been *ignorant*. But that is not the sort of fact about his upbringing that Socrates thinks Crito needs to recognize. ("Unbeknownst to you, Crito, I was brought up, not by my folks, but by the Laws of Athens.") And in the case of each of the other two arguments as they are expounded by Frankena, the factual premise, or supposedly factual premise, raises comparable questions.

Frankena is convinced, in advance of actually looking at the *Crito*, that moral thought about a particular case consists of bringing principles and rules to bear on *the facts* of the case. He does not envisage as a possibility that any moral thinking goes on in what one takes to be the facts of a case, how one comes to see them or describe them. He chooses as an example of moral thought one in which it is quite conspicuously the case that terrifically original moral thinking is involved in describing the facts of the case—describing them in such a way that they *can* be connected with familiar principles—and he totally ignores that. Facts are facts. Socrates says that his escaping would be breaking an agreement. If that is a premise in the argument, and it is not a moral principle, it must be a statement of fact—so *that* cannot be where any moral thinking is. That is how Frankena sees the case. And this is despite the fact that the moral originality of the description of the facts is underlined by Plato. When Socrates asks Crito whether, if he escapes without persuading the State to let him go, he would be treating someone badly, and not *just* treating *someone* badly but treating badly those whom least of all he should, when Socrates follows that with the question whether he must stand by his agreements or no, Crito has no idea how to answer; he does not understand the questions, does not know how to bring the terms of the questions into connection with the case before him. Socrates then by an exercise of moral imagination involving the personification of the Laws enables Crito to see the situation differently. All of which is regarded by Frankena as nothing to do with moral thinking. Facts are facts; describe them, and then comes the moral work: apply your principles. What interests me is that the case of Socrates in the *Crito* is not a case in which it is easy to miss the work of the moral imagination. We see *Crito's* imagination at work at the beginning of the dialogue. He describes life after Socrates's death, what that will be like for Socrates's friends and his children. Socrates then enables him to redescribe that future; he wants to teach Crito and his other friends to see what he is doing, wants to give them a way into his story. Professor Nussbaum quotes James's remark about Adam Verver: "he had read his way so into her best possibility"; and we can use that remark to describe what Socrates aims at: he enables his friends to read *their* way into his best possibility. His imaginative description of his situation, including the personification of the Laws, is an exercise of his moral creativity, his artistry. It is as much a significant moral *doing* as is his choosing to stay rather than to escape, or, rather, it in fact goes to any full characterization of *what* Socrates is doing in staying: the story of his death includes the imaginative understanding of the death by his friends, the understanding to which they are led by his remarkable redescription of the situation. Using the phrase that Professor Nussbaum quotes from Henry James, "to 'put' things is very exactly and responsibly and interminably to do them":[5] to ignore *how* Socrates puts things, the very particular way he puts them, to leave that out of the *doing*, is to be ignorant of *what* it was he was doing, what he was making of his death in prison.

It takes some doing to ignore that side of the *Crito* entirely, and I shall consider later what is going on in Frankena's failure of attention. But now I need to look further at what Socrates does, taking from Professor Nussbaum's paper the notion of improvisation. She wants to show how Maggie Verver's standing obligations to her father are related to her understanding the particular situation in which she finds herself, her capacity to *see* it. Maggie's perception is aided by the general principles she recognizes, and Professor Nussbaum introduces the idea of improvisation at just this point; she speaks of the improvisation of an actress who must, far more than someone going by an external script, be responsively alive to the other artists, to the evolving narrative, to the laws and constraints of the genre and its history. She must, like an improvising musician, in contrast with one who works from a score, be actively responsible and responsive, a person who will not let the others down. The description fits Socrates: he makes his death part of an evolving narrative to which his earlier talks with Crito and other friends belong. He takes up themes of the earlier parts of that narrative, like his own theme that one must not treat people badly, a theme itself sounded earlier by Crito, who has accused Socrates of planning to do what will bring disgrace on his friends and harm his sons. He takes up that theme and makes something entirely unexpected of it. He will not let the other players down, and this in a situation in which the other players were sure he was going to let them down. An extraordinary improvisation shows something to be possible that the others had not even imagined was there.

And it is that connection between improvisation and possibility that I want to insist on. It is essential in contrasting Frankena's view of what moral activity is, what moral thought is, with the view that is expressed in Martha Nussbaum's paper. As Frankena sees moral thought, it goes on in a situation with fixed, given possibilities; the terms of choice, the alternatives, are something for which one has no responsibility (except so far as one has by one's previous actions brought into existence certain now fixed elements of the situation). The moral agent must take these now fixed alternatives as they are and must determine which of them is supported by the strongest moral reasons. The notion of improvisation signals an entirely different view of what is involved in moral life, in life *simpliciter*, in which possibility and the exercise of creativity are linked. What is possible in Socrates's story is something unthought of by his friends, and depends on his creative response to the elements of his situation, his capacity to transform it by the exercise of creative imagination, and thus to bring what he does into connection with what has happened in his life. The idea of possibilities as fixed in advance and built into the situation locates the moral agent's responsibility and his freedom in quite a different place from where one sees it if one takes the capacity for improvisation as essential in any account of our moral life. The link that Professor Nussbaum makes between the task of the literary artist and the ethical task is implicitly denied when moral thought is limited to the direction of choice between fixed and readily grasped possibilities, with the idea that it is not for us as moral agents to struggle to make sense of things.

Here I find myself in the midst of an argument that Professor Nussbaum made in her earlier paper on *The Golden Bowl*, where she developed the idea of deliberation as an *adventure* of the personality "undertaken against terrific odds and among frightening mysteries."[6] In this present paper, she quotes a very striking remark of Henry James's about *adventure*: through our attentive reading of George Eliot's novels, James says, the emotions, the stirred intelligence, the moral consciousness of her heroes and heroines become our own very adventure.[7] "Adventure" is for James a significant word, used repeatedly in the Preface to *The Princess Casamassima*, from which the quoted remark comes. James describes himself as the writer of *adventures*. This may seem odd, because if someone asked you to recommend a good adventure story, it would be unlikely that you would say "Go read *The Princess Casamassima* or *The Golden Bowl*." But James did not mean "adventure" in a peculiar sense. I can explain why I say that by quoting the mountain climber George Mallory, asked why mountaineers climb mountains. "Our case," he said, "is not unlike that of one who has, for instance, a gift for music. There may be inconvenience, and even damage, to be sustained in devoting time to music; but the greatest danger is not in devoting enough, for music is this man's adventure. . . . To refuse the adventure is to run the risk of drying up like a pea in its shell. Mountaineers, then, take opportunities to climb mountains because they offer adventure necessary to them."[8] The sense of adventure, expressed there, is closely linked to the sense of life, to a sense of life as lived in a world of wonderful possibilities, but possibilities to be found only by creative response. The possibilities are not lying about on the surface of things. Seeing the possibilities in things is a matter of a kind of transforming perception of them. The possibilities yield themselves only as it were under pressure. There you are, let us say, at the end of a long day's climb, with your earlier 'confident enjoyment' shattered by the finally impossible unyielding obstacle, knowing your own spirit unwilling at last to tackle the alarming perpendicular wall. Mallory described how in such circumstances one's active sense of possibilities may flow back, not as it were first with a seeing, then a doing; it is rather a moving directly into an intensity of effort of mind and body which is an intensity of awareness, the expressive response in the face of great danger and difficulty. This response is, for Mallory, analogous to the dancer's response to music, involving also all of mind and body; it is analogous as well to the appreciative response to great art. Like a work of art, "[a] great mountain is always greater than we know: it has mysteries, surprises, hidden purposes; it holds always something in store for us."[9]

Here is how Henry James puts his own way of using the word "adventure":

> A human, a personal 'adventure' is no *a priori*, no positive and absolute and inelastic thing, but just a matter of relation and appreciation—a name we conveniently give, after the fact, to any passage, to any situation, that has added the sharp taste of uncertainty to a quickened sense of life. Therefore the thing is, all beautifully, a matter of interpretation and of the particular conditions; without a view of which latter some of the most prodigious adventures, as one has often had occasion to say, may vulgarly show for nothing.[10]

James intended his words there about *adventure* to make clear the link between such adventures as Jim Hawkins's exciting and terrifying discovery that Long John Silver is a pirate and Isabel Archer's suddenly *seeing* the conditions in which she has been living, in the great central scene of *The Portrait of a Lady*.[11] His account gives us the link, too, between Mallory's adventures as a climber and moral life as Martha Nussbaum describes it: both involve the response of the quickened sense of life to what is appreciated as having its mysteries and depths and uncertainties and dangers; both involve an openness to surprise. But James's remarks also bring us back to the subject of obtuseness: he says that "the thing is a matter of interpretation"; "without a view of the particular conditions"—and not just *any* view—"some of the most prodigious adventures may vulgarly show for nothing"; and he pointedly adds that this is something he has often had occasion to say. We may add his comment about Isabel Archer's adventures. If you look at them simply from the outside, and in comparison with battles, murders, and sudden deaths, they are "next to nothing at all": it is through her sense of what is happening, her imaginative conversion of them into the stuff of adventure, that they are the prodigious adventures he wants his readers to see them to be.[12]

What happens to her becomes adventure, becomes interesting, exciting, through the quality of her attention to it, the intensity of her awareness, her imaginative response. What happens, though, if we are *bad* readers? Two things joined together. We do not see what that is exciting happens to her. *That* passes for nothing with us; and we also do not see what is exciting, what is fine, what is secret and hidden in the book. A novel or poem, James says, does not give out its finest and most numerous secrets, except under the closest pressure, except when most is demanded from it, looked for in it;[13] in other words, when what is in the book, through the quality of the reader's attention, becomes his own very adventure. The inattentive reader then misses out doubly: he misses the adventures of the characters (to him they "show for nothing"), and he misses his own possible adventure in reading.

Actually he misses out in a third way as well. In James's novel, *The Europeans,* Gertrude Wentworth is different from the other American characters. The difference is marked at the beginning of the novel by her not going to church with the others and by her reading *The Arabian Nights* instead. She is reading about the love of Prince Camaralzaman and Princess Badoura when her European cousin, previously unknown to her, turns up. When she looks up and sees this totally unexpected visitor, he is transformed by her imagination into Prince Camaralzaman. Her active imagination is repeatedly linked in the novel with her difference from the other Americans in her wish for awareness of what life offers. She will not turn away from adventure, nor dry up like a pea in its shell. Her 'charmed perusal' of the tales goes with her seeing the world as fit home for such marvellous stories: the world she actually inhabits. *It* is an enchanted place, anything can happen, anything can have its story. Prince Camaralzaman can turn up if you are ready to see him.

This is not to say that the magic worked by a vivid imagination will not lead you into deep trouble. *The Portrait of a Lady* is about just that. My point now, though, is a different one: that for James, the adventurous reader is one who delights in there being more in things than meets the eye, who delights in the invitation the tale offers to find, to make, adventure in reading. That spirit is linked by James with imaginative perception in life, the capacity and the wish to bring to what befalls one an attention that makes it adventure, with all the dangers that may bring. The greater danger is *in*attention, the refusal of adventure. The risk there, as Mallory puts it, is of drying up like a pea in its shell. And that, for James, is the characteristic danger of New England life, the danger of the Puritan spirit: one misses out on life through unconsciousness, unawareness, linked to moralism and to a falsifying view of art.

In her other discussions of *The Golden Bowl,* Professor Nussbaum has explored these themes; in particular, she has drawn attention to Maggie Verver's moralism in the first half of the novel as a 'refusal of life': she meets what happens to her in a spirit that leaves no room for anything that cannot be fitted into her moral scheme. In her social situation there are not allowed to lurk alarming and unprecedented possibilities, inviting, demanding, improvisation.[14]

Martha Nussbaum has argued that we need texts like James's novels to show us the refusal of life in any attempt to fix in advance a scheme of moral rules for dealing with any situation we may meet. But the problem is that so far as we *need* such texts, so far (that is) as we are likely to pass over, as next to nothing at all, the moral life as the scene of adventure and improvisation, just so far are we also unlikely to make our reading of the texts our adventure, unlikely to find in such texts what they might offer a different reading. Our own conception of deliberation and of the moral life will shape our reading and make the values in moral improvisation invisible to us.

This affects us as readers of novels; it affects us as philosophers; but in different ways. The contrast can be brought out if I consider *The Portrait of a Lady*. We (and I do not here mean we philosophers but we readers) may find ourselves reading the novel with the question: Should Isabel or should she not go back to Osmond? Is going back really required of her? We think of her as confronted by a question whose terms are fixed, the possibilities are fixed. On one side: back to Osmond, fulfilment of her obligation to Pansy and to her marriage vows; on the other, freedom and self-fulfilment with Caspar Goodwood, and an end to her suffering. We do not look at all at the question what becomes of her situation under the strongest imaginative pressure she can put on it; we do not ask what the situation yields, thus pressed, in the way of possibilities and even opportunities. Not to ask is not to put our own pressure on the novel itself. The moral issue *what she should do* so interests us, we like her so much, we hate so much her having to go back or thinking she must go back to that horrible man, that we do not actually see *her* fully: do not see her as the great maker of something out of what happens to her, we do not see the relevance of her genius for *appreciation*.[15] We may miss the sense of what she does, miss her adventure, impoverish our own, through our very concern for her; but the concern is *faulty*, in something like the way Crito's concern for Socrates's fate is shown to be faulty.[16] Our care for her is not informed by any live sense of moral life as containing more possibilities, more wonderful, more interesting, more attaching, possibilities than can readily be seen. But our obtuseness here need not be obtuseness *on principle*.

Philosophical obtuseness is different. It may fail to see even the possibility of the kind of obtuseness I have been talking about. Earlier I ascribed to Frankena a view of moral thought as concerned with choice between fixed and readily graspable possibilities; in deliberation, the question, the terms in which deliberation can proceed, are fixed: obligations clash *so* with other obligations or desires. The outcome of deliberation is not a different understanding of the question. That view goes with an implicit conception of each of us as having a sort of belief-forming subperson, who uses the data available to him or her to come to beliefs about matters of fact, the minor premises, which can then be handed over to the moral-thinker-subperson for use in arriving at moral conclusions. The belief-forming subperson can be *ignorant* of straightforward matters of fact, but blindness of the sort Crito exemplifies in his blinkered care for Socrates, of the sort we may exhibit in our blinkered care for Isabel Archer—such blindness, such obtuseness, has no place in the philosophical scheme. Crito is at first blind to possibilities in Socrates's situation, possibilities Socrates appreciates; but philosophical blindness like Frankena's is blindness to such blindness. James spoke of the constant force that makes for muddlement, and Martha Nussbaum of Maggie's early dependence on moral rules as refusal of life. The constant force, the refusal of life, takes a particular shape in philosophy, where it is the principled attempt to conceive the moral faculty independently of what James and, following him, Martha Nussbaum refer to as the active sense of life.

Notes

1. Read at a meeting of the American Philosophical Association, December 1985, in reply to Martha Nussbaum, "'Finely Aware and Richly Responsible': Moral Attention and the Moral Task of Literature." Professor Nussbaum's piece appeared in *The Journal of Philosophy* **82** (1985). A revised version, "'Finely Aware and Richly Responsible': Literature and the Moral Imagination" is in A.J. Cascardi, ed., *Literature and the Question of Philosophy* (Baltimore and London, 1987) and is reprinted in Professor Nussbaum's *Love's Knowledge: Essays on Philosophy and Literature* (Oxford, 1990).
2. Henry James, *The Art of the Novel* (New York, 1934), p. 149.
3. James, pp. 149–150.
4. William Frankena, *Ethics* (Englewood Cliffs, N.J., 1963), pp. 1–3.
5. Henry James, p. 347.
6. Martha Nussbaum, "Flawed Crystals: James's *The Golden Bowl* and Literature as Moral Philosophy," *New Literary History* **15** (1983), p. 44. "Flawed Crystals" is reprinted in Nussbaum, *Love's Knowledge*.
7. Henry James, p. 70.
8. George Mallory, in a manuscript; quoted in David Robertson, *George Mallory* (London, 1969), pp. 216–7.
9. See Robertson, pp. 138–9, 219, 142.
10. Henry James, p. 286.
11. See also James, pp. 56–7.
12. ibid.
13. James, pp. 346–7.
14. Martha Nussbaum, "The Discernment of Perception: an Aristotelian Conception

of Personal and Public Rationality," in *Proceedings of the Boston Area Colloquium in Ancient Philosophy*, ed. J. Cleary (New York, 1985), revised version in Nussbaum, *Love's Knowledge*; also "Flawed Crystals" (supra, note 6), especially p. 43.

15. I have lifted the phrase from a letter of Lady O'Malley's, in which it was used of George Mallory; see Robertson, op. cit., pp. 253–4.

16. *Crito*, 46b.

Chapter 13
Eating Meat and Eating People

This paper is a response to a certain sort of argument defending the rights of animals. Part I is a brief explanation of the background and of the sort of argument I want to reject; Part II is an attempt to characterize those arguments: they contain fundamental confusions about moral relations between people and people *and* between people and animals. And Part III is an indication of what I think can still be said on—as it were—the animals' side.

I

The background to the paper is the recent discussions of animals' rights by Peter Singer and Tom Regan and a number of other philosophers.[1] The basic type of argument in many of these discussions is encapsulated in the word "speciesism." The word, I think, is originally Richard Ryder's, but Peter Singer is responsible for making it popular in connection with an obvious sort of argument: that in our attitude to members of other species we have prejudices which are completely analogous to the prejudices people may have with regard to members of other races, and these prejudices will be connected with the ways we are blind to our own exploitation and oppression of the other group. We are blind to the fact that what we do to them deprives them of their rights; we do not want to see this because we profit from it, and so we make use of what are really morally irrelevant differences between them and ourselves to justify the difference in treatment. Putting it fairly crudely: if we say "You cannot live here because you are black," this would be supposed to be parallel to saying "You can be used for our experiments, because you are only an animal and cannot talk." If the first is unjustifiable prejudice, so equally is the second. In fact, both Singer and Regan argue, if we, as a justification for differential treatment, point to things like the incapacity of animals to use speech, we should be committed to treating in the same way as animals those members of our own species who (let us say) have brain damage sufficient to prevent the development of speech—committed to allowing them to be used as laboratory animals or as food or whatever. If we say "These *animals* are not rational, so we have a right to kill them for food," but we do not say the same of *people* whose rationality cannot develop or whose capacities have been destroyed, we are plainly not treating cases alike. The fundamental principle here is one we could put this way (the formulation is based on Peter Singer's statements): we must give equal consideration to the interests of any being which is capable of having interests; and the capacity to have interests is essentially dependent only on the capacity for suffering and enjoyment. This we evidently share with animals.

Here I want to mention a point only to get it out of the way. I disagree with a great deal of what Singer and Regan and other defenders of animals' rights say, but I do not wish to raise the issue how we can be certain that animals feel pain. I think Singer and Regan are right that doubt about that is, in most ordinary cases, as much out of place as it is in many cases in connection with human beings.

It will be evident that the form of argument I have described is very close to what we find in Bentham and Mill; and Mill, in arguing for the rights of women, attacks Chartists who fight for the rights of all men and drop the subject when the rights of women come up, with an argument of exactly the form that Singer uses. The confinement of your concern for rights to the rights of *men* shows that you are not really concerned with equality, as you profess to be. You are only a Chartist because you are not a lord.[2] And so too we are told a century later that the confinement of moral concern to human animals is equally a denial of equality. Indeed the description of human beings as 'human animals' is a characteristic part of the argument. The point being made there is that just as our language may embody prejudices against blacks or against women, so may it against non-human animals. It supposedly embodies our prejudice, then, when we use the word "animal" to set them apart from us, just as if we were not animals ourselves.

It is on the basis of this sort of claim, that the rights of all animals should be given equal consideration, that Singer and Regan and Ryder and others have argued that we must give up killing animals for food, and must drastically cut back—at least—the use of animals in scientific research. And so on.

That argument seems to me to be confused. I do not dispute that there are analogies between the case of our relations to animals and the case of a dominant group's relation to some other group of human beings which it exploits or treats unjustly in other ways. But the analogies are not simple and straightforward, and it is not clear how far they go. The Singer-Regan approach makes it hard to see what is important *either* in our relationship with other human beings *or* in our relationship with animals. And that is what I shall try to explain in Part II. My discussion will be limited to eating animals, but much of what I say is intended to apply to other uses of animals as well.

II

Discussions of vegetarianism and animals' rights often start with discussion of human rights. We may then be asked what it is that grounds the claims that people have such rights, and whether similar grounds may not after all be found in the case of animals.

All such discussions are beside the point. For they ask why we do not kill people (very irrational ones, let us say) for food, or why we do not treat people in ways which would cause them distress or anxiety and so on, when for the sake of meat we are willing enough to kill *animals* or treat them in ways which cause them distress. This is a totally wrong way of beginning the discussion, because it ignores certain quite central facts—facts which, if attended to, would make it clear that *rights* are not what is crucial. *We do not eat our dead*, even when they have died in automobile accidents or been struck by lightning, and their flesh might be first class. We do not eat them; or if we do, it is a matter of extreme need, or of some special ritual—and even in cases of obvious extreme need, there is very great reluctance. We also do not eat our amputated limbs. (Or if we did, it would be in the same kinds of special circumstances in which we eat our dead.) Now the fact that we do not eat our dead is not a consequence—not a direct one in any event—of our unwillingness to kill people for food or other purposes. It is not a direct consequence of our unwillingness to cause distress to people. Of course it *would* cause distress to people to think that they might be eaten when they were dead, but it causes distress because of what it is to eat a dead person. Hence we cannot elucidate what (if anything) is wrong—if that is the word—with eating people by appealing to the distress it would cause, in the way we can point to the distress caused by stamping on someone's toe as a reason why we regard it as a wrong to him. Now if we do not eat people who are already dead and also do not kill people for food, it is at least prima facie plausible that our reasons in the two cases might be related, and hence must be looked into by anyone who wants to claim that we have no good reasons for not eating people which are not also good reasons for not eating animals. Anyone who, in discussing this issue, focuses on our reasons for not killing people or our reasons for not causing them suffering quite evidently runs the risk of leaving altogether out of his discussion those fundamental features of our relationship to other human beings which are involved in our not eating them.

It is in fact part of the way this point is usually missed that arguments are given for not eating animals, for respecting their rights to life and not making them suffer, which imply that there is absolutely nothing queer, nothing at all odd, in the vegetarian eating the cow that has obligingly been struck by lightning. That is to say, there is nothing in the discussion which suggests that a cow is *not* something to eat; it is only that one must not help the process along: one must not, that is, interfere with those rights that we should usually have to interfere with if we are to eat animals at all conveniently. But if the point of the Singer-Regan vegetarian's argument is to show that the eating of meat is, morally, in the same position as the eating of human flesh, he is not consistent unless he says that it is just squeamishness, or something like that, which stops us eating our dead. If he admitted that what underlies our attitude to dining on ourselves is the view that *a person is not something to eat*, he could not focus on the cow's right not to be killed or maltreated, as if that were the heart of it.

I write this as a vegetarian, but one distressed by the obtuseness of the normal arguments, in particular, I should say, the arguments of Singer and Regan. For if vegetarians give arguments which do not begin to get near the considerations which are involved in our not eating people, those to whom their arguments are addressed may not be certain how to reply, but they will not be convinced either, and really are quite right. They themselves may not be able to make explicit what it is they object to in the way the vegetarian presents our attitude to not eating people, but they will be left feeling that beyond all the natter about 'speciesism' and equality and the rest, there is a difference between human beings and animals which is being ignored. This is not just connected with the difference between what it is to eat the one and what it is to eat the other. It is connected with the difference between giving people a funeral and giving a dog one, with the difference between miscegenation and *chacun à son goût* with consenting adult gorillas. (Singer and Regan give arguments which certainly appear to imply that a distaste for the latter is merely that, and would no more stand up to scrutiny than a taboo on miscegenation.) And so on. It is a mark of the shallowness of these discussions of vegetarianism that the only tool used in them to explain what differences in treatment are justified is the appeal to the capacities of the beings in question. That is to say, such-and-such a being—a dog, say—might be said to have, like us, a right to have its interests taken into account; but its interests will be different because its capacities are. Such an appeal may then be used by the vegetarian to explain why he need not in consistency demand votes for dogs (though even there it is not really adequate), but as an explanation for the appropriateness of a funeral for a child two days old and not for a puppy it will not do; and the vegetarian is forced to explain that—if he tries at all—in terms of what it is *to us,* a form of explanation which for him is evidently dangerous. Indeed, it is normally the case that vegetarians do not touch the issue of our attitude to the dead. They accuse philosophers of ignoring the problems created by animals in their discussions of *human* rights, but they equally may be accused of ignoring the hard cases for their own view. (The hardness of the case for them, though, is a matter of its hardness for any approach to morality deriving much from utilitarianism—deriving much, that is, from a utilitarian conception of what makes something a possible object of moral concern.)

I do not think it an accident that the arguments of vegetarians have a nagging moralistic tone. They are an attempt to show something to be morally wrong, on the assumption that *we all agree* that it is morally wrong to raise people for meat, and so on. Now the objection to saying that *that* is morally wrong is not, or not merely, that it is too weak. What we should be going against in adopting Swift's "Modest Proposal" is something we should be going against in salvaging the dead more generally: useful organs for transplantation, and the rest for supper or the compost heap. And "morally wrong" is not too weak for that, but in the wrong dimension. One could say that it would be impious to treat the dead so, but the word "impious" does not make for clarity, it only asks for explanation. We can most naturally speak of a kind of action as morally wrong when we have some firm grasp of what *kind* of beings are involved. But there are some actions, like giving people names, that are part of the way we come to understand and indicate our recognition of *what* kind it is with which we are concerned. And "morally wrong" will often not fit our refusals to act in such a way, or our acting in an opposed sort of way, as when Gradgrind calls a child "Girl number twenty." Doing her out of a name is not like doing her out of an inheritance to which she has a right and in which she has an interest. Rather, Gradgrind lives in a world, or would like to, in which it makes no difference whether she has a name, a number being more efficient, and in which a human being is not *something to be named, not numbered.* Again, it is not 'morally wrong' to eat our pets; people who ate their pets would not have pets in the same sense of that term. (If we call an animal that we are fattening for the table a pet, we are making a crude joke of a familiar sort.) A pet is not something to eat, it is given a name, is let into our houses and may be spoken to in ways in which we do not normally speak to cows or squirrels. That is to say, it is given some part of the character of a person. (This may be more or less sentimental; it need not be sentimental at all.) Treating pets in these ways is not at all a matter of recognizing some *interest* which pets have in being so treated. There is not a class of beings, pets, whose nature, whose capacities, are such that we owe it to them to treat them in these ways. Similarly, it is not out of respect for the interests of beings of the class to which we belong that we give names to each other, or that we treat human sexuality or birth or death as we do, marking them—in their various ways—as significant or serious. And again, it is not respect for our interests which is involved in our not eating each other. These are all things that go to determine what sort of concept 'human being' is. Similarly with having duties to human beings. This is not a consequence of what human beings are, it is not justified by what human beings are: it is itself one of the things which go to build our notion of human beings. And so too—very much so— the idea of the difference between human beings and animals. We learn what a human being is in—among other ways—sitting at a table where *we* eat *them*. We are around the table and they are on it. The difference between human beings and animals is not to be discovered by studies of Washoe or the activities of dolphins. It is not that sort of study or ethology or evolutionary theory that is going to tell us the difference between us and animals: the difference is, as I have suggested, a central concept for human life and is more an object of contemplation than observation (though that might be misunderstood; I am not suggesting it is a matter of intuition). One source of confusion here is that we fail to distinguish between 'the difference between animals and people' and 'the differences between animals and people'; the same sort of confusion occurs in discussions of the relationship of men and women. In both cases people appeal to scientific evidence to show that 'the difference' is not as deep as we think; but all that such evidence can show, or show directly, is that the differences are less sharp than we think. In the case of the difference between animals and people, it is clear that we form the idea of this difference, create the concept of the difference, knowing perfectly well the overwhelmingly obvious similarities.

It may seem that by the sort of line I have been suggesting, I should find myself having to justify slavery. For do we not learn—if we live in a slave society—what slaves are and what masters are through the structure of a life in which we are here and do this, and they are there and do that? Do we not learn *the difference between a master and a slave* that way? In fact I do not think it works quite that way, but at this point I am not trying to justify anything, only to indicate that our starting point in thinking about the relationships among human beings is not a *moral agent* as an item on one side, and on the other *a being capable of suffering, thought, speech,* etc; and similarly (*mutatis mutandis*) in the case of our thought about the relationship between human beings and animals. We cannot point and say, "This *thing* (whatever concepts it may fall under) is at any rate capable of suffering, so we ought not to make it suffer." (That sentence, Jonathan Bennett said, struck him as so clearly false that he thought I could not have meant it literally; I shall come back to it.) That 'this' is a being which I ought not to make suffer, or whose suffering I should try to prevent, constitutes a *special* relationship to it, or rather, any of a number of such relationships—for example, what its suffering is in relation to me might depend on its being my mother. That I ought to attend to a being's sufferings and enjoyments is not *the* fundamental moral relation to it, determining how I ought to act towards it—no more fundamental than that this man, being my brother, is a being about whom I should not entertain sexual fantasies. What a life is like in which I recognize such relationships as the former with at any rate some animals, how it is different from those in which no such relationships are recognized, or different ones, and how far it is possible to say that some such lives are less hypocritical or richer or better than those in which animals are for us mere things would then remain to be described. But a starting point in any such description must be understanding what is involved in such things as our not eating people: no more than our not eating pets does *that* rest on recognition of the claims of a being simply as one capable of suffering and enjoyment. To argue otherwise, to argue as Singer and Regan do, is not to give a defence of animals; it is to attack significance in human life. The Singer-Regan arguments amount to this: knee-jerk liberals on racism and sexism ought to go knee-jerk about cows and guinea-pigs; and they certainly show how that can be done, not that it ought to be. They might reply: If you are right, then we are, or should be, willing to let animals suffer for the sake of significance in *our* life— for the sake, as it were, of the concept of the human. And what is that but speciesism again—more high-falutin perhaps than the familiar kind but no less morally disreputable for that? Significance, though, is not an end, is not something I am proposing as an alternative to the prevention of unnecessary suffering, to which the latter might be sacrificed. The ways in which we mark what human life is belong to the source of moral life, and no appeal to the prevention of suffering which is blind to this can in the end be anything but self-destructive.

III

Have I not then, by attacking such arguments, completely sawn off the branch I am sitting on? Is there any other way of showing anyone that he does have reason to treat animals better than he is treating them?

I shall take eating them as an example, but want to point out that eating animals, even among us, is not just one thing. To put it at its simplest by an example, a friend of mine raises his own pigs; they have quite a good life, and he shoots and butchers them with help from a neighbor. His children are involved in the operations in various ways, and the whole business is very much a subject of conversation and thought. This is obviously in some ways very different from picking up out of the supermarket freezer one of the several billion chicken-breasts we Americans eat every year. So when I speak of eating animals I mean a lot of different cases, and what I say will apply to some more than others.

What then is involved in trying to show someone that he ought not to eat meat? I have drawn attention to one curious feature of the Peter Singer sort of argument, which is that your Peter Singer vegetarian should be perfectly happy to eat the unfortunate lamb that has just been hit by a car. I want to connect this with a more general characteristic of the utilitarian vegetarians' approach. They are not, they say, especially fond of, or interested in, animals. They may point that out they do not 'love them'. They do not want to anthropomorphize them, and are concerned to put their position as distinct from one which they see as sentimental anthropomorphizing. Just as you do not have to prove that underneath his black skin the black man has a white man inside in order to recognize his rights, you do not have to see animals in terms of your emotional responses to people to recognize their rights. So the direction of their argument is: *we* are only one kind of *animal*; if what is fair for us is concern for our interests, that depends only on our being living animals *with* interests—and if that *is* fair, it is fair for *any* animal. They do not, that is, want to move from concern for people to concern for four-legged people or feathered people—to beings who deserve that concern only because we think of them as having a little person inside.

To make a contrast, I want to take a piece of vegetarian propaganda of a very different sort.

Learning to be a Dutiful Carnivore[3]
Dogs and cats and goats and cows,
Ducks and chickens, sheep and sows
Woven into tales for tots,
Pictured on their walls and pots.
Time for dinner! Come and eat
All your lovely, juicy meat.
One day ham from Percy Porker
(In the comics he's a corker),
Then the breast from Mrs Cluck
Or the wing from Donald Duck.
Liver next from Clara Cow
(No, it doesn't hurt her now).
Yes, that leg's from Peter Rabbit
Chew it well; make that a habit.
Eat the creatures killed for sale,
But never pull the pussy's tail.
Eat the flesh from 'filthy hogs'
But never be unkind to dogs.
Grow up into double-think—
Kiss the hamster; skin the mink.
Never think of slaughter, dear,
That's why animals are here.
They only come on earth to die,
So eat your meat, and don't ask why.
Jane Legge

What that is trying to bring out is a kind of inconsistency, or confusion mixed with hypocrisy—what it sees as that—in our ordinary
ways of thinking about animals, confusions that come out, not only
but strikingly, in what children are taught about them. That is to say,
the poem does not ask you to feel in this or the other way about
animals. Rather, it takes a certain range of feelings for granted. There
are certain ways of feeling reflected in our telling children classical
animal stories, in our feeding birds and squirrels in the winter, say—
in our interfering with what children do to animals as we interfere
when they maltreat smaller children: "Never pull the pussy's tail."
The poem does not try to get us to behave like that, or to get us to
feel a 'transport of cordiality' towards animals. Rather, it is addressed
to people whose response to animals already includes a variety of
such kinds of behavior, and taking that for granted it suggests that
other features of our relationship to animals show confusion or hypocrisy. It is very important, I think, that it does not attempt any

justification for the range of responses against the background of which certain other kinds of behavior are supposed to look hypocritical. There is a real question whether justification would be in place for these background responses. I want to bring that out by another poem, not a bit of vegetarian or any other propaganda. This is a poem of Walter de la Mare's.

> *Titmouse*
>
> If you would happy company win,
> Dangle a palm-nut from a tree,
> Idly in green to sway and spin,
> Its snow-pulped kernel for bait; and see
>   A nimble titmouse enter in.
>
> Out of earth's vast unknown of air,
> Out of all summer, from wave to wave,
> He'll perch, and prank his feathers fair,
> Jangle a glass-clear wildering stave,
>   And take his commons there—
>
> This tiny son of life; this spright,
> By momentary Human sought,
> Plume will his wing in the dappling light,
> Clash timbrel shrill and gay—
> And into Time's enormous Nought,
>   Sweet-fed will flit away.

What interests me here is the phrase "This tiny son of life." It is important that this is connected in the poem with the bird's appearing out of earth's vast unknown of air, and flitting off into Time's enormous Nought. He is shown as fellow creature, with this very striking phrase "son of life." I want to say some things about the idea of a fellow creature.

First, that it indicates a direction of thought very unlike that of the Singer argument. There we start supposedly from the biological fact that we and dogs and rats and titmice and monkeys are all species of animal, differentiated indeed in terms of this or the other capacity, but what is appropriate treatment for members of our species would be appropriate to members of any whose capacities gave them similar interests. We are all equally animals, though, for a start—with, therefore, an equal right to have whatever our interests are taken into account. The starting point for our thought is what is general and in common and biologically given. Implicitly in the Jane Legge poem, and explicitly in the de la Mare, we have a different notion, that of living creature, or fellow creature—which is *not* a biological concept.

It does not mean, biologically an animal, something with *biological life*—it means a being in a certain boat, as it were, of whom it makes sense to say, among other things, that it goes off into Time's enormous Nought, and which may be sought as *company*. The response to animals as our fellows in mortality, in life on this earth (think here of Burns's description of himself to the mouse as "thy poor earthborn companion,/An' fellow mortal"), depends on a conception of *human* life. It is an extension of a non-biological notion of what human life is. You can call it anthropomorphic, but only if you want to create confusion. The confusion, though, is created only because we do not have a clear idea of what phenomena the word "anthropomorphic" might cover, and tend to use it for cases which are sentimental in certain characteristic ways, which the de la Mare poem avoids, however narrowly.

The extension to animals of modes of thinking characteristic of our responses to human beings is extremely complex, and includes a great variety of things. The idea of an animal as company is a striking kind of case; it brings it out that the notion of a fellow creature does not involve just the extension of moral concepts like charity or justice. Those are, indeed, among the most familiar of such extensions; thus the idea of a fellow creature may go with feeding birds in winter, thought of as something akin to charity, or again with giving a hunted animal a sporting chance, where that is thought of as something akin to justice or fairness. I should say that the notion of a fellow creature is extremely *labile*, and that is partly because it is not something over and above the extensions of such concepts as justice, charity and friendship-or-companionship-or-cordiality. (I had thought that the extension of the 'friendship' range of concepts was obviously possible only in some cases, titmice and not hippopotamuses, e.g.; but recent films of the relation between whales and their Greenpeace rescuers show that I was probably taking an excessively narrow view.) Independence is another of the important extended concepts, or rather, the idea of an independent life, subject, as any is, to contingencies; and this is closely connected with the idea of something like a *respect* for the animal's independent life. We see such a notion in, for example, many people's objections to the performance of circus tricks by animals, as an *indignity*. The conception of a hunted animal as a 'respected enemy' is also closely related. *Pity* is another central concept here, as expressed, for example, in Burns's "To a Mouse"; and I should note that the connection between pity and sparing someone's life is wholly excluded from vegetarian arguments of the sort attacked in Part I—it has no place in the rhetoric of a 'liberation movement'.

It does normally, or very often, go with the idea of a fellow creature, that we do eat them. But it then characteristically goes with the idea that they must be hunted fairly or raised without bad usage. The treatment of an animal as simply a stage (the self-moving stage) in the production of a meat product is not part of this mode of thinking; and I should suggest also that the concept of 'vermin' is at least sometimes used in excluding an animal from the class of fellow creatures. However, it makes an importantly different kind of contrast with 'fellow creature' from the contrast you have when animals are taken as stages in the production of a meat product, or as "very delicate pieces of machinery" (as in a recent BBC program on the use of animals in research). I shall have more to say about these contrasts later; the point I wish to make now is that it is not a *fact* that a titmouse *has a life*; if one speaks that way it expresses a *particular relation* within a broadly specifiable range to titmice. It is no more biological than it would be a biological point should you call another person a "traveller between life and death": that is not a biological point dressed up in poetical language.

The fellow-creature response sits in us alongside others. This is brought out by another poem of de la Mare's, "Dry August Burned", which begins with a child weeping her heart out on seeing a dead hare lying limp on the kitchen table. But hearing a team of field artillery going by to maneuvers, she runs out and watches it all in the bright sun. After they have passed, she turns and runs back into the house, but the hare has vanished—"Mother," she asks, "please may I go and see it skinned?" In a classic study of intellectual growth in children, Susan Isaacs describes at some length what she calls the extraordinarily confused and conflicting ways in which we adults actually behave towards animals in the sight of children, and in connection with which children have to try to understand our horror at the cruelty they may display towards animals, our insistence that they be 'kind' to them.[4] She mentions the enormously varied ways in which animal death and the killing of animals are a matter-of-course feature of the life children see and are told about. They quite early grasp the relation between meat and the killing of animals, see insect pests killed, or spiders or snakes merely because they are distasteful; they hear about the killing of dangerous animals or of superfluous puppies and kittens, and are encouraged early to fish or collect butterflies—and so on.

I am not concerned here to ask whether we should or should not do these things to animals, but rather to bring out that what is meant by doing something *to an animal*, what is meant by something's being an animal, is shaped by such things as Mrs. Isaacs describes. Animals—these objects we are acting upon—are not given for our thought independently of such a mass of ways of thinking about and responding to them. This is part of what I meant earlier when I dismissed the idea of saying of something that whatever concepts it fell under, it was capable of suffering and so ought not to be made to suffer—the claim Bennett found so clearly false that he thought I must not have meant it. I shall return to it shortly.

This mass of responses, and more, Mrs. Isaacs called confused and contradictory. But there are significant patterns in it; it is no more just a lot of confused and contradictory modes of response than is the mass which enables us to think of our fellow human beings as such. For example, the notion of vermin makes sense against the background of the idea of animals in general as not mere things. Certain groups of animals are then singled out as *not* to be treated fully as the rest are, where the idea might be that the rest are to be hunted only fairly and not meanly poisoned. Again, the killing of dangerous animals in self-defence forms part of a pattern in which circumstances of immediate danger make a difference, assuming as a background the independent life of the lion (say), perceived in terms not limited to the way it might serve our ends. What I am suggesting here is that certain modes of response may be seen as withdrawals from *some* animals ('vermin'), or from animals in *some* circumstances (danger), of what would otherwise belong to recognizing them as animals, just as the notion of an enemy or of a slave may involve the withdrawing from the person involved of some of what would belong to recognition of him as a human being. Thus, for example, in the case of slaves, there may be no formal social institution of the slave's name in the same full sense as there is for others, or there may be a denial of socially significant ancestry, and so on. Or a man who is outlawed may be killed like an animal. Here then the idea would be that the notion of a slave or an enemy or an outlaw assumes a background of response to persons, and recognition that what happens in *these* cases is that we have something which we are *not* treating as what it—in a way—is. Of course, even in these cases, a great deal of the response to 'human being' may remain intact, as for example what may be done with the dead body. Or again, if the enemyhood is so deep as to remove even these restraints, and men dance on the corpses of their enemies, as for example in the 1970s in the Lebanon, the point of this can only be understood in terms of the violation of what is taken to be how you treat the corpse of a human being. It is because you know it *is* that, that you are treating it with some point as that is *not* to be treated. And no one who does it could have the slightest difficulty—whatever contempt he might feel—in understanding why someone had gone off and been sick instead.

Now suppose I am a practical-minded, hardheaded slaveholder whose neighbor has, on his deathbed, freed his slaves. I might regard such a man as foolish, but not as batty, not batty in the way I should think of someone if he had, let us say, freed his cows on his deathbed. Compare the case Orwell describes, from his experience in the Spanish Civil War, of being unable to shoot at a half-dressed man who was running along the top of the trench parapet, holding up his trousers with both hands as he ran. "I had come here to shoot at 'Fascists', but a man who is holding up his trousers is not a 'Fascist', he is visibly a fellow-creature, similar to yourself, and you do not feel like shooting at him."[5] The notion of enemy ('Fascist') and fellow creature are there in a kind of tension, and even a man who could shoot at a man running holding his trousers up might recognize perfectly well why Orwell could not. The tension there is in such cases (between 'slave' or 'enemy' and 'fellow human being') may be reflected not merely in recognition of the point of someone else's actions, but also in defensiveness of various sorts, as when you ask someone where he is from and the answer is "South Africa and you do not treat them very well here either." And that is like telling someone I am a vegetarian and getting the response "And what are your shoes made of?"

What you have then with an image or a sight like that of the man running holding his trousers up is something which may check or alter one's actions, but something which is not compelling, or not compelling for everyone who can understand its force, and the possibility, even where it is not compelling for someone, of making for discomfort or of bringing discomfort to awareness. I should suggest that the Jane Legge poem is an attempt to bring a similar sort of discomfort closer to the surface—but that images of fellow creatures are naturally much less compelling ones than images of 'fellow human beings' can be.

I introduced the notion of a fellow creature in answer to the question: How might I go about showing someone that he had reason not to eat animals? I do not think I have answered that so much as shown the direction in which I should look for an answer. And clearly the approach I have suggested is not usable with someone in whom there is no fellow-creature response, nothing at all in that range. I am not therefore in a weaker position than those who would defend animals' rights on the basis of an abstract principle of equality. For although they purport to be providing reasons which are reasons for anyone, Martian or human being or whatnot, to respect the rights of animals,

Martians, and whatnot, in fact what they are providing, I should say, is images of a vastly more uncompelling sort. Comically uncompelling, as we can see when similar arguments are used in *Tristram Shandy* to defend the rights of homunculi. But that takes me back to the claim I made earlier, that we cannot start thinking about the relations between human beings and animals by saying "Well, here we have me the moral agent and there we have it, the thing capable of suffering" and pulling out of that "Well, then, so far as possible I ought to prevent its suffering." When we say that sort of thing, whatever force our words have comes from our reading in such notions as human being and animal. I am not now going to try to reply to Bennett's claim that my view is clearly false. I shall instead simply connect it with another clearly false view of mine. At the end of Part II I said that the ways in which we mark what human life is belong to the source of moral life, and no appeal to the prevention of suffering which is blind to this can in the end be anything but self-destructive. Did I mean that? Bennett asked, and he said that he could see no reason why it should be thought to be so. I meant that if we appeal to people to prevent suffering, and we, in our appeal, try to obliterate the distinction between human beings and animals and just get people to speak or think of 'different species of animals', there is no footing left from which to tell us what we ought to do, because it is not members of one among species of animals that have moral obligations to anything. The moral expectations of other human beings demand something of me as other than an animal; and we do something like imaginatively read into animals something like such expectations when we think of vegetarianism as enabling us to meet a cow's eyes. There is nothing wrong with that; there *is* something wrong with trying to keep that response and destroy its foundation.

More tentatively, I think something similar could be said about imaginatively reading into animals something like an appeal to our pity. Pity, beyond its more primitive manifestations, depends upon a sense of human life and loss, and a grasp of the situations in which one human being can appeal for pity to another, ask that he relent. When we are unrelenting in what we do—to other people or to animals—what we need is not telling that their interests are as worthy of concern as ours. And the trouble—or a trouble—with the abstract appeal to the prevention of suffering as a principle of action is that it encourages us to ignore pity, to forget what it contributes to our conception of suffering and death, and how it is connected with the possibility of relenting.

My non-reply to Bennett then comes to an expansion of what he would still take as false, namely that our *hearing* the moral appeal of an animal is our hearing it speak—as it were—the language of our fellow human beings. A fuller discussion of this would involve asking what force the analogy with racism and sexism has. It is not totally mistaken by any means. What might be called the dark side of human solidarity has analogies with the dark side of sexual solidarity or the solidarity of a human group, and the pain of seeing this is, I think, strongly present in the writings I have been attacking. It is their arguments I have been attacking, though, and not their perceptions, not the sense that comes through their writings of the awful and unshakeable callousness and unrelentingness with which we most often confront the non-human world. The mistake is to think that the callousness cannot be condemned without reasons which are reasons for anyone, no matter how devoid of all human imagination or sympathy. Hence their emphasis on rights, on capacities, on interests, on the biologically given; hence the distortion of their perceptions by their arguments.[6]

Notes

1. See especially Peter Singer, *Animal Liberation* (New York, New York Review, 1975), Tom Regan and Peter Singer, eds., *Animal Rights and Human Obligations* (Englewood Cliffs: Prentice-Hall, 1976), Stanley and Roslind Godlovitch and John Harris, eds., *Animals, Men and Morals* (New York: Grove, 1972), and Richard Ryder, "Speciesism: The Ethics of Vivisection" (Edinburgh: Scottish Society for the Prevention of Vivisection, 1974).
2. 'The Enfranchisement of Women', *Dissertations and Discussions* (Boston: Spencer, 1864), vol. III, pp. 99–100. Mill's share in writing the essay is disputed, but his hand is evident in the remarks about Chartism. (For the origin of the remark, see also Mill, *Collected Works*, ed. J. M. Robson (Toronto: University of Toronto Press, 1963–89), vol. VI, p. 353n.)
3. *The British Vegetarian*, Jan/Feb 1969, p. 59.
4. *Intellectual Growth in Young Children* (London: Routledge, 1930), pp. 160–2.
5. *Collected Essays, Journalism and Letters* (London: Secker and Warburg, 1968), Vol. II, p. 254.
6. For much in this paper I am indebted to discussions with Michael Feldman. I have also been much helped by Jonathan Bennett's comments on an earlier version of Part II.

   Permission to quote the poems on pp. 327–8 was kindly given by the Vegetarian Society, and by the Society of Authors as representative of the Literary Trustees of Walter de la Mare.

Chapter 14

Experimenting on Animals: A Problem in Ethics

My aim in this essay is to clarify our continuing disputes about experimentation on animals. Someone from Mars trying to make sense of it all—the televised debates, the speeches at public meetings and addresses to learned societies, the demonstrations, the lobbying, the books and articles—might at first take it that on one side there were defenders of the freedom of investigators, and on the other, the defenders of animals. That would be one way of dividing up the combatants, but it is oversimple, and I want to look at the dispute differently. I want to represent it as having two 'sides', but each of the two sides is meant to include a range of views.

The Two Sides of the Dispute

I can represent one side by using this diagram:

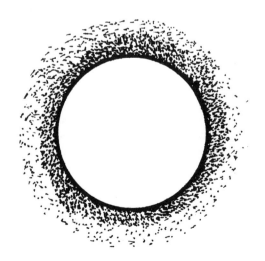

The circle represents the limits of the justifiable use of animals in experiments. Outside the circle are to be found various sorts of unjustifiable modes of treatment of animals. One is positively sadistic treatment, and another would be wanton indifference to the welfare of the animals. Also outside the realm of the justifiable, on this view, would be the handling of animals by those without real technical competence, and, in general, neglect due to ignorance or inadequate training.

The side of the dispute which I want to characterize using the diagram can be put this way: so long as a scientist's use of animals remains *within the circle*, there is no real basis for criticism from the point of view of ethics. On this view, then, there are certain minimal standards which animal experimentation has to meet to be justifiable, but once those standards are met, there is no further need for the scientist to try, for example, to minimize his use of animals. His own professional judgment is to be relied on here as it is in his decision to use any piece of complicated and expensive equipment. Sir John Eccles has stated such a view very clearly.[1] He contrasts the conditions which must be met if we are to carry out experiments on human beings with those which must be met if an experiment on animals is to be justified. In the case of experiments on human beings, we must consider the relation between risks to the subject and the possible benefits to the subject and others; we must be certain the importance of the objective is in proportion to the risk to the subject. But such considerations have no place at all, he claims, in connection with experiments on animals. We must indeed take precautions about pain (presumably with the qualification: so far as is consistent with the purposes of the investigation), but that is all we have to do: beyond that we can do what we wish on the animal. Thus Eccles's example: the experimental implantation of electrodes in the brains of human beings is unethical because it is destructive and not at all therapeutic, but exactly the same sort of investigation carried out on primates is highly desirable. It involves no pain, the animals can be experimented on, if well looked after, for weeks or months, and there should be far more of such experimentation. A similar view of animal experimentation was taken by several people in a 1977 BBC television program on the subject.[2] For example, a Home Office spokesman claimed that callousness in experiments on animals is unlikely because one's colleagues would disapprove. The idea is that pressure from one's peers would keep one from moving off outside the circle. Again, in the BBC program, the view was expressed that pain can muck up your experimental results, so experimenters will naturally want to safeguard against it as far as they can. Here we have the idea that departures in the outward direction from the circle will result in diminished effectiveness of the experiment as well as increased costs; the same point has been made by many others.

The conception just sketched of what is justifiable in experiments on animals goes with a certain view of the training of those engaged in such experiments. They ought to know the fundamental physiological and psychological needs of the kinds of animals they will work with, and the ways in which various kinds of stress, discomfort, pain, and so on can arise and how they can be prevented, just as they ought to know the proper use and care of any kind of equipment they will use. But there is no idea here that they ought to be trained in such things as how to avoid using animals. An animal on this view is fundamentally a delicate and expensive piece of equipment, and apart from any economies there might be in replacing it with something else, there is no particular reason to think one ought to use, or try so far as possible to use, something else instead. *Which* instrument to use is fundamentally a matter for scientific and economic considerations to decide, assuming one stays within the circle—and in any case there are scientific and economic pressures to stay within it.

People who accept this view of animal experimentation (which I shall call the First View) may nevertheless be divided on whether there is any need for change in the laws covering research (or for change in social policy more generally—including here the organization of medical, veterinary, or scientific education). Some may be reformers. For example, they may think that the current legislation is outdated and inadequate to ensure against abuses, or that something should be done to ensure that the training of those who will deal with animals is not wholly inadequate: "a very delicate piece of machinery needs *specialists* to look after it."[3] Others, though, who accept the First View may feel that any attempt to strengthen regulations dealing with animal experimentation is the thin end of the antivivisectionist wedge. John Dewey was *still*—in 1975—being quoted with approval on this:

> The point at issue on the subjection of animal experimentation to special supervision and legislation is thus deeper than at first sight appears. In principle it involves the revival of the animosity to discovery and to the application to life of the fruits of discovery which, upon the whole, has been the chief foe of human progress. It behooves every thoughtful individual to be constantly on the alert against every revival of this spirit, in whatever guise it presents itself.[4]

Someone who accepts Dewey's view might then recognize that there are some—or even many—things done to animals in the name of science which ought not to be done, but he would nevertheless be opposed to any kind of regulation to prevent such abuses. Any tidying up in the house of science that needs to be done should not be imposed from without. So there is room for quite a lot of *practical* disagreement on the part of those who share the same fundamental view of animal experimentation.

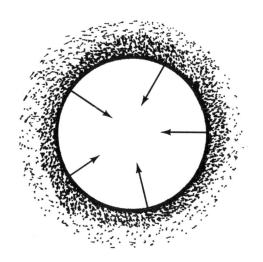

I shall represent the opposed view of animal experimentation by the diagram above. Here the sphere of justifiable experimentation on animals is under a sort of pressure or tension, tending to narrow the sphere of what is allowable so far as possible. And an animal is perceived here, not as a delicate instrument, but as a creature with a life of its own, so that the systematic interference by us with an animal's life for our ends, and equally the creation of such life for our ends, is seen as quite unlike the manufacture and use for our ends of a microscope, say, or other piece of technical equipment. There are on this Second View questions which can appropriately be raised about how we are justified in interfering with an animal's life or creating such life for our ends, questions which cannot be raised about the use and manufacture of machinery. Even if an experiment would lie within the allowable sphere of animal experiments on the First View, the Second View would require us to ask further questions before we could conclude that the procedure was justified: could we at perhaps some increased cost substitute a procedure which did not use animals or which did not subject them to such-and-such treatment? Is the value of the result in terms of human knowledge (or whatever other benefit may be in view) really sufficient to justify the kind of interference that is proposed?—which is not a question which science itself can answer. Such questions imply a mode of thinking about animals quite different from that implicit in the First View. On the First View, once certain standards of attention to the welfare of the animal have been met, the only further questions which arise are ones for the professional judgment of the scientist; on the Second View, questions do arise about the animal's treatment which are not for the scientist as a scientist, and which take the animal as a center of moral claims in something *like* the way a human being is. Again, Sir John Eccles provides a way of characterizing the distinction between the two sides: experimentation on human beings involving risk of any sort should be diminished so far as possible; on the First View (his), nothing corresponding can be said about animal experimentation. On the Second View, something of the same sort can and indeed should be said about animal experimentation.

Just as there can be wide practical disagreement among those who share the First View, so there can be among those who hold the Second. Just as holders of the John Dewey version of the First View are in principle opposed to any governmental supervision of animal experiments as antiscientific and the thin end of the antivivisectionist wedge, so holders of an equally extreme version of the Second View (far fewer in number than they once were) are in principle opposed to any governmental supervision of animal experiments short of abolition—as an implicit recognition of the principle that animals *may* justifiably be used merely as instruments in the pursuit of scientific knowledge. So the extremes meet—but only because each takes *any* governmental regulation as granting some recognition to the other side.

In summary, then, we have these two ways of looking at the use of animals in experiments:

Within certain limits, experimental animals may be regarded as delicate instruments, or as analogous to them, and are to be used efficiently and cared for properly, but no more than that is demanded.	Within certain limits, animals may be regarded as sources of moral claims. These claims arise from their capacity for an independent life, or perhaps from their sentience, but in either case the moral position of animals is seen as having analogies with that of human beings.

The Dispute Not Over a Moral Issue but Over Whether There Is a Moral Issue

I have mentioned that on the First View of animal experimentation, there is no moral need to justify the use of animals in experimentation, provided that certain kinds of abuse (arising from willful sadism or ignorance) are avoided. This means that from the First point of view, holders of the Second View, who do regard at least some of what goes on 'within the circle' as morally unjustifiable, are not so much mistaken in the *particular* moral view they take, but in making or trying to make a moral issue where there is none. In this part of the paper I want to show the significance in the First View of the idea that there *is no moral issue* about the use of animals 'within the circle' and its connection with other characteristic features of the First View.

The dispute between holders of the First View and holders of the Second should *not* be conceived as a dispute between those who attach greater and those who attach lesser weight to the interests of animals in the clash between their interests and ours. Let me explain by considering a contrasting case, in which animals are used in scientific investigation, but in a setting in which their interests are taken into account—given weight, but less weight than ours. Sled dogs have been used in the course of scientific work in the Antarctic, during which they have undergone serious risks, considerable pain, and prolonged discomfort. Most people would of course think that if, during such an expedition, a situation arose in which a dog's interests and a person's clashed (say, only one could be rescued from a crevasse) the dog's would properly be sacrificed. But many people would *also* think that at the end of the expedition the dogs should not be killed (however painlessly) merely to save the money it would cost to ship them back. They might think in terms of something 'owed' to the dogs in such a case, and indeed in the actual case I have in mind all the dogs involved were adopted. What then is the difference between the treatment of such animals and the treatment of dogs in experiments? It is not that the latter are necessarily treated *worse* or are subject to more *pain*. This need not be so at all. The point is that in the experimental setting, the dog may come to be thought of merely as a useful and disposable object; we may come automatically to take it that there simply is *no room* for thinking of it as a being with a life of its own. We do not then see it (for example) as a being to which something may be owed, in at least that minimal sense in which we may feel something—analogous, at least, to gratitude—*is* owed to the sled dog after what *it* has gone through. The animal seen in the laboratory setting becomes something we may respond to in accordance with quite a different set of ideas from those which are natural and quite common with the sled dog. The person who thinks this way need not deny that it is wrong to be cruel to dogs or indeed to other animals. But he believes that there *is* cruelty only when the laboratory animal is subject to some treatment *outside* the circle, like wanton abuse. On this view, when the animal is treated in the laboratory as a delicate instrument, to be used properly and disposed of painlessly, no question of cruelty, no moral question at all, arises.

This way of thinking of the laboratory context, and the animal viewed as an instrument in it, is in some ways analogous to the mode of thought of such slaveholding societies as the *ante bellum* American South. Slaveholders may recognize some modes of treatment of slaves as morally wrong, but these will be *outside* what they take to be the circle of appropriate economic use of the slave, and would include wanton cruelty. As in the case of laboratory animals, there is economic pressure to stay within the circle. From the slaveholder's point of view, modes of treatment which are within the circle, and belong to the proper use of the slave as economic tool, can raise no moral issue, and do not properly speaking involve *cruelty.* In both cases, people who may be perfectly kindly set apart an area of practical activity in which beings of a sort which they themselves regard in *some* contexts as proper objects of moral concern, can be treated as practicality dictates, and no moral concern, it is held, is appropriate, provided the treatment involves no *gratuitous* suffering.

The First View then does not differ from the Second in giving *less* weight to the costs borne by laboratory animals: provided the minimal conditions for justifiable animal experimentation are met, the costs borne by the animals are seen as having no moral significance. The idea is not of a clash between their interests and ours, in which ours must take precedence, but of an area in which we can simply get on with the job of asking and answering scientific questions, treating animals solely as our instruments in doing so.

This feature of the First View is reflected not only in direct assertions that animal experimentation does not really raise any moral questions but also in other ways; I shall look at five of them.

(a) Later on, I shall discuss the accusation made by those who hold the First View that the other side is guilty of *sentimentality.* What is relevant now is that one basis on which that charge is made is that holders of the Second View do precisely regard experimental animals as properly objects of moral concern, even within the setting of well-conducted experiments. They are thought of as sentimental because they bring a type of concern for animals which might be appropriate in the sled dog context into what is, on the First View, a wholly inappropriate context for *that* sort of concern. The basis of accusation is not that they care *as much* about animals as about people—they mostly do not—but that they make a moral issue where, on the First View, there is none.

(b) If you conceive of a certain sort of situation as one in which two groups of beings come into conflict, and if you think that such situations are likely to occur frequently, then a test whether you really do think that there is at least some weight on *both* sides is: Are you concerned to find some way of avoiding such conflicts? Thus, for example, in the case of abortion: If you think of the situation as one in which the mother's interests outweigh those of the fetus, but you think the interests of the fetus do count for *something,* you might show that that was what you believed by, say, an interest in making adoption an easily available and attractive option. On the other hand, so far as you are totally uninterested in preventing the occurrence of situations in which there is a clash between the interests of the mother and those of the fetus, situations, that is, in which one's interests cannot be respected unless the other's are sacrificed, you tend to show that you do not take abortion as raising any real moral questions, with real costs to be borne on both sides.—This argument is based on a discussion of moral dilemmas by Ruth Barcan Marcus, and I have drawn on her use of the abortion example. She has argued that there is a fundamental moral principle: "As rational agents with some control over our lives and institutions, we ought to conduct our lives and arrange our institutions so as to minimize predicaments of moral conflict."[5] If that is indeed a fundamental principle, then there is a strong implication that a total *lack* of concern with institutional arrangements intended to prevent conflicts of some sort must tend to show that such conflicts are not being seen as ones in which there is serious moral weight on both sides. Thus someone might hold that in a conflict between the interests of mice and those of people, the interests of people must win, but if he *also* regards it as quite unnecessary, or even wrongheaded, that training for medical or scientific research be such as to incline people to use alternatives if they possibly can, to design experiments to limit the number of animals used or the kind of interference involved—this would tend to show that there is on his view no real moral conflict. The First View goes with the idea that it is not worth human ingenuity or resources or concern to work out ways of diminishing animal experimentation, and that it is not worth trying to alter social institutions like scientific or medical education so that people are inclined to look for alternatives and to use them when they can. Anyone who accepts that does *not* think of animals as having merely *less* moral significance than people, but thinks of the context of scientific experimentation as one in which the animals' lives have no moral significance. This is an important point because proponents of the First View often attempt to enlist support by appealing to the generally accepted idea that a rat's life or suffering, or a dog's, matters less than a person's. But someone who holds that generally accepted view should not on that account alone be willing to support the First View. The idea that an animal's life or suffering matters less than a person's is entirely compatible with the Second View.

(c) If, as I have said, the holder of the First View does not regard animal experimentation as a moral issue, this will be reflected in the way he looks at statements of the Second View. He will tend not to regard them as *moral claims* with which he disagrees (for that would go with the idea that animal experimentation within the circle raises moral issues on which there are different positions) but will put them in some other category. Usually they will be seen as expressions of irrational or non-rational likes and dislikes, but occasionally they may be seen as expressions of an eccentric theological or metaphysical position. Again the comparison with the case of abortion may be useful. Those who believe the interests of the fetus to have *some* moral weight will see the expression of their own position as one within what we might call the arena of moral discussion. But those for whom the fetus is no more than a collection of tissues which may or may not be wanted by its bearer will see that the fetus may well be the center of great *emotions* of different sorts for different people, but cannot (cannot usually, that is) take seriously that the view opposed to their own is a view in the *moral* arena at all. It appears as *merely* an emotional response (or a religious reflex), and any attempt to protect the interests of the fetus is seen as a fundamentally illegitimate attempt to interfere, on merely emotional or religious grounds, in what is a personal decision for the pregnant woman. To recognize someone else's position as *moral* disapproval of a course of action one favors is to accept at least this much, that the kind of conduct falls into the arena of moral discussion. And this the holders of the First View often show they do not do, in their ways of describing their opponents' ideas. Thus, for example, in the 1977 BBC program, the advantages and limits of tissue culture as an alternative to the use of animals in medical research were being discussed; the advantages were said to be that it was cheap and pleasing for those who find animal experimentation distasteful. The use of the words "pleasing" and "distasteful" here takes for granted that the issue is one in which *taste* is all that is involved. (Compare a discussion of war in which pacifists were described as finding killing *distasteful* and other methods of settling disputes more *pleasing*.)

(d) Holders of the First View insist that the choice whether or not to use animals in some experiment is a choice which can be judged appropriate or inappropriate only by an *expert*. This idea is closely related to the last: describing one's opponents as merely expressing their emotions is one way of emphasizing that the issue is not in the moral arena at all, as far as you can see, and the idea that it is a field *for experts* is simply the other side of the same notion. Once an area is recognized as one in which there are genuine moral problems, it is *eo ipso* recognized as one not to be left to experts in the particular field. If (for example) there *are* moral problems concerning euthanasia, it follows that the position and training of the doctor does not *as such* qualify someone to decide such matters; if it is urged that the expertise of scientific investigators *is* sufficient and necessary for judging what use of animals in science is appropriate, it is being assumed that there is no significant moral issue. It is interesting that the people doing research for the BBC Horizon program on animal experiments had assumed, beforehand, that the licensing procedure for such experiments involved some kind of judgment whether the likely benefits of the result of some proposed experiment balanced the suffering for the animal subjects. But they found to their surprise that the licensing procedure involves no such judgment at any point, and "the scientist is not licensed to conduct a given experiment at all, but is licensed for a period of time to *carry out certain procedures on animals*," and indeed may alter the program of investigation without needing any change of license.[6] We can see in the present licensing system a reflection of the idea that once certain minimal standards are met in animal experiments, no further issues arise in which society might properly be interested. On the other hand, the suggestion made by the Littlewood Committee in 1965, and strongly supported by many people in animal welfare groups, that there be a standing body *involving four laymen* to advise the Home Office on matters to do with the use of animals in scientific work, and concerned not only with the ways in which animals are treated but also with the *purposes* for which they are used—this recommendation reflects a position opposed to the First View.

(e) One further reflection of the First View can be seen by anyone who looks at the literature in the field now called bioethics. It is certainly true that articles concerned with animal experimentation turn up *occasionally* in the professional journals concerned with ethics and the life sciences. But for many working in the field, the phrases "ethical problems posed by research" and "ethical problems posed by research *on human subjects*" are treated as simply interchangeable. Again, a large (79-page) bibliography on society, ethics, and the life sciences, described by its publishers as containing the most pertinent references on precisely such subjects as experimentation, contains nine pages on ethical and legal problems of experimentation, including, besides general material, sections specifically on experimentation on fetuses, prisoners, mental patients, and children—but does not include references to the ethical problems of animal experimentation.[7] The explanation I was offered of this omission is that references to a particular problem would be put either in a section devoted to the subject—but this would be done only if the bibliographers found 10 to 15 relevant pieces, and apparently they had not done so—or under some more general heading—but this had not been done either: Peter Singer's *Animal Liberation*, for example, "fell between the cracks in the structure of the bibliography."[8] But major discussions *can* fall between the cracks, the articles (which certainly do exist, on both sides) *can* fail to be noticed by bibliographers, because the subject itself is perceived as merely a peripheral one in bioethics—at best. For many scientists with strong interests in bioethics, it simply is not an ethical problem at all, and the professional 'ethicist' often shows by ignoring the issue that he tacitly shares the view that it is not one of the things we need to be thinking about. This is striking, because in a sheer numerical sense, animal experimentation is an enormously bigger thing than human experimentation (far bigger in the number of experimental subjects involved, in the number of experimenters and technicians and of people indirectly involved, and in the amount of money spent) or indeed than most of the other problems bioethicists discuss. It is not merely big in numerical terms, but a feature of so many parts of our social life: it is hard to think of anything produced in our society except jokes that is not tried out on animals! It is partly the very *normality* of animal experimentation that helps make it invisible to the bioethicist, but it is also the acceptance by many of some version of the First View, and the prestige the view gains by its connection with the research establishment.

Neither Side is More Rational than the Other

People who take the First View do sometimes tend to regard it as more rational. But how could this be shown? What we can see right off is that there are the two different analogies which play a role in thinking about animal experiments—the delicate-instrument analogy, and the person-with-moral-claims analogy. A laboratory rat *is neither* a machine *nor* a person; if it really were one or the other there would be no problem how to draw the boundaries of morality. Just simply looking at the two views as two different views, it cannot be said that one is rational and the other merely emotional, or that one is a matter of taste and the other appropriately scientific. Until something more is said, there is a considerable symmetry: we have the two views.

One thing that is often said by holders of the First View is that the Second cannot be held to consistently, or that if its implications were clearly seen it would lose all popular appeal. The idea is this: in many parts of our lives, we *do* treat animals as mere instruments. Most significantly, we manipulate their lives and kill them off for food—food which is not essential to our health. If we think that to please our palates, we may justifiably treat animals pretty much as mere objects serving our needs and wishes, how can we think that the free use of them in scientific experimentation should be questioned? As one well-known experimenter on primates has put it: "there is no more need to seek alternatives to the use of animals for medical research than to search for non-flesh substitutions for meat in our diets."[9] So the idea is that only a vegetarian could *consistently* object to the use of animals in research, and, if this is once clear, ordinary folk should see that, given their own basic views (including their views about the justifiability of eating meat), they have no reason to treat the use of animals in science as a moral issue.

To clarify the issues which this line of argument raises, recall the summary description of the two sides. As I stated the First View, it was that *within limits* it is appropriate to treat animals as any other instrument that might be used in scientific investigation, and the Second View was that *within limits* it is appropriate to treat animals as sources of moral claims and in that respect like human beings. As a matter of fact, there are people who take an extreme version of the First View and do not recognize *any* limits on the circumstances in which animals may be regarded as mere things giving rise to no moral claims on their own account, and there are people who take an extreme version of the Second View and do not recognize *any* limits on the circumstances in which an animal is to be treated as a source of moral claims analogous to those made on us by another human being. *Most* people taking the First View, though, do not hold the extreme version of that view—nor do most taking the Second View hold the extreme version of *it*. It is perhaps worth noting how very unattractive the extreme version of each is. The extreme version of the Second View involves holding that there is no duty to frighten off a wolf (say) stalking a human baby, or to try to get the baby out of harm's way, *unless* there is a comparable duty to frighten off a wolf stalking some other sort of animal, or to try to get *it* out of harm's way. Anyone who thinks that one might have a duty to a human being in such circumstances but that one does not have a comparable duty with respect to other animals does not hold the extreme version of the Second View. The extreme version of the First View holds that we may have a duty to an animal's owner not to molest it, or again we may have a duty to other human beings not to treat an animal in a way that would increase the likelihood that we would treat *human beings* badly, but that just considering the animal itself and leaving aside all the ways injury to an animal indirectly injures human beings, we have *no* reason at all to think there are moral constraints (of kindness or justice or of any other sort) on how the animal should be treated. On this extreme view, if you and a dog were, let us say, the only surviving living things on the planet, so nothing you could do to it could injure anyone else, and if it amuses you—helps you pass the time—to torment the dog, there is no possible moral objection to this. Indeed, if your amusement takes the form of tying tin cans and so on to the dog while it is asleep, so that it does not take in at all that you are the source of its daily miseries and it never gives up its pathetic affection for you—this refinement is equally morally all right.—I do not think one needs to try to decide *which* extreme view is more unacceptable. The point is that most people who hold the First View have something important in common with most people who hold the Second: they regard animals as a source of moral claims analogous to those arising from human beings in *some* circumstances but not others. Holding such a view is not *itself* a sign of inconsistency on either side. We can no more assume that a holder of the Second View who eats meat is inconsistent than we can assume that there must be inconsistency if a holder of the First View says to a child tormenting an animal, "How would you like it if someone did that to you?" in the same spirit in which he might say it if the victim had been a smaller child. There is, you could say, a built-in tension in our modes of treatment of animals. From childhood on, we are familiar with animals treated sometimes as within the sphere of morality, and sometimes as mere things, sometimes as companions, sometimes as lamb chops on the hoof—and so on.[10] One may, on reflection, alter some of one's views about animals; for example, one might go from thinking that using animals for food raises no real moral issues to thinking it does—or the other way. That is, I am not suggesting that whatever we are brought up to accept we should go on thinking is acceptable. I *am* suggesting that the complex of beliefs which the typical holder of the First View might accept is not in any obvious way a more rational collection than that which might be accepted by his typical opponent; there is no reason at all to think that considerations of consistency ought to drive one to give up the Second View. Further, if we distinguish, as we should, between consistency in moral response and mere singlemindedness, we should also see that *neither* extreme view is forced on us by the demands of consistency.

The accusation of inconsistency brought against the non-vegetarian holder of the Second View may be based on the different idea that the cases—of the use of animals for food, and their use as laboratory instruments—cannot be morally distinguished on any reasonable grounds. A vegetarian myself, I should nevertheless argue that the accusation is ill-founded, and that it can be shown to be so by appeals to examples. One such example would be the views of G. K. Chesterton, which I shall not discuss in detail. His moral position, a coherent and in many ways attractive one, includes opposition to animal experiments *and* to vegetarianism—his views on both subjects being connected with his hatred of snobbery.[11]

The Specialness of Human Beings

Proponents of the First View often claim that it is based on our recognition of the immense gulf that separates human beings from all other animals, while many of those who hold the Second View argue that what makes a being an appropriate object of moral concern is its possession of sentience or of the capacity to live its own life—things, that is, shared by human beings and animals. Their argument continues: what makes it morally questionable to carry out risky experiments on people is not their rationality but the fact that they have interests, interests to which we may not be giving adequate consideration, and, animals equally having interests, there must be a moral question whether *theirs* may be overridden. A common and closely related argument is that there is *no* feature of human beings, such as rationality of such-and-such a level, which is actually shared by *all* human beings and *no* other animals, and which could be used as the basis for giving human beings a specially privileged position in morality. The basic idea in this argument is that if you put the level of rationality low enough to include the senile or hopelessly retarded among us, many animals such as primates (at the very least) will come out *higher*. How then can we treat experimentation on primates as perfectly all right because of the great gap between them and us in rationality, and experiments on seriously retarded people as a great big moral problem? Again, we *ignore* differences in rationality when we consider whether a human being is a proper object of moral concern; the Nazis are criticized for (among other things) taking the senile and insane as things that were a mere drain on the nation's resources and that should be painlessly disposed of. If we regard such people as entitled to the same moral concern as other people, despite their absence of rationality, how can we say that animals may be treated in scientific experimentation as mere instruments for the satisfaction of our wants and needs, because they have not got *our* rationality? It has been further argued on the same lines that only if we invoke some sort of *theological* doctrine can we give any justification for taking the boundary between human beings and other animals as of any moral significance. If you believe in an immortal soul that people and not animals have, that idea might back up the claim that people, being very special, can use other animals, which are not at all special, for experimentation, but cannot use the retarded, the senile, or the insane. But then the criticism is that the idea of the specialness of *human* life cannot be maintained without its theological backing.

I believe that neither sort of argument will do: the First View cannot be supported by arguments from the gulf between animals and ourselves, and the Second View cannot be supported by the arguments that without theological support, there is no basis on which to defend a morally significant distinction between human beings and other animals, and that men and many animals share those empirical characteristics (like sentience) in virtue of which moral concern about what is done to them is justified. We do not need to discuss *either* how far Mozart is from the most musical whales, *or* how far Washoe the chimpanzee is ahead of some severely retarded children. There are two claims I should wish to make against these bad arguments offered by both sides.

(a) It is possible to combine a recognition of human life as terribly special with the Second View—they are perfectly compatible. The bad arguments offered by both sides share the false assumption that the First View is supported by the idea of human life as special—special in some morally significant way.

(b) The bad arguments offered on both sides involve the same confused picture of morality. It is a confusion about what would be involved in any attempt to justify treating human beings and animals differently. The bad arguments suppose that any attempted justification would have two elements. You would have to be able to point to some empirical difference between human beings and animals—say, that human beings have x and animals do not—and you would further have to accept some general moral principle to the effect that *any* beings with x can properly be treated differently in such-and-such circumstances from *any* beings which lack it. Take a simple parallel to illustrate the general point: the idea is that we might offer a justification of "Kicking stones is okay and kicking people is not" by (i) pointing out that stones do not feel pain when kicked and people do, and then (ii) appealing to the principle that things that feel pain ought not to be treated in ways that cause them pain. The bad argument for the First View is an attempt to give such a justification for distinguishing between how people and how animals should be treated, and the bad argument for the Second is that any such attempted justification would have to appeal to a principle justifying experiments on lower grade people, and that there is *no* principle which really would be acceptable, if its consequences were thought through, to proponents of the First View and which would justify treating animals as they think we should.

The heart of the shared idea of morality held by those putting forward such arguments on both sides is that what is involved in moral thought is knowledge of empirical similarities and differences, and the testing and application of general principles of evaluation. The maker of a moral evaluation is 'the moral agent', and the essence of a moral agent is that it can find out facts and understand and accept general principles and apply them to actual cases. Thus the idea is that if a Moral Agent believes it is wrong to torment a cat, this must depend on his having some such general principle as that The Suffering of a Sentient Being is a Bad Thing and that one ought therefore to prevent such bad states of affairs from existing.

Against this, I should claim that we are not Moral Agents in that sense at all—and thank heavens for it. We have resources in our moral thinking which the story I have just told forgets all about. We can, for example, ask what human beings have *made of* the difference between human beings and animals. A difference like that may indeed start out as a biological difference, but it becomes something for human thought through being taken up and made something *of*—by generations of human beings, in their practices, their art, their literature, their religion, their ethics. This is true of any difference. If you want to know whether it is a good thing to treat men and women differently, or to treat the old with respect simply because they are old, or to treat dogs differently from other animals, or cows differently from other animals—it is absurd to think these are questions you should try to answer in some sort of totally general terms, quite independently of seeing what particular human sense people have *actually* made out of the differences or similarities you are concerned with. And this is not predictable. If the Nuer, for example, had not actually made something humanly remarkable out of giving cows a treatment quite different from that accorded other animals, one could not know that 'singling cows out for special treatment' could come to that. It would be foolish to raise the question "Should cows be treated differently from other animals?" as a general abstract question, because one would not know what it could come to to do so. As the Nuer have made something quite remarkable out of their special relationship with their cattle, so our culture has made something (which we might recognize as remarkable if it were not so familiar) of treating dogs, and to a lesser extent cats and horses, differently from other animals. Much more important, of course, we have made something of human significance and great depth out of the difference between men and women—and we have never made anything humanly valuable of the differences between races, the mythology of the American South notwithstanding.

The view I am putting forward is that we are never confronted merely with the existence of 'beings' with discoverable empirical similarities and differences, towards which we must act, with the aid of general principles about beings with such-and-such properties deserving so-and-so. The modes of life and thought of our ancestors, including their moral thinking, have *made* the differences and similarities which are now available for us to use in our thinking and our emotions and decisions. We have available to us, not for example the mere biological notion of difference-of-sex, but a human notion of that difference, made by literature, art, and common thought and life over centuries—and we can make something more or less of it in our turn. Far from it being the case that we have moral principles which can be given in purely general terms, and which are then applied in a world of empirically given similarities and differences, what differences there are *for us in our thought* is a matter created in part by past moral thought, marking and making something with human sense of such things as male/female, human/non-human. What we have made of these differences may be valueless or valuable or a mixture of good and bad.

That was intended as a general point about morality. The specific point is that we have made something of great human significance out of the very notion of *human life*. People think the invention of the wheel was a great thing. But so was the invention of the idea of human life as something special. (I do not mean "invention" to imply that someone sat down and came up with it as a good idea. I mean that it is something made by us.) Chesterton expresses the idea I have in mind this way:

> Ordinary things are more valuable than extraordinary things; nay, they are more extraordinary. Man is something more awful than men; something more strange. The sense of the miracle of humanity itself should be always more vivid to us than any marvels of power, intellect, art, or civilization. The mere man on two legs, as such, should be felt as something more heartbreaking than any music and more startling than any caricature. Death is more tragic even than death by starvation. Having a nose is more comic even than having a Norman nose.[12]

The bad arguments for both the First and Second Views suggest that you could justify making a moral distinction between how people are to be treated and how animals are to be if there were some specially significant characteristic of human beings that animals lack. Against this I am claiming that making such distinctions in our mode of treatment is not grounded on a prior recognition of differences but is itself one of the complex of human activities through which we come to have the concept of the heartbreaking specialness of human life, of which Chesterton spoke.

Two further brief points:

(i) We do not need *theology* to back up the idea of the specialness of human life, any more than we need it to back up the idea of the human nose as comic. The idea of human life as poignantly special did not rest, for Chesterton, on his religious views. The relation between that idea of human life and Christian doctrine may be seen very clearly in Hopkins's "That Nature is a Heraclitean Fire." The poet exclaims with pity and indignation at the disappearance in the fire of nature of man and all the marks of his mind that shine out, but then is comforted by the resurrection. The significance of the resurrection here depends on a prior sense of the tragedy of death as such.

(ii) The capacity to feel the heartbreakingness of the mere man on two legs as such—this is a main source of that moral sensibility which we may *then* be able to extend to animals. We can come to think of killing an animal as in some circumstances at least similar to homicide, but the significance of doing so depends on our already having an idea of what it is to kill a man; and for us (as opposed to abstract Moral Agents) the idea of what it is to kill a man does depend on the sense of human life as special, as something set apart from what else happens on the planet. There is then a possibility of extending that sense of what life is to animals, without this involving any going back on the idea of human life as special. I should want to claim (though I am not going to argue for this here) that the idea of the specialness of human life is not merely compatible with the Second View, but essential to all except the most unattractively simple-minded versions of that view.

An Accusation Against the First View

I have argued in the two preceding sections that neither view is more rational than the other nor more securely grounded in the actual empirical similarities or differences between human beings and animals. Is there any more fruitful approach to the dispute? Yes; and it requires us to notice one difference between the two views that I have not yet touched on at all. Those who hold the Second View usually regard experimentation on animals as likely to harden those who engage in it, and to do the same to others as well, for whom it will serve as a model—leading, it is suggested, to a general increase in callousness. Proponents of the First View usually deny that this is so. It is worth attending to this issue; it will lead us to the heart of the dispute about animal experimentation. In the rest of this section, I shall explain the charge of callousness as conceived from the Second View, and in the following section I shall show its significance for us.

The first thing to note is that the question whether animal experimentation makes one more callous is not a purely empirical one. As I pointed out on page 341, there are ways of treating animals which will be regarded as cruel on the Second View but not on the First (in which there is cruelty only when pain or distress is imposed on an animal through sadism or neglect or ignorance). Thus, for example, the removal of a monkey from its natural habitat to a cage in a laboratory might be regarded as cruel on the Second View but not on the First. In the absence of agreement on what counts as cruelty, there can clearly be no agreement on what counts as increasing people's callousness (their indifference to cruelty, or willingness to treat it as acceptable), and so it is no wonder the two sides disagree whether animal experimentation does so.

It may be useful to consider an actual example in which the importance of what one takes to be callousness comes out. In 1912, Stephen Paget, the founder and secretary of the Research Defence Society, published a collection of excerpts from the testimony given to the Royal Commission on Vivisection, which had just completed its work.[13] Among his main aims was to show that experimenters were not inhumane and that virtually all experimentation met the tests of humanity towards animals. One passage which he singled out for inclusion was from the testimony of the eminent pharmacologist Sir Lauder Brunton. Brunton himself was concerned to bring out that much experimentation involves no pain to speak of, and to illustrate his point he described a dog on whom he had made a gastric fistula, and "which never showed the slightest sign of pain." Brunton went on that whenever he went to examine the dog

> it showed great delight—just like a dog that has been sitting about the house, and wants to run out for a walk. When it saw that I was going to look into its stomach, it frisked about in the same way as if I was going to take it out for a walk.[14]

These daily examinations were not only painless but, Brunton explained, eagerly anticipated by the dog, because it liked to be made much of and shown around.—Now one possible reaction to this story is that it is a miserable life for a dog to have nothing to look forward to but the daily examination of the interior of its stomach. Of course such things happen to people too, in hospitals—but it is pathetic in either case. It is clear that neither Brunton nor Paget (who selected Brunton's testimony for the collection) saw the pathos of the case, the possibility of its eliciting not, "Oh good, no pain," but, "What a miserable life for an animal." Paget, note, was concerned especially to show that animal experimentation was carried out by humane men. Humane men in his society, including (let us grant) himself and Brunton, would no doubt have regarded it as deplorable, *outside* the context of scientific experimentation, to deprive a dog of a normal sort of dog's life, and would not think that 'no pain' made it *un*deplorable. The charge, that animal experimentation makes one callous, is (among other things) the charge that one can come to think like Brunton and Paget, that is, can cease to take in that what one is doing to animals is something which one would oneself in other circumstances regard as deplorable, and which one therefore should, at the very least, notice, be concerned about, regret, and regard as something one should try to avoid, and so on. It is possible for humane men to set apart the area of experimentation as one in which one simply cannot bring in the sorts of consideration that play a role in judging how animals are treated outside that area. The judgment "What a pathetic life!" which they themselves might make in connection with a confined animal outside the sphere of experimentation they do not make, and do not see as appropriate, when the confinement and deprivation of normal life is for the sake of scientific knowledge. But the animal's life is not made any *less* pathetic by the fact that its deprivations are for the sake of science. We may think, given that we *are going* to treat animals this way, it is impractical to respond as the humane man would in other cases of confinement and deprivation of normal life. This is to say that the humane person who is involved in experimentation on animals had better become inured to it, had better set up these compartments, as it were, in his mind—so that he comes quite naturally to apply quite different standards of what counts as humane treatment in the context of scientific experimentation from those he uses in other contexts. He no longer thinks, "How pathetic!" of treatment like that of Brunton's dog. It is part of the normal life of animals in laboratories; and one simply does not see this normal laboratory life as itself raising any questions.

What I have tried to bring out with this example is how the same case can be seen (as by Brunton and Paget) as meeting all the requirements of humanity in the treatment of animals, and (from a different point of view) as illustrative of the way animal experimentation can make experimenters callous by encouraging a compartmentalization of mind in which the experimenter can simply get on with the job. Once you have accepted this sort of compartmentalization, you simply do not *look at* the treatment of animals in science as you otherwise might: here is an animal, here is how it is treated, and my gracious, is it really justifiable to do *this*? The 'this' in the particular case is something we no longer bring to realization. Our powers of imagination and judgment are not brought to bear on the case; and this (it is suggested) is a form of callousness. We do without fully thinking what we do.

Supporters of the First View sometimes mention that 'even' Albert Schweitzer allowed that animal experimentation could not be given up. But it is important to see that his position is opposed to the First

View at what really is its central point: that we can give a *general* justification for animal experimentation and then *get on with the job*, provided only we meet the minimal conditions. The heart of Schweitzer's view is that no such *general* justification can be given, but only justifications which take fully into account what we are doing to particular animals in the particular case, justifications that recognize them as individual animals with their own lives. In other words, to experiment in the spirit of Schweitzer, one would have fully to recognize the morally problematic character of even routine experiments—not to speak of heroic ones; one would have to recognize also the need to fight against a tendency to separate one's way of judging the treatment of animals in science from the way one would judge it in other contexts.

I have tried to show that the accusation made by holders of the Second View, that animal experimentation makes for callousness, should be connected with the idea that it leads to a harmful compartmentalization of mental life, in which one does not bring to full imaginative realization what one is doing. I want now to turn to the other part of the accusation: the increase in callousness is supposed to affect not just the experimenter but others. I have in front of me, as I write, a popular scientific journal put out by the Museum of Natural History in New York. In an article on why food rots, there is a description, quoted from a pharmacological journal, of an experiment in which moldy maize was fed to farm animals. Several refused it, and post-mortem examination showed that they were in fact starving rather than eating; others were force fed and got very ill (showing depression, weakness, and bloating, and undergoing seizures) before dying.[15] What I am interested in is the way the experiment is described, both in the original report and by the writer of the popular article incorporating the quotation. The language is the language of the normal, of the not-in-need-of-any-comment even. The reader is not supposed to think, as he would, reading in the newspaper of a farmer who treated his animals so, "How horrible!" He is not supposed to think that treating animals like *that* must need some very weighty justification. The misery caused the animals was unavoidable, given the nature of the experiment, and so the investigation falls 'within the circle'. The reader is expected, or, one might say, invited, by the language of the description, to share the compartmentalization of mind in which there is 'no point' in allowing oneself to realize fully in imagination what was being done.

This compartmentalization of mind is also imparted in schools, to an extent which is perhaps difficult to appreciate in Britain, where there has never been the American combination of absence of legis-lative control and affluence capable of providing large numbers of living animals for children to learn science on. In my school, for ex-ample, each pair of 13-year-olds in the biology classes had a living but pithed frog to cut up. Two years after doing this in school, I wanted to give younger children at a summer camp a biology lesson. Inca-pable of pithing anything, I battered a snake's head—it seemed about the same—and then showed the children all the pieces inside the snake. I could do this because I thought of it as science. Heaven knows it was not, but what a child can pick up all too easily is the idea that in 'science' one can irresponsibly treat the world and what is in it as *interesting things*. I want to emphasize that my claim is not that the scientific spirit involves treating animals as *things* to be in-vestigated in a state of moral anesthesia, but that the practice of animal experimentation is in our society accompanied by the com-partmentalization I have spoken of, and that biology teaching using living animals imparts, besides impressive—unforgettable—knowl-edge of what a beating heart looks like, the idea, impressive in a dif-ferent way, that if you are doing science, you are in a situation in which you do not take seriously the lives of the animals used—do not see them as individual animals with lives of their own at all.

Consider a different example, again an American one. "Send a mouse to college" was used several times as the official slogan for cancer research collections in my community. "Grow a tumor in a mouse" would not have quite done. If holders of the First View can claim that experimentation is not connected with callousness, how can the apparent callousness of such a slogan be taken? The answer would be that a humane person has in the end to be more concerned about the sufferings of human beings from cancer than about the suf-ferings of mice. But that is no answer; a humane person should in-deed be more concerned about men than about mice, but does not therefore have to take mice as joke animals, with no more reality to them than the happy pigs dancing on a sausage van.

It has been claimed that the result of contact with laboratory ani-mals in one's work is heightened respect for them, "likely to be fol-lowed by considerate treatment and a general enrichment of life for both man and animals." This from Dr Lane-Petter,[16] one of the very few scientists working with animals who has written or spoken with real sympathy for the Second View. There is no doubt that for many scientists such contact teaches respect for the marvelous complexity of animals: of their physiology and their behavior; and such respect may breed contempt for those who treat such marvelous things sloppily or carelessly. But considerate and feeling treatment is different, and has a different source—imagination, not characteristically scientific imagination, but the imagination exemplified here:

> Now and again I caught and brought home in a glass bottle some miserable minnow or stickleback. A wooden bucket—if not a large wooden tub—would then be filled with the best of cool well water fresh pumped; a stone or two, a crock or two, would be dropped in to make a comfortably uneven floor and there—Why would the wretched stickleback never live? Ah—why rather did it linger so long? The laceration of its mouth by the hook was probably the least of the horrors. Cold and motionless well water replaced the limpid freedom of the running water; and the company of other fishes, and all the homeliness of a well known environment, had been lost. What knowledge the fish had was no longer of any use to it; it might as well have been blinded. In vain I dropped worms into the water. No longer served by its own senses, the lonely captive swam round and round, turned whitish; and at last, after hours, died. And I never dreamt that the whole enterprise on my part was sheer cruelty from beginning to end. . . . But intentional cruelty horrified me if I had eyes to see it.[17]

The Disagreement Explored Further

In the preceding section I explained the charge brought by holders of the Second View that animal experimentation makes for an increase in callousness, in experimenters and others. The charge should not be taken to mean that people become less humane *in general* but that they set apart an area insulated from the kinds of thought which they themselves (granting now that they are indeed humane people in general) would bring to bear on at any rate some other situations involving the treatment of animals.

Holders of the First View do not just deny that animal experimentation increases callousness. There is a counteraccusation they bring: that the Second View is essentially sentimental. One version of this charge is comparatively unimportant: it may be claimed that holders of the Second View are sentimental in that their attacks on animal experimentation reflect a fantasy of what animals are. This might be called the Bambi version of the sentimentality charge. It applies, no doubt, to some antivivisectionists, especially Victorian ones, but is no more applicable to most than is the charge of 'wanton sadism' to most experimenters. Far more important, and worth taking seriously, as the Bambi accusation is not, is a charge of sentimentality on other and indeed hardly compatible grounds: the accusation is that holders of the Second View think it appropriate to go in for imaginative realization of what the individual animals experimented on go through or are deprived of, when it is sentimentally self-indulgent to bring this to mind at all. Here the "How pathetic!" said of Brunton's dog because it had nothing in its life but a daily stomach examination would be seen as the bringing to bear on that dog of considerations appropriate to *pet* animals but totally inappropriate to it, and even more glaringly out of place, let us say, in connection with such laboratory creations as the nude mouse.

It is confused to reply to such charges in the traditional style of defenders of the Second View. The traditional reply is that sentimentality consists in *not* looking at reality, but in self-indulgently inventing what you prefer. The holder of the Second View then adds: I am not sentimental; for I look at the reality of what is done to animals: I bring it to attention, if I can, that these are ways of treating animals that no humane person can view with equanimity.

The confusion of such a reply lies in not seeing the heart of the accusation, which is not that one has been putting fantasies of what animals are for facts, but that one has been treating certain facts as worth attention and concern when they should be treated as things we should learn to take in our stride, as the way things have to be done. It is sentimental, the accusation is, to take these animals' lives seriously, when the serious business of our lives requires that we treat the area of experimentation as one in which such considerations are simply irrelevant. The accusation is indeed that the holder of the Second View substitutes a fantasy for reality, not a fantasy about animals but a fantasy about human life. He fails to treat scientific investigation in an appropriate and realistic way, taking into account its enormous significance to us.

I said this is the counteraccusation to the charge that experimentation on animals leads to callousness. I can now state the reason. From the First View, the imaginative realization of what is done in experimentation to the individual animals is self-indulgent sentimentality; from the Second View, it is a form of callousness to set this area apart as one in which imaginative attention to what is done is out of place. One view, that is, takes to be callous exactly what the other takes to be required by the practicalities of scientific investigation. One side takes to be sentimental exactly what the other takes to be required by humanity.

I should emphasize that by 'imaginative realization' I do not mean 'thinking about all that pain'. Pain is not what the problem is about, though it comes in. A neurophysiologist once mentioned in a lecture to philosophers about his work that he was distressed by all the death of animals that was part of that work—important as he recognized his work to be. When I mentioned this to a colleague of his, *he* was bothered that any fellow-worker should feel that or say so. The idea was that a scientist should not take the deaths so, should not think "All these deaths!" and be distressed by their inseparability from the kind of work he does.

What I hope is clear is the very deep disagreement that is reflected in the two accusations; a disagreement about how people should live, about the place of science in life and the place of imagination in it, and the role of the spirit of practicality, of getting on with the job. It is this disagreement which lies at the root of the question discussed on pages 340–6: whether the use of animals 'within the circle' should be thought of as a moral issue.

The matter need not be left with a mere statement of the depth and extent of the disagreement. For we can also ask: *is* it sane and practical, or is it a kind of callousness, to be untroubled by the enormous amount of animal experimentation that is 'within the circle'? The idea that it is sane and practical has two sources, and I shall, very briefly, criticize each.

The first source is the conception of scientific investigation itself as a special sort of activity, whose special character is marked by (among other things) its immunity from some sorts of ordinary moral criticism. This immunity is not seen simply in connection with the use of animals. Social scientists, for example, routinely use deception in experiments on people, with the idea that normal standards of honesty in dealing with other people do not apply if one is conducting a scientific experiment meeting certain minimal conditions. That is, there is the idea here too of a circle (experiments 'within the circle' here are those not involving serious risk of harm to the subject)—and lies to the subject when the experiment falls 'within the circle' are not thought of by the experimenter as involving *dishonesty*. They occur in what has become for him a moral enclave, analogous to the enclave of animal experimentation 'within the circle'. And indeed—no accident—critics of such experimentation claim it increases the callousness of those who engage in it and of others influenced by them. The source of the callousness is the same in both cases: the conception of scientific research as conferring a special moral status on what one does. The point was made in Victorian language by George Rolleston, Professor of Anatomy and Physiology at Oxford, and a member of the group of distinguished scientists from whom nineteenth century experimenters expected support on the vivisection issue:

. . . I must say that with regard to all absorbing studies, that it is the besetting sin of them, and of original research, that they lift a man so entirely above the ordinary sphere of daily duty that they betray him into selfishness and unscrupulous neglect of duty.[18]

The removal from the 'ordinary sphere' which Rolleston speaks of is removal *to* a sphere in which the things the scientist is investigating exist in their wonderful complexity, their endlessly complicated and fascinating relationships. In this sphere, one can attend with the highest and truest scientific respect—or even awe—to the reality of the things one is investigating, and nevertheless fail to take the things one is studying seriously *except* as things it is fascinating and rewarding, or frustrating, to study. That is, in this sphere, attention to their reality is scientific attention, in the fullest sense of that term, which indeed has an ethical element: but it is quite distinct from ordinary ethics, which ceases fully to apply—or so it seems. For the scientist using laboratory animals, they provide no moral counterweight to his own wish to pursue his investigations; the only considerations which are seen as applying are scientific ones. Rolleston, speaking with the splendid certainty of Victorian ethics, implies that it is a bad thing for any man to regard any of his activities as taking place in a special sphere, free from the sorts of consideration which otherwise apply to human activities. The criticism, though, is not grounded in some special feature of Victorian thought, but in common human sense—which rejects the pretension of any activity to special moral status. The most forceful arguments for the Second View are those which rest on this bit of common sense.

What is being criticized, note, is not the desire for knowledge, but the significance which that motive may be given, and the view that actions from that motive have a special and superior status: the view that a man is not *dishonest* who lies to others only in the course of experiments, or *hard* who would deafen birds only because we do not know how they learn to sing. Some defenders of the freedom of scientists have construed any such criticism as Rolleston's as an attack on *science*—but this is balderdash, of the same sort as that which identifies patriotism with the doctrine that ordinary moral considerations fail to apply to what is done for the sake of one's country. Again, it may be argued that treating scientific investigation as having some morally special status is justified by its results. But what are *its* results? It is a complete non sequitur to argue from the desirable results of scientific investigations which have used animals, or which have involved deception, to the desirability of continuing to view scientific investigation as an activity insulated from certain kinds of moral criticism. Is the idea that we should probably have far fewer valuable scientific discoveries if scientists were encouraged (by legislation, education, and the structure of institutions) to resist the temptation to view research as a special sort of sphere, morally insulated in the way I have been discussing? If that is the idea, I do not see that it has ever been seriously argued for.

I said that the view that it is not a kind of callousness but good sense to be untroubled by what is done to animals in experiments 'within the circle' had two sources. One is the idea that scientific investigation is properly marked off as a special sort of activity, within which one's subject matter may be viewed purely in a scientific spirit. The other source is quite different. Here the idea is not that science, as a human activity, is a special one and properly treated differently, but that certain kinds of moral consideration are inappropriate in the practical conduct of life, of which scientific activities are part. This second line of thought is especially important when it is physiological investigations using animals that are being defended; the first is more important in the defence of animal experimentation where practical applications are not seriously in view. But the two lines of thought are often combined.

What is this idea that it is a virtue to be practical and hardheaded? Practicality *is* a virtue, if what is meant is that one does not *just* sit about and consider moral difficulties, but does what one can, what needs doing, as well. But what is sometimes called 'practicality' and boasted of is not a virtue at all: when it means getting on with the job, ignoring questions of any moral complexity, putting any difficulties out of view, treating them as a sort of luxury to be left to those who like that sort of thing and have the time for it. Thus Albert Schweitzer, who would count as a deeply practical man if the term is used in the first sense, has been described as *impractical*—which indeed he was, in the second sense. Scientists do sometimes boast of practicality in this second sense, in which it is nothing to boast of. Thus if a biologist, working on in vitro fertilization, is aware that it is regarded as a morally problematic area by many, he may say or think with some complacency, "These are not problems for me; I cannot try to resolve them. I am basically a biologist, I have no moral qualms about this."[19] This conception of practicality does not involve the rejection of moral considerations altogether, but drastic oversimplification: the side of humanity is the side of the battle against disease, deformity, and death, so let us get on with the job. With blinkers on. One example of what I mean is the nineteenth and twentieth century history of medical support for social policies intended to fight venereal disease, policies distinguished by insensitivity to any other considerations than public health, notably to liberty and respect for persons.[20]

For those who use animals in experiments and who see practicality in this sense as central in their own work, consciousness of their own humanitarian motives may be combined with impatience at those who insist on bringing up problems—problems that may appear to the practical humanitarian spirit as so much gas, when there is *all this good* to be done by moving full speed ahead. Thus, for example, brisk impatience at restrictions on animal experimentation is sometimes combined with similar impatience at those restrictions on human experimentation (requiring consent, say, or barring experiments on children or prisoners) which may seem to be merely hindrances to the achievement of great good, and unethical on that account.

In a somewhat different and extreme form, the ideal of practicality involves the relegating of moral concern and imagination entirely to the peripheries of life: on this view it would be sentimental and unrealistic to criticize the administration of a colony, say, because it failed to adhere to standards of justice in its treatment of colonial subjects, or the conduct of a war, because it failed to respect the humanity of the enemy. This conception of practicality as an ideal is implicitly cruel: it involves being prepared to overlook cruelty, to call it necessary, and to regard its recognition as sentimental or hypocritical; Chesterton aptly called such a view brutalitarian. As an ideal of character it is contemptible, but the same cannot be said of the ideal of simplistic practical humanitarianism mentioned earlier. But *it* takes one-eyedness for a virtue and treats deadness of imagination as admirable.

Conclusion

In the opening section, "The Two Sides of the Dispute," I characterized two ways of looking at the use of animals in experiments. The heart of the First View was the idea that within certain limits, laboratory animals may properly be regarded as delicate instruments; the heart of the Second View was that even in laboratories, animals are to be regarded as sources of moral claims, analogous to those of which human beings are the source. Each view goes with an accusation: the First with the accusation that opponents of animal experimentation are sentimental, precisely in insisting that laboratory animals not be thought of merely as instruments, and the Second with the accusation that animal experimentation makes for callousness. In the last two sections I tried to make clear the lines of thought involved in each accusation. In particular, I tried to show that the accusation of sentimentality has two sources: ideas about scientific activity which indeed underlie the First View. One is a view of scientific activity as special and set apart from other activities in the inapplicability to it of certain kinds of moral criticism. The scientist is seen as engaged in an objective investigation of reality; and by a non sequitur this suggests that he is not called upon to bring moral imagination to bear on what he does—to animals or, indeed, to other people. The other source was a simplistic ideal of practicality: *not* the idea that doing what needs doing is important, but the idea that a practical person need not bother overmuch with the problematic character of the area in which he acts, indeed need not try fully to see *what* he is doing, if that might slow him down. Worrying about it is for theologians, philosophers, and other such 'idealists', while biological science is 'immutably practical'.[21] These views of science and of the practical underlie the First View and the idea of an area, scientific work 'within the circle', in which the imaginative realization of what one is doing is unnecessary and inappropriate. They further underlie the idea that discussion of animal experimentation as a moral issue is itself unnecessary: that there is no serious issue to be discussed. To reject these views—indeed to reject the idea of there being any area to which we should not bring our thought and imagination as best we can—is not to deny in any way the value of scientific work, either as a rewarding human activity or as the source of great practical benefits. It is simply to say that there is a great self-indulgent cop-out in treating what is done to animals in science as nothing worth thinking about.

Notes

1. J. C. Eccles, "Animal Experimentation versus human experimentation," in *Defining the Laboratory Animal* (International Committee on Laboratory Animals and the Institute of Laboratory Animal Resources, National Research Council, National Academy of Sciences, Washington, D.C., 1971), pp. 285–93.
2. BBC, "The Guinea-pig and the Law," *Horizon* program, broadcast on 2 February, 1977. All references to this program are based on my notes, taken during the program.
3. ibid.
4. M. B. Visscher, *Ethical Constraints and Imperatives in Medical Research* (Springfield, Illinois, 1975), pp. 78–9.
5. R. B. Marcus, "Moral Dilemmas and Consistency," *Journal of Philosophy* **77**, pp. 121–36.
6. S. Harris, "The Guinea-pig and the Law," *The Listener* **97** (1977), pp. 226–8.
7. S. Sollitte and R. M. Veatch, *Bibliography of Society, Ethics and the Life Sciences, 1979–80* (Hastings-on-Hudson, New York, 1978).
8. R. M. Veatch, in a letter.

9. R. J. White, "Antivivisection: the reluctant hydra," *The American Scholar* **40** (1971) pp. 503–7.

10. See S. Isaacs, *Intellectual Growth in Young Children* (London, 1930), pp. 160–70 and D. Sperlinger, "Natural Relations—Contemporary Views of the Relationship Between Humans and Other Animals," in D. Sperlinger, ed., *Animals in Research: New Perspectives in Animal Experimentation* (Chichester, Sussex, 1981), pp. 79–101.

11. See, for example, G. K. Chesterton, *George Bernard Shaw* (New York, 1910), pp. 79–86.

12. G K. Chesterton, *Orthodoxy* (New York, 1959), pp. 46–7.

13. S. Paget, *For and Against Experiments on Animals: Evidence Before the Royal Commission on Vivisection* (New York, 1912).

14. op. cit., p. 90.

15. D. H. Janzen, "Why Food Rots," *Natural History* **88** (1979), pp. 60–4.

16. W. Lane-Petter, "The Ethics of Animal Experimentation," *Journal of Medical Ethics* **2** (1976), pp. 118–26, at p. 119.

17. G. Sturt, *A Small Boy in the Sixties* (Hassocks, Sussex, 1977), p. 157.

18. G. Rolleston, in "Report of the Royal Commission on the Practice of Subjecting Live Animals to Experiments for Scientific Purposes," *Parliamentary Papers* C. 1397, **xli** (London, 1876), p. 277, qn. 1287.

19. B. L. Colen, "Norfolk Doctors Ready to Implant Embryo," *Washington Post* (September 28, 1979).

20. See, for example, S. Amos, *A Comparative Survey of Laws in Force for the Prohibition, Regulation and Licensing of Vice in England and Other Countries* (London, 1875) and B. Yanovsky, *The Dark Fields of Venus: From a Doctor's Logbook* (New York, 1972).

21. See, for example, White, op. cit., p. 507.

Chapter 15

Having a Rough Story about What Moral Philosophy Is[1]

If we are to say anything about the relation between moral philosophy and literature we must, as Professor Nussbaum makes clear, "have some rough story about what moral philosophy and the job of moral philosophy are" (p. 40). I propose to discuss why it is difficult to characterize moral philosophy—and in particular difficult when what we are aiming at is clarity about its relation to literature.

Professor Raphael alludes to one of the difficulties, quoting A. J. Ayer's Editorial Foreword to P. H. Nowell-Smith's *Ethics:* "There is a distinction . . . between the activity of the moralist . . . and that of a moral philosopher."[2] For Ayer that distinction was a straightforward one. The moral philosopher as such makes no moral judgments; the moralist, on the other hand, "sets out to elaborate a moral code, or to encourage its observance." Thus Ayer went on to describe Nowell-Smith as a moral philosopher: he "shows how ethical statements are related to, and how they differ from, statements of other types, and what are the criteria which are appropriate to them." Ayer's idea was that this could be done without the philosopher's taking sides on any moral or practical issue. For Ayer, then, three things were closely linked: the distinction between moralist and moral philosopher, the ethical neutrality of the philosopher, the characterization of his aim as linguistic or conceptual clarification. It has now gone out of fashion to hold that the moral philosopher as such makes no moral judgments, and Nowell-Smith himself in that very book (back in 1954, when it *was* fashionable) rejected any such idea: "Moral philosophy," he said, "is a practical science; its aim is to answer questions in the form 'What shall I do?'"; to help you answer such questions, it can "paint a picture of various types of life in the manner of Plato and ask which type of life you really want to lead."[3] There is clearly no suggestion there that the philosophical task requires ethical neutrality; and indeed Nowell-Smith's remarks leave open the possibility that such "painting" might be carried on as well in literature as in explicitly philosophical works. Going along with fashion, then, we give up ethical neutrality, and recognize it to be neither desirable nor indeed possible. With it, we drop the idea that the aim of moral philosophy is limited to conceptual clarification. But there is still the matter of the distinction between the activity of the moralist and that of the moral philosopher. If it is no longer to be drawn in Ayer's way, do we still want to draw it, and if so, how? This is a question not only for Raphael, who has an explicit answer, but for Martha Nussbaum, who has a different but largely implicit one. Hers reflects a willingness to let works of literature teach us something about what moral philosophy can be. But that conclusion I shall need to argue for later.

Why is it a question for her? She wants to argue that *The Golden Bowl* may be regarded as a text in moral philosophy; and for that purpose she needs (or thinks she does) a characterization of moral philosophy which will be widely acceptable. She offers us one derived from Aristotle: "Ethics is the search for a specification of the good life for man" (p. 40). An objection that some philosophers would surely bring is that the characterization includes too much. For (it will be said) a *moralist* may engage in just such a search; and if she shows us that Henry James in *The Golden Bowl* communicates something about how to live well, she will not thereby have shown that he is to be taken seriously as a moral philosopher but will merely have illustrated his powers as a moralist. I think that this objection misses the point, but it serves in any case as an illustration of the difficulties here.

Let me turn back to Raphael, to *his* way of handling the distinction between moralist and moral philosopher. He first contrasts the activity of the moralist with that of the moral philosopher, then makes (as if it were the same) a contrast between moral*ism* and moral philosophy, and later (as if it were the same again) a contrast between moral*izing* and moral philosophy. It may by now be unclear quite *what* should be distinguished from moral philosophy—but let us turn to Raphael's actual way of drawing his distinction. *Mere* preaching of moral doctrine goes on one side; moral doctrine presented as the outcome of structured argument he puts on the other, the moral philosophy, side—and that leaves him with some significant cases undecided, cases in which moral doctrine is presented in a new perspective. If the author uses *rational* methods of persuasion, we should, Raphael thinks, recognize his work as moral philosophy. It is not the label, though, that matters, on his view: it is the points of resemblance to clear examples of moral philosophy. Applying this distinction, Raphael is then willing to claim that literary works can contribute to moral philosophy.

There are still difficulties here, and one is what is supposed to be at stake. What does it matter whether we say that literature can be moral philosophy, or moral philosophy literature? Let me pursue this further.

Raphael supports his claim that moral philosophy may be done in literature by discussing three examples, the *Oresteia*, *Tom Jones*, and *Erewhon*. He argues that the *Oresteia* explores the concept of justice, develops it—and that it thus shows there to be *room* for the kind of conceptual exploration we see when moral philosophy proper, 'the real thing', comes into existence. The possibilities for moral philosophy in literature are different once 'the real thing' does exist (p. 9). A novelist like Fielding, aware of the ideas of contemporary moral philosophers, can in a novel take sides in a philosophical dispute. Thus we can see the rationalist/sentimentalist controversy pursued in *Tom Jones*. Rationalism in the person of Mr. Square is satirized, and sentimentalism supported. And, finally, Raphael discusses both the explicit philosophizing in *Erewhon* and the use in it of satirical transposition to make philosophical points.

To bring out the limiting assumptions in Raphael's account, we may contrast his view of philosophy in *Tom Jones* with Wolfgang Iser's.[4] Iser sees the relation of the novel to the philosophical systems of the day as much more 'indirect' than does Raphael. Rationalism is indeed embodied in Mr. Square, and other philosophical positions are associated with Allworthy, Thwackum, Squire Western, and Mrs. Western. The inadequacies of any such systematic account of human nature, of any such attempt to fix it in some single principle, rationalist or sentimentalist or whatever, can be brought to light by literature, Iser suggests, "not by systematic discourse." Through a reading of the novel, we can come to recognize the gulf between all such systems and the 'fluidity' of human experience, as we repeatedly encounter the limited character of each of the principles, bearing in mind each time the previous encounters.[5] What we learn of human nature is not the truth or falsity of any particular view in the repertoire; rather, reading the novel teaches us how to think about human nature by making us think about it, in response to its 'constant intertwining' of perspectives.[6] Its criticism of philosophical views is not separable from the very different sort of demand it makes on the reader from that made by ordinary philosophical works. If we can say that it makes a contribution to philosophy, the argument would be different from Raphael's and would have to reflect a different view of moral philosophy, including a different view of the reader of moral philosophy. In philosophy as Raphael sees it, we are concerned to develop certain ideas, to work out their consequences and systematic relations, to see their rational justification. The training a reader of philosophy needs will develop in him the capacity to grasp, formulate, and examine critically the philosophical ideas present in a text. The differences between Raphael's reading of *Tom Jones* and Iser's are not just differences about that novel. If Raphael does not see what Iser does, if he describes differently the relation of the novel to the philosophical systems of the day, it is partly because he is not looking for, or even looking at, the same thing. He is looking for ideas in the text, for the views it presents, while Iser looks at what the reader— of a certain sort—*does* because certain things are *not* in the text. For Raphael, if some of the ideas or issues in the three works he discusses are philosophical, their definition as philosophical issues lies outside the works; one might say that their validation as philosophical is external. Our experience is, for Raphael, the touchstone of the rationality of the perspectives they employ: their philosophical seriousness does not lie in what they can do, as works of art, to make us reshape that experience.

We can approach the same questions by turning to Raphael's brief remarks about Kierkegaard and Nietzsche. One of the reasons he gives for allowing that literary works may count as philosophy is that "there are acknowledged philosophers who make their mark by means of novel perspective rather than structured argument"; he is referring to Nietzsche and Kierkegaard (p. 5). But even so, Raphael is not happy calling them philosophers, because the novel perspectives their work depends on are not rational ones. But if he will not himself call what they do philosophy, what weight has their acknowledgment by others as philosophers? To take that acknowledgment as a reason for shaping the definition of moral philosophy one way rather than another leaves the whole issue pretty muddy.

Let us ask whether a philosopher may invite philosophical thought in his readers by defeating some of their expectations of a philosophical text. Wittgenstein, interestingly, once claimed that that is *all* a philosopher should do: "The correct method in philosophy would really be this: to say nothing except what can be said, i.e., propositions of natural science—i.e., something that has nothing to do with philosophy—and then whenever someone else wanted to say something metaphysical, to demonstrate to him that certain signs in his propositions had been given no meaning. This method would be unsatisfying for the other person—he would not have the feeling that we were teaching him philosophy—but *this* method would be the only strictly correct one."[7] What is to be learned by the reader of such a philosophical text would not be anything in the text; the person to whom such philosophy is addressed must take philosophically seriously the use of a literary technique, that of *not* enabling the reader to find what he expects in a certain sort of work. Just as Iser, reflecting on *Tom Jones*, emphasizes that the novel teaches us how to think about human nature by making us think about it and not by giving us *what* to think, so a philosophical text may aim to make us think about things in a new way, not by giving us *what* to think about them, not by presenting new views or doctrines. What philosophical readers, trained to extract and examine critically the ideas and arguments in a philosophical text, make of such works might easily be guessed, though there is no need to. An important example is P. F. Strawson's review of Wittgenstein's *Philosophical Investigations*. Only a "very specialised view of the nature of philosophical understanding" would, he thinks, block the attempt to treat that text as containing extractable views on a set of philosophical topics.[8] The 'very specialised view' would be one which regarded as *part* of the philosophy of Wittgenstein the distance between the way it is written and the way academic philosophers write; it is to be connected with Iser's remark that only literature and not systematic discourse can bring to light the inadequacy of certain philosophical ways of thinking about human life and with Martha Nussbaum's claim that clarity about the role of mystery and risk in the 'stories' of our moral lives requires the abilities and techniques of a teller of stories and cannot be done through the 'plainness' of traditional moral philosophy (pp. 43–4).

Raphael says that a philosophical work may "have merit as a work of literature," and he gives examples, including several of Plato's dialogues (p. 2). We may ask what the interest is of the literary quality of such works. Is it that the response demanded or invited by the work as a work of literature contributes to what we may learn from it as moral philosophers? The only example Raphael goes into is that of the *Phaedo*, which leaves the matter obscure. That is because Plato's philosophical aim, as Raphael describes it, is so very different from the aim of most moral philosophers. The *Phaedo* was intended, he says, to be a sort—a new, reformed sort—of tragic drama: 'philosophical' tragedy *replacing* 'poetical' (pp. 3–4). We may be able to see how literary features of the work are necessary for the fulfillment of that aim—but that does not help us much to see their bearing on moral philosophy when it is not taking over, or trying to, the place of poetry.

Raphael's remarks about possible literary merits of philosophical works leaves unasked a significant question: What about literary weaknesses and their relevance to philosophical aims? May failings of a sort we can come to notice through what we might refer to vaguely as literary sensibility (i.e., whatever those abilities are we need to read literary works adequately, whatever it is to do that) be relevant to a philosophical evaluation? Can a literary critic draw to our attention signs of *philosophical* trouble? Dorothea Krook's critical remarks about Hume's *Enquiry Concerning the Principles of Morals* may serve as an example.[9] She tries to make clear the unreality of Hume's vision of the good life, bringing to his philosophical writings the sensibility and tools of a student of literature. Perhaps we may see here again, in Raphael's not raising such questions, evidence of the view of philosophy I ascribed to him earlier: that the essential thing in it is the development and criticism of ideas. Literary skill, if a philosopher has it, may then make his ideas strike us more forcefully (if we have the requisite sensibility as readers), but the important thing for a philosophical reading is the ideas themselves, and whatever considerations may rationally support them. Such a view of philosophy may then go with a *narrow* conception of the kind of weakness we need literary sensibility to see: a narrowing of the notion to weaknesses of style in a fairly superficial sense, which might make philosophical ideas less striking, less immediately attractive, but not less *cogent.* Failure of style as *philosophical* failure has then no place.[10] Perhaps I have pushed too far the attempt to make Raphael's remarks the expression of a particular view of moral philosophy. But it is the prevalent view, even if he himself is not as committed to it as I have suggested.

Let me turn now to some other features of the prevalent view of moral philosophy, important for understanding its relation to literature. Earlier I quoted P. H. Nowell-Smith's similar remarks about the aim of moral philosophy being to help us answer questions about what to *do.* It is a striking fact that many moral philosophers wish to define the sphere of the moral by tying it in some such way to action. How deep a difference is there between such accounts and characterizations like Martha Nussbaum's, in which the central notion is not action but the good human life? It might be argued that the difference is not significant. Those philosophers—so the argument might begin—who define the subject matter of moral philosophy in terms of action may, like Nowell-Smith, assign an important place to philosophical description of types of human life. Such descriptions subserve the end of moral philosophy by helping us to act and choose as well as we can. On Nowell-Smith's own view, we come, through philosophy, to see what kind of life we want to lead, and we then act, or try to act, in accordance with the decision to live so. Or that part of the story might go somewhat differently: we come to know, through philosophy, what makes a good human life, and that knowledge is what enables us to answer questions about what to do, how to act, how to choose. The argument might then continue: just as philosophers who define the moral sphere in terms of *action* might give a central place to the description of kinds of life, or to the attempts to specify the good human life, so philosophers whose definition links moral philosophy or moral thought directly to the specification of *the good human life* must give a central place to principles of action. For it is our actions, our choices, which give a particular shape to the life we lead; to be able to lead whatever the good life for a human being is *is* to be able to make such choices well. So the argument concludes that there is no real difference between the two types of definition: specifying the good life for human beings and enabling us to answer questions of the form "What shall I do?" are inseparable or perhaps even equivalent.

But the argument begs the question—and might serve as a perfect example of something Iris Murdoch warned us of. There is, she argued, a peculiar difficulty in ethics (in contrast with other parts of philosophy) in specifying the phenomena to be studied. Our moral judgments themselves shape our conception of the field of study. We thus come up with a "narrow or partial" selection of phenomena; that selection then suggests particular philosophical approaches, which in turn support the initial selection: "A circle is formed out of which it may be hard to break."[11] The argument of the last paragraph illustrates these dangers: it reflects a particular evaluation of action, and accordingly represents what is morally significant in life in terms of actions and choices.

"A particular evaluation of action"—but action as opposed to *what?* What is being left out, ignored, played down? We may look for an answer to Miss Murdoch—but in the essay I have quoted she puts her answer in several different ways.[12] She points out that when we use the notions of action and choice to specify the sphere of morality, it may be action as what is observable, public—opposed, then, to what is private, to the 'inner life'. But "inner life" itself may be understood to mean what goes on in our minds and is knowable through introspection—or to mean "private or personal vision which may find expression overtly or inwardly." There are already then two contrasts: between the publicly observable and the inner world, and between action and vision. There is a third, brought in as part of her explanation of the second:

> When we apprehend and assess other people we do not consider only their solutions to specifiable practical problems, we consider something more elusive which may be called their total vision of life, as shown in their mode of speech or silence, their choice of words, their assessments of others, their conception of their own lives, what they think attractive or praiseworthy, what they think funny: in short, the configurations of their thought which show continually in their reactions and conversation. These things, which may be overtly and comprehensibly displayed or inwardly elaborated and guessed at, constitute what, making different points in the two metaphors, one may call the texture of a man's being or the nature of his personal vision.[13]

The two metaphors do indeed make different points, different contrasts with action. Iris Murdoch is herself more interested in the second metaphor. In *The Sovereignty of Good* she connects the significance of vision in moral life with Simone Weil's use of the word *attention* "to express the idea of a just and loving gaze directed upon a particular reality," and she takes such attention to be "the characteristic and proper mark of the active moral agent."[14]

But we need also to turn to the other metaphor if we are concerned with the relation between moral philosophy and literature. Moral philosophers have been obsessively concerned with action and choice, and do occasionally refer to moral vision. But 'texture of being' hardly gets a mention; and yet it is surely enormously characteristic of many novelists that *that* is what they give us—and out of an interest we may properly call moral. The opening chapters of *Anna Karenina*—what do they give us so much as the texture of Stiva's being? His good-hearted, silly smile when he is caught at something shameful, his response to the memory of the stupid smile, the failure of his attempt to look pathetic and submissive when he goes back to Dolly—what he blushes at, what he laughs at, what he gives an ironical smile at, what he turns his eyes away from: this is Stiva. Such things, as Iris Murdoch points out, are what we consider when we 'apprehend and assess' another person; but if we refer to them as the person's 'total vision of life', the word "vision" is used in a far looser sense than she gives it elsewhere. I could put the problem here this way. One may properly be concerned how one sees another person, whether one's mode of vision is just—and Iris Murdoch has described such a case in detail, showing the significance both of the inner life (as contrasted with observable actions) *and* of vision (as contrasted with action).[15] Many philosophers might be willing to be persuaded that vision in such a case *is* morally assessable—but what a man finds funny? What kind of blushes he gives? His precision of expression? Here they would find it far harder to see that they are dealing with something of moral interest. If a case can be made it will be a different one, a harder one, because it runs up against deeper prejudices. But we cannot see the moral interest of literature unless we recognize gestures, manners, habits, turns of speech, turns of thought, styles of face as morally expressive—of an individual or of a people. The intelligent description of such things is part of the intelligent, the sharp-eyed, description of life, of what matters, makes differences, in human lives. Martha Nussbaum's Aristotelian specification of ethics leaves room (or is intended to leave room) for attention to these things; an account of ethics, or of moral philosophy, which takes action as definitive of the moral does not.

"Texture of being" is a useful expression for this area; it also allows for an extension of Miss Murdoch's general point. Moral reflection may be directed not just towards individual human beings but towards forms of social life. The social phenomena that are usually regarded by moral philosophers as their concern are familiar enough; they do *not* include what corresponds on the social side to 'texture of being' *or* 'vision' on the individual side. Income distribution or the death penalty count for moral philosophers as properly of concern to them; styles of furniture, for example, as expressive of the 'texture of life' do not. Yet surely Henry James's interest in furniture in *The Europeans* is an interest in it as expressive of attitudes to life. Just as what a person is *like*, his complex attitude to life, shows continually in how he thinks, what he says, what he laughs at, and the like, so the complex attitudes of a people to life show continually in their manners, habits, styles of utterance, dress, architecture. Martha Nussbaum touches very briefly in her discussion of *The Golden Bowl* on the 'international theme' in that novel: the significance of the fact that moralism and excessive simplicity characterize an *American* character. Her main interest, though, is what the novel shows about human moral experience and whether we need such texts in moral philosophy—and here the 'international theme' drops out of sight, or seems to. There is a further question then whether the same kind of argument she makes about James's explorations of the lives of individual human beings can be made about his explorations of contrasting forms of social life. I thought at first that she implied that it could: ethics, understood as she proposes, cannot "in any way be cut off from the study of the empirical and social conditions of human life" (p. 40). But the question remains how *particular* the things may be that ethics is concerned with. Is its concern limited to what *generally* belongs to the empirical and social conditions of human life? Can it include in its phenomena the contrasts between European and American life, not taking these as examples of anything more generally human? Professor Nussbaum remarks that even in order to raise the question whether *The Golden Bowl* can be regarded as an important text for moral philosophy, we need to drop the Kantian insistence that moral philosophy as such (as opposed to 'practical anthropology') be concerned only with what is independent of specifically *human* experience (p. 40). The Kantian definition even more obviously rules out James's explorations of his 'international theme'; they do not even make it (as far as I can see) into practical anthropology.

There may even be a tension between Martha Nussbaum's account of ethics in terms of the good life for human beings and James's interests. His description of his aim (the production of an 'intelligent report' of experience, i.e., of "our apprehension and measure of what happens to us as social creatures") brings him, she says, "into intimate connection with the Aristotelian enterprise" (p. 40). But is the relation so close? That James and Aristotle can both be described as concerned with the 'appearances,' with people's 'experiences and sayings,' does not settle the question. James's interest is that of a 'painter'; his 'report of people's experience' is essentially his 'appreciation' of it, and to appreciate is to avoid as far as possible all simplification (simplification which would be in place if one's concern were action and practical application), to convey the sense and taste of a situation through intimacy with a man's specific behavior, intimacy with his given case, and so to see that case as a whole.[16] He certainly does not explicitly say anything about the good life for human beings, nor even imply that there *is* such a thing. And even if he did believe that there is such a thing, an interest in moral features of human life need not (in general) be an interest in what the good human life would be.

I have argued, following Iris Murdoch, that any specification of the sphere of morality, of the phenomena of interest to moral philosophy, in terms of action and choice is a limited and limiting one. How we define the sphere of the moral bears in several different ways on the relation of literature to moral philosophy.

It bears first of all on the question *where* in works of literature a moral philosopher can see an exploration of something of moral significance. A narrow definition of the moral will, for example, enable us to recognize a moral interest in the account, in *Portrait of a Lady*, of Isabel's decision to return to Osmond, but not in the description of architecture and furniture in *The Europeans*. It may also lead to crude views of the moral implications of literary works.

Secondly, if we say that the sphere of the moral is not limited to action but includes thought and imagination, the moral significance of works of literature is not reducible to their connection, direct and indirect, with action, but includes also what kind of thought and imagination they express and what they invite. Take as an example Martha Nussbaum's argument that *The Golden Bowl* elicits from us as readers an acknowledgment of our own imperfection. We are, she says, repeatedly struck, while reading it, by the inadequacies of our own attention and thus learn something of ourselves (p. 46). This self-knowledge may itself be regarded as a good thing for us, irrespective of any bearing it may have on what we go on to *do*.

There is a third point. Any discussion of a practical issue, of what to do, exhibits thought or thoughtlessness. Regardless of the right or wrong of what is argued for, the thought itself may be criticized. If we limit the sphere of morality to action, we leave no room for criticizing thought about action except so far as it involves mistakes of reasoning or premises against which some rational argument may be brought. On the other hand we may treat, let us say, a too great knowingness, a refusal to acknowledge mystery or adventure in deliberation (to use once more Martha Nussbaum's discussion of *The Golden Bowl* [p. 44]), as failures of thinking, failures subject themselves to moral criticism. Here the significance of works of literature for moral philosophy is that we may learn from our reading of such works, and from reflection on them, terms of criticism of thought applicable to discussions of practical issues and to moral philosophy itself.

I want to turn to one last difficulty about what moral philosophy is—a difficulty about the sort of world it goes on in. Again I shall begin from something Iris Murdoch has said. If we treat action as the central notion in defining the sphere of morality, this may, she suggests, have as one of its sources a view of the world as in a fundamental sense comprehensible, and of the facts constituting the situations in which we act as straightforwardly describable.[17] Comprehension, description, appreciation of the facts will not be seen as tasks for which moral energy, discipline, imagination, creativity, wit, care, patience, tact, delicacy, . . . may be required. The problem here should be treated separately from the last. What sort of subject we think moral philosophy is depends on whether we accept or not some such view of the world. Is there not a taking for granted that whatever philosophical questions there may be about knowing what the world is like, they belong to epistemology (as traditionally conceived) or philosophy of science and are not seriously troubling ones for moral philosophy? Is there not a taking for granted that *saying* what the world is like, what the situations are in which we find ourselves, is a 'plain' business, in that sense of "plainness" which Martha Nussbaum used in speaking of traditional moral philosophy? If in philosophy we see the moral life of human beings against such a background, we shall surely greet with disbelief the idea that the *un*plainness of literary works is itself important for moral philosophy.

Consider Professor Raphael's remarks: "If someone says that literature feeds moral philosophy, he may mean that characters or situations in a work of literature can be used as evidence for some issues in moral philosophy. This is the most obvious, the richest, and the most satisfying way in which literature and moral philosophy are connected" (p. 1). It is the most obvious; to suggest that it is the richest and most satisfying reflects a particular view of moral philosophy, of how far it is concerned with a world whose deepest difficulties include difficulties of description. What, let us ask, is it to use a character or situation in a novel as evidence for an issue in moral philosophy? Prior to reading it, we may, as philosophers, have been concerned with questions, for example, about the significance of rules; the novel, let us imagine, describes a situation involving adultery and marriage, and we may take the novel to bear upon the general questions we had had. After reading it, we may recognize that our previous answers to those questions were inadequate, that we had failed to take into account certain human possibilities or what we can now see to be likelihoods, certain ways in which situations may be resolved or possible explanations for their being irresolvable, possible kinds of background or complications of character—and we may accordingly modify or refine our general principles or our systematic account of how principles bear on cases. The contribution of the novel is then a greater understanding of how things can and do happen—an understanding which could also have come from keeping one's eyes open to similar things happening in the world. What is here 'food' for moral philosophy is the story itself, what happens, and to what kind of people, in what sort of situation; what plays no role is *how* the story is told, the 'unplainness' of the telling, its 'density,' the kinds of demand that that makes on the reader. Here I am going over Professor Wollheim's line of reasoning (in his commentary on Martha Nussbaum's piece); such a contribution by a novel to philosophical thought is, for the reasons he gives, not *specifically* a contribution as novel but rather as Story, in his sense (p. 186). The Story provides evidence, bearing on issues and questions already there in moral philosophy; the effect of reading is the difference the evidence makes to judgments, conclusions, answers we reach.

An argument for a richer kind of connection between moral philosophy and literature is provided by Martha Nussbaum; what I want to bring out is that her argument supposes a different view of moral philosophy from Professor Raphael's. What we are to get from the experience—the 'adventure'—of reading such a text as *The Golden Bowl* is not *evidence* bearing on philosophical conclusions about the nature of deliberation. What philosophical thought does a novel like that call for, then, if she is correct? It calls for an attempt to connect features it has specifically as a novel with the character of what in human life the novel is about; it calls, that is, for an attempt to show the relation between the thought it invites and the author's relation to his characters, the ambiguity, the 'dissonance,' the complications it presents of possible treatings as salient, and so on. The task is not one belonging to the philosopher as such, drawing on things in the novel, as opposed to that of a literary critic, nor that of a critic as opposed to that of a philosopher. The question being thought about is of the form, "How is it that *this* (whatever feature of the novel it may be) is an illuminating way of writing about *that* (whatever feature of human life)?" And what we can see in Martha Nussbaum's essay is the combination of that question with, "How is it that *this* is so much more illuminating a way of writing about it than are the familiar ways of moral philosophy?" The implication is that it is no plain business finding how to write illuminatingly about human experience—and no plain business reading about it either. But these are not issues or questions which belong to moral philosophy on the prevalent view of the subject; if they are questions for it, it is only through our familiarity with unplain ways of using language, through our responses to those ways of using language, that we can recognize them as such questions.

Let met put the matter with a different kind of example. Lawrence spoke of *the novel* as a great discovery: ". . . it won't *let* you tell didactic lies"; it shows them up, shows *you* up if you try to put them in.[18] Here is a view (true or false does not matter for my present concerns) about the relation between forms of thought and expression, and what we try to think about. But it is not on every view of philosophy that what Lawrence says will seem to call for philosophical discussion. Philosophers can easily see as a conceptual innovation relevant to their concerns a new way of thinking about justice (let us say); but that *the novel* (or particular forms, particular kinds of novel, styles of narration and the like) might be thought of as a kind of moral discovery, that modes of describing or presenting life are significant from the moral philosopher's point of view: this is not something that fits into their current conception of their subject matter.

I have two points in conclusion. First, that Martha Nussbaum's attempt to take as a starting point a widely agreed and inclusive notion of the aim of moral philosophy is pretty much doomed. No one knows what the subject is; most widely agreed accounts of it depend on suppositions that are not obvious and that reflect particular evaluations and views of the world, of human nature, and of what it is to speak, think, write, or read about the world. The more inclusive an account is, the more likely it will include what many philosophers would not dream of counting as part of their subject. Fortunately, her essay, and more particularly her attempt to show us how we may take *The Golden Bowl* as a text of moral philosophy, do not depend on finding such an agreed account. By thinking philosophically about literature in a way that breaks the rules of what counts—on many views—as moral philosophy, she goes some way toward showing that we should not take those rules seriously, or the conception of moral philosophy which they determine.

In the essay I quoted earlier, Iris Murdoch said of the moral philosophy of the 1950s: "What these linguistic analysts mistrust is precisely language."[19] She had in mind their idea of philosophy as mere analysis of moral concepts, in contrast to the development of new modes of understanding, new moral visions. As they saw matters, the moralist or the ordinary man, in making moral judgments, labels certain things "good" or "right"; the moral philosopher then shows how the use of such terms is related to the facts on the one hand and to action and choice on the other. It is striking that, although such an approach in moral philosophy has virtually disappeared, although the notion of neutral analysis of moral terms is dead or moribund, what she meant by "mistrust of language" is as present as ever it was; and that is the second point I wanted to reach. The focus is *still* on "evaluations," "judgments," on explicit moral reasoning to conclusions that something is worthwhile, or a duty, or wrong, or ought to be done; our conception of what are 'issues' for moral thought is still "x is wrong" versus "x is permissible"; the abortion debate is our paradigm of moral utterance. 'Mistrust of language' is a reluctance to see all that is involved in using it well, responding well to it, meeting it well, reluctance to see what kind of failure it may be to use it badly. How do our words, thoughts, descriptions, philosophical styles let us down or let others down? How do they, used at full stretch—and in what spirit or spirits—illuminate? Moral philosophy may no longer be called "linguistic" (it rarely called itself that anyway), but the narrowness of focus has not changed.

Notes

1. This essay comments on papers in an issue of *New Literary History* (Vol. 15, no. 1, Autumn 1983) on Literature and/as Moral Philosophy. The papers to which I refer are Martha Nussbaum's "Flawed Crystals: James's *The Golden Bowl* and Literature as Moral Philosophy," pp. 25–50, reprinted in Nussbaum, *Love's Knowledge* (Oxford, 1990), pp. 125–47; D. D. Raphael's "Can Literature be Moral Philosophy?" pp. 1–23; and Richard Wollheim's "Flawed Crystals: James's *The Golden Bowl* and the Plausibility of Literature as Moral Philosophy," pp. 185–91. Page references in the text are to that issue of *New Literary History*.

2. Raphael (p. 3) quotes A. J. Ayer, Editorial Foreword to P. H. Nowell-Smith, *Ethics* (Harmondsworth, 1954), p. 7.

3. Nowell-Smith, p. 319.

4. Wolfgang Iser, *The Act of Reading* (Baltimore, 1978); Iser, "Interaction between Text and Reader," in S. R. Suleiman and I. Crosman, eds., *The Reader in the Text* (Princeton, 1980), pp. 106–19.

5. Iser, *The Act of Reading*, pp. 76–7.

6. Iser, "Interaction between Text and Reader," p. 113.

7. L. Wittgenstein, *Tractatus Logico-Philosohicus* (London, 1961), 6.53.

8. P. F. Strawson, "Critical Notice: L. Wittgenstein, *Philosophical Investigations*," *Mind*, 63 (1954), pp. 70–99, at p. 70.

9. Dorothea Krook, *Three Traditions of Moral Thought* (Cambridge, 1959), chapter 6. See also Michael Tanner, "The Language of Philosophy," in L. Michaels and C. Ricks, eds., *The State of the Language* (Berkeley, 1980), pp. 458–66.

10. On these issues, see W. Hart, "How are we to read philosophy?" *Haltwhistle Quarterly* No. 3 (Spring 1975), pp. 47–56.

11. Iris Murdoch, "Vision and Choice in Morality," *Proceedings of the Aristotelian Society*, Supplementary Vol. 30 (1956), pp. 32–58, at pp. 32–3.

12. op. cit., pp. 35–40.

13. op. cit., p. 39.

14. Iris Murdoch, *The Sovereignty of Good* (London, 1970), p. 34.

15. op. cit., pp. 17–40. The importance of this notion of vision is emphasized in Martha Nussbaum's recent work. See especially "The Discernment of Perception: An Aristotelian Conception of Personal and Public Rationality," revised version in Nussbaum, *Love's Knowledge* (Oxford, 1990) pp. 54–105, "'Finely Aware and Richly Responsible': Moral Attention and the Moral Task of Literature," revised version in Nussbaum, *Love's Knowledge*, pp. 148–67, and Section E2 (pp. 37–40) of the Introduction to *Love's Knowledge*, with further bibliographical references. My comments on an earlier version of "'Finely Aware'" are in "Missing the Adventure."

16. The remarks are drawn from the Preface to *The Princess Casamassima* (Harmondsworth, 1977), p. 12; the paragraph from which they are drawn follows that quoted by Martha Nussbaum.

17. Murdoch, "Vision and Choice," pp. 49–50; see also pp. 42–3.

18. D. H. Lawrence, "The Novel," in Lawrence, *Phoenix II* (London, 1968), pp. 416–26, at pp. 416–7.

19. Murdoch, "Vision and Choice," p. 42n.

Bibliography

Ambrose, A., ed. *Wittgenstein's Lectures, Cambridge 1932–1935* (Totowa, New Jersey, 1979).

Amos, S. *A Comparative Survey of Laws in Force for the Prohibition, Regulation and Licensing of Vice in England and Other Countries* (London, 1875).

Anscombe, G.E.M. "The Reality of the Past," in M. Black, ed., *Philosophical Analysis* (Ithaca, 1950), pp. 38–59. Reprinted in Anscombe, *Metaphysics and the Philosophy of Mind* (Minneapolis, 1981), pp. 103–19.

Anscombe, G.E.M. "Modern Moral Philosophy," *Philosophy* 33 (1958), pp. 1–19. Reprinted in Anscombe, *Ethics, Religion and Politics* (Minneapolis, 1981), pp. 26–42.

Anscombe, G.E.M. *Introduction to Wittgenstein's Tractatus* (London, 1959).

Anscombe, G.E.M. "On Sensations of Position," *Analysis* 22 (1961–62), pp. 55–8. Reprinted in Anscombe, *Metaphysics and the Philosophy of Mind* (Minneapolis, 1981), pp. 71–4.

Anscombe, G.E.M. "The Intentionality of Sensation," in R.J. Butler, ed., *Analytical Philosophy*, Second Series (Oxford, 1965), pp. 158–80. Reprinted in Anscombe, *Metaphysics and the Philosophy of Mind* (Minneapolis, 1981), pp. 3–20.

Anscombe, G.E.M. *Metaphysics and the Philosophy of Mind* (Minneapolis, 1981).

Anscombe, G.E.M. and Geach, P.T. *Three Philosophers* (Oxford, 1963).

Anselm. *Proslogion*, ed. and trans. M.J. Charlesworth (Oxford, 1965).

Anselm. *Monologion*, in Anselm, *Basic Writings*, trans. S.N. Deane (La Salle, Illinois, 1968).

Ayer, A.J. Editorial Foreword to P.H. Nowell-Smith, *Ethics* (Harmondsworth, Middlesex, 1954), p. 7.

Ayer, A.J., ed. *Logical Positivism* (London, 1959).

Baier, A.C. "Nonsense," in *Encyclopedia of Philosophy*, ed. P. Edwards (New York and London, 1967), vol. 5, pp. 520–22.

Barth, K. *Anselm: Fides Quaerens Intellectum* (Cleveland and New York, 1962).

Benacerraf, P. and Putnam, H., eds. *Philosophy of Mathematics* (Englewood Cliffs, New Jersey, 1964).

Berkeley, G. *Philosophical Commentaries, Works*, ed. A.A. Luce and T.E. Jessop (Edinburgh, 1948–57), vol. I.

Berkeley, G. *Principles of Human Knowledge, Works*, ed. A.A. Luce and T.E. Jessop (Edinburgh, 1948–57), vol. II.

Berkeley, G. *Three Dialogues between Hylas and Philonous, Works*, ed. A.A. Luce and T.E. Jessop (Edinburgh, 1948–57), vol. II.

Berkeley, G. *Alciphron, Works*, ed. A.A. Luce and T.E. Jessop (Edinburgh, 1948–57), vol. III.

Bernays, P. "Comments on Ludwig Wittgenstein's *Remarks on The Foundations of Mathematics*," *Ratio* 2 (1959–60), pp. 1–22. Reprinted in P. Benacerraf and H. Putnam, eds., *Philosophy of Mathematics* (Englewood Cliffs, New Jersey, 1964), pp. 510–28.

Black, M., ed. *Philosophical Analysis* (Ithaca, 1950).

Black, M., ed. *Philosophy in America* (London and New York, 1965).

Blackburn, S., ed. *Meaning, Reference, and Necessity* (Cambridge, 1975).

Bloch, M. *Feudal Society* (London, 1965).

Block, I., ed. *Perspectives on the Philosophy of Wittgenstein* (Oxford, 1981).

Bradley, M. "On the Alleged Need for Nonsense," *Australasian Journal of Philosophy* 56 (1978), pp. 203–18.

Butler, R.J. "A Wittgensteinian on 'The Reality of the Past'," *Philosophical Quarterly* 6 (1956), pp. 304–14.

Butler, R.J., ed. *Analytical Philosophy*, Second Series (Oxford, 1965).

Carnap, R. "The Elimination of Metaphysics through Logical Analysis of Language," in A.J. Ayer, ed., *Logical Positivism* (London, 1959), pp. 60–81.

Cavell, S. "The Availability of Wittgenstein's Later Philosophy," *Philosophical Review* 71 (1962), pp. 67–93. Reprinted in Cavell, *Must We Mean What We Say?* (New York, 1969), pp. 44–72.

Cavell, S. "Aesthetic Problems of Modern Philosophy," in M. Black, ed., *Philosophy in America*, pp. 74–97. Reprinted in Cavell, *Must We Mean What We Say?*" pp. 73–96.

Cavell, S. *Must We Mean What We Say?* (New York, 1969).

Chadwick, N. *The Age of the Saints in the Early Celtic Church* (London, 1961).

Chesterton, G.K. *George Bernard Shaw* (New York, 1910).

Chesterton, G.K. *Orthodoxy* (New York, 1959).

Clark, S.L.R. *The Moral Status of Animals* (Oxford, 1977).

Clogan, P.M., ed. *Medieval Hagiography and Romance. Medievalia et Humanistica*, New Series, 6 (Cambridge, 1975).

Craig, E.J. "The Problem of Necessary Truth," in S. Blackburn, ed., *Meaning, Reference, and Necessity* (Cambridge, 1975), pp. 1–31.

Currie, G. *Frege: An Introduction to his Philosophy* (Brighton, 1982).

Davidson, D. "Truth and Meaning," *Synthese* 17 (1967), pp. 304–23. Reprinted in Davidson, *Inquiries into Truth and Interpretation* (Oxford, 1984), pp. 17–36.

Delehaye, H. *The Legends of the Saints* (New York, 1962).

Diamond, C., ed. *Wittgenstein's Lectures on the Foundations of Mathematics, Cambridge 1939* (Ithaca, 1976; reprinted Chicago, 1989).

Diamond, C. "Ethics, Imagination and the Method of Wittgenstein's *Tractatus*," in R. Heinrich and H. Vetter, eds., *Bilder der Philosophie, Wiener Reihe* 5 (Vienna, 1991).

Diamond, C. "Rules: Looking in the Right Place," in D.Z. Phillips and P. Winch, eds., *Wittgenstein: Attention to Particulars* (Basingstoke, Hampshire, 1989), pp. 12–34.

Donagan, A. "Wittgenstein on Sensation," in G. Pitcher, ed., *Wittgenstein: The Philosophical Investigations* (Garden City, New York), 1966, pp. 324–51.

Dummett, M. "Wittgenstein's Philosophy of Mathematics," *Philosophical Review* 68 (1959), pp. 324–48. Reprinted in Dummett, *Truth and Other Enigmas*, pp. 166–85; in P. Benacerraf and H. Putnam, eds., *Philosophy of Mathematics* (Englewood Cliffs, New Jersey, 1964), pp. 491–509.

Dummett, M. "The Reality of the Past," *Proceedings of the Aristotelian Society* 59

(1968–69), pp. 239–58. Reprinted in Dummett, *Truth and Other Enigmas*, pp. 358–74.

Dummett, M. *Frege: Philosophy of Language* (London, 1973).

Dummett, M. *Truth and Other Enigmas* (London, 1978).

Dummett, M. *The Interpretation of Frege's Philosophy* (London, 1981).

Eccles, J.C. "Animal Experimentation Versus Human Experimentation," in *Defining the Laboratory Animal* (International Committee on Laboratory Animals and the Institute of Laboratory Animal Resources, National Research Council), National Academy of Sciences, Washington, D.C., 1971, pp. 285–93.

Empson, W. *The Structure of Complex Words* (London, 1951).

Evans, G. *The Varieties of Reference*, ed. J. McDowell (Oxford, 1982).

Evans-Pritchard, E.E. *The Nuer* (New York and Oxford, 1974).

Frankena, W. *Ethics* (Englewood Cliffs, New Jersey, 1963).

Frege, G. "On the Scientific Justification of a Concept-Script," trans. J.M. Bartlett, *Mind* 73 (1964), pp. 155–60.

Frege, G. *Translations from the Philosophical Writings of Gottlob Frege*, ed. P.T. Geach and M. Black (Oxford, 1966).

Frege, G. "Function and Concept," in *Translations from the Philosophical Writings of Gottlob Frege*, pp. 21–41. Also in Frege, *Collected Papers on Mathematics, Logic and Philosophy*, pp. 137–56.

Frege, G. "On Concept and Object," in *Translations from the Philosophical Writings of Gottlob Frege*, pp. 42–55. Also in Frege, *Collected Papers on Mathematics, Logic and Philosophy*, pp. 182–94.

Frege, G. "On Sense and Reference," in *Translations from the Philosophical Writings of Gottlob Frege*, pp. 56–78. Also (as "On Sense and Meaning") in Frege, *Collected Papers on Mathematics, Logic, and Philosophy*, pp. 157–77.

Frege, G. *Basic Laws of Arithmetic*, ed. and trans. M. Furth (Berkeley and Los Angeles, 1967).

Frege, G. *Begriffsschrift*, trans. S. Bauer-Mengelberg, in J. van Heijenoort, ed., *From Frege to Gödel* (Cambridge, Massachusetts, 1967), pp. 1–82.

Frege, G. *On the Foundations of Geometry and Formal Theories of Arithmetic*, ed. and trans. E.-H.W. Kluge (New Haven, 1971).

Frege, G. "On the Foundations of Geometry," First Series (1903), in Frege, *On the Foundations of Geometry and Formal Theories of Arithmetic*, pp. 22–37. Also in Frege, *Collected Papers on Mathematics, Logic and Philosophy*, pp. 273–84.

Frege, G. "On the Foundations of Geometry," Second Series (1906), in Frege, *On the Foundations of Geometry and Formal Theories of Arithmetic*, pp. 49–112. Also in Frege, *Collected Papers on Mathematics, Logic and Philosophy*, pp. 293–340.

Frege, G. *The Foundations of Arithmetic*, trans. J.L. Austin (Oxford, 1974).

Frege, G. *Wißenschaftliche Briefwechsel*, ed. G. Gabriel et al. (Hamburg, 1976).

Frege, G. *Posthumous Writings*, ed. H. Hermes et al., trans. P. Long and R. White (Oxford and Chicago, 1979).

Frege, G. "[Dialogue with Pünjer on Existence]," in Frege, *Posthumous Writings*, pp. 53–67.

Frege, G. *Philosophical and Mathematical Correspondence*, ed. G. Gabriel et al., trans. H. Kaal (Oxford, 1980).

Frege, G. *Collected Papers on Mathematics, Logic and Philosophy*, ed. B. McGuinness (Oxford, 1984).

Frege, G. "Thoughts," in Frege, *Collected Papers on Mathematics, Logic and Philosophy*, pp. 351–72.

French, R.D. *Antivivisection and Medical Science in Victorian Society* (Princeton, 1975).

Geach, P.T. *Mental Acts* (London, 1957).

Geach, P.T. "Frege," in G.E.M. Anscombe and P.T. Geach, *Three Philosophers* (Oxford, 1963), pp. 127–62.

Geach, P.T. *Reference and Generality* (Ithaca, 1968).

Geach, P.T. "Names and Identity," in S. Guttenplan, ed., *Mind and Language* (Oxford, 1975), pp. 139–58.

Geach, P.T. "Saying and Showing in Frege and Wittgenstein," in *Essays on Wittgenstein in Honour of G.H. von Wright*, ed. J. Hintikka, *Acta Philosophica Fennica* 28 (Amsterdam, 1976), pp. 54–70.

Godlovitch, S. and R. and Harris, J., eds., *Animals, Men and Morals* (New York, 1972).

Goldfarb, W. "Objects, Names, and Realism in the *Tractatus*," unpublished.

Goldfarb, W. "I Want You to Bring Me a Slab: Remarks on the Opening Sections of *Philosophical Investigations*," *Synthese* 56 (1983), pp. 265–82.

Goodstein, R.L. "Proof by Reductio Ad Absurdum," in Goodstein, *Essays in the Philosophy of Mathematics* (Leicester, 1965), pp. 1–11.

Guttenplan, S., ed. *Mind and Language* (Oxford, 1975).

Haack, R. "No Need for Nonsense," *Australasian Journal of Philosophy* 49 (1971), pp. 71–7.

Haack, S. "Pragmatism and Ontology: Peirce and James," *Revue Internationale de Philosophie* 31 (1977), pp. 377–400.

Haaparanta, L. and Hintikka, J., eds. *Frege Synthesized* (Dordrecht, 1986).

Hacker, P.M.S. *Insight and Illusion* (Oxford, 1972).

Hacker, P.M.S. "Semantic Holism," in C.G. Luckhardt, ed., *Wittgenstein: Sources and Perspectives* (Ithaca, 1979), pp. 213–42.

Harman, G. "Logic and Reasoning," *Synthese* 60 (1984), pp. 107–27.

Harris, S. "The Guinea-Pig and the Law," *The Listener* 97 (1977), pp. 226–8.

Hart, W. "How are we to read philosophy?" *Haltwhistle Quarterly* No. 3 (Spring 1975), pp. 47–56.

Hawthorne, N. "The Birthmark," in Hawthorne, *Young Goodman Brown and Other Tales*, ed. B. Harding (Oxford and New York, 1987), pp. 175–92.

Heist, W.W. "Irish Saints' Lives, Romance and Cultural History," in P.M. Clogan, ed., *Medieval Hagiography and Romance*, pp. 25–40.

Hick, J., ed. *The Existence of God* (New York, 1964).

Hintikka, J., ed. *Essays on Wittgenstein in Honor of G.F. von Wright*. *Acta Philosophica Fennica* 28 (Amsterdam, 1976).

Holtzman, S.H. and Leich, C.M., eds. *Wittgenstein: To Follow a Rule* (London, 1981).

Hume, D. "Of Suicide," in Hume, *Two Essays* (London, 1777).

Isaacs, S. *Intellectual Growth in Young Children* (London, 1930).

Iser, W. *The Act of Reading* (Baltimore, 1978).

Iser, W. "Interaction between Text and Reader," in S.R. Suleiman and I. Crosman, eds., *The Reader in the Text* (Princeton, 1980), pp. 106–19.

Ishiguro, H. "Use and Reference of Names," in P. Winch, ed., *Studies in the Philosophy of Wittgenstein* (London, 1969), pp. 20–50.

James, H. *Portrait of a Lady* (New York, 1908).

James, H. *The Letters of Henry James*, ed. P. Lubbock (New York, 1920).

James, H. *The Art of the Novel: Critical Prefaces* (New York, 1934).

James, H. "Guy de Maupassant," in James, *Selected Literary Criticism* (London, 1963), pp. 87–111.

James, H. "The New Novel," in James, *Selected Literary Criticism* (London, 1963), pp. 311–42.

James, H. *Selected Literary Criticism*, ed. M. Shapira (London, 1963).

James, H. *The Princess Casamassima* (Harmondsworth, Middlesex, 1977).

Janzen, D.H. "Why Food Rots," *Natural History*, 88 (1979), pp. 60–4.

Kant, I. *Metaphysics of Morals*, Part II. Trans. by M.J. Gregor as *The Doctrine of Virtue* (Philadelphia, 1969).

Kant, I. *Logic*, trans. R. S. Hartman and W. Schwarz (Indianapolis and New York, 1974).

Kripke, S.A. *Wittgenstein on Rules and Private Language* (Oxford, 1982).

Kripke, S.A. "Wittgenstein on Rules and Private Language," in I. Block, ed., *Perspectives on the Philosophy of Wittgenstein* (Oxford, 1981), pp. 238–312.

Krook, D. *Three Traditions of Moral Thought* (Cambridge, 1959).

Lane-Petter, W. "The Ethics of Animal Experimentation," *Journal of Medical Ethics* 2 (1976), pp. 118–26.

Lawrence, D.H. "The Novel," in Lawrence, *Phoenix II* (London, 1968), pp. 416–26.

Leavis, F.R. *The Great Tradition* (New York, 1964).

Lee, D., ed. *Wittgenstein's Lectures, Cambridge 1930–1932* (Totowa, New Jersey, 1980).

The Little Flowers of Saint Francis, ed. G.L. Passerini, trans. L. Sherley-Price (Harmondsworth, 1959).

Macdonald, M. Notes on Wittgenstein's Lectures on 'Personal Experience', 1935–36, unpublished.

Malcolm, N. "Anselm's Ontological Arguments," *Philosophical Review* 69 (1960), pp. 41–62. Reprinted in Malcolm, *Knowledge and Certainty* (Ithaca, 1963), pp. 141–62.

Malcolm, N. *Nothing is Hidden* (Oxford, 1986).

Marcus, R.B. "Moral Dilemmas and Consistency," *Journal of Philosophy* 77 (1980), pp. 121–36.

McDowell, J. "On the Sense and Reference of a Proper Name," *Mind* 86 (1977), pp. 159–85.

McDowell, J. "Non-Cognitivism and Rule Following," in S.H. Holtzman and C.M. Leich, eds., *Wittgenstein: To Follow a Rule* (London, 1981), pp. 141–62.

McGuinness, B. "'I Know What I Want'," *Proceedings of the Aristotelian Society* 57 (1956–57), pp. 305–20.

McGuinness, B. "The So-Called Realism of the *Tractatus*," in I. Block, ed., *Perspectives on the Philosophy of Wittgenstein* (Oxford, 1981), pp. 60–73.

Michaels, L. and Ricks, C., eds. *The State of the Language* (Berkeley, 1980).

Mill, J.S. and H.T. "The Enfranchisement of Women," in Mill, J.S., *Dissertations and Discussions*. Boston, 1864, vol. 3, pp. 93–131. Also in Mill, J.S., *Collected Works*, ed. J.M. Robson (Toronto, 1963–89), vol. 21, pp. 393–415.

Murdoch, I. "Vision and Choice in Morality," *Proceedings of the Aristotelian Society*, supp. vol. 30 (1956), pp. 32–58.

Murdoch, I. *The Sovereignty of Good* (London, 1970).

Nowell-Smith, P.H. *Ethics* (Harmondsworth, Middlesex, 1954).

Nussbaum, M.C. "Flawed Crystals: James's *The Golden Bowl* and Literature as Moral Philosophy," *New Literary History* 15 (1983), pp. 25–40. Reprinted in Nussbaum, *Love's Knowledge: Essays on Philosophy and Literature*, pp. 125–47.

Nussbaum, M.C. "The Discernment of Perception: An Aristotelian Conception of Personal and Public Rationality," in J. Cleary, ed., *Proceedings of the Boston Area Colloquium in Ancient Philosophy* 1 (New York, 1985), pp. 151–201. Revised version in Nussbaum, *Love's Knowledge: Essay on Philosophy and Literature*, pp. 54–105.

Nussbaum, M.C. " 'Finely Aware and Richly Responsible': Moral Attention and the Moral Task of Literature," *Journal of Philosophy* 82 (1985), pp. 516–29. Revised version, " 'Finely Aware and Richly Responsible': Literature and the Moral Imagination," in A.J. Cascardi, ed. *Literature and the Question of Philosophy* (Baltimore and London, 1987), pp. 169–91. Reprinted in Nussbaum, *Love's Knowledge: Essays on Philosophy and Literature*, pp. 148–67.

Nussbaum, M.C. *Love's Knowledge: Essays on Philosophy and Literature* (Oxford, 1990).

O'Connor, F. Foreword to N. Gogol, *Dead Souls* (New York, 1961), pp. v–x.

O'Neill, O.R. Review of S.L.R. Clark, *The Moral Status of Animals*, *Philosophical Review* 77 (1980), pp. 440–46.

O'Neil, O.R. "The Power of Example," *Philosophy* 61 (1986), pp. 5–29.

Orwell, G. "Charles Dickens," in Orwell, *A Collection of Essays* (Garden City, New York, 1954), pp. 55–111.

Orwell, G. "Looking Back on the Spanish War," in Orwell, *Collected Essays, Journalism and Letters*, ed. S. Orwell and I. Angus (London, 1968), vol. 2, pp. 249–67.

Paget, S. *For and Against Experiments on Animals: Evidence Before the Royal Commission on Vivisection* (New York, 1912).

Pap, A. "Types and Meaninglessness," *Mind* 69 (1960), pp. 41–54.

Pascal, B. *Pensées*, trans. J.M. Cohen (Harmondsworth, 1961).

Peacocke, C. "Reply [to G. Baker]: Rule Following: The Nature of Wittgenstein's Arguments," in S.M. Holtzman and C.M. Leich, eds., *Wittgenstein, To Follow a Rule* (London, 1981), pp. 72–95.

Peirce, C.S. *Collected Papers of Charles Sanders Peirce*, ed. C. Hartshorne, P. Weiss and A.W. Burks (Cambridge, Massachusetts, 1931–58).

Plato. *Crito*, trans. A.D. Woozley, in Woozley, *Law and Obedience* (London, 1979), pp. 141–56.

Prior, A. "Entities," *Australasian Journal of Philosophy* 32 (1954), pp. 159–68. Reprinted in Prior, *Papers in Logic and Ethics*, ed. P.T. Geach and A.J.P. Kenny (London, 1976), pp. 25–32.

Quine, W.V. "Two Dogmas of Empiricism," in Quine, *From a Logical Point of View* (Cambridge, Massachusetts, 1953), pp. 20–46.

Quine, W.V. *Word and Object* (Cambridge, Massachusetts, 1960).

Ramsey, F.P. *The Foundations of Mathematics* (Totowa, New Jersey, 1965).

Ramsey, F.P. "General Propositions and Causality," in Ramsey, *The Foundations of Mathematics*, pp. 237–55.

Raphael, D.D. "Can Literature be Moral Philosophy?" *New Literary History* 15 (1983), pp. 1–12.

Regan, T. and Singer, P., eds. *Animal Rights and Human Obligations* (Englewood Cliffs, New Jersey, 1976).

Rhees, R. "Some Developments in Wittgenstein's View of Ethics," *Philosophical Review* 74 (1965), pp. 17–26. Reprinted in Rhees, *Discussions of Wittgenstein*, pp. 94–103.

Rhees, R. *Discussions of Wittgenstein* (London, 1970).

Rhees, R. " 'The Philosophy of Wittgenstein'," *Ratio* 8 (1966), pp. 180–93. Reprinted in Rhees, *Discussions of Wittgenstein*, pp. 37–54.

Ricketts, T.G. "Frege, The *Tractatus*, and the Logocentric Predicament," *Noûs* 15 (1985), pp. 3–15.

Ricketts, T.G. "Generality, Meaning and Sense in Frege," in *Pacific Philosophical Quarterly* 67 (1986), pp. 172–95.

Ricketts, T.G. "Objectivity and Objecthood: Frege's Metaphysics of Judgment," in L. Haaparanta and J. Hintikka, eds., *Frege Synthesized* (Dordrecht, 1986), pp. 65–95.

Ricketts, T.G. "Facts, Logic, and the Criticism of Metaphysics in the *Tractatus*," unpublished.

Robertson, D. *George Mallory* (London, 1969).

Royal Commission. "Report of the Royal Commission on the Practice of Subjecting Live Animals to Experiments for Scientific Purposes," Parliamentary Papers C. 1397, xli (London, 1876).

Ruskin, J. *Ruskin Today*, ed. K. Clark (New York, 1964).

Russell, B. *Principles of Mathematics* (London, 1937).

Russell, B. *An Enquiry into Meaning and Truth* (London, 1940).

Russell, B. "The Philosophy of Logical Atomism," in Russell, *Logic and Knowledge*, ed. R.C. Marsh (London and New York, 1956), pp. 175–281.

Ryder, R. *Speciesism: The Ethics of Vivisection* (Edinburgh, 1974).

Shakespeare, W. *Measure for Measure*, ed. S. Nagarajan. In S. Barnet, general ed., *The Complete Signet Classic Shakespeare*, pp. 1137–73.

Shwayder, D. "Wittgenstein on Mathematics," in P. Winch, ed., *Studies in the Philosophy of Wittgenstein* (London, 1969), pp. 66–116.

Singer, P. *Animal Liberation* (New York, 1975).

Sluga, H. *Gottlob Frege* (London, 1980).

Sollitte, S. and Veatch, R.M. *Bibliography of Society, Ethics, and the Life Sciences, 1979–80* (Hastings-on-Hudson, New York, 1978).

Sperlinger, D. "Natural Relations—Contemporary Views of the Relation Between Humans and Other Animals," in Sperlinger, ed., *Animals in Research: New Perspectives in Animal Experimentation* (Chichester, Sussex, 1981), pp. 79–101.

Stock, B. "Propaganda for the Holy Men" (review of P.M. Clogan, ed., *Medieval Hagiography and Romance, Medievalia et Humanistica* 6), *Times Literary Supplement*, February 25, 1977, p. 224.

Strawson, P.F. "Critical Notice: L. Wittgenstein, *Philosophical Investigations*," *Mind* 63 (1954), pp. 70–99. Reprinted in Strawson, *Freedom and Resentment and Other Essays* (London and New York, 1974), pp. 133–68.

Sturt, G. *A Small Boy in the Sixties* (Hassocks, Sussex), 1977.

Tanner, M. "The Language of Philosophy," in L. Michaels and C. Ricks, eds., *The State of the Language* (Berkeley, 1980), pp. 458–66.

Tooley, M. "A Defence of Abortion and Infanticide," in J. Feinberg, ed., *The Problem of Abortion* (Belmont, California, 1973), pp. 51–91.

Vesey, G., ed. *Understanding Wittgenstein*, Royal Institute of Philosophy Lectures, vol. 7 (London 1974).

Visscher, M.B. *Ethical Constraints and Imperatives in Medical Research* (Springfield, Illinois, 1975).

Waismann, F. *The Principles of Linguistic Philosophy* (London, 1965).

Waismann, F. "Notes on Talks with Wittgenstein," trans. M. Black, *Philosophical Review* 74 (1965), pp. 12–16. (The notes, with trans. by J. Schulte and B. McGuinness, are in Waismann, *Wittgenstein and the Vienna Circle*, pp. 68–9, 115–18).

Waismann, F. *Wittgenstein and the Vienna Circle*, ed. B. McGuinness, trans. J. Schulte and B. McGuinness (Oxford, 1979).

Weiner, J. "On Concepts, Hints and Horses," *History of Philosophy Quarterly* 6 (1989), pp. 115–30.

Weiner, J. *Frege in Perspective* (Ithaca, 1990).

White, R.J. "Antivivisection: The Reluctant Hydra," *The American Scholar* 40 (1971), pp. 503–7.

Whitehead, A. N., and Russell, B. *Principia Mathematica to *56* (Cambridge, 1962).

Williams, B. A. O. "Wittgenstein and Idealism," in G. Vesey, ed., *Understanding Wittgenstein*, pp. 76–95. Reprinted in Williams, *Moral Luck* (Cambridge, 1981), pp. 144–63.

Winch, P., ed. *Studies in the Philosophy of Wittgenstein* (London, 1969).

Winch, P. "Language, Thought and World in Wittgenstein's *Tractatus*," in Winch, *Trying to Make Sense* (Oxford, 1987), pp. 3–17.

Wisdom, J. "The Modes of Thought and the Logic of God," in John Hick, ed., *The Existence of God* (New York, 1964), pp. 275–98.

Wittgenstein, L. *Remarks on the Foundations of Mathematics*, ed. G.H. von Wright, R. Rhees and G.E.M. Anscombe, trans. G.E.M. Anscombe. Oxford, 1956 (first edition); 1967 (second edition); 1978 (third edition).

Wittgenstein, L. *Philosophical Investigations*, trans. G.E.M. Anscombe (Oxford, 1958).

Wittgenstein, L. *Notebooks, 1914–1916*, ed. G.H. von Wright and G.E.M. Anscombe, trans. G.E.M. Anscombe (Oxford, 1961).

Wittgenstein, L. "Notes Dictated to G.E. Moore in Norway," in Wittgenstein, *Notebooks, 1914–1916*, pp. 107–18.

Wittgenstein, L. *Tractatus Logic-Philosophicus*, trans. D.F. Pears and B. McGuinness (London, 1961).

Wittgenstein, L. *The Blue and Brown Books* (Oxford, 1964).

Wittgenstein, L. "A Lecture on Ethics," *Philosophical Review* 74 (1965), pp. 3–12.

Wittgenstein, L. *Lectures and Conversations on Aesthetics, Psychology and Religious Belief*, ed. C. Barrett (Oxford, 1966).

Wittgenstein, L. *Zettel*, eds. G.E.M. Anscombe and G.H. von Wright, trans. G.E.M. Anscombe (Oxford, 1967).

Wittgenstein, L. *Philosophical Grammar*, ed. R. Rhees, trans. A. Kenny (Oxford, 1974).

Wittgenstein, L. *Philosophical Remarks*, ed. R. Rhees, trans. R. Hargreaves and R. White (Oxford, 1975).

Wollheim, R. "Flawed Crystals: James's *The Golden Bowl* and the Plausibility of Literature as Moral Philosophy," *New Literary History* 15 (1983), pp. 185–91.

Wordsworth, W. *Lyrical Ballads*, with expanded Preface (1802 and subsequent editions).

Wordsworth, W. *The Prelude: 1799, 1805, 1850*, ed. J. Wordsworth, M.H. Abrams and S. Gill (New York and London, 1979).

Wright, C. *Wittgenstein on the Foundations of Mathematics* (London, 1980).

Yanovsky, B. *The Dark Fields of Venus: From a Doctor's Logbook* (New York, 1972).

Index